The title of this artfully written book is a subtle play on words—it is about both the sociology of traditions and the traditions of sociology. The author is one of India's premier sociologists, and to read his interpretations is to see a master at work. Madan explores significant features of the social body of Hinduism, Islam, and Sikhism, and also of Gandhian ideals and Indian secularism. He discusses various approaches to their study, and makes us reconsider what is distinctive about India's understanding of the relationship between religious traditions and the secular state.

The second half of the book is devoted to four scholars who have greatly influenced the field of Indian sociology. Madan skilfully presents the perspectives of Radhakamal Mukerjee who strove for interdisciplinary integration; D.P. Mukerji, who applied interests of class formation to India's religious communities; M.N. Srinivas, who gave us a sophisticated understanding of the role of religion and caste in changing society; and Louis Dumont, who unearthed the religious assumptions underlying India's enduring social structure.

Madan ends with reflections on the development of the most important journal, *Contributions to Indian Sociology*, and on his own intellectual autobiography as a cultural anthropologist and sociologist. *Sociological Traditions* may well become the most influential of Madan's many excellent books.

Mark Juergensmeyer
Professor of Sociology
University of California
Santa Barbara

This marvellous book is T.N. Madan's journey through the sociology of Indian sociology. As researcher, teacher, and founder-editor of the second series of India's premier journal of sociology, *Contributions to Indian Sociology*, Madan has redrawn the contemporary landscape of the discipline. It is only appropriate that he should now look back on it with intimacy and professional detachment. And he does so with unfailing sensitivity to the ways in which cultures of knowledge and individual biographies intersect.

The first half of the book can be read as a comparative perspective on some of the major concerns of Indian sociology. The emphasis is on how the larger issues of social change and modernization in India have been refracted through, and epitomized by, the changing perspectives on the study of religion. The second half explores, through the intellectual biographies of four intriguing but gifted exemplars, the emergence of a new social science, and new, often strange, templates of scholarship in a less than appreciative, somewhat wary, intellectual climate. Together, the two parts of the book constitute a fascinating cultural biography of a knowledge system and reconfirm Madan's stature as one of the most insightful intellectuals of our time.

Ashis Nandy
Emeritus Senior Fellow
Centre for the Study of Developing Societies
Delhi

Sociological Traditions

70

T.N. Madan

Sociological Traditions

Methods and Perspectives in the Sociology of India

⊛SAGE www.sagepublications.com
Los Angeles • London • New Delhi • Singapore • Washington DC

Copyright © T.N. Madan, 2011

All rights reserved. No part of this book may be reproduced or utilized in any form or by any means, electronic or mechanical, including photocopying, recording or by any information storage or retrieval system, without permission in writing from the publisher.

First published in 2011 by

SAGE Publications India Pvt Ltd
B1/I-1 Mohan Cooperative Industrial Area
Mathura Road, New Delhi 110 044, India
www.sagepub.in

SAGE Publications Inc
2455 Teller Road
Thousand Oaks, California 91320, USA

SAGE Publications Ltd
1 Oliver's Yard, 55 City Road
London EC1Y 1SP, United Kingdom

SAGE Publications Asia-Pacific Pte Ltd
33 Pekin Street
#02-01 Far East Square
Singapore 048763

Published by Vivek Mehra for SAGE Publications India Pvt Ltd, typeset in 10.5/12.5 Times New Roman by Tantla Composition Services Pvt. Ltd., Chandigarh and printed at Chaman Enterprises, New Delhi.

Third Printing 2012

Library of Congress Cataloging-in-Publication Data

Madan, T.N.
  Sociological traditions : methods and perspectives in the sociology of India / T.N. Madan.
     p. cm.
  Includes bibliographical references and index.
  1. Sociology—India. 2. Religion and sociology—India. I. Title.

HM477.I4M33   301.0954—dc22   2011   2011002887

ISBN: 978-81-321-0575-6 (HB)

The SAGE Team: Gayatri Mishra, Madhula Banerji, Amrita Saha, and Deepti Saxena

In Memoriam

P.S. Jayasinghe, Ravi Dayal,

and

Tejeshwar Singh

Architects of Social Science Publishing in India

*Thinking too has a time for ploughing and a time
for gathering the harvest.*
  —WITTGENSTEIN, *Culture and Value*

*And yet a line of thought that has matured
over many years has its own stability.*
  —HANS-GEORG GADAMER, *Truth and Method*

Thank you for choosing a SAGE product! If you have any comment, observation or feedback, I would like to personally hear from you. Please write to me at contactceo@sagepub.in

—Vivek Mehra, Managing Director and CEO,
SAGE Publications India Pvt Ltd, New Delhi

Bulk Sales

SAGE India offers special discounts for purchase of books in bulk. We also make available special imprints and excerpts from our books on demand.

For orders and enquiries, write to us at

Marketing Department
SAGE Publications India Pvt Ltd
B1/I-1, Mohan Cooperative Industrial Area
Mathura Road, Post Bag 7
New Delhi 110044, India
E-mail us at marketing@sagepub.in

Get to know more about SAGE, be invited to SAGE events, get on our mailing list. Write today to marketing@sagepub.in

This book is also available as an e-book.

Contents

Preface xi
Acknowledgements xix

PART I *Cultural Traditions, Sociological Perspectives*

ONE Indian Secularism in a Post-secular Age 3
TWO Hinduism: The Book View and the Field View 23
THREE Islam: The Universal and the Particular 45
FOUR Sikhism: The Sacred and the Secular 75
FIVE Gandhi and Weber: The Work Ethic, Capitalism, and Conscience 101

PART II *Sociological Traditions: Exemplars, Interpreters*

SIX Radhakamal Mukerjee and His Contemporaries 119
SEVEN D.P. Mukerji: Towards a Historical Sociology 146
EIGHT M.N. Srinivas: Empiricism and Imagination 174
NINE Louis Dumont: The Man and His Work 195
TEN *Contributions to Indian Sociology*: Towards Methodological Pluralism 217

Epilogue: **Engagements and Passages—
   An Exercise in Reflexivity**   240
References   266
Index   290
About the Author   307

Preface

This is a book about tradition—about dynamic cultural traditions as subjects of study and about intellectual traditions as evolving approaches to their study—in the context of the sociology of India. I do not employ the term 'tradition' to suggest the completeness or closure of a stock of ideas and perspectives, or an unthinking adherence to particular styles of thinking. In his celebrated book, *The Sociological Tradition* (1966), Robert Nisbet did indeed suggest that a set of core concepts (namely, community, authority, status, the sacred, and alienation) may well be said to constitute *the* sociological tradition. Needless to emphasize that, for him, the Western sociological tradition is universal. I do not follow that trail in this book, although I am very much concerned in it with the idea of the sacred in non-Christian cultural traditions and the crafting of appropriate methods for its study.

To use the phraseology of an earlier, related book of mine, *Pathways: Approaches to the Study of Society in India* (1994c), the present work is about sociological 'pathways' and 'path makers'. The foregoing clarifies, I trust, my use of the term 'tradition'. It suggests that significant ideas usually emerge from collective endeavours or may be put forward by gifted individuals who never are so original as to be wholly independent of their sociocultural and intellectual settings. Such ideas grow by being interrogated and refined by interested interlocutors and interpreters. Thus conceived, intellectual traditions are alive and, therefore, as much contemporary as they are of the past.

Edward Shils insightfully observes in his masterly book *Tradition* (1981) that social scientists generally have been wary of traditionalism and self-consciously 'progressivistic' in their outlook (p. 137); yet, and ironically, they have transformed this critical attitude itself into a tradition. Generally agnostic, they have recognized the role of religious traditions in history, whether as inhibiting or promoting social progress. If Marx believed that in his times religiosity served the interests of the exploiter class in European bourgeois society by drawing a veil upon social reality, standing it on its head as it were, Weber thought that religious values bestow meaning and significance on human existence, and Durkheim saw in them the moral basis for sociality.

What is more, sociologists throughout the twentieth century and today have been so rooted in the ideas of the founding fathers as to invite the charge of necrophilia! In the field of sociology, Shils observes, Weber and Durkheim are studied with the same seriousness as Kant and Hegel among philosophers, or Machiavelli and Hobbes among political theorists. 'Their own past is still very much alive in the thought of contemporary social scientists and they do not hide it from themselves' (Shils 1981: 140).

What is true of the 'greats' of the Western sociological tradition everywhere is not, however, similarly true of the founders of other sociological traditions. In India, succeeding generations have condescendingly neglected the work of their predecessors. As far as I know, only one formal account of the genesis of the discipline in India is available. Ramkrishna Mukherjee's 'Trends in Indian Sociology' (1977) devotes a twenty-four-page chapter to the 'pioneers'. As for books other than college-level textbooks, I know of only three studies: Swapan Kumar Bhattacharya's painstaking *Indian Sociology: The Role of Benoy Kumar Sarkar* (1990); S.K. Pramanick's *Sociology of G.S. Ghurye* (1994); and Surajit Sinha's rather slim *Nirmal Kumar Bose: Scholar Wanderer* (1986). A more recent volume, *Anthropology in the East: Founders of Indian Sociology and Anthropology* (2007), edited by Patricia Uberoi, Nandini Sundar, and Satish Deshpande, contains some excellent essays. The editors acknowledge that notwithstanding an interest in the work of contemporaries (or perhaps because of it?) 'historicizing the disciplinary past appears to have been neglected' (Uberoi et al. 2007: 2). It is surprising that they themselves have not included in their book a discussion of the contributions of Radhakamal Mukerjee.

It is regrettable that, not only has no one written at length about Mukerjee's work, many of his books are not available even in the libraries of the University of Lucknow, where he established the Department of Economics and Sociology in 1922. Surely, the large corpus of his writings on economics, demography, sociology, and ecology—notwithstanding their repetitiveness and lack of scholarly rigour—demand attention. Is disciplinary insularity that characterizes our times responsible for the neglect of Mukerjee's work? Since his work is difficult to appreciate, if it is compartmentalized, scholars find it easier to put it aside. And this is so in spite of the fact that his work finds renewed relevance in the context of current debates about ecology and the limitations of the economic science. The sociological traditions of India have yet to find their historians.

Turning to this book, it has been written piecemeal, essay by essay; eight of the ten chapters were written over five years, between 2005 and 2010, and two in the late 1990s. Except the three not yet published, all the others have been revised and in some cases expanded over the last one year. The book is now offered to the reader as not a collection of essays, but a unified work about themes, methods, and perspectives.

Part I addresses the problem of the study of India's major religious traditions (Hinduism, Islam, and Sikhism) from a variety of sociological perspectives and, in their setting, explores the character of Indian secularism as a religio-sacred ideal. Gandhi's religious pluralism and his concern for ethics in public no less than private life also is briefly discussed in both the chapter on Indian secularism and the one on the work ethic related issues. In the study of Hinduism, the complementarity of the book and field views is stressed; in the study of Islam, a hierarchical view of the relationship of the universal and local expressions of the faith is recommended; and in the study of Sikhism, a similar, hierarchical perspective on the relationship of the sacred and the secular is shown, I hope convincingly, to be self-suggestive. In other words, the first five chapters of the book are about cultural traditions of belief and value as well as about various sociological traditions available for their study, the former as part of the vast subject matter of Indian sociology, and the latter as methodological perspectives on the same.

At this point I may digress to briefly comment on the fact that Indian sociologists generally have been more concerned with social forms and processes rather than cultural traditions, with interests rather than values. The separation of sociology from cultural anthropology (a Western import) has been mainly responsible for this. Be that as it may, it has resulted in a relative neglect of the study of religion, which is regrettable given the importance of religion in the private and public domains, for good or evil, in our times. Referring to this lack of interest, M.N. Srinivas, himself a believer, and author of a major study of a community's religion, observes in *The Remembered Village* (1976) that, 'leading Indian anthropologists and sociologists profess to be rationalists' (p. 290). Max Weber (1930: 183) too noticed this failing a hundred years ago: 'The modern man is in general unable to give religious ideas a significance for culture and national character that they deserve.' Weber himself, it has been noticed, saw the possibility of 'refuge' in religion, but, as a rationalist, did not take this road. Nevertheless, he contributed more than anyone else of his time and since to our understanding of the structures and implications of religious belief.

Part II of the book proceeds along a different but parallel track. It focuses on the making of sociological traditions, and addresses the work of four distinguished scholars, namely, Radhakamal Mukerjee, D.P. Mukerji, M.N. Srinivas, and Louis Dumont, all four of them outstanding exemplars. After all, intellectual traditions grow in practice through the collective exertions of participating contributors from the interplay of concurrence and contestation among them. Such traditions (any traditions) never arise full blown from a single source, nor do they have a moment of creation. They are built of diverse materials, brick by brick, over time. The idea of completion, the putting in place of a capstone, also is alien to traditions. They exist in a continuous present, although their genesis lies in a fluid past, and are perpetuated through renewal and reinvention (somewhat like Pierre Bourdieu's intellectual fields).

In the discussion of the works of Mukerjee, Mukerji, and Dumont, I have tried to be synoptic in my approach, highlighting their major substantive and methodological concerns, and indicating the lines along which critical assessment has proceeded or may proceed. Mukerjee's is a unique case: his sociology began as a corrective perspective on economic theory, the major assumptions of which, he insisted, were rooted in Western cultural traditions and historical specificities. A 'general' economics could be constructed only on the basis of a comparison of 'regional' economic systems. From this, he proceeded to develop an institutional theory of economics and alongside of it, social ecology. These eventually matured into a sociology of values in his hands. Finally, in his last years, he went beyond the social sciences and endeavoured to produce a synthesis of different civilizational traditions. In this he was less than successful.

Mukerji's original project was a general sociology, but gradually with his attraction to Marxism, and his conclusion that the essence of the Marxist method lay in specification, he moved on to the study of India. It is this that led him to argue for the study of tradition. Dumont arrived at the importance of traditions through the comparative method characteristic of the French school established by Émile Durkheim and Marcel Mauss; the latter was his teacher. Dumont publicly acknowledged in the opening pages of his magnum opus, *Homo Hierarchicus*, that in his work he owes everything to that sociological tradition. The chapter on Srinivas focuses on a specific methodological issue, namely, the relationship of sociology and literature, of real and imagined worlds, in the context of his allegiance to the empirical tradition of British social anthropology. This allegiance is brought out clearly in the chapter on the sociology of Hinduism.

It is important to note here that, I had discussed the work of three of these scholars, alongside that of some others, in my *Pathways: Approaches to the Study of Society in India* (1994c). The two sets of chapters, in the earlier and the present books, are not, however, identical but complementary. The discussion here is broader in the case of Mukerji and Dumont, and, as stated earlier, focuses on both a broader and a narrower but significant problem in the case of Srinivas, which were not addressed in the earlier work.

The Epilogue of the book strikes a personal note. The beginnings of my career as a sociologist and cultural anthropologist go back to the early 1950s, when I was a student in the Department of Economics and Sociology at the University of Lucknow. Among my teachers there, Radhakamal Mukerjee, D.P. Mukerji, and D.N. Majumdar were particularly influential in my case. What I learnt there was in some respects (notably the empirical tradition of the social sciences) reinforced during my doctoral research in the Department of Anthropology and Sociology at the Australian National University (ANU). Subsequently, the encounter with the work of Louis Dumont turned out to be a turning point. Although I was not a student of M.N. Srinivas, for Indianists of my generation, he was a major exemplar. Discussions of the contributions of Mukerjee, Mukerji, Srinivas, and Dumont have led me to reflect on my own intellectual journey in its various dimensions, including that of interpretation as creative work.

The passage of years in a scholar's life is, or should be, a fulfilling experience; it has been so for me, and in ample measure. It is also, however, an exacting experience, particularly because one is rarely wholly in control or entirely satisfied. And it cannot go on and on; the slowing down that comes with the passage of time is a natural process and, therefore, not unwelcome. Surely, writing is, inter alia, a confession of one's limitations.

This book celebrates the making of another tradition also, that of social science publishing in India. It is dedicated to the memory of three great architects of this tradition, namely, P.S. Jayasinghe, Ravi Dayal, and Tejeshwar Singh. Unfortunately, each one of them died before it was time for him even to retire from publishing activity. Jayasinghe showed us in the 1950s that good scholarly work by Indians could be produced well for both the home and overseas markets. Asia Publishing House, which he founded in the early 1950s, was headquartered in Bombay, and had offices in London and New York. My first book was accepted for publication by Asia's very able editorial director, Samuel Israel (who died recently), and I came to know them both quite well. Unfortunately, Jayasinghe allowed enterprise to be overwhelmed by its arch enemy, recklessness.

Even as Asia Publishing was folding up in the late 1960s, Ravi Dayal began the process of transforming the Indian branch of the Oxford University Press (OUP) from a publishing house known mainly for atlases, dictionaries, and textbooks, into the country's premier publisher of high quality academic books. I became an OUP author in 1983 at Ravi Dayal's invitation, and we became good friends. I still publish with OUP.

It was my privilege to have been in Delhi when Tejeshwar Singh established SAGE Publications India Pvt. Ltd in 1980, at the invitation of Sara and George McCune, the visionary founders of SAGE companies in the USA and the UK, and with their manifold support. I welcomed the initiative, and handed over *Contributions to Indian Sociology* (New Series), then sixteen years old, to him. It was one of the first two social science journals published by SAGE India (the other being *Indian Economic and Social History Review*), and there they have stayed ever since, to the satisfaction of everybody concerned.

When Tejeshwar Singh retired from the position of Managing Director of SAGE India in 2006, after having secured it an honoured place as one of the country's topmost publishing companies, he wrote graciously to thank me for my support, but complained that I had never given a book to SAGE. I responded saying that I would do so. This, then, is that book, but, alas, Tejeshwar Singh is no longer with us.

I would like to conclude by noting that the intellectual debts incurred in writing this book are numerous; some of them are acknowledged chapter-wise. I would also like once again to place on record my indebtedness to the Institute of Economic Growth (IEG)—to the colleagues and the directors—for unstinting encouragement and support over the last forty years. In preparing this book for the publisher, I have received invaluable assistance from Rajesh Chatwal and Aradhya Bhardwaj. I thank them both most warmly.

T.N. Madan

New Delhi
March 2010

Acknowledgements

Of the chapters comprising this book, all except Chapter Eight are revised and, in some cases, are extended versions of essays published earlier elsewhere. I thank the publishers, and where relevant the editors, of the earlier versions. The details of each chapter are given as follows:

- **Chapter One**: 'Indian Secularism in a Post-secular Age' appeared as 'Indian Secularism as a Religio-secular Ideal' in Linell Cady and Elizabeth Hurd (eds), *Secularism and Politics in a Global Age*, pp. 258–76. New York: Palgrave-Macmillan, in 2010.
- **Chapter Two**: 'Hinduism: The Book View and the Field View' appeared as 'The Sociology of Hinduism: Reading Backwards from Srinivas to Weber' in *Sociological Bulletin*, 55(2): 215–36, in 2006.
- **Chapter Three**: 'Islam: The Universal and the Particular' appeared as 'One from Many: Explorations in the Anthropology of Islam' in *The Eastern Anthropologist* 60(1): 1–25, in 2007. This is the revised text of the first D.N. Majumdar Endowment Fund Lecture delivered under the auspices of the Department of Anthropology, University of Lucknow, on 23 November 2006. I owe thanks to Professor Indu Sahai, Head of the Department, and her colleagues for their many courtesies.

I am also indebted to Raymond Jamous, M. Ishaq Khan, Roddam Narasimha, Margrit Pernau, Asim Roy, Satish Saberwal,

Farzana Shaikh, Sudhir Chandra, and Nur Yalman for their careful reading of an earlier draft of this chapter and for their excellent advice. I am particularly grateful to Roy for his patient support and to Narasimha, a physicist, for his insightful observations on the theme of hierarchical relationships, whether within cultural traditions or between the scales of turbulent fluid motion.

- **Chapter Four**: 'Sikhism: The Sacred and the Secular' appeared as 'The Sikh Religious Tradition: Three Meanings of Secularism' in T.N. Madan, *Modern Myths, Locked Minds: Secularism and Fundamentalism in India*, pp. 39–62. New Delhi: Oxford University Press, in 1997.
- **Chapter Five**: 'Gandhi and Weber: The Work Ethic, Capitalism, and Conscience' appeared in a shorter version as 'Moral Choices: Gandhi and Weber on Capitalism and Conscience' in Jyotirmaya Sharma and A. Raghuramaraju (eds), *Grounding Morality: Freedom, Knowledge and Plurality of Cultures*. New Delhi: Routledge, in 2010.
- **Chapter Six**: 'Radhakamal Mukerjee and His Contemporaries' is a slightly modified version of the First Radhakamal Mukerjee Memorial Lecture, delivered on 28 December 2010, at the 35th All India Sociological Conference at Ravenshaw University, Cuttack. The original text is being published simultaneously in *Sociological Bulletin*, 60(1), in 2011. I am grateful to the President of the Indian Sociological Society, Professor John Jacob Kattakayam, and the Editor, *Sociological Bulletin*, Professor N. Jayaram, for their consent to simultaneous publication of the lecture.
- **Chapter Seven**: 'D.P. Mukerji: Towards a Historical Sociology' appeared as 'Search for Synthesis: The Sociology of D.P. Mukerji' in Patricia Uberoi, Nandini Sundar, and Satish Deshpande (eds), *Anthropology in the East: Founders of Sociology and Social Anthropology in India*, pp. 256–89. Nainital: Permanent Black, in 2007.
- **Chapter Eight**: 'M.N. Srinivas: Empiricism and Imagination' is forthcoming as 'The Real and Imagined Worlds of M.N. Srinivas' in a Festschrift in honour of Ashis Nandy, edited by Shail Mayaram and Ravi Sundaram. I owe thanks to

Arindam Chakrabarti, Uma Madan, Ashis Nandy, Gananath and Ranjini Obeyesekere, and Sudhir Chandra for their helpful reading of an earlier draft of this chapter.
- **Chapter Nine**: 'Louis Dumont: The Man and His Work' appeared as 'Louis Dumont: A Memoir' in *Contributions to Indian Sociology*, 33(3): 473–501, in 1999.
- **Chapter Ten**: '*Contributions to Indian Sociology*: Towards Methodological Pluralism' appeared as '*Contributions to Indian Sociology* at Fifty' in *Contributions to Indian Sociology*, 42(1): 9–28, in 2008.
- **Epilogue**: 'Engagements and Passages—An Exercise in Reflexivity' is mostly newly written, but partly based on 'Discovering Anthropology: A Personal Narrative' in Meenakshi Thapan (ed.), *Anthropologial Journeys*, pp. 143–62. New Delhi: Orient Longman, in 1998.

Part I

CULTURAL TRADITIONS, SOCIOLOGICAL PERSPECTIVES

In its ordinary use in English 'culture', which is much the same idea as cultivation, refers to a process, and we can define it as the process by which a person acquires, from contact with other persons or from such things as books or works of art, knowledge, skill, ideas, beliefs, tastes, sentiments. In a particular society we can discover certain processes of cultural tradition, using the word tradition in its literal meaning of handing on or handing down.

—A.R. RADCLIFFE-BROWN, *Structure and Function in Primitive Society*

This part of the book comprises discussions of the character and appropriate sociological approaches to the study of various religious and value traditions of India. The lead chapter argues that, paradoxical though it may seem, Indian secularism as a political ideology is predicated on the existence of a plurality of religions in the public domain. The next three chapters address select aspects of the study of Hinduism, Islam, and Sikhism. In each case, the argument is in favour of methodological pluralism, or, put otherwise, recognition of the complementarity of seemingly opposed perspectives. In a sense, these three chapters carry forward my discussion of the major religious traditions of India in an earlier work, *Modern Myths, Locked Minds: Secularism and Fundamentalism in India* (1997). In fact, Chapter Four is reproduced here from that book. There the focus was on the relationship of the sacred and the secular; here it is on methods of study. The last chapter briefly engages with the manner in which Gandhi and Weber tackled certain value concerns associated with Western civilization generally, but capitalism in particular. Taken together, the first five chapters of the book are explicitly concerned with the study of cultural traditions. Since the methods of study discussed, employed, or advocated are sociological, these exercises are also concerned with sociological traditions.

Chapter One

Indian Secularism in a Post-secular Age

[The secular state] is a state which honours all faiths equally and gives them equal opportunities....
—JAWAHARLAL NEHRU, *An Anthology*

I use this term ['post-secular Europe'] not as designating an age in which the declines in belief and practice of the last century would have been reversed, because this doesn't seem likely, at least for the moment; I rather mean a time in which the hegemony of the mainstream master narrative of secularization will be more and more challenged. This I think is now happening.
—CHARLES TAYLOR, *A Secular Age*

I claim no originality, only certain timeliness.
—GREGORY BATESON, *Angels Fear*

Is Indian secularism the Indian version of a universal conceptual category—secularism *in* India—with its own defining characteristics in addition to some essential general features which it shares with secularism elsewhere? Or, is it significantly distinctive for us to be wary of its being treated as just a variant without, however, asserting its uniqueness? Bhargava (2007: 20f.) has argued forcefully for Indian secularism being 'a distinctively Indian and differently modern variant of secularism'. While broadly in agreement with Bhargava's formulations, particularly his emphasis on the multivocality of secularism in the West, I will develop my argument somewhat differently, focusing for heuristic purposes more on the specificity of Indian secularism than its generality. Let me recall Max Weber's (1949a: 78) insightful observation that whatever is 'historical' is so because it is 'significant in its individuality'. Moreover, it seems to me, the method of civilizational comparison through 'typification' with a view to revealing the universal by focusing on difference (see Dumont 1980a; Madan 2006a: Chapter 12) is appropriate for this endeavour.

THE HISTORY OF INDIAN SECULARISM

The specificity of Indian secularism, I would like to argue, lies in a combination of historical and contemporary circumstances. The limitation of space permits only a brief outline.

Whether Indians have for very long considered religion a determinant of group and individual identities, or only from the nineteenth century onward after the colonial intrusion, such identification is today universal among the more-than-one-billion inhabitants of India. In the last census (2001), only a fraction of one-half per cent respondents refused to answer the question about religious affiliation. It will not do to dismiss such responses, as is often done, as thoughtless gut reactions to enumerators' insistent questions. The pervasiveness of religion as personal faith, or as political ideology, or as both simultaneously, is a basic sociological and political fact about India today.

What makes this demographic datum potentially dangerous to the civil society and the polity is the very uneven distribution of religious identities: approximately 82 per cent Hindus, 13 per cent Muslims, and 2 per cent each Christians and Sikhs. The remaining 1 per cent accounts for dozens of communities including Buddhists, Jains, Jews, and Zoroastrians. The overwhelming majority of Hindus and by no means the small population of Muslims call for a fine tuning of governmental policies; errors of judgement in what is appropriate and what can be implemented can be costly. I will not go into the internal heterogeneity of Hindus and Muslims beyond mentioning that a considerable number of politically mobilized, traditionally oppressed, lower-caste communities do not consider themselves Hindus any more, nor is it right to regard all tribal religions as Hindu in some sense.

Now, the religious traditions of Hindus and Muslims, and Sikhs too, who together account for 95 per cent of the population, do not recognize the autonomy of the domains of economics and politics, but consider them governed by moral or religious values. In the classic Brahmanical formulation of the goals and value orientations of life, *dharma*, or morality, encompasses *artha*, that is the rational pursuit of economic and political goals, and provides its legitimizing principle (see Madan 1982a, particularly the chapters by Charles Malamoud and K.J. Shah). The Islamic tradition is absolutely unequivocal in its rejection of Western formulations of the sacred–secular dichotomy (see Madan 1997, Chapter 5). The religious traditions notwithstanding, secularization (in the sense of an increasing range of activities such as agriculture, education, healthcare, and governance being 'released' from the control of traditional knowledge and specialists and conducted in accordance with modern science, technology, and bureaucratic procedures) are proceeding apace everywhere, but secularism as a worldview does not therefore automatically become acceptable.

Indians like other peoples elsewhere are quite comfortable living with contradictions. They do not seem to think that religious beliefs and practices have to be strictly separated from secular (so-called) activities or, in some sense, privatized. My contention (Madan 1987b) is that religiousness in India is publicly acknowledged and pursued, and that its privatization is an alien idea and, therefore, secularism as a worldview providing an ideological backdrop for the secular state would not find easy acceptance—this attracted much criticism from secularist intellectuals in India. My conclusion, which clearly stated that for the success of the secular state we need to take both religion (as worldview) and secularism (as political ideology/practice) seriously, was generally ignored. Secularism as political ideology and practice obviously does not stand for the separation of religion/church and the state in India, but rather for a non-discriminatory state, which is constrained to treat its citizens in certain contexts (where religious beliefs and/or identities are at stake) differentially rather than uniformly.

At this point, I must briefly mention the long history of inter-religious conflict (Indianists call it communalism), which in modern, colonial India overrode the sociocultural reality of peaceful coexistence. The term that is generally used for the latter is *composite* culture, but I find it ambiguous, and am, therefore, sceptical about its usage. My fieldwork experience in the Kashmir Valley has convinced me that Hindus and Muslims may situationally recognize cultural differences (no common worship, intermarriage, or commensalism) and yet construct non-conflictual, even harmonious, social arrangements on its basis (see Madan 2001a).

The national movement for freedom from colonial rule split early in the twentieth century and followed two tracks. On the one side were the pluralists or multi-religious nationalists, led by Mahatma Gandhi and Jawaharlal Nehru, and included Muslim nationalists, who constructed their political agenda in terms of common interests. The term secular was hardly ever used to characterize such interests. On the other side were the mono-religious nationalists, called communalists by their opponents and more prominent among Muslims than among Hindus, who regarded religious communities as nations and stressed the incompatibility of both their interests and their values. Resentful of the loss of political power in the subcontinent, which they had enjoyed for 800 years, and apprehensive of Hindu dominance in a one person–one vote democratic polity, Muslim separatists, inspired by a path-breaking ideological statement by the poet-philosopher Mohammad Iqbal (see Mukherjee 2007: 119–42), and led by M.A. Jinnah, ironically a secularist in the Western sense of the term (see Wolpert 1988), eventually forced the partition of the country in 1947. Independence from British colonial rule thus coincided with the emergence of two sovereign nation states, India and Pakistan, in the subcontinent.

Expectedly, although contrary to the wishes of its founder (who died in September 1948), Pakistan was proclaimed and remains until today an Islamic but non-theocratic state. And, again quite expectedly, the leaders of the new Indian state set out to fashion a polity in consonance with the ideals of the freedom movement, notably democracy and religious pluralism.

Legislatures elected under restricted franchise in the last year of colonial rule (1946) assumed the responsibility of constitution-making in both countries. Pakistanis ran into many and protracted difficulties after the initial proclamation of the Islamic state; Indians, after two years of diligent deliberations, gave themselves the world's most liberal constitution. Proclaiming India a democratic republic, 'freedom of conscience and free profession, practice and propagation of religion' (Article 25) was granted to the citizens as a fundamental right. Additionally, another fundamental right

(Article 15) forbade discrimination by the state against any citizen on the basis of religious identity. There is no specific prohibition of the establishment of a state religion, but such a limitation is entailed by other relevant provisions. Indeed, the spirit of the Constitution is against it. Like it had seldom been used in the pluralist rhetoric of the freedom movement, the word secularism found no place in the Constitution either despite the repeated pleas of a member (K.T. Shah) to mention it. The pleas of another vocal member (H.V. Kamath) to open the Constitution with a reference to god were also rejected.

It is clear that secularism even in its limited sense of non-religiousness, not to mention its connotation of opposition to religion, was not an idea that would find acceptance among the constitution-makers who were drawn from all the religious communities of India. Even agnostics and rationalists like Nehru had to concede that Indians were by and large religious. This is how he put it in 1948 a few months after independence: 'India will be a land of many faiths, equally honoured and respected, but of one national outlook' (Madan 1997: 233). Here, then we have the definition of Indian secularism: religious pluralism as a positive value combined with the affirmation of national unity within a democratic framework. Thus defined, secularism was subsequently declared by the Indian Supreme Court to be a basic and, therefore, unalterable feature of the Constitution. The qualifying term 'secular' in describing the Republic was added to the Preamble after an amendment in 1976 to identify India as 'a Sovereign Socialist Democratic Republic'. The Hindi version of the Constitution pinpoints the connotation of the term secular (*laukik*; cf. Greek *laikos*) by using the phrase *pantha nirpeksha*, which translated back into English would read as denominationally neutral, using the word 'denomination' in a general rather than its specific Christian connotation.

Today, the public display of symbols of religious identity has become a major contentious issue in many countries. In France, the Muslim headscarf and the Sikh turban are not allowed in public (which is currently faced with problems similar to India's), and in Turkey, the headscarf has failed to make it to the university campus. In Denmark, the government is contemplating a ban on the wearing of Christian crosses, Jewish skull caps, and veils and turbans by judges in its law courts, and in Quebec (Canada), according to media reports, the Gérard Bouchard-Charles Taylor Commission recently (in 2008) recommended removal of the crucifix atop the speaker's chair in the Quebec provincial parliament to protect the state's secular image.

In sharp contrast, the Indian parliament—a microcosm of the Indian nation—affords the viewer an eye-catching spectacle. Christian crosses, Jain robes, Hindu forehead marks, Muslim and Sikh beards, varieties of headgear including veils and turbans, and even swords proclaim the religious identity of every such honourable member's wish to display it. What is true of the Parliament is also true of other public spaces including schools, banks, and government offices. Religious symbols do indeed thickly populate the public square in India.

How could the ideal of national unity binding religious communities into a nation with a common outlook, which could not be achieved through the years of the freedom movement, be attained in the wake of independence? The appeal to economic interests consistently repeated over many years had failed to overcome communal differences and prevent partition. Ten years after independence, in 1958, Nehru did have to confess to André Malraux that 'creating a secular state in a religious society' was no easy task (Malraux 1968: 145). Whether Nehru used the phrase 'secular state' in the Western or the Indian sense of the term to connote a separation of the domains of religion and politics/governance or to convey equal respect for all religions, he made it clear that the ideal was not easily achievable. And who would know better?

Secular considerations were not to be abandoned, but could perhaps be reinforced by drawing upon the resources of religious traditions and also of early and medieval Indian history (see Bhargava 2010). Indian secularism was to be a religio-secular ideology. It is noteworthy that Nehru himself felt constrained to invest economic and political developments with the aura of the sacred. He famously called the big dams and other development works 'temples of the new age' (Mukherjee 2007: 222, 225), and described 'secular democracy' as a 'sacred cause' (Abdullah 1993: 122). He personally chose the Buddhist wheel of righteousness (*dharma chakra*) as the centrepiece of the national flag and the Sarnath pillar of the third century BC, depicting three religious images including the *dharma* wheel as the national emblem. Here, then, we have that 'intimate union of the spirit of religion and the spirit of liberty', which

Alexis de Tocqueville found in North America and missed in his own country. In this formulation, needless to emphasize, primordial identity and democracy are not antagonistic categories.

The most outstanding and influential spokesman of the traditional Hindu point of view during the formative years of the Republic was the philosopher Radhakrishnan (who was chosen by Nehru to be the second President). And he thought it would be 'strange that our government should be a secular one while our culture is rooted in spiritual values'. Secularism, Radhakrishnan maintained, had to be given a culturally appropriate definition in India to emphasize that 'the universality of spiritual values may be attained in a variety of ways' (Madan 1997: 245). This was a throwback to the Rig Veda (c. 1500 BC): *ekam sad viprah bahudhā vadanti* (the Truth or Absolute is one, but has been variously described by the wise).

This is the doctrine of religious pluralism that modern Hindu intellectuals have invoked over centuries in promotion of religious pluralism and tolerance. In the late nineteenth century, a charismatic Hindu religious reformer, Vivekananda, who sought to recast Vedantic (late Vedic) Hinduism as a global religion, cited the aforementioned Vedic aphorism and much else from traditional sources to stress its tolerant, even accommodative character. And in the twentieth century, Gandhi presented it thus: 'All religions are divinely inspired, but they are imperfect because they are products of the human mind and taught by human beings' (Iyer 1986: 543).

I do not have the space here to more-than-barely mention that many Muslim traditionalists who totally reject Western secularism as a worldview, support Indian secularism as state policy, for it is expedient to do so. For example, the Jamā'at-i Islāmī of India considers Indian secularism a 'blessing' and a 'guarantee for a safe future of Islam' in modern India (Ahmad 1991). Obviously, this is a tactical compromise offset by an explicit commitment to the ideal of a universal Muslim community of faith (*ummah*). In contrast, their counterparts in Pakistan and Bangladesh campaign for an Islamic state. Moreover, many traditionalists selectively cite the Qur'ān itself to derive from it the doctrine of religious pluralism and tolerance (see Madan 1997: Chapter 5 for a discussion of the views of Maulana Azad).

Scripture is not, however, what the orthodox secularists would fall back upon. Indeed, some Indian Marxist intellectuals have denounced Indian secularism in no uncertain terms: 'It is in fact no secularism at all—it is far more a celebration of all kinds of religion and religiosity, ignorance, obscurantism and social oppression' (Singh 1993: 49). Others have observed that the notion of *samabhāva*, or equal treatment, does not necessarily imply respect or goodwill, or *sadbhāva*, but that it could more reasonably stand for the eventual rejection of all religions as error and falsehood.

The liberals appeal to secular history, and trace a tradition of inter-faith dialogues and religious tolerance back to the policy of the emperor Ashoka (c. 268–233 BC), who, although born a Hindu himself embraced Buddhism, did not make it the state religion. Instead, he commended 'religious concord' to his subjects so that they may 'hear one another's principles'; by honouring another's sect 'one increases the influence of one's own sect' (Thapar 1961: 255). He declared 'all men are my children (*savve munisse pajā mamā*)', thus presenting himself as a parent rather than a prophet (Thapar 1961: 147). His policy of *dhamma*, although undoubtedly inspired by his understanding of the Buddha's teaching, was largely his own formulation. Thapar (1961: 163) calls it 'a secular teaching', 'an attempt ... to suggest a way of life', which was 'practical' as well as 'highly moral' (Thapar 1961: 149).

Nearly two millennia later, the Muslim emperor Akbar (1543–1605 CE), breaking with the established policy of treating non-Muslims in India as protected but morally and politically inferior subjects,[1] pursued a policy of religious tolerance and even syncretism, and peace towards all (*sulh-i-kul*). He decreed that 'no man should be interfered with on account of religion, and anyone is to be allowed to go over to a religion that pleases him' (Sen 2005: 18). Akbar's exemplary policies suffered fairly rapid erosion after his death. Needless to add, orthodox Muslim opinion was severely critical of him, even accusing him of apostasy (see Sharma 1962).

---

[1]The medieval period of Indian history is marked by persistent admonitions by religious leaders (*Ulamā'*), advocating that the kings establish a theocratic state. The kings generally were, however, more concerned about secular gains (territory, stability, revenues, and so on) than religious merit through the propagation of Islam and the elimination of infidels. Persecution in various forms of those not yet converted was common however (see Jackson 1999: 275–98).

Amartya Sen, among others, finds 'echoes' of Ashoka's and Akbar's (particularly the latter's) promotion of inter-religious harmony 'in the later history of India' (Sen 2005: 16). He maintains that Akbar 'laid the formal foundations of a secular legal structure and of religious neutrality of the state' (Sen 2005: 18), a kind of 'secular state which was yet to be born in India or for that matter anywhere in the world' (Sen 2005: 287).[2]

Attention has also been drawn to the emergence of a syncretistic religious culture in north India in the medieval period, at the local level, which had Hindu gurus and Muslim pīrs as its charismatic preceptors. They preached 'a message not only of tolerance but also of social equality and a concern for the human condition' (Thapar 2007: 100). It is argued that this tradition provides a credible historical basis for contemporary Indian secularism. But this too is problematic mainly because of the other-worldly character of these sects (see Schomer and McLeod 1987).

I think one has to be cautious, and not project, even inadvertently, conceptual similarity as historical continuity. It is fine to see in Ashoka's or Akbar's ideas, or in medieval folk religions, alternative, non-Western conceptions of secularism as religious pluralism, and build a comparative typology of secular (or religious) ideologies and states, but only just that. The immediate antecedents of the Indian secular state lie elsewhere.[3]

---

[2] It may be noted here that the innovations of Ashoka and Akbar were not inherent in their respective religious traditions as Nandy (2001a: 8) rather brusquely suggests, but were the outcome of their situational predicaments and spiritual struggles (see Moosvi 2007; Thapar 1961).

[3] Judging by a carefully assembled anthology of Gandhi's moral and political writings (Iyer 1986) and Nehru's *The Discovery of India* (1961), Ashoka and Akbar were, of course, significant presences in the thinking of these two founding fathers of Indian secularism, but much more so in Nehru's than in Gandhi's case. Both of them noted Ashoka's efforts to spread Buddhism. Akbar received more attention in the context of inter-religious harmony. Interestingly, Gandhi attributed Akbar's tolerance to the influence of Hinduism on him (Iyer 1986: 470). Nehru mentions Akbar's attempts to 'start a new synthetic faith to suit everybody' and to promote a composite Hindu–Muslim culture (Nehru 1961: 273) and 'to interpret religion in a rational spirit' (Nehru 1961: 278). Both leaders viewed Ashoka and Akbar as important historical personalities, but also noted that their innovations were short-lived.

THE SOURCES OF CONTEMPORARY INDIAN SECULARISM

A religiously neutral, non-discriminatory state made its appearance only in the middle of the nineteenth century, when the British crown assumed full responsibility of the governance of those areas of the subcontinent that had been seized by the East India Company. A royal proclamation in London in 1858, inspired largely by the perception that the soldiers' mutiny and the subsequent mass uprising of the previous year had been triggered by official disregard of the religious sensibilities of Indians generally, and committed the government to abstention from any interference in the religious beliefs and practices of the empire's Indian subjects: 'We declare it to be our royal pleasure that none be in any wise favoured, nor molested or disquieted, by reason of their religious faith or observances, but that all shall alike enjoy equal and impartial protection of the law' (Smith 1963: 72). The proclamation did not, however, grant to Indian religions moral equality with Christianity as true faiths, and evangelical activities, allowed by an act of the British parliament in 1813, continued as before. Not everyone, however, considered the proclamation sincere or gracious. The wife of the deposed King of Oudh, issued a counter proclamation later in the year 1858, totally rejecting its genuineness (see Sen 1957: 382–84). Even so, the British statement of policy did indeed influence the thinking of a nascent national leadership.

A society characterized by religious pluralism and governed by a non-discriminatory state is what Indian secularism has come to mean under the constitution of free India adopted in 1949. Non-discrimination does not mean, however, that there shall be no intervention in the religious practices of the people to secure justice for all. Bhargava (2007: 39–41) calls this the policy of 'principled distance' and argues cogently in favour of it, but does not consider the difficulties in implementing such a policy. The government has on many occasions ended up tying itself in knots, trapped in uncomfortable proximity instead of maintaining reasonable distance. The real problem is the absence of a general consensus on how to define principled distance in a pluralist setting.

Thus, the Constitution outlawed the immemorial Hindu practice of untouchability (Article 17), under which some of the lower castes were denied access to upper caste places of worship, wells, village commons, and so on, and physically avoided because they were considered ritually polluting. Besides, after the promulgation of the Constitution, and in furtherance of social justice, the Indian parliament enacted a series of laws which overturned centuries-old Hindu customs in respect of the inferior or non-existent rights of Hindu women with regard to marriage, divorce, maintenance, inheritance of property, and so on. British rulers had refrained from interfering with such customs and, in fact, froze them by codifying them as Hindu personal law. The policy of non-interference was uniformly applied to all communities.

Although the Constitution requires, under the Directive Principles of State Policy, that the state shall 'endeavour to secure for the citizens a uniform civil code' (Article 44), successive governments have generally refrained from intervening in the personal laws of minority communities. Such restraint is not an expression of principled distance, but political caution, which its critics call, not entirely without justification, political opportunism or 'vote bank' politics. Differential treatment of the majority and minority communities, defined primarily in terms of religious identity, has thus emerged as a defining feature of Indian secularism. Articles 29 and 30 grant the minorities the fundamental, inalienable right to establish and administer educational institutions, which are exempted from taxation and other liabilities, and are subject to certain limitations.

In this regard, it has been argued by some political scientists that the state should compensate the religious minorities for the conditions of economic and political deprivation that cannot reasonably be said to be their own creation. It should also enable them to preserve their cultural and religious heritage through the creation of 'supportive structures' (Chandhoke 1999). This is highly problematic; I will not go into that here beyond pointing out that such a policy could lead to a vastly enlarged and proactive role for the state generally, to the detriment of individual liberty and civil society initiatives. Moreover, it would hinder the growth of a national identity (see Madan 2006a: 130f.).

A major conclusion that the foregoing, necessarily brief discussion of the evolution of Indian secularism yields is that its institutional expression, namely, the secular state, is meaningful *only* in the presence of a continuing plurality of religious communities. This is, of course, broadly true of the USA also, but in India, in the absence of the kind of cultural homogeneity that prevails in North America, the state is expected to honour all religions and not construct a wall of separation between them and itself. The secular state exists here not because the society at large has turned its back on religion as a public phenomenon, but because religion is generally important and not as personal faith alone. The state is not emancipated from religion: this was the constitutional choice and is the governmental practice. It should be added, however, that the general processes of secularization proceed in India independently of the political ideology of secularism. To trust an agronomist rather than an astrologer, a doctor rather than a faith healer, or a banker rather than a traditional money lender has nothing to do with secular politics.

The majority–minority conundrum that divided the national movement in the first half of the twentieth century and led to the partition, is the spectre that haunts India today at the beginning of the twenty-first century. The last twenty-five years have been witness to the re-articulation of Hindu revivalism as cultural nationalism under the auspices of a family (so-called) of organizations, among which the Rashtriya Swayamsevak Sangh (RSS, National Volunteer Corps), founded in 1925, is the parent body, and the Bharatiya Janata Party (BJP, Indian People's Party), founded in 1980, the political front (see Jafferlot 1996). Claiming to be the representative body of Hindus, although including a sprinkling of non-Hindus, it has not so far been able to win, at the national level, the support of more than approximately one-fifth of the total electorate. In terms of its presence in the parliament, however, it made great strides in just fourteen years, from 1984 when it had two members, to 1998 when it emerged as the single largest party ahead of the Congress, the self-proclaimed torch bearer of Indian secularism. It may be added that, throughout its career, BJP has made extensive use of religious symbolism in political mobilization, drawing upon mythology, old beliefs, and current practice.

BJP has characterized the concern of other political parties, including notably the Congress and the Left parties, for the minorities as the policy of appeasement. The emergence of Muslim terrorism in various parts of the country since the late 1980s has provided grist to its mill. BJP headed a coalition government at the centre (federal level) from 1998 to 2004, which soft-pedalled its agenda of Hindu hegemony presented as Indian cultural nationalism, and rather focused on economic and foreign policy issues. BJP's national leadership failed to take action against the government of the state of Gujarat run by the party for its failure to prevent mass murder, rape, and loot in early 2002, following an incident of arson on a train carrying Hindu political workers, suspected to have been engineered by Muslim terrorists. According to revised official estimates (in 2008), the carnage left about 1,100–1,200 Muslims dead (see Vardarajan 2002 for early, detailed reports).

The most authoritative leader of BJP, L.K. Advani, recently summed up the party's stand on secularism thus:

> Unfortunately, for decades now, in the name of secularism, politicians have been wanting the nation to disown its essential personality. For the left inclined, secularism has been a euphemism to cloak their intense allergy to religion and more particularly to Hinduism. It is this attitude which BJP characterizes as pseudo-secularism. This attitude is wrong and unscientific [*sic*]. (Advani 2008: 371)

Needless to emphasize, the 'essential personality' of Advani's conception is rooted in pre-Islamic indigenous cultural values.

Now, Partha Chatterjee pointed out in 1994 that '[t]he majoritarianism of the Hindu right is perfectly at peace with the institutional procedures of the "western" or "modern state"' ([1994] 1998: 346). The question that therefore arises is whether 'the defence of secularism [is] an appropriate ground for meeting the challenge of the Hindu right?' Or, whether the emphasis should be on 'the duty of the democratic state to ensure policies of religious toleration' (Chatterjee [1994] 1998: 348)? He argued tolerance 'premised on autonomy and respect for persons', so that the minorities can 'resist homogenization from outside and push for democratization from inside' (Chatterjee [1994] 1998: 375, 378).

Although it is now fifteen years since Chatterjee put forward the foregoing argument, it retains its validity. But one needs to recognize that governmental policies often err on the side of excessive protectionism, giving some credence to the charges of minority appeasement and reverse discrimination against the majority (that is, the Hindus). The most recent example of this is the decision (in 2009) of the Left Front government in the state of Kerala that 11 per cent equity of an Islamic financial service company shall be held by the Kerala State Industrial Development Corporation. According to a public interest application currently being heard by a division bench of the Kerala High Court, the company is to be set up in accordance with Sharī'ah, the canon law of Muslims, and, thus, violates certain articles of the Indian constitution, notably Article 14, which provides for equality before the law and Article 15, which prohibits 'discrimination on grounds of religion, race, caste, sex or place of birth'. The issue is more than one of constitutional validity and political rectitude; it has a deep moral dimension also. And that takes us back to Gandhi, who maintained that: 'A society or group, which depends partly or wholly on state aid for the existence of its religion, does not deserve or, better still, does not have any religion worth the name' (see Bose 1948: 287).

GANDHI AND INDIAN SECULARISM

Mahatma Gandhi is generally considered the patron saint, as it were, of Indian secularism—this is an oversimplification. And often he is bracketed with Nehru as a secularist—this is quite misleading. Gandhi's conception of religion could be called secular since he demystified it and bracketed it with reason, but not otherwise. Nehru was, as I have already said, an agnostic, and Gandhi was an intensely religious person. 'For me,' he affirmed quite early in his life, 'every, the tiniest, activity is governed by what I consider my religion' (Iyer 1986: 391). In 1940, as on numerous other occasions during his life, he reiterated his position: 'I cannot conceive politics as divorced from religion. Indeed religion should pervade every one of our actions' (Madan 1997: 235).

The state was, another thing, however, much narrower in scope and less accessible than politics. The politics of a country is a field of activity that is in principle open to every citizen. The state, in contrast, is an arena of institutionalized activity governed by rules and procedures regarding who will operate it and how. It follows that if Gandhi affirmed the inseparability of religion (understood as morality, *dharma*) and politics, and the *separability* of religion (as denominational faith) and the state, he did not contradict himself. It is hardly necessary to add that Gandhi's observations on the character of the state belong to the last years of his life, while those about the moral nature of politics of his conception reflected a lifelong concern. They surely were influenced by the violent communal riots of 1946–48. A few months before his assassination, Gandhi said that 'the state should undoubtedly be secular. Everyone ... should be entitled to profess his religion without let or hindrance, so long as the citizen obeys the laws of the land' (Iyer 1986: 395). In Gandhi's judgement, the moral individual was the cornerstone of the good society, provided that he or she was an other-regarding rather than self-oriented individual—a *satyāgrahī* (a truth agent) and not a *sannyāsī* (a renouncer)—and in such a society the state's functions obviously would be limited.

Two clarifications are in order here. First, what was Gandhi's conception of religion? His answer was that 'religion does not mean sectarianism. It means a belief in ordered moral government of the universe.... This religion transcends Hinduism, Islam, Christianity, etc. It does not supersede them. It harmonizes them and gives them reality' (Madan 1997: 235f.).

Second, and in view of the foregoing statement, what was the rationale for religious plurality? For this Gandhi appealed to, among other ideas, the combined Jain doctrine of 'many sidedness' (*anekantavād*) and 'qualified certainty' (*syādavād*), which, he said, he made 'peculiarly his own' (see Chatterjee 2005: 306), and according to which no absolute or unqualified statements can be made about existential reality because of its multi-dimensional and complex nature. Various kinds of specification are necessary. It is this doctrine, he affirmed, which had taught him 'to judge a Mussalman from his own standpoint and a Christian from his.' And it was *syādavād* that had taught him 'the unity of all religions' (Jordens 1998: 151f.).[4]

---

[4]It is perhaps noteworthy that these specifically Jain ontological and epistemological perspectives are claimed by some commentators to be Hindu perspectives. Thus, P.B. Gajendragadkar, one of the most articulate and influential Justices (eventually the Chief) of the Supreme Court wrote in a landmark judgement of 1966 (quoted in Sen 2010: 17):

> Naturally enough it was realized by Hindu religion from the very beginning of its career that truth was many-sided and different views contained different aspects of truth which no one could fully express. This knowledge inevitably bred a spirit of tolerance and willingness to understand and appreciate the opponent's point of view.

Interestingly, Gajendragadkar based his formulation on S. Radhakrishnan's view of Hinduism rather than on Gandhi's (see Sen 2010: 17). Needless to add, both Gajendragadkar and Radhakrishnan, and Gandhi too, and now the Indian constitution, consider Jainism as a member of the larger Hindu family.

Gandhi also argued that a truly religious person would always be open to what religions other than the one he or she is born into had to teach. What may be missing or latent in one tradition could be present or manifest in another. One's tradition does not say it all or always get right what it says. Put otherwise, no religion is complete without significant others. This led Gandhi not towards some kind of religious syncretism, but to the recognition of the value of religious plurality—which is what Indian secularism primarily is all about. Contrary to what is often maintained, Gandhi did not argue that the followers of all religions should become a single community of faith, but rather that such a community should be, as it were, many, for one cannot be truly religious in moral isolation. As early as in 1921, Gandhi said, in the context of Hindu–Muslim unity for which he was then striving, that the objective was not 'uniting the religions', but 'uniting hearts, despite the separateness of religions' (Gandhi 1966a: 305). Nothing could be more explicit than this. Twenty-six years later, under the menacing shadow of the mass killings that defined Partition, he spoke in deep anguish at one of the prayer meetings held by him in Delhi on 13 September 1947. Addressing Hindus in particular, he said: 'I am a Hindu, a true Hindu, a *sanatani* [orthodox, traditional] Hindu. *Therefore*, I am also a Muslim, and a Parsi, and a Christian, and a Jew too' (Gandhi 1954: 307, my translation of the original Hindi, emphasis added). The implication surely is that anyone who is truly religious is, *ipso facto*, multi-religious. In holding such a view, he was radically different from religious thinkers like the Hindu Vivekananda (see Basu 2002) or the Muslim Maulana Azad (see Madan 1997, Chapters 5 and 6), who regarded their respective religions as the most perfect, but granted the right of other true religions to exist. Indeed, Vivekananda maintained that Vedantic Hinduism included in itself all that was true in every other religion.

Gandhi's pluralism was marked by humility rather than condescension. He found the notions of tolerance and respect for all religions inadequate: tolerance seemed to him to 'imply a gratuitous assumption of the inferiority of other faiths to one's own', and respect was, he said, 'patronising'. What satisfied him was (to quote his own words again) *samabhāva* or the resolve 'to entertain *the same respect* for religious faiths of others as we accord to our own, thus *admitting the imperfections of the latter*', which he said was in conformity with *ahimsa* (Jordens 1998: 154, emphasis added).[5] In other words, for Gandhi the value of others lies in their otherness. By embracing otherness, one may hope to move gradually from truths, which are relative, closer to Absolute Truth, which remain, however, only an ideal and difficult to realize because of the limitations of the human condition.[6]

It is pertinent to note here that Gandhian pluralism minimizes the state. It is concerned more with collective (people's) attitudes and individual responsibility. The history of the Indian state over the last sixty years is, however, one of increasing involvement and interference in the religious affairs of the people: in this, all three branches of the state (parliament, government, and judiciary) have been complicit (on the Supreme Court, see Sen 2010). While Gandhi's view of future society envisaged a religiously diverse political community comprising moral, responsible individuals, the Nehruvian state has moved unfailingly in the direction of a secularized, culturally homogenized, political community of citizens, defined by fundamental rights. One would have to admit that the chances of redefining the goals of India's political elite of any hue or shade are at present remote. The Gandhian perspective, however, remains relevant for civil society and a decentralized polity. The latter could well be the imperative of a not too distant future.

Gandhi's concept of the minimalist secular state (small government), re-envisaged as a decentralized polity, harmonizes well with *participatory* pluralism within civil society. His secularism was a religious idea, a moral value, implying reference to a transcendental principle. It was not a matter of political necessity or prudence, but

---

[5]Many contemporary scholars have arrived at similar but differently argued positions. Thus, Seligman (2000) in an insightful discussion recommends '[h]umility ... in all directions—of both faith and reason', and a willingness to 'question the very "givenness" of each's certitudes'. He calls this attitude 'a skeptical toleration—an epistemological modesty whose very uncertainty would prevent intolerance of the other' (Seligman 2000: 128).

[6]It has been pointed out by some perceptive scholars, most notably Rudolph (2006), that Gandhi's thought anticipated many significant strands of postmodernism, particularly his refusal 'to privilege modernism's commitment to the epistemology of universal truths, objective knowledge and master narratives' (Rudolph 2006: 4).

could become so. It must be added that religious ideas in Gandhi's reckoning were not self-certified, nor was the sanction of scripture sufficient: they were essentially open to the scrutiny of moral reason and, in his own case, conscience (see Chapter Five).[7] And unlike many other religious reformers such as Dayananda Sarasvati, the founder of the revivalist Arya Samaj (see Jordens 1978), or Martin Luther for that matter, Gandhi's inner voice was not silent on politics and economics. His vision of the good society was holistic. And, what is more, it remains vital for the future of Indian secularism.

CONCLUDING REMARKS

What about the future of Indian secularism as a religio-secular ideal?

Its most serious challenges could, perhaps ironically, come from the secular state's concern for the religious sensibilities of the people, particularly of the minorities, and from its democratic character. Thus, currently (in 2008–10), the Indian Supreme Court is seized of the problem of whether to allow the cutting through of a submarine rock formation between the southern tip of India and the northern tip of Sri Lanka to allow the passage of large cargo and passenger ships. This will very considerably shorten the sea route from the west coast of India to the east coast, which at present requires going round Sri Lanka, and contribute to economic development and be useful in other ways too. The Hindu Right, including the BJP, opposes the move on the ground that the orthodox among the Hindus believe this geological formation, popularly called Ramar Sethu (Rama's Bridge), was constructed by the god Rama. To cut through it, they maintain, will amount to its desecration and hurt the religious feelings of the majority community, which should be no less sacrosanct than similar feelings of the minorities.

---

[7]Thus, Gandhi wrote on one occasion (see Mathur 2008: 359):

> I exercise my judgement about every scripture, including the Gita. I cannot let a scriptural text supersede my reason whilst I believe that the principal books are inspired, they suffer from a process of double distillation. Firstly, they come through a human prophet and then through the commentaries of interpreters.... I cannot surrender my reason whilst I subscribe to divine revelation.

The Hindu case was argued in the Supreme Court by some of the country's most eminent constitutional lawyers, including a former Attorney General, Soli Sorabji, himself a Parsee. To reject their argument would amount to allowing secular considerations to violate freedom of religion, they suggested, because Hindus offer worship at Ramar Sethu, and would no longer be able to do so if it is desecrated. To accept it would mean the subordination of secular concerns, including developmental activities, to the dictates of the purveyors of religious traditions, without regard for the historical authenticity of such traditions and contemporary national interest. For the time being the Court has chosen evasion; it gave an interim order asking the government to suspend work on the project, assess its environmental impact, and examine alternatives to the proposed sea passage and then report back to it. This has not yet happened at the time of writing (December 2009).

Should the Court eventually give the green signal to the project, an angered and mobilized Hindu Right could, perhaps, gain politically. It is, of course not certain that this will happen; many Rama bridges would be needed to provide passage to the Hindu Right to its promised land. One cannot, however, entirely rule out the possibility that India may gradually slide into a situation comparable in some respects to the situation in Turkey, where the guardians of the nearly 100-year-old secular legacy of Kemal Ataturk, that is, the army and the judiciary, have often been at loggerheads with legally elected, popular governments, notably the present Justice and Democratic Party (AKP) government, which has been many times charged by the country's top courts of diluting or even seeking to undermine the secular character of the state. While historical and ideological differences between the BJP and AKP should not be minimized, the fear that Islamist ideological fervour is gaining ground is not unfounded. At a deeper level, therefore, the current Indian and Turkish political scenarios are two of several worldwide that question the conventional wisdom on the relationship of politics and the state in settings of religious resurgence (see Cady and Hurd 2010).

I do not mean to suggest that the future of Indian secularism will be decided by any particular event or issue, although it may highlight the dilemmas. That would obviously be absurd. The point I am trying to make is that the character and cross-cultural relevance of Indian secularism are not as yet finally settled issues. The conceptual snarls are many and the policy snares numerous. There is no easy and sure way of predicting its future course as a religio-secular ideal in a post-secular age. Of two things, we can be certain however. One, there can be no going back to Western liberal or Marxian notions of the relation between the religious beliefs and practices of the people and the state. Elements of these notions may appear here, but not the totalities. Second, to render Indian secularism historically and sociologically intelligible, and, thereby, to anticipate its future, we have to take India's religious traditions seriously as legitimate subjects of scholarly study. Accordingly, in the following three chapters, I highlight select methodological issues in the sociology of Hinduism (see Chapter Two), Islam (see Chapter Three), and Sikhism (see Chapter Four), and underline the importance of the pluralist perspective that is vital to the survival of Indian secularism.

Chapter Two

Hinduism:
The Book View and the Field View

> *Do not stay in the field!*
> *Nor climb out of sight.*
> *The best view of the world*
> *Is from a medium height.*
> —NIETZSCHE, *The Gay Science*

It should be obvious, in principle, that a Sociology of India lies at the confluence of Sociology and Indology.
—LOUIS DUMONT, 'For a Sociology of India'

It is a sociological truism that the bearers of a cultural tradition usually are not also the bearers of a critical consciousness of its character. It is outsiders who bring this gift to them, whether by being told of inter-cultural similarities or differences, or both. Put otherwise, what is lived reality to the insider is an observable and describable way of life to the outsider. And it is the sociologist's and, particularly, the cultural anthropologist's vocation to adopt an outsider perspective even when they may be insiders. Comparison is the crucial element of sociological understanding. Thus, Dumont observes: 'The sociologist has to construct a view in which the representation [the insider's view] is preserved as it presents itself and at the same time seen in relation to its non-conscious counterpart' (1970a: 8). He further adds:

In this task it is not sufficient to translate indigenous words, for it frequently happens that the ideas which they express are related to each other by more fundamental ideas *even though these are unexpressed*. Fundamental ideas 'go without saying' and have no need to be distinct, that is tradition. (Dumont 1970a: 7, emphasis added)

The peoples of India have had for thousands of years both kinds of awareness—an *affirmative*, insider awareness embodied in oral and textual traditions, and an *interrogative* awareness generated by the narratives of outsiders. Greek ambassadors, Chinese pilgrims, Arab chroniclers, European travellers, Christian missionaries, and colonial administrators have made significant contributions to the corpus of outsider accounts of India. Even when biased, because they were self-interested, the value of the genre lies in the wealth of detail. Orientalists like William Jones in Bengal (see Mukherjee 1968) and Max Müller in Oxford (see Chaudhuri 1974), through their translations and commentaries, not only brought classical, Sanskrit texts (religious as well as secular) to the notice of interested scholars in the West, they also helped Indians to renew contact with their pasts in innovative ways (see Halbfass 1988; King 1999).

Among missionaries, we have the remarkable work of the Abbé Dubois, admired by Max Müller among others, who believed that 'a faithful picture of the wickedness and incongruities of polytheism and idolatory would by its ugliness help greatly to set off the beauties and perfections of Christianity' (Dubois [1906] 1959: 9). Whatever his motives, the Abbé gave us one of the richest accounts of everyday Hinduism, based on his thirty years' stay in south India, where, in his own words: 'I have noted down just what I saw, just what I heard, just what I read' (Dubois [1906] 1959: 8). He learnt Tamil, and perhaps some Sanskrit too, and lived among the people, and dressed much like an upper-caste Hindu. He kept his opinions to himself. In all these respects, he was an exemplary fieldworker. Needless to add, all this did not save him from his ethnocentrism or his account from the resultant distortions.

The inequities and wilful distortions of the massive colonial archive too have been highlighted in recent times (see, for example, Dirks 2002), but this also contains an enormous wealth of detail that is corroborated by other sources such as folklore and mythography (see Shah 2002). The information, qualitative as well as quantitative (district gazetteers, census reports, and so on), was, of course, primarily intended to serve the interests of the administration, but it is valuable nonetheless, and the like of it is not available in any other source. Indology, missionary accounts, and colonial records have truly been the forerunners, as it were, of the sociology and cultural anthropology of India.

In their efforts to steer clear of the normative formulations of Indological and other traditional texts, and focus on lived reality, sociologists of the Hindu religious traditions have remained focused on what is observable through fieldwork or other methods of empirical inquiry. The gains of this approach have been enormous, but not an unmixed blessing. The losses of information and insight have been far less severe in cases where local communities have had only oral traditions, but where textual traditions are available and alive, even if only partially, it makes good sense to treat them as a valuable resource, but not the whole story. To borrow Dumont's words (employed by him in a much broader context) the sociology of Hinduism should 'in principle' lie at 'the confluence' of its book and field views, keeping in mind the imperative of spreading one's textual net more widely than he did. The argument in favour of this complementarily is, I think, hard to refute. To illustrate my position, I will focus in this chapter on select aspects of the studies of Max Weber and M.N. Srinivas, reading backwards, as it were, from the latter to the former.

IS A SOCIOLOGY OF HINDUISM POSSIBLE?

To begin, I would like to briefly address two objections to the project of a sociology of Hinduism. First, Hinduism, it is said, is not a religion, for it does not have a founder, or a single foundational scripture, or a set of fundamentals of belief and practice. A notion of the supernatural is not central to it and the idea of moral law that may be considered a substitute is highly relativistic. Moreover, if etymologically religion (from *relegere* or *religare*) points to 'bonding', *dharma* (from *dhri*) betokens 'upholding' or 'maintenance'. In place of the 'other', the focus is on the 'self', on one's moral duty. These and other similar doubts have been around for a long time.

One such doubter, the Indologist R.N. Dandekar, concludes: 'And yet Hinduism has persisted through centuries as a distinct religious identity' (1971: 273). Srinivas, too, acknowledged them; he wrote about the 'amorphousness' and 'complexity' of Hinduism and the difficulty of defining it (Srinivas 1952, 1958; Srinivas and Shah 1968). All this did not, however, deter him from writing about it. In my reading of the ethnographic literature, I have come across several instances of the explicit avoidance of the term 'religion', for example, by David Pocock (1973: xiii), who prefers to write about 'belief and practice', or of its restricted use (for example, in Parry 1994). The terms 'Hindu' and 'Hinduism', as also caste names, are more freely used, however. In his comprehensive analysis of the relevant, intensive fieldwork-based literature, Fuller describes 'popular Hinduism' as 'the living religion of the vast majority of the population [of India]' (Fuller 1992: xi). I think the matter should be allowed to rest there.

As for the issue of core beliefs, Weber considered reverence for the Vedas and belief in the sacredness of the cow-defining features of Hinduism (Weber 1958: 27). He too noted, however, the virtual lack of dogma in it (Weber 1958: 21), and the fact that the term itself was a recent Western coinage (Weber 1958: 4). He observed: 'Hinduism simply is not a "religion" in our [Christian?] sense of the word. What the Occidental conceives as "religion" is closer to the Hindu concept of *sampradāya*' (Weber 1958: 23). He paid no further attention to the issue. Wilfred Cantwell Smith, distinguished scholar of comparative religion, has argued that if we were to 'define' Hinduism, for instance, as a religion, it would 'deny the Hindu his right to the freedom and integrity of his faith. What he may do tomorrow no man can say today' (Smith 1978: 145). Whether Hinduism is a religion or not, and whether religion itself is a meaningful cross-cultural category or not, it would be pointless to deny that Hinduism is a cultural tradition and, thus, a legitimate subject for study. This should suffice for the present discussion.

The second objection, voiced by some historians is that Hinduism is not an old, existential tradition, that it is only a nineteenth century fabrication of Christian missionaries, Orientalists, builders of the colonial archive, and would-be makers of an Indian nationalism. 'What has survived over the centuries,' Thapar writes, 'is not a single monolithic religion but a diversity of sects which we today have put under a uniform name' (Thapar 1997: 56). This, I am afraid, amounts to throwing away the baby with the bath water.

There are other historians who have documented the continuities as well as the discontinuities between the early religion of the

Vedas and the later religion of the Smritis, Shastras, Puranas, and the epics and, indeed, of the modern times. They have also drawn attention to the 'family resemblance' among the regional traditions of myth and ritual to come to the conclusion that 'around the period [AD] 300–600', a complex cultural tradition took 'a recognizably Hindu shape' and that 'Hinduism was not invented by anyone, European or Indian' (Lorenzen 1999: 655; see also Michaels 2005). It does indeed have a history. Whatever may have been the earlier connotations of the Persian–Arabic term 'Hindu', by the medieval times, it certainly identified most of the known peoples of India by their religious beliefs and practices.

For this we have the testimony of the great traveller scholar al-Biruni, who came to India with Mahmud Ghaznavi and composed his famous work, *Tarikh-ul Hind*, around AD 1030, after having lived in India as a kind of participant observer for a dozen years (see Sachau [1914, 1988] 2002). Beginning with the Hindu conception of god, his wide-ranging ethnography covers, among other topics, sacred texts, mythology, metaphysics, ritual, custom, law, and the sciences to distinguish and even contrast the Hindus as a sociocultural and religious category from the Muslims. He sarcastically notes the Hindus' willingness to argue with words in defence of their religion, but not die for it, as apparently every good Muslim would.[1] The focus is on difference, the emphasis, on specificities.

There have been other regional witnesses of the differentiation of Hindus and Muslims as distinct religious communities. Thus, the Shaiva mystic Lalla of the Kashmir Valley (early fourteenth century) called upon the thoughtful and the wise to abandon the distinction between Hindu and Muslim as followers of different faiths, and recognize the common, in-dwelling divinity in all human beings. Her insights were echoed by the greatest exponent of Islam in that part of

---

[1]Alberuni (as Sachau spells the name) wrote:

> [T]hey [the Hindus] totally differ from us in religion, as we believe in nothing in which they believe, and *vice versa* [an echo of the Qur'ān 109]. On the whole, there is very little disputing about theological topics among themselves; at the most they fight with words, but they will never stake their soul or body or property on religious controversy. (Sachau [1914, 1988] 2002: 3)

the world, Shaikh Nur-ud-din, who knew of her sayings, acclaimed her as an *avatār*, and wondered why Muslims and Hindus were divided when they were but one, united in the same creator. By the sixteenth century, the religious connotation of the terms Hindu and Muslim was well established, for instance, in the vernacular literatures of eastern, northern, central, and western India, as terms of self-reference and designation of others. In the seventeenth century, Shivaji spoke of his sacrifices for the protection of 'Hindu *dharma*' against what he considered the Muslim (or Islamic) onslaught.

Lorenzen sums up the outcome of the Hindu–Muslim encounters by pointing out that during the centuries of Muslim rule, beginning with the Sultans in the early thirteenth century, 'the Hindus developed a consciousness of a shared religious identity based on the family resemblance among the variegated beliefs and practices', cutting across the boundaries of 'sect, caste, chosen deity or theological creed' (Lorenzen 1999: 655). I find this formulation very persuasive. The point is that more than any other historical religion, Hinduism is characterized by its dynamism or processual character. The establishment of Pax Britannica in the eighteenth century contributed to the unification of the country in territorial, administrative, and communication (railways, postal services, newspapers, and so on) terms on an unprecedented scale. This coming together, as it were, of peoples and regions promoted sociocultural unification also, but the religious divide survived; indeed it became sharper.

The term 'Hinduism' was an import from the West, but it described an existing historical consciousness (see Saberwal 2008). Rammohan Roy, often called the first modern Indian, was perhaps the first Indian to use it in 1816 (see King 1999: 100). The roots of the authentic (as against the degenerate) 'Hindooism' lay, he argued, in the Vedanta. He regretted that the 'ancient religion had been disregarded by the moderns' (see Kopf 1979: 13). Here, we also find a crucial distinction between the earlier (Vedantic) and the later (Puranic) textual traditions.

SRINIVAS ON THE 'SPREAD' OF HINDUISM AND 'SANSKRITIZATION'

In short, the recognition of the diversities of belief and custom among self-acknowledged Hindus over the *longue durée* and on a regional or local basis—the proverbial trees of ethnographic description—does not require us to deny the existence of a more-than-a-millennium-old evolving subcontinental religious heritage—the sociological wood. Put otherwise, the dream of the ethnographer does not have to be the sociologist's nightmare. An insightful way of doing this was provided by Srinivas in his classic study of religion among the Coorgs of South India (Srinivas 1952). Summing up towards its end, he recalls his use of the concept of 'spread' throughout the book, categorizing Hinduism for heuristic purposes as 'All-India', 'Peninsular', 'Regional', and 'Local'. 'All-India Hinduism,' he writes, 'is Hinduism with an all-India spread, and this is chiefly Sanskritic in character' and 'it spreads in two ways: by the extension of Sanskritic deities and ritual forms to an outlying group, as well as by the greater Sanskritization of the ritual and beliefs of groups inside Hinduism' (Srinivas 1952: 214). After drawing attention to the step-by-step change of scale, Srinivas continues: 'In a very broad sense it is true that as the area of spread decreases, the number of ritual and cultural forms shared in common increases. Conversely, as the area increases, the common forms decrease' (Srinivas 1952: 213–14). That is, they do not disappear completely. The processes Srinivas mentions are, in his opinion, empirically observable and their significance inheres in them. Put otherwise, they are accessible to the attentive fieldworker and are self-explanatory.

The sceptical historians will perhaps fault Srinivas for making the methodological error of category assumption, illicitly smuggling in a fictional, subcontinental Hinduism into his analytical framework. The charge will not stick, for he provides ethnographic ballast for his framework by pointing out that the different levels of Hinduism are not hermetically sealed, but are the stages of a two-way social process characteristic of the caste-based social structure of South Asia. While Sanskritic (or Brahmanical) Hinduism, the one with the all-India spread, had shown a remarkable capacity for absorbing local cultural elements, 'local' Hinduisms too have borrowed from the Sanskritic reservoir of belief and practice. This latter process has had its roots deep in history with significant consequences; Srinivas famously called it 'Sanskritization'. He wrote the following:

The caste system is far from a rigid system in which the position of each caste is fixed for all time. Movement has always been possible, and especially so in the middle regions of the hierarchy. A low caste was able, in a generation or two, to rise to a higher position in the hierarchy by adopting vegetarianism and teetolism, and by Sanskritizing its ritual and pantheon. In short, it took over, as far as possible, the customs, rites, and beliefs of the Brahmins, and the adoption of the Brahmanic way of life by a low caste seems to have been frequent, though theoretically forbidden. (Srinivas 1952: 30)

The extreme caution that marks this initial formulation of the notion of Sankritization is noteworthy. It generated an enormous body of ethnographic work—more, perhaps, than any other theoretical construct in the history of the sociology of India—and was, in the process, refined by Srinivas himself and by others in the mid-1950s. Notable among these were Marriott (1955a), who used the terms 'universalization' and 'parochialization' for the two-way process, Bailey (1958), who introduced the important notion of limits, showing how those below the barrier of pollution do not have this route of upward mobility open to them, and Sinha (1962), who wrote about Rajputization or state formation among the tribal peoples. Srininvas (1966a) himself presented more nuanced formulations, linking Sanskritization to Westernization and secularisation, almost in linear progression, as strategies of status enhancement. His virtually unqualified, positive assessment of Sanskritization as productive of sociocultural cohesion (Srinivas 1967a) provoked some criticism of his failure to unmask the hegemonic character of the process. My concern here is not to make an overall assessment of his paradigm of social change, but only to look at it for the light it throws on the processual and internally complex nature of Hinduism.

All this is of course well known; let me just add that some of the most significant long-term evidence of the two-way process of cultural borrowing has been provided by historians themselves. One of the richest such works is Chakrabarti's (2001) insightful account of the cultural and religious histories of medieval Bengal, in which the wily Brahmans are shown to have played a most significant role in the creation of what, in Srinivas's terms, is an example of regional Hinduism, combining the itinerant Brahmanical and the rooted, local traditions in a rich synthesis.

SRINIVAS ON RITUALS AND SOCIAL
SOLIDARITY: A FIELD VIEW

Let me now turn to another crucial aspect of Srinivas's study of Hinduism. A casual look at his bibliography reveals not more than about ten titles that would suggest that Hinduism, or, more generally, religion was one of his principal concerns as a sociologist; but titles can be deceptive. If one were to think of him as primarily a sociologist of caste, one would have to note that, in his judgement, caste as a social institution derives its legitimacy from religious values. His first major publication was *Marriage and Family in Mysore* (1942), but the focus, as he himself states at the very beginning, is very much on the family as a site for the performance of rituals: puberty rites; marriage rites; delivery and naming rites; and celebratory periodical rites (fasts and festivals) are described. The practices of the Brahmans are distinguished from those of the 'non-Brahmans' among the Kannada castes. Little is said about the economic side of family life, although there is a short chapter on bride price, or of interpersonal relations beyond a brief discussion of the conflict-ridden relations between mothers-in-law and daughters-in-law. What is equally noteworthy is that the beliefs that go with the rites receive little attention. Thus, 'the purpose of death ceremonies' is described in a short quotation from Monier-Williams (Srinivas 1942: 150–51); in other words, Indology is briefly invoked to fill in a gap in fieldwork data.

In continuation of this emphasis, religion in the Coorg book also is structured around what Srinivas calls the 'ritual idiom'. 'Every society,' he writes, 'has a body of ritual, and certain ritual acts forming part of the body of ritual repeat themselves constantly. Not only ritual acts but also ritual complexes, which are wholes made up of several individual ritual acts, frequently repeat themselves' (Srinivas 1952: 70). It is thus that ritual contributes to social solidarity. What we have here is near reification of ritual, as if the act moves under its own steam. The connected beliefs, notably ritual purity and pollution, with which the book is significantly concerned, and notions like *dharma* and *karma*, *pāpa*, and *punya* provide only an underpinning. The same cluster of values finds mention again in *The Remembered Village* (Srinivas 1976: 312–19) and, in a likewise manner, as a backdrop of behaviour. There are no detailed descriptions of rituals here, presumably because processed fieldnotes of the observations made may have been lost in arson in his office at Palo Alto (Srinivas 1976: xi).

I find the emphasis on observable behaviour an intriguing aspect of Srinivas's methodology and would like to dwell on it briefly. We have been told that Srinivas's impressionable childhood was spent in the setting of a long house in the city of Mysore in which five Sri Vaishnava Brahman families had their abode (Shah 1996: 198). Writing himself about the life of the Brahman families of the village of Rampura, Srinivas observes that it was 'permeated by ritual' (Srinivas 1976: 293); so must have been, one imagines, the daily life of his own natal household. The preoccupation of the Brahmans everywhere with *karmakānda*, that is, with the performance of lifecycle rituals, as householders is well known. Moreover, the *karmakānda* is behaviouristic insofar as the efficacy of the *mantra* is believed to lie in the utterance and of the associated bodily movements and gestures (*mudra*) in correct procedure. Any search for the meaning of the ritual act as a whole is considered redundant if not injurious to the purpose of the ritual.

The writing of Srinivas's doctoral dissertation under the supervision of Radcliffe-Brown at Oxford must have been a felicitous meeting of minds. In his Foreword to the Coorg book, Radcliffe-Brown wrote:

> For the social anthropologist the religion of a people presents itself in the first instance not as a body of doctrine, but as what we may call 'religious' behaviour as a part of social life. Social anthropology is behaviouristic in the sense that we seek to observe how people act as a necessary preliminary to trying to understand how they think and feel. (Radcliffe-Brown 1952b: vi)

There would be little to complain about this procedure if all it meant was that it is in social activity that the meaning of concepts and beliefs is located, not in themselves. But in practice it has usually resulted in religious beliefs being pushed into the background, and rendered secondary.

At the very commencement of the post-Enlightenment study of religion, some of the pioneers were sceptical about the existence of religious belief outside the fold of what they considered the fully-evolved religions. Thus, William Robertson Smith stated that 'antique religions had for the most part no creed; they consisted entirely of institutions and practices' ([1894] 2002: 16–17). Earlier, Fustel de Coulanges had affirmed 'the necessity of studying the earliest beliefs of the ancients in order to understand their institutions' ([1864] n.d.: 11ff.), only to conclude that in those cultural settings, beliefs (for example, about the inseparability of body and soul) were forgotten in course of time and the connected rites alone (for example, burial and the building of tombs) survived as evidence of their existence. 'Thus a complete religion of the dead was established,' he wrote, 'whose dogmas might soon be effaced, but whose rites endured until the triumph of Christianity' (Coulanges [1864] n.d.: 21).

Coulanges was one of the teachers of Durkheim, who defined religion as a unified 'complex system of myths, dogmas, rites, and ceremonies' ([1915] 1995: 33). It was Durkheim's analysis of the modes of ritual conduct that, however, distinguished his approach to the subject. Tylor's ([1871] 1913) speculation about the origin of primitive religion in the notion of the individual soul, and the earlier characterization of belief as an 'act of the mind' by Hume ([1757] 1957), would have stood precisely for the kind of psychologism, and in effect reductionism, to which Durkheim was firmly opposed. For him the social fact, comprising both collective representations and group activities, could be legitimately explained only in sociological, not psychological, terms. Durkheim in turn influenced Radcliffe-Brown, who wrote in his ethnography of the Andaman Islanders (Radcliffe-Brown [1922] 1964) about their beliefs (for example, in 'a class of supernatural beings'), but by his own declaration he foregrounded ritual.

The point of the digression is to suggest that, intellectually, Srinivas belongs to a celebrated, but not uncriticized, tradition in the sociological study of religion, which valourizes behaviour at the cost of belief. To be fair, I must mention that in his studies of Hinduism there are references to beliefs, but these are brief and remain confined to a mention of sectarian differences in the conception of deities (theology) and to a more general set of metaphysical ideas, notably *samsāra*, *karma*, *dharma*, and *moksha*. The practical notions of ritual purity and pollution, however, receive rich treatment in the Coorg book, and this is done exclusively on the basis of observations made during fieldwork. Textual sources are not considered necessary. Only one classical (Sanskrit) textual source, namely, the Kāveri Mahātmya (from the Skanda Purāna), is mentioned in the monograph (Srinivas 1952: 33–34, 215, 217, 219–21), in connection with the mythic origin of the Coorgis. It may be noted, however, that the Kāveri myth is described in some detail in an appendix, and its functional value elaborated (Srinivas 1952: 241–46).

It is likely that Srinivas's distrust of 'bibliocentrism' in the study of Hindu society, which he considered characteristic of upper castes, even when they may not be well-informed about 'the sacred literature' (Srinivas 2002a: 282), held him back. But the 'field view' itself would have revealed a great deal more about beliefs than is to be found in his book had he been theoretically differently oriented than he was, beliefs of the kind that we find in the doctoral dissertation of Jayanthi Beliappa, a Coorgi scholar. I should add here parenthetically that Srinivas (1973a) himself later expressed dissatisfaction with the limitations of the functionalist framework.

Like Srinivas, Beliappa too set out 'to comprehend the nature of the relationship between religion and social reality'. Bypassing Radcliffe-Brown, she turns directly to Durkheim to emphasize that, for him 'the concreteness of social reality was embedded in a cognitive system', just as 'systems of knowledge were grounded in a social framework' (Beliappa 1979: 1.9). This is elaborated to lead one to the study of how the Coorgis 'comprehend and construct their cosmology in order to derive from it a system of meanings that help their social life as a small community to endure'. She explores 'areas of religious experience in which there is a clear delineation of religious discourse for the routines of everyday life' (Beliappa 1979: 2.1). Beliappa acknowledges the great value of Srinivas's pioneering study, but suggests that an alternative approach, grounded in structuralism rather than functionalism, may reveal to us more about how the Coorgis themselves *conceptualise* their social life. For instance, birth and death are, for them, 'meaningful' events besides being occasions for the performance of appropriate rituals. 'Function' and 'meaning' are of course intertwined aspects of these rituals. And, as is so well known, the question of 'meaning'—the question of making sense of the world—engaged Max Weber deeply.

WEBER ON THE PLACE OF BELIEFS IN HINDUISM: A BOOK VIEW

I would like to begin my discussion of some aspects of Max Weber's 'view from afar' of Hinduism with the thought that he nailed to the masthead of his celebrated (although in some respects flawed) study of the rise of the spirit of capitalism in the West. In the opening paragraph of the book, he maintained that, the offspring of 'modern European civilization, studying any problem of universal history' were bound to reflect on the circumstantial uniqueness of certain 'cultural phenomena' that have 'appeared' there, and which they would 'like to think ... lie in a line of development having *universal* significance and value' (Weber 1930: 13, emphasis original). Paradoxically, uniqueness is here considered generalizable, and the history of the West is privileged. As Marx put it, it was the mirror in which the rest of the world could see the face of its future.

Given such a point of departure for his massive project of the study of the economic ethics of world religions, Weber's study of Hinduism was inevitably cast in the mould of otherness. While Srinivas was born into Hindu society and studied it from within although as an anthropologist—he wrote eloquently about 'the study of one's society' (Srinivas 1966b)—Weber was distant from it in every conceivable respect—the absolute outsider. Srinivas wrote about Hinduism from personal experience and fieldwork study. He used secondary sources also in both the Mysore and Coorg books but sparingly, and these were contemporary English language rather than traditional texts.

Weber drew heavily upon the colonial archive (including descriptive and census reports), but he also delved into the traditional texts (in German or English translation). The Brahmanical ideas that he examined for their secular, sociological significance came from his obviously selective reading of the Vedic corpus, the *smriti*, *shāstra*, and *nīti* literatures, the Mahābhārata and the Rāmāyana, the Upanishads, and even the *tantra* texts. He also consulted contemporary exegeses and commentaries by Western and Indian scholars. In short, Weber's view of Hindu society and religion was the 'book view' par excellence. Now, as I have already said, Srinivas was deeply suspicious of 'bibliocentrism'; he was equally wary of 'paleocentrism'— they were for him two sides of the same counterfeit coin. The aridity of the book view, its lack of contact with lived reality, were known to him from the work of some of his Bombay University colleagues. That Weber's approach was different was not known to Srinivas when he formulated his early views, because although Weber's original work was published in 1920, Srinivas did not read German, and the English translation, *The Religion of India*, was published only in 1958.[2]

Differences of method notwithstanding, what I find striking in the first place is the similarity of substantive conclusions arrived at by Srinivas and Weber, but there are significant differences too. For both, the caste system was the fundamental institution of Hinduism and the Brahmans, the crucial mediators in the relationship of religion and society. Both recognized them as ritual specialists and repositories of sacred knowledge, but Weber especially stressed their role as the 'cultural literati', weaving out their webs of metaphysics that had for very long ensnared the 'masses'. What the creative minority thought up, the mimetic majority acquiesced in one way or the other.

'All Hindus,' Weber wrote, 'accept two basic principles: the *samsara* belief in the transmigration of souls and the related *karman* doctrine of compensation. These alone are the truly "dogmatic" doctrines of Hinduism' (Weber 1958: 118). Such acceptance had become manifest in the ordering of social relations, in the caste system. The bond between 'idea' and 'action' is summed up in one of the most memorable passages of *The Religion of India*:

> Karma doctrine transformed the world into a strictly rational, ethically determined cosmos; it represents the most consistent theodicy ever produced by history. The devout Hindu was accursed to remain in a structure which made sense only in this intellectual context; its consequences burdened his conduct. *The Communist Manifesto* concludes with the phrases 'they (the proletariat) have nothing to lose but their chains, they have a world to win'. The same holds for the pious Hindu of low castes. He too can 'win the world', even the heavenly world; he can become a Kshatriya, a Brahman, he can gain heaven and become a god—only not in this

---

[2] I regret never having asked Srinivas when he learnt, and what exactly, about Weber's study of Hinduism. Discussion of Weber's considerations was, of course, available to him in English commentaries on them when he was formulating his own views on the Hinduism at Bombay and Oxford universities. Among Oxford anthropologists, Durkheim, rather than Weber, had been influential in the study of religion (see Evans-Pritchard 1965).

life, but in the life of the future after rebirth into the same world pattern.³ (Weber 1958: 121–22)

I would like to draw attention to two aspects of Weber's statement. First, he highlights a view of society that emphasizes its embeddedness in a morally determined universe in which good fortune, or bad fortune, is a deserved condition, and society is not a matter of customs and transactions, but of moral imperatives and social obligations. One does what one ought to do and not what is personally pleasing or profitable: one must be true to one's group *dharma*.

But—this is the second aspect—*dharma* is absent in the passage, although it is almost invariably bracketed with *karma* by most authorities including Srinivas. *Dharma* is, in fact, introduced at the very beginning of the work, given the broad connotation of all social action as ritual, a kind of social liturgy, and contrasted to dogma (Weber 1958: 21). 'Hinduism is primarily ritualism,' Weber observed, 'a fact implied when modern authors state that *mata* (doctrine) and *marga* (holy end) are transitory and ... freely elected, while *dharma* is "eternal"—that is, unconditionally valid.' But '*dharma* differs according to social position ... *dharma* depends upon the caste into which the individual is born ... *dharma* can be developed ... by finding thus far unknown but eternally valid consequences and truths' (Weber 1958: 24–25). Weber's conception of

---

³It may be helpful here to quote Weber's gloss of the notion of theodicy (1948a: 122):

> The age-old problem of theodicy consists of the very question of how it is that a power which is said to be at once omnipotent and kind could have created such an irrational world of undeserved suffering, unpunished injustice, and hopeless stupidity. Either this power is not omnipotent or not kind, or, entirely different principles of compensation and reward govern our life—principles we may interpret metaphysically, or even principles that forever escape our comprehension.

Weber acknowledges the inspiration of the Upanishads in arriving at the quoted formulation. We owe the word 'theodicy' to the late nineteenth century German philosopher Gottfried Liebniz, who derived it from Greek roots (*theos*, *dikē*) to connote 'justice of gods'. Such justice was for him proof that the world we live in is the best of all possible worlds.

Hinduism as ritualistic is not the same, it should be emphasized, as Srinivas's conception of it, as a configuration of domestic and extra-domestic rituals associated with the human lifecycle and religious devotion.

Srinivas regards the 'ideas of *karma, dharma* and *moksha*' as 'intimately related to the caste system', and acknowledges that, their Sanskritic origin notwithstanding, they have reached 'the common people' through various channels of communication (Srinivas and Shah 1968: 359). In the Rampura book, he describes how in the judgement of the villagers generally, *dharma* refers to good, liberating conduct and *karma* to evil actions which have consequences that hold one in karmic bondage (Srinivas 1976: 312–19). But he does not engage with these ideas in any great detail.

Srinivas rather focuses, as I said earlier, on another set of ideas in his writings, particularly in the Coorg book: these are the ideas of good-sacred and bad-sacred, of ritual purity and pollution (*madi* and *polé* in Coorgi speech). It is these that he sees as the principal determinants of interpersonal and intergroup relations in the contexts of the family and caste. Needless to emphasize, these ideas are more readily discernible in everyday behaviour—relating to, for example, food taboos, bodily contact, and occupational choice—but not more important than the more abstract ideas of *dharma* and *karma* that Weber focused on. In this, Srinivas anticipated Louis Dumont's later valorization of ritual purity as the cardinal value that defines hierarchy (Dumont 1970a). It is not, therefore, surprising that Dumont (1959: 9) should have hailed the Coorg book as a modern classic in just about half a dozen years after its publication. Notwithstanding his programmatic declaration that the sociology of India lies at the confluence of Indology and sociology (Dumont and Pocock 1957: 7), Dumont the fieldworker is closer to Srinivas than Dumont the textualist is to Weber. I cannot, however, pursue this trail here (but see Chapter Nine), beyond noting that Dumont called Weber's book on Indian religions 'the richest and most fine-drawn comparison between the Western and the Hindu universes', notwithstanding the fact that 'the work drew only on secondary sources' (Dumont 1970a: 30). I must return to Weber.

Weber was not, of course, a fieldworker, but he was sensitive to such ethnography as was available to him, and his perspective was processual. The best way to illustrate this is to recall what he wrote about the diffusion of Hindusim over time, and here he anticipated

Srinivas most remarkably. He called this process 'Hinduization' and believed that Hindu 'propaganda in the grand manner' or simply 'missionary propagation' (Weber 1958: 9) had been going on for close to a millennium. Hinduism had, thus, spread from the heart of northern India (Āryāvarta) to the rest of the country. This extensive Hinduization (as he called it) sucked local tribal communities into a subcontinental religio-social milieu. Indeed, the propagators were 'met halfway' by the 'outsiders' (Weber 1958: 14).

The process, Weber noted, was multi-stranded, involving the selective but expanding use of the expert services of the Brahmans, adopting new kinds of work and occupations, altering dietary habits and social customs, and accepting new modes of religious behaviour. Gradually, the outsiders would usually find themselves transformed into impure Hindu castes. Within the broader framework of extensive Hinduization, Weber noted, there was a tendency to engage in intensive (or internal) Hinduization in pursuit of status enhancement (Weber 1958: 11). If material gain motivated the Brahman to be accommodative (a player of the game), the quest for social legitimation drove the climbers forward and upward, hoping to bridge 'the abysmal distance Hinduism establishes between social strata'. Weber called it the peculiar 'religious promise' of Hinduism (1958: 17).

What all this means we know very well indeed, thanks to the vast body of ethnographic studies generated by Bose's seminal essay on 'the Hindu method of tribal absorption' (Bose 1941) and, of course, Srinivas's discussions of Sanskritization. Weber appreciated as well as Bose and Srinivas that the processes were collective and not individual and that it could not be 'otherwise' since individuals can never rise except as a 'caste' (Bose 1941: 11ff.). The similarity between Weber and Srinivas's views is so striking that it is puzzling that not much attention has been paid to it (Kulke 1986 is a notable exception). Srinivas himself never mentions it in his published work.

The only references to Weber in Srinivas's writings that seem to exist are with reference to the argument about the lack of appropriate ideological resources in Hinduism for the endogenous development of capitalism. A very short comment (in a coauthored article), criticizes Weber for 'a partial view of Hinduism', but notes that 'Weber himself [had] identified a few elements of "rational ethic" in Hinduism', and concludes with a reference to the managerial and administrative abilities often displayed by 'Hindu ascetics' who head 'large and wealthy monasteries and temples' (Srinivas and Shah 1968: 364). A somewhat more detailed, but really quite short, reference is Srinivas's (1973b) discussion of a seminar paper by Milton Singer, who argued that Weber's views on the relationship of Hinduism and capitalism were ill-informed and misleading; Srinivas agreed and, further, criticized Weber's understanding of Hinduism as a religion. His criticisms are, however, based on a rather hasty reading of Weber's work. What is more regrettable is the fact that Srinivas totally ignores the convergence of their views in the context of Sanskritization (Srinivas) and Hinduization (Weber).

Weber's views about Hinduism and capitalism have been subjected to much criticism, some of it based on misreading what he actually wrote. This is how he describes the scope of his study: 'Here we shall inquire as to the manner in which Indian religion, *as one factor among many, may have prevented capitalistic development* (in the Occidental sense)' (Srinivas 1973b: 4, emphasis added). Could any formulation be more cautious even if it is not wholly open minded? Nor can Weber's thesis be disproved by describing what Indian entrepreneurs achieved in the nineteenth century often in competition with British entrepreneurs. Weber's concern was with *initial* development (or the first appearance), and he held the hereditary and non-innovative character of caste-based division of work as much responsible for the non-emergence of the spirit of capitalism as any religious ideas as such. It is not my contention that Weber's thesis, whether about Europe or its generalizability, is above criticism (see, for example, Munshi 2003 for an excellent recent critique), but thematic considerations do not permit fuller discussion here.

In any case, the question about capitalism with which Weber begins *The Religion of India* is not all that interested him in Hinduism. In the first part of the book, after introducing the ideological backdrop, he discusses the Hindu social system comprising tribe, caste, sect, and so on. It is in this discussion that the convergences between him and Srinivas are pronounced. Part Two, which is about as long as the first, focuses on 'orthodox and heterodox holy teachings'; in the concluding part, he moves into east Asia with the Buddhist missions to return to nineteenth century India's restoration movements.

For a final comment on Weber's work, to illustrate his interest in the role of ideas, I would like to recall his insightful discussion of the

Bhagavadgītā (Weber 1958: 180–91), which, he says, 'in a certain sense represents the crown of the classical ethics of Indian intellectuals' (Weber 1958: 185). Here he lays bare 'the inner conflict' of the Hindu tradition, notably that between the Brahmanical and Kshatriya ways of life, and between two modes of salvation represented by, first, the moral agent's assumption of responsibility for breaking out of the karmic chain and, second, his seeking refugee in divine grace (*prasāda*) (Weber 1958: 187), a radical departure from the classical Brahmanical tradition.

A key question is posed by Draupadī in the Mahābhārata, writes Weber, when, apropos Yudhishthira's 'blameless misfortune', she tells him that 'the great God only plays with men according to his whims'. Yudhishthira's response is: '[O]ne should not say such things, for by the grace of God the good receive immortality and, above all, without this belief people would not practice virtue' (Weber 1958: 182). And without virtue there is no social life: social norms ultimately arise when individuals learn to care and give, trust, and conform.

But, then, how does one practice virtue? The Bhagavadgītā teaches the ethic of conformity to one's *varna dharma* or obligations established by nature, Weber notes: right knowledge (*jnānyoga*) for the Brahman and right action (*karmayoga*) for the rest. The Kshatriya must wage war and rule—'without any concern for consequences', especially not for personal success (Weber 1958: 184). 'The innerworldly ethic of the *Bhagavadgita*,' Weber observes, 'is "organismic" in a sense hardly to be surpassed. Indian "tolerance" rests upon this absolute relativising of all ethical soteriological commandments' (Weber 1958: 189–90, see Note 4 in Chapter 1). In his apprehension of absolute relativism in Hindu ethics, and the resultant tolerance, Weber is of course mistaken: maybe fieldwork in an Indian village would have brought to his notice the widely known fact, recorded by ethnographers (see, for example, Mathur 1965), that there are shared values also, the *sādhāran dharma* that defines one's humanity and cuts across *varna* boundaries. And there is exploitation, oppression, and violence. Weber obviously did not know certain things and got others wrong. (I wonder if he ever knew a Hindu or met one.) That is not remarkable: what is so is how much he knew right and how comprehensive his outline of a sociology of Hinduism—and indeed of the comparative sociology of religion—was. In Dumont's words, although *The Religion of India* is based 'only on secondary sources, it is a miracle of empathy and sociological imagination' (Dumont 1970a: 30).

CONCLUDING REMARKS

I trust I have been able to bring out in the foregoing discussion, in some small measure, that while the field, or contemporary, ethnographic view of Hinduism brings into sharp focus the lived social reality, the book, or traditional, bibliographic view provides the background that illumines at least some aspects of the foreground. Combining the two views is not a retreat from fieldwork and the personally observed microcosm from the concreteness of rituals to the abstraction of beliefs. The effort rather is to establish a balance between the two perspectives, even a fusion of perspectives. Needless to emphasize, the dialectic of perspectives generates questions and yields answers that neither of its two constituents does on its own. If *Religion and Society among the Coorgs of South India* is the one bookend, as it were, of the rather sparse sociological corpus on Hinduism (sparse compared to what sociologists and cultural anthropologists have written on other world religions), then *The Religion of India* is the other. What we need to do is to bridge the bookends, not merely to hold the shelf together, but to enrich it too.

In this context, a comment on sociological and social anthropological studies of Hinduism in the relatively recent past is in order. Primary reliance on fieldwork continues to be their defining characteristic; this is exactly as it should be. And we have some truly insightful studies of this kind, such as Pocock's (1973). Gold's (1987) highly empathetic account of Rajasthani pilgrims also is a product of dedicated fieldwork and refers to a couple of textual sources, such as the Garuda Purāna; the latter, she informs us, is known to the villagers themselves. The growing recognition of relevant textual sources is also gaining ground among the more thoughtful scholars: this is welcome. A limitation is the lack of proficiency in classical languages, where such knowledge would be useful. Every serious fieldworker, of course, knows the spoken language of the area of fieldwork. Illustratively, I would like to mention a few studies that are, I think, methodologically innovative and ethnographically rich.

In many ways a pioneer in opening new approaches to the study of Hinduism in the post-Srinivas period, Marglin's (1985) excellent study of the ritual complex of the Jagannatha temple in Puri would never have been as insightful as it is if she had not drawn upon the relevant Sanskrit and Oriya texts, the former in translation. (Some of the translations were actually done at her request.) Certain aspects of these rituals are known only to the specialists, who themselves rely upon the texts, although all significant participants (such as the temple dancers, *devadāsī*s) do not. I would also like to refer to Jonathan Parry's (1994) ethnographically thick, theoretically nuanced, fieldwork based study of the ritual complex associated with death among Hindus in the city of Banaras. He selectively draws upon the textual sources that seem relevant to him, for example, the Sanskrit Garuda Purāna (with a contemporary Hindi commentary), the Kāshī Khanda, and the Kāshī Mahimā Prakāsh.

Students of Hinduism from a background of language and civilization studies also are, on their part, engaging in fieldwork in more numbers than before, without being too concerned about the theoretical and methodological issues that engage the sociologist. Thus, we have a wide-ranging and widely read work on the same city by a scholar of Sanskrit and comparative religion, Diana Eck (1982), which includes, among other topics, a discussion of death rituals. The classical literature she cites is extensive, but the first-hand data she gathered during visits to Banaras understandably do not have the same richness (or 'thickness') as Parry's. In short, the two types of studies, namely, the primarily textual and the primarily contextual, will continue to remain distinct in scope, methodology, and orientation, even as they hopefully get into a dialogue, as it were, with each other—as Parry and Eck have done.

One more example, and a special one, should suffice for my present purpose. While Marglin and Parry studied ritual traditions that, respectively, have their roots in the less or more remote past, Mark Juergensmeyer (1991) in another, path-breaking work analyses for us 'the logic of a modern faith', namely, the Radhasoami movement of north India, which has an overseas following also. Emerging out of the teachings of Kabirpanthi, Sikh, Nath Yogi, and Hindu Vaishnava orders in the late nineteenth century, the new cult has generated a considerable body of its own textual materials in English and

Hindi (see Juergensmeyer 1991: 253–60). Juergensmeyer combined the skills of a fieldworker and a multilingual student of texts to give us one of the finest studies of religion in India. Its methodological interest lies in a fine balancing of perspectives. That, of course, is the right way to go ahead in the sociology of Hinduism.[4] The combining of complementary theoretical perspectives, I will argue in the next two chapters, is as relevant to the study of Islam and Sikhism in India as it is in the sociological study of Hinduism.

---

[4]In my reading of the anthropological literature on South Asian religions, there is not a more comprehensive work than Gananath Obeyesekere's (1984) magnum opus on the cult of the goddess Pattini, who has been worshiped in south India and Sri Lanka by Buddhists, Jains, and Hindus for 1,500 years. Obeyesekere engaged in fieldwork and had also to reckon with the fact that the cult has a fairly large and well-preserved textual tradition, comprising thirty-five ritual manuals. His anthropologically, historically, and psychoanalytically grounded analysis makes deft use of both the data generated from his fieldwork and textual materials. The latter constitute Part Two of the monograph and run into about 250 pages.

Mention may also be made here of Robert Levy's (1990) study of the traditional Hindu city of Bhaktapur in Nepal. The fieldwork lasted two-and-a-half years and the author draws almost exclusively on the data he himself generated. His principal informant–collaborator, a Brahman ritual specialist, was, however, obviously well-versed in the textual tradition.

Chapter Three

Islam:
The Universal and the Particular

Moses said: 'I will journey on until I reach the land where the two seas meet, although I may march for ages.'
—Qur'ān 18, 60

Orientalists are at home with texts. Anthropologists are at home in villages. The natural consequence is that the former tend to see Islam from above, the latter from below.
—ERNEST GELLNER, *Muslim Society*

ISLAM, ONE OR MANY

Sociologists and social anthropologists (I use the two terms synonymously) are primarily interested in what people actually do in their lives, and not in what is given in their traditions, whether textual or oral. Needless to say, Muslim communities around the world have both kinds of traditions. The hiatus between the given and the actual provides for flexibility of action; without such flexibility a culture would just freeze. The Qur'ān is, of course, the cornerstone of the Great Tradition of Islam. Its text was canonized in the time of Usman (assumed khilāfat in AD 643), and this considered initiative made Islam the religion of the book *par excellence*.

Although the Qur'ān is a guide to the everyday life of all, even illiterate Muslims, the sociologist should first recognize that historically Islamic orthodoxy is much more than what is said in the revealed scripture, and is *always* in the making. The sociocultural setting and the role of politics are both very significant. It follows that the sociologist must focus on what the believers of the holy book have learnt to regard as its purport. It is the latter more than the text received through qualified interpreters that guides behaviour. In other words, Islam *as social reality* resides in the dialectic of Qur'ānic traditions and the 'lived' traditions. Needless to add, the notions of the pure text (uncontaminated by interpretation) and, concomitantly, of the single Qur'ānic tradition, are what the fundamentalists advocate. In India, the sociological study of Islam requires that the community being studied be squarely situated in its historical, regional, cultural, and linguistic settings; whether it belongs to Bengal or Gujarat, Kashmir or Kerala, does indeed make a crucial difference. In principle universal and one, the *ummah* or the universal 'community' of Muslims, is actually internally heterogeneous. The pluralist perspective and the comparative approach are, therefore, imperative.

The Qur'ān seemingly insists that Islam is a particular form of submission (*al-islām*) to god's command and guidance. The true believer is identified by being such a submitter, which is what being a Muslim literally means (Qur'ān 2: 128; 3: 19 et passim). What was revealed to Muhammad through 'Word descent' (*tanzīl*) had earlier been told to Moses and other apostles (Qur'ān 41: 43–45), but obviously not in the same fullness. In Verse 3 of Chapter 5 of the holy book, which is a homily to the 'true believers', we read: 'This day I have perfected your religion for you and brought to its completion my mercy upon you; I have chosen for you Islam as your religion.' The Islamic way of life is thus the paradigm of perfection crafted by Allah Himself for the Muslims to follow, and Muslims are the chosen people (see also Qur'ān 2: 214; 3: 16; 3: 105). In other words, by faith (*imān*) alone should a Muslim be truly known; any other identity, whether of race (*quam*), language (*zubān*), or native land (*watan*) is ideally irrelevant. The Qur'ānic text is believed to be transparent and the ideals it embodies do not admit of multiple expressions.

In the history of the Muslim peoples, however, the category of the believers has always been open and their identity, layered. Believers do not spring ready-made from the head of god, as it were; they come to be in the state, or are 'made' so, in diverse sociocultural settings. Since the first Muslims were Arabs, who spoke Arabic and lived in

Arabia, ethnic identity, language, and native land remained in the background overshadowed by the enthusiasm for the new religious identity, signifying the end of their state of ignorance (*jahiliyya*). But as Islam was rapidly carried by its crusaders and missionaries beyond the place of its origin, other peoples were encountered in other lands, including India (al-Hind) who spoke other languages and indeed professed other faiths (*dīn*). Apart from the requirement that the convert affirm the doctrine of the unity of god (*tauhīd*), believed to have been first taught by Abraham, and say the prescribed daily prayers (*namāz*) in Arabic, no custom or practice had to be abandoned unless it explicitly was contrary to the Qu'rān and the emerging tradition (*Hadīs*). The contrariness was a matter of interpretation, and this opened the way for variation. To put it otherwise, variant interpretations of the true faith follow from the fact that, although the Qur'ānic text is the same everywhere, its interpretations at the hands of culturally situated human beings are contingent and, therefore, various. Indeed, the Prophet himself is believed to have said that the differences of opinion among the interpreters was itself god's blessing (Nasr 1993: 431).

One who travels, desirous of making friends and followers, would know the limits of coercion and appreciate the virtues of accommodation. When the Prophet Muhammad migrated in AD 622 from Makkah to Yathrib, later renamed al-Madīnah (the City), he entered into a covenant (*mu'ahadah*) with the Jews (and even the pagans) there, according to which the Muslims and the Jews constituted a single community, not yet of faith (the *ummah* was to come later, but before Muhammad's death), but of one city, and were committed to its defence against any attack from outsiders (for the text of the constitution of Madīnah, see Williams 1971: 11–15). That the Jews turned against him before long does not affect the argument about accommodation. Actually, in Verses 82 and 83 of the fifth chapter of the Qur'ān, a preference is expressed for Christians as the people closest in affection to Muslims over Jews and the pagans, the relentless enemies.

When Muhammad returned to Makkah as a victor, he immediately acknowledged the supreme sanctity of the ancient pre-Islamic house of worship called the Ka'bah. Earlier, before the migration to Madinah, he had looked upon the Rock of Jerusalem as the direction (*qiblah*) in which one was to offer prayers, obviously in order to distinguish the true believers from the recalcitrant pagans of Makkah, who prayed at the Ka'bah (Qur'ān 2: 43). Eventually, the Ka'bah, its polytheistic and idolatrous rituals notwithstanding, was under divine command, Muhammad averred ('cleanse our house', Qur'ān 2: 125), reestablished as the *qiblah*, and its pristine *tauhīdic* character was restored when all the 360 stone idols inside it were destroyed under his command. It then became the centre of prayer and pilgrimage—*hajj*—(Qur'ān 2: 144; 3: 95–97), for were not the foundations of the temple originally raised by Abraham (Qur'ān 2: 127; 14: 36–40), who was no idolater (Qur'ān 3: 95), nor Jew or Christian (Qur'ān 2: 135–41)? The Prophet and his followers performed the lesser pilgrimage (*'umrah*) there in AD 628, marking the final break with the Jews (see Rodinson 1973: 186–87). The point is that, as the distinguished Islamicist Fazlur Rahman (1979: 23, 28) has written, Muhammad was a strategist as well as an intensely spiritual person.

Developments in the early history of Islam, after Muhammad's death, testify to the importance of regional variations in the expanding world of Islam, most notably in the manner the Qur'ān was interpreted in the light of local customary law. These juridical interpretations gave rise among the Sunnīs to the famous four schools of law (*mazhāhib*), namely, the Malikite, the Hanbalite, the Hanafite, and the Shafiite, which were, however, rooted in the same basic principles. Moreover, the scope of such interpretations was gradually closed. Of these schools, the latter two prevail in the Indian subcontinent. In other ways too, internal pluralities in the Islamic tradition became manifest, for example, through the early emergence of Sūfīsm and sectarian divisions, notably the Khawārij ('revolters') and the Shī'ah ('followers' or partisans of Ali, who developed their own jurisprudence) and later of secular law (*qānūn*) in different countries (see Rahman 1979: Chapters 4 and 10). By the close of the eleventh century, orthodox Islamic scholarship had taken a stand regarding plurality within the *ummah* and more generally in the world. Although al-Ghazālī (d. 1111) had successfully persuaded the Ulamā' to admit Sūfīsm within the pale of orthodoxy, he had severely limited the scope of *ijtihād*, that is, logical reasoning by the qualified individual on matters of orthodoxy (particularly theological questions).

Then on, there was but one true religion, namely, Islam as expounded by the Ulamā' (specialists in the interpretation of Sharī'ah, Islamic law). Departures from it were held to be due to the corruption of true faith, which had been made available to every people (see, for example, al-Biruni's discussion of idolatry in Sachau [1914, 1988] 2002: 95–108). Such claims to authority have been, however, contested throughout the history of Islam as a world religion. In fact, the Ulamā' themselves have never been a homogeneous category, and often one interpretation has been opposed by another. There is no scripturalist tradition without reference to a centre of political power to which it has been related either positively or negatively.

Moreover, it should be noted that the Sūfī orders survived, as oases in a flat landscape of uniformity, upholding the authenticity of the individual seeker's quest for spiritual illumination, as against the authority of the opinion of the doctors, guided only by his conscience. The Prophet himself ruled out intermediaries between Man and his God, but in practice, we know, there are always all kinds of 'intermediaries' (see Yalman 2007). Indeed, it has been suggested that, had the Ulamā' had their way, they might have 'even created an overall religious authority for the Islamic community similar to that of the Vatican for Western Christianity' (Baldock 2006: 83). As it happened, however, their domineering tendencies were contested everywhere by the Sūfī Sheikhs and, as I will describe below, by many local spiritual orders, such as the Pīrs of Bengal and the Rishīs of Kashmir. From the sociological perspective, these dissenters were the real makers of Islam as a world religion by carrying it to the local communities in far-flung places. Their approach was marked by juxtaposition of the old and the new rather than by displacement of the former by the latter.

To conclude the argument, the history of Islam from the cultural, sociological, and political perspectives is the history of the meeting of peoples of diverse origins—the nations and the tribes recognized in the Qur'ān itself (49: 13)—and the contact of cultures. The establishment of Muslim rule in pagan lands was, therefore, not only a story of accommodation, compromise, and adaptation, but also of intolerance, rigidity, and exclusivism. In 2009, only about 20 per cent of the 1.5 billion Muslims of the world were Arabs. Everywhere, they hold fast to the three-fold identity of faith (*al-dīniyah*), ethnic group (*al-qaumiah*), and native land (*al-wataniah*). The emergence of ethnic nationalism among Muslims, beginning with the rise of post-Caliphate Turkey, and including the birth of Bangladesh, has been one of the defining features of the twentieth century.

If one were to say that god created humanity and the earth too for its abode, and designed Islam as its faith to guide it to 'the straight path' (*sirat al-mustaquīm*, Qur'ān 1: 6), one could also truthfully say that human beings (god's creatures) have all along set out to create many Islamic lands and cultures, without consciously pretending to be god's partners, which is the ultimate heresy according to Islamic orthodoxy. And in this they have been eminently successful.[1] What is true of everywhere else is, of course, true of the Indian subcontinent also. It may be said that the hubris that makes man dare challenge god must have a fall, that such a relapse of Muslims into ignorance can be only a temporary aberration, and that the making of an undifferentiated *ummah* bound together by common faith and practice that override every variable tendency is the destiny of Islam. But we are not there yet.

ISLAM IN MOROCCO, INDONESIA, AND THE PHILIPPINES

Illustratively, I would like to briefly recall Clifford Geertz's seminal comparison of Islam in Morocco and Indonesia in his *Islam Observed* (1968), which is a modern classic of anthropological literature and an exemplary study for anyone who wishes to describe on the basis of observation the character of Islam as a *lived* religion.

The background obviously is crucially important. Islam reached north-west Africa under the auspices of the Umayyads as early as the late seventh century, about fifty years after the death of Muhammad. In a short span of time, local Islam, a product of Arab–Berber (the latter name was derived from the word 'barbarian') interaction, encountered, across the Gibraltar, Spanish Islam early in the eighth century. Between the middle of the eleventh century and the middle of the fifteenth century, Morocco was shaped into a nation with Islam as its creed. While settled agriculture at the centre provided sustenance, tribal communities constituting the frontiers of the country

---

[1]So much so indeed that a poet (Iqbal?) makes Allah speak plaintively to man, 'the whole world I made of one water and one soil; it is you who have carved out countries out of it (*jāhān ra ze yak āb-o-gil āfrīdam/ tu irān-o-tātār-o-zang āfrīdī*)'.

emerged as the principal makers of a vibrant culture. Today, almost all of Morocco's 31 million people are Muslims.

In the midst of 'Andalusian decorations, Berber folkways, and Arabian state craft,' says Geertz, a 'strenuous, fluid, violent, visionary, devout and unsentimental but, above all, self-assertive' way of life was cultivated, with Islam as its spiritual core and the warrior saint as its 'axial figure' (Geertz 1968: 7–9). Out of these beginnings grew a culture of cities and an Islam that was mystical, a variety of Sūfīsm, with its saints and their miracles, *barakah* (grace), shrines, and chains of descendants. These saints are, in the words of Ernest Gellner (quoted by Geertz 1968: 51), 'the Prophet's flesh and blood. Koranic propriety emanates from their essence, as it were. Islam is what they do. They *are* Islam.'

That may well be the final word on the 'classical' style of Moroccan Islam, but we must also reckon with the impact of French colonialism. Whatever its political and economic implications, in the domain of religion it contributed to a turn, not away from Islam, but towards scripturalism. This meant the assertion that the true Islamic way of life is based on the Sharī'ah, which in turn is grounded in the Qur'ān and the *Hadīs*, that is, what the Prophet, inspired by god, said and did, and enjoined others to do (Geertz 1968: 65). Today, the religionists have one more concern, namely, the in-roads of secularization, which are by no means insignificant. But then the fundamentalists, too, have arrived, and the monarchical state continues to claim legitimacy from the assertion that the ruling family is descended from the Prophet. The monarch is called 'the commander of the faithful', a title of great significance in the political history of Islam.

The Indonesian story is different. The focus of Geertz's study is on the 'overpowering heartland of Java'. Here we have a productive, wet, rice-based peasant economy, about 2,000 years old, of which the 'archetype' is 'the settled, industrious, rather inward plowman' (Geertz 1968: 11). Islam was brought here by Arab traders, active in the area since the ninth century, and later by Sūfī missionaries from about the fifteenth century onward via Persia, Gujarat, and the Malabar coast, to confront 'one of Asia's greatest political, aesthetic, religious, and social creations, the Hindu-Buddhist Javanese state' (Geertz 1968: 11). It succeeded in putting an end to the 'Hindu times', or almost; much has survived in language (Bahāsā is a delectable mixture of Malay, Sanskrit, and Arabic), folk culture, classical theatre, symbols of the state (Garuda, derived from Hindu mythology, is the national emblem), and in virtually everybody's memory.[2] Islam acquired 'many forms' in Indonesia, writes Geertz, but 'whatever it brought to the sprawling archipelago, it was not uniformity' (Geertz 1968: 12). Indeed, the Islam of Java, as noted, is 'rather different in style from that of Malaysia or Sumatra' (Ricklef 1993: 4–6).

To make any impact at all, Islam had to be 'malleable', 'multivocal', and 'syncretistic'. Its approach had to be 'pragmatic' and 'gradualistic'—a matter of, in Geertz's words, 'compromises, halfway covenants, and outright evasions. The Islamism which resulted did not pretend to purity; it pretended to comprehensiveness; not to intensity but to a largeness of spirit' (Geertz 1968: 16). Indonesian Islam, like the Moroccan, developed a mystical ethos that was all its own. It was rooted in, according to tradition, the redemptive mystical experience of an individual of wicked ways, who underwent an inner change and became a Muslim even without ever having heard the Qur'ān read or the Muslim prayers said. He then set out, it is said, single-handedly and peacefully to convert others to *his* Islam. The story is obviously apocryphal, at least partly. But it anticipates the character of classical Indonesian Islam, which matured between the middle of the sixteenth and nineteenth centuries. It consisted of, as Geertz puts it, 'renditions of medieval Islam, now occult and emotional, now crabbed and scholastic, now dogmatic and puritan', held together, alongside the folk religion of the masses, in 'a sort of spiritual balance of power' (Geertz 1968: 42–43).

In the twentieth century, Islamicists as well as secularists played a significant role in the making of the country's nationalism. The former, however, had reluctantly to retreat after independence from

---

[2] I once discovered to my embarrassment that an Indonesian (Muslim) anthropologist knew more about the symbolism of skin colour in the Rāmāyana than I did—that Hanuman was red and Sugriva white! The Rama story, widely known throughout Southeast Asia, finds expression in Indonesia and Malaysia through textual adaptation as the story of a native hero, even a model Islamic prince; indeed the Rama story becomes their own utopia (see Raghavan 1980). This is the tradition and it is alive. As recently as in 1998, the State Bank of Indonesia issued currency notes with an image of Ganesha, the Hindu god of auspiciousness. Ganesha calendars are, of course, a common sight in business establishments in India, including banks.

Dutch rule when the political leadership of the new nation opted for a state, which was not strictly secular, nor was it theocratic either. The five foundational principles (*Pancasila*) were: Belief in one supreme god (Maha Esa; cf. Sanskrit Īsha or Maheshvara); humanity; national unity; democracy; and social justice. This decision had the support of the miniscule Hindu and relatively larger Christian communities. Simultaneously, a considerable number of Muslims (about 2 million) converted to Christianity and Hinduism, a most unique event.

Today, Indonesia, the world's largest Muslim country, with 87 per cent of its over 240 million strong population being followers of Islam, faces a serious challenge from Islamic fundamentalists (the most formidable organizations are Jamā'at-i Islāmī and Nahdlatul Ulamā') who raised their heads in the 1980s, and have succeeded in introducing Sharī'ah laws in many of the country's thirty-three provinces, in violation of the 1945 broadly secular constitution. They are strong, but they face opposition from the moderates such as the Liberal Islamic Network (Jaringan Islam Liberal) founded in 2001, who consider the traditionally inclusivist Islam superior to what they call 'Arab Islam'. Being revivalist does not mean, however, being against modernity in all its aspects: the Nahdlatul presents itself as pluralist in relation to non-Muslims and a promoter of democracy. Given Indonesia's internal ethnic, cultural, and religious diversities, pluralism is inherent in the social fabric. But the crucial and destabilizing fact is that the Sharī'ahization agenda of radical Islamic groups is *essentially* homogenizing and anti-democratic. Its seeds were sown in the repressive 1960s and 1970s when President Soeharto, a Javanese Muslim, dealt with communism and Islam as the two principal political enemies of the state. This, and the fact that the ideological inspiration of the radical parties comes from the Middle East, may remind one of Iran, but the comparison is of limited relevance, because liberal Islamic groups in Indonesia are not a pushover (see Anwar 2007).

What, then, is the point of the comparison of Moroccan and Javanese Islam (obviously ideal types rather than mirror images) set up for us by Geertz? Simply but most significantly this: the two Islamic 'classical' styles stood for 'rather different things in the two cases. On the Indonesian side, inwardness, imperturbability, patience, poise, sensibility, aestheticism, elitism, and an obvious self-effacement, the radical dissolution of individuality; on the Moroccan side, activism, fervour, impetuosity, nerve, toughness, moralism, populism, and an almost obsessive self-assertion, the radical self-assertion of individuality' (Anwar 2007: 54). In short, *one* scriptural tradition, but *two* lived Islams.

With that insight in mind, let us now take leave of Clifford Geertz, but stay a little while longer in Southeast Asia to look for further elaboration of the pluralist thesis. Indonesian (that is, Javanese–Sumatran) Islam is part of a larger religio-cultural complex. Moving north east, Islam pushed into what is now known as Malaysia, and into the Sulu archipelago, and then into the coastal areas of southern Mindanao, one of the largest of the hundreds of islands that comprise the Philippines, making converts among the animists (so called) everywhere. The Muslim states of Sulu and Maguindanao came into being by the end of the fifteenth century, and a composite culture of immigrant Islam and local ways of life became widely pervasive.

Further immigrants, including Arabs, Malays, and Indians followed, and more conversions also took place. Manila in the northern province of Luzon was a Muslim kingdom when the Spaniards arrived as conquerors in the late sixteenth century. They went about aggressively proselytizing the people to Roman Catholicism, and would have driven Islam out but for the stiff resistance put up by the Muslims, who are now no more than 5 per cent of the total population of the Philippines. This is quite unlike the situation in Indonesia (87 per cent Muslim) and Malaysia (60 per cent Muslim). Christians and Muslims have never really been at peace with each other in the Philippines, and the former dominate society and the state. Although the Muslim secessionists of the south now seem reconciled to a unified multicultural country, Islamic fundamentalists have emerged as a considerable force and attracted the supportive attention of many Muslim countries.[3]

According to Islamic orthodoxy (acknowledged as such by Sunnīs as well as Shī'ahs), the Islamic way of life should everywhere be based on the Sharī'ah. Anthropological research among the Muslim

---

[3]In the predominantly Buddhist Thailand also, again in the south, Muslim insurgency has been one of the factors that destabilized the democratic political system of the country during 2005–06.

communities of Southeast Asia has shown that pre-Islamic conventions and customary law (*adat*) survive among them in many areas of life, notably interpersonal relations, settlement of disputes, management of sickness, and coping with contingencies. It has been said that 'in Muslim Filipino jurisprudence, Qur'ānic law is so intermixed with *adat* law as to be in some places unrecognizable' (Gowling 1974: 285). The great majority of Muslim Filipinos are not proficient in Arabic, and their ability to read the Qur'ān is limited, if not wholly lacking. Even the imams who lead at the congregational prayers, are often 'unschooled in the subtleties of Islam' (Gowling 1974: 287). It is these deficiencies that have today created the space for fundamentalist rhetoric. Nevertheless, most Filipinos sincerely believe that 'there are no people on earth more Muslim than the Muslim Filipinos' (Gowling 1974: 292).

'By adopting Islam, a segment of the population of the Philippines became,' writes the distinguished Filipino Muslim scholar Cesar Majul (1973: 78), 'part of a wider religious community extending from the Pillars of Hercules to the borders of China'. Indeed, many of them prefer to be called just Muslims, and the adjective Filipino is applied by them to Christians. The *particular* in their identity is thus played down in their self-ascription and the *universal* valorized. The traditional way of life, as it was evolved locally, is honoured and preserved through a linguistic strategem, and the fundamentalist call to orthodoxy considered redundant. I have heard the very same argument in the Kashmir Valley. Let us then turn to South Asia, to Bengal and Kashmir, two regions that witnessed the emergence of large Muslim populations in the subcontinent during the medieval period (Sindh and western Punjab was the third).

ISLAM IN SOUTH ASIA: BENGAL

Islam arrived in Sindh early in the eighth century under the auspices of the very same Umayyad Caliphate that, as noted earlier, had overseen the march of Islam to Morocco. Its spread all over South Asia during the medieval period has been attributed to a multiplicity of factors including coercive conversion, the appeal of an egalitarian social order to the unprivileged among the Hindus, the tolerant message of total peace (*sulh-i-kul*) of most Sūfī orders, and the status climbing or preserving strategies of certain non-Muslim elite groups. Which of these routes is emphasized often only reflects the perspective that an author chooses. The exemplary researches of Asim Roy (1983) and Richard Eaton (1994) into the mass conversion that occurred in East Bengal (more or less coterminous with what is now Bangladesh, where Muslims account for 88 per cent of the total population of 147 million) have been an eye opener and reveal, as they do, that factors other than religious ideology and political control could also be significantly involved, as ecology and economics undoubtedly were in the area under consideration.

Thus, Roy draws attention to the demographic and economic consequences of a major shift in the course of the Ganges, which turned eastern and southern Bengal into a fertile delta. He stresses both the 'specific demands of the new deltaic land' and the role of the local cult of Pīrs in explaining 'the great Muslim preponderance' in East Bengal (Roy 1983: 48–51). Eaton elaborates the story, pointing out that the supernatural powers of the Sūfīs allegedly came handy in 'subduing' the 'wild and dangerous' forests (Eaton 1994: 218), and Islam spread through a multiplicity of processes (inclusion, identification, and displacement) (Eaton 1994: 269–81).

As elsewhere in the Indian subcontinent, so also in Bengal, Muslim society comprised relatively small numbers of immigrants, whose cultural roots were outside Bengal, even outside India, and who considered themselves superior in every way, and a mass of converts belonging to Bengal itself, drawn predominantly from Hindu lower castes and tribal communities. This is the well-known distinction between the Ashrāf and the Ajlāf, the nobility and the commoners. The latter retained their mother tongue and did not entirely abandon their customs, manners, and dietary habits, and even some of their religious beliefs and practices. So significant indeed was the cultural distinctiveness of the Bengalis that the Mughal Ashrāf showed 'a disinclination to convert [them] to Islam' (Eaton 2000: 252). On their part, the converts did not look upon Islam as 'a closed, exclusive system to be accepted or rejected as a whole' (Eaton 2000: 274).

A Bengali Muslim community thus came into being, which was culturally schizophrenic, alien as well as native Muslim, as well as Bengali. The 'Muslim-ness' of the converts was understandably shallow; their conversion had less to do with 'spiritual illumination' and more with social mobility and economic advantage (see Roy 1983: 41).

Conscious of the contempt of the immigrants, the converts felt obliged to present themselves as Muslims, leaving out the qualifying term Bengali, and indeed applying it exclusively to Hindus (Roy 1983: 65). The similarity in this regard between Filipino Muslims and Bengali Muslims is telling and bears testimony to a general identity problem. An additional and significant reason for them to stress the Muslim component of their identity was the Bengali peasantry's wish to distance themselves from their oppressive Hindu landlords. Indeed, places of worship that were sacred to both communities were attacked or desecrated during the disturbances that were widespread in Bengal in the 1830s (see Guha 1983: 74).

The innovative manner in which this problem was tackled by the converts has been insightfully described by Asim Roy on the basis of early Muslim writings in Bengali. He writes that in the sixteenth and seventeenth centuries, a category of 'Muslim cultural mediators' attempted to present classical Islam to the masses in a familiar language, namely, Bengali, and in a familiar cultural idiom, that of the Hindu epics and purānas, paradoxically with a view to disseminate the knowledge of Islamic tradition among them, and to improve the quality of their faith. To quote Roy (1983: 81–82):

> The dogmas of Islam fell far short of meeting the demands of [the converts'] passion for traditions in which they could hear about the glorious and miraculous exploits of the champions of their religion. They knew next to nothing about their new idols, who remained prisoners in the 'ivory tower' of Arabic and Persian literatures, whereas the entire cultural atmosphere of Bengal was saturated with the traditions of the *Mahābhārat*, the *Rāmāyan*, *nāthism*, and the *mangal-kāvya*, centring around the exploits of Manasā, Chandī, Dharma, Śiv, and hosts of minor religious personalities or spirits.

It followed that the only significant way in which Islam could be made a vibrant religion was to bring it 'into line with the cultural traditions of people' (Roy 1983: 82). Thus, the foundations of what Roy calls the Islamic syncretistic tradition in Bengal were laid. One of the key texts of a new genre is Saiyid Sultan's work *Nabī-vamśa*, in which the roles of *nabī* (prophet) and *avatār* (incarnation) are merged, and Muhammad is presented as the Kali *avatār*, and Krishna as a *nabī*. Muhammad is enshrined in a biographical narrative that draws upon the Bhāgavat Purāna. In this daring spiritual venture, Islam and Hinduism retained their mutual exclusiveness as religions, but shared a common regional culture.

Lack of space precludes further detail, fascinating though it is, but I must briefly recall that the syncretistic culture that was thus deliberately and creatively constructed eventually evoked a reformist response in the early nineteenth century, known as the Farāizī and Tariqā-i Muhammadiya movements, which strove for an Islam in its pristine purity, free from Hindu contamination, and emphasized the fundamental obligations of the faithful (see Ahmed 1981). In the first half of the twentieth century, Bengali Muslims generally provided support to separatist politics: the Muslim League was founded in Dhaka in 1906, and Fazlul Huq, a popular peasant leader moved the resolution demanding the parts of India on a communal (Hindu and Muslim) basis at the Muslim League meeting in Lahore in 1940. Pakistan came into being in 1947, comprising two wings, West Pakistan and East Pakistan, separated by the entire breadth of India. Advocates of a common Bengali nationalism among the Muslims were present, however, throughout the first half of the twentieth century.

In 1971 the Bengali *Muslims* of the 1940s reincarnated as Muslim *Bengalis* in East Pakistan, and rediscovered the high qualities of Bengali culture, of which Bengali language was the inalienable bearer. The setting within which this transformation occurred was that of a clash of secular (economic, political) interests between the two wings of Pakistan (the phrase 'internal colonialism' was much in vogue among political analysts) buttressed by, on the part of the West Pakistan, the cultural slur that the Bengalis were inferior Pakistanis because they were not good Muslims. The fervour of the post-liberation days, when Tagore's song 'Shonār Bānglā' (Golden Bengal) was adopted as the national anthem and a secular state established, has faded now (see Madan 1994a). The fundamentalist Jamā'at-i Islāmī, Jamā'atul Mujāhidīn, Islami Oikya Jote, and associated organizations are major political and cultural forces in Bangladesh today. Apart from a hostile attitude towards non-Muslim minorities (Buddhists, Christians, and Hindus), who were one-third of the population of East Pakistan when it came into existence in 1947, and are now only a little more than one-tenth, the non-conformist Ahmaddiya Muslims and their places of worship also are under attack. Even the Bengali language, which was the rallying symbol of Bangladeshi identity in 1971, is now receiving supposedly invigorating doses of Arabic. In short, efforts are afoot to homogenize the traditionally composite Bengali Muslim culture in the cauldron of an intolerant, universalist Islam. Some writers have warned that Bangladesh could go the Taliban way and even become 'a global exporter of terrorism' (Karlekar 2006).

The story of the Islamization of Bengal makes it clear that a religion that is universal in its geographical spread is bound to appear before us in myriad cultural forms. The precision and compactness of the dogmatic core of a single, universal Islam (represented best by the well-known five pillars of *kalimah, namāz, rohza, zakāt,* and *hajj*) itself entails the emergence of many lived Islams, for 'the true believers' come from many ethnic, cultural, and linguistic backgrounds, and these can be obliterated no more than Arabic can be made the sole language of every Muslim community everywhere. Take the crucial case of prayers: the *namāz* must of course be said in Arabic, that is the unalterable practice of the *ummah* worldwide, but what else one may offer by way of devotion and thanksgiving is a matter of individual choice. The fundamentalists, however, frown upon such latitude, with tragic consequences, for instance, in the Kashmir Valley.

ISLAM IN SOUTH ASIA: KASHMIR

Kashmir preceded Bengal in going through the experience of mass conversion, but Kashmiris have followed their own distinctive path in coping with it. Like Bengal, Kashmir also had earlier been the meeting ground of Brahmanical and Buddhist religions. The impact of Buddhism had softened the caste-based social organization, which inevitably goes hand-in-hand with Brahmanical orthodoxy, before the arrival of Islam. The excesses of ritualism, particularly in the *tantrika* mode, had generated an internal reaction, which reiterated the basic non-dualistic theology and philosophy of Shaivism that had been expounded by such notable teachers as Abhinavagupta (AD 960–1050). He, of course, wrote his treatises on aesthetics and religion in Sanskrit; his teaching did not, therefore, reach the masses, who were readily manipulated by the wily priesthood.

In the midst of what was a period of cultural and political decay, there emerged a person of rare wisdom, who presented the essential teachings of Shaivism in the Kashmiri language, in the form of quartrains, known as *vākh* (from Sanskrit *vākya*, sayings). She was a woman by the name of Lalla (born c. AD 1320), and would have been of a mature age when the first Sūfī missionaries arrived in Kashmir (see Kaul 1973). Her monistic theology may well have readied many disgruntled Hindus to be receptive to the message of theological 'one-ness', or non-dualism (*wahdat*), brought by Islamic preachers. She obviously was witness to the early phase of conversions and lamented (Kaul 1973: 107):

> Shiva resides everywhere,
> Do not distinguish the Hindu from the Muslim;
> If you are wise, know thy true Self,
> Which indeed is to know the Lord!

It is clear from the twelfth century chronicle of the kings of Kashmir, *Rājataranginī*, written by Kalhana, that Hindu society in Kashmir as everywhere else was marked by caste divisions. The fact that the only Hindus who survived mass conversion were Brahmans (some of them were perhaps only pretenders), is ample proof of the scale and speed of conversions. From my reading of select primary and secondary sources, I have identified the following set of mutually reinforcing causes of mass conversion: (i) mutual antagonism and internal corruption of the Brahmanical and Buddhist traditions; (ii) acute socioeconomic and political degeneration of Kashmir in the closing years of Hindu rule; (iii) severe intolerance of some of the early Muslim kings and of their advisers, some of the latter themselves converts; (iv) sustained peaceful exertions of immigrant Sūfī masters to propagate their faith; and (v) the emergence of an eclectic and accessible version of folk Islam preached by sons of the soil through the medium of a common mother tongue.

Among the Sūfī masters, the contributions of Mir Sayid Ali Hamadani of the Kubrawi order, a zealous missionary, who arrived in Kashmir around AD 1384 and stayed there less than a year, and of his son Mir Muhammad a decade later, are believed to have been crucial. According to popular legend, the senior Hamadani and Lalla met; what they talked about and who influenced whom are wholly in the realm of speculation, and do not concern me here.

What does concern me is that Kashmir's transition to Islam proceeded along two complementary channels of communication. On the one hand, there were the rather awe-inspiring foreigners from Central Asia and Persia, the Ulamā' and the Sūfī, who were well-versed in Arabic and Persian; on the other, the local Rishīs, a mystical order founded by Shaikh Nur-ud-din (AD 1379–1442), son of a convert, popularly remembered to this day as Nunda Rishī. He was perhaps proficient only in his mother tongue, Kashmiri, for he was illiterate, but obviously remembered the Qur'ān by heart, and emphasized the importance of its recitation. His choice of the Sanskrit designation 'rishī', an ascetic sage, for himself and his followers obviously recognized the unity of the spiritual quest across religious traditions, and maintained the continuity of select aspects of the Brahmanical tradition of ritual practices (including meditation in forests and caves, breath control, celibacy, and vegetarianism) beyond conversion. In this regard, it is most noteworthy that Nur-ud-din claimed the Prophet Muhammad himself to be the founder of his order and counted himself as the seventh Rishī.[4] He also hailed the Shaiva devotee Lalla as an *avatār* for the Rishīs and prayed for spiritual powers such as, he believed, she had been bestowed with (see Khan 1994: 45, 77). Given the uncompromising monotheism of Islam, this was an extraordinary conceptualization, and reminds us of the Bengali Saiyid Sultan's reference to Muhammad himself as an *avatār*. Obviously, Nur-ud-din's mysticism was partly derived from Lalla's. Echoing the spiritual anguish of Lalla, he asked: '[W]hen will the Hindu and Muslim cut the tree of dualism?' (Khan 1994: 81).

Here then, perhaps, is the Kashmiri equivalent of the Bengali syncretistic tradition, but the Rishīs were, it seems, not quite as self-conscious as the 'cultural mediators' of Bengal. As in the case of Bengal, conversion was initially conceived in terms more of gradual social change than a dramatic spiritual transformation, 'little more than shifting of camps' (Wani 2004: 232; see also Khan 2004: 79).

---

[4]It is noteworthy that the Purānic notion of seven seers (*sapta rishī*) is widely known among upper caste Hindus. Kashmiri Pandits offer them prayers at a rock shelter midway between where Ganesha and the goddess Sharika are worshiped on the Hari Parbat hillside. The seven rishīs are Kashyapa, Atri, Vasishtha, Vishvamitra, Gautama, Jamadagni, and Bhardvaja. One may further recall that, within the Shaiva tradition, all knowledge is traced through a line of gurus to Shiva himself.

The role of the Rishīs in Kashmir in providing content to this change recalls that of the Pīrs in Bengal (see Roy 1983: 50–57). Total transformation may have been the ultimate goal of some external missionaries, but no insiders would have even thought about it. As for the missionaries, no two groups of them have ever been in complete agreement over the details of perfection, ruling out a single definition of orthodoxy.

Nevertheless, there is no Muslim society in which the tension between the ideal and practice is absent; the differences are of degree, ranging from a benign sense of one's distinctive identity in some cases to an aggressive assertion of it in others. One of the best examples of this difference is that of the Meos before and after the impact of the Tablīghī Jamā'at on them (see Mayaram 1997). In short, the process of Islamization is both variable in its content and 'never-ending' in time (see Khan 1994: 167, 222; 1997: 91). Its ebb and tide are influenced by external stimuli (for example, the arrival of a charismatic preacher) or new experiences (for example, the pilgrimage to Makkah, where the *ummah* is encountered in flesh and blood).

If the call to embrace Islam given by the Sūfī missionaries and the Ulamā' may be regarded to have been the external challenge to the religious sensibilities of the Kashmiris in the late fourteenth and early fifteenth centuries, the teachings of the native Rishīs were the positive response. They were by and large endorsed by the Sūfīs, contributing in no small measure to their acceptance among the people (see Wani 2004: 268), but the Ulamā' remained hostile. The Rishīs were simultaneously receptive to the fundamentals of the Islamic faith and social order, represented notably by the Sharī'ah, and self-consciously rooted in the religio-cultural heritage of Kashmir, aspects of which, notably caste distinctions, were, however, rejected.

The mosque (*mashīd* from *masjid*) and the shrine, which is usually a holy man's hospice (*asthān*) or tomb (*dargah*), both represent Islam in the public domain; but from the very beginning they have done so in two different idioms, namely, the universal (common to the *ummah*) and the local (peculiar to Kashmiri Muslims). Unlike the grand mosques that often are remote from the countryside, concentrated as they are in towns and cities (such as the Jāma' Masjid in Srinagar), the small shrines, honouring the memory of Sūfī saints or Rishīs, are usually within walking distance anywhere and accessible to man, woman, and child alike. If the daily (usually daybreak) visit to a shrine provides the pious individual the opportunity for quiet prayers said in Kashmiri, the annual *'urs* (death anniversary) is a festive occasion of collective celebration of and thanksgiving for the revered saint's everlasting grace (*barakat*, from *baraqah*), comparable to the two 'Īds. One can say, in other words, if the mosque and the austere prayers within its precincts represented the challenge of the homogenizing orthopraxis, the shrine and the celebratory *'urs* associated with it were a culturally specific response to the same (see Khan 2004: 62, 66, 80).

Now, orthodoxy, which is allegedly a set of fixed beliefs, or a consensual 'body of opinion' of the day (*ijma'*), is actually a structure of power, that enables some people to coerce others (see Asad 1986: 15). Its partisans strongly disapprove of the celebrations mentioned above, particularly the dance and music that characterize them, and the veneration of relics enshrined in the tombs (*ziārats*) of saints. Doing so amounts to both *bida'h*, innovation, and *shirk*, giving god partners, which are not permissible.[5] The lack of proficiency in Arabic among the general populace even today and, therefore, in the recitation of the Qur'ān and the saying of daily prayers (*namāz*)

---

[5]The holy hair of the Prophet at the *dargah* of Hazratbal is another matter (see Amin 2001), for these actions, the critics maintain, accord to human beings, even though they may be acclaimed as saints, honours that are due only to god and the Prophet. In this connection, Professor M. Ishaq Khan writes (in a personal communication dated 17 August 2006):

> [O]ne has to differentiate between partners and the major Partner in a creative sense. The supposed 'partners', in my view, respond to the message of Allah, no matter that their response at the societal level is laden with characteristics quite unknown to Islam in its Arabic setting.

Khan's reference to creativity recalls to one's mind Roy's richly documented study of syncretism in Bengal discussed above. Eaton also concludes likewise: 'It is testimony to the *vitality of Islam*—and one of the clues to its success as a world religion—that its adherents in Bengal are so *creative* in accommodating local socio-cultural realities with the norms of religion' (2000: 275, emphasis added). Elsewhere, Eaton suggests that 'the non-translatability of the Qur'ān may well have compelled Muslims to be *creative* ... in devising ways to adapt the content of the Qur'ān to Indian literary genres and modes of communication' (2003: 3, emphasis added). This observation illumines our understanding of the significance of the sayings of Shaikh Nur-ud-din of Kashmir.

is, perhaps, what originally led to and has since helped to retain the congregational practice of reciting aloud in Kashmiri, in a standing position with folded hands (like their Hindu compatriots), devotional hymns in praise of Allah, Prophet Muhammad, and the Kashmiri saints. This is also frowned upon by the purists (see Khan 1994: 82, 234). Also recited aloud are *aurād* (invocatory prayers), *durūd* (benedictions on the Prophet), and *dhikr* (recitation of the names of Pīrs); this too appears to be peculiar to Kashmiri devotional practice, but may not actually be so (see Wani 2004: 263–68).

The opposition of the orthodox to Kashmiri religious practices has assumed violent expressions in recent years with tragic consequences. Among the Rishī shrines of Kashmir none has been more deeply venerated than the tomb of Shaikh Nur-ud-din himself in the town of Chrar-i-Sharif. It was believed to have been originally built by a Buddhist devotee in the decorative style of a pagoda, and was subsequently rebuilt several times. There are at least five other shrines in Kashmir that commemorate different events of the saint's life. Now, two groups of armed *jihādī*s, led by Pakistanis, owing allegiance to Jamā'at-i Islāmī and Harkat-ul-Ansār, respectively, camped in the shrine complex in the winter of 1994. Military action followed in the form of a siege; eventually the shrine and many surrounding buildings were gutted in May as a result of fires started by the *jihādī*s and worsened by retaliatory action by the security forces (see Joshi 1999: 352–66). The relevance of the incident from the point of view of the present discussion is that the *jihādī*s showed scant respect for the sacred shrine, in keeping with the negative attitude of the fundamentalists to Kashmiri Islam. The struggle continues.[6]

In short, two Islams confront one another in Kashmir today, a purist Islam, which in the hands of some is militantly fundamentalist, and a peaceful, popular Islam. The former is espoused by a minority, led by the Ahl-i-Hadīs, a 100-year-old organization (see Zutshi 2003: 150), and the more recent Jamā'at-i Islāmī, both of non-Kashmiri

---

[6]In 2006, a Lashkar-e-Tayyiba operative bombed a religions congregation in Sopore in northern Kashmir; the target apparently was a mystic called Ahad Sa'ab, but he escaped unhurt. In 2005, another Lashkar operative bombed a Sūfī congregation in Bijbehara in southern Kashmir, killing fifteen devotees. Such examples are too numerous to cite here.

origin; the latter is the religion of the great majority of the people (see Khan 2004: 62). The question that arises here is whether the majority has been all along misguided, and the reformists are their saviours, leading them along the path of Islamization to their salvation or the destroyers of their Kashmiri tradition.

This is not a new question, it is not merely a Kashmiri question, but also a Moroccan, Indonesian, Filippino, and Bangladeshi question; in today's world, it is a universal question, and it demands an answer. I will conclude my discussion with an attempt to formulate an answer in the light of what I have said so far, supplemented by a brief recapitulation of the views of a few contemporary scholars, some of them anthropologists and others historians.

CONCLUSION: TOWARDS A HIERARCHICAL MODEL

The author of a pioneering study of caste among Indian Muslims, Ghaus Ansari, was born and brought up in Lucknow, and later studied anthropology there and in London and Vienna. The social environment of north India in which he grew up, with caste standing at its centre among Hindus as well as Muslims, obviously had made such a deep impact upon him that he chose Muslim caste as the subject of his doctoral dissertation (Ansari 1960).

Ansari recalls in his autobiography that, soon after he had been awarded the degree in 1957, he was approached by the distinguished Pakistani archaeologist A.H. Dani (an emigrant from India), who was a professor at Dhaka University, to start the teaching of anthropology there. But the offer was conditional: having read Ansari's doctoral dissertation, Dani told Ansari that he would have to suppress it because it went against the 'two-nation theory', which was the basis for partition (Ansari 2004: 88–89; see also Shaikh 2009, particularly Chapter 2). Hindus and Muslims were, in terms of social organization, much too alike one another in his study, whereas they should have been different, for caste is fundamentally incompatible with the ideal of social egalitarianism in Islam. The implication of the argument is that Muslim identity is properly defined only in terms of adherence to a supposedly unchanging Sharī'ah and by membership of a monolithic, internally undifferentiated, *ummah*.

Ansari's pioneering work was followed by others,[7] including three influential volumes of essays edited by Imtiaz Ahmad (1973, 1976, 1981), respectively dealing with caste and social stratification, marriage and family, and religion and ritual among the Muslims of India. A fundamental problem in the anthropology of Islam in India, and indeed elsewhere, was highlighted in these works, namely, the nature of the relationship of a single, scriptural Islam and a variety of lived Islams. The merit of these studies was that they focused on the duality at the heart of the Muslim society, and did not try to brush it under the carpet as Islamicists have been wont to do.

In a paper on Kashmiri Hindus and Muslims, I had pointed out that intercommunity relations were rooted either in ideological considerations resulting in mutual avoidance, or in the compulsions of living in shared cultural, social, and economic spaces (Madan 1972a). The totality of everyday life, which is the focus of sociological research, may not be captured if these compulsions are dismissed as temporary aberrations or, in the case of Muslims, incomplete Islamization. The present of a society is, of course, a product of its history, but as a functioning, meaningful social system it is already complete.

Ahmad, after identifying an 'ultimate and formal' scriptural Islam and a 'proximate and local' Islam 'validated by custom' as the two 'distinct elements' that comprise the religious tradition of Indian Muslims, observes that it was perhaps the 'resistance and resilience' of 'the indigenous traditions [that] encouraged Islam in India to accept and retain the local cultural traditions, but adapt them to its own requirements and needs by putting an Islamic content into them'. This 'logical *modus operandi*' presumably enabled Islam to be 'eventually successful in establishing its integrity and at the same time stabilizing itself on the otherwise religiously clustered [*sic*] Indian scene'

---

[7]Satish Misra's (1964) historical study of the processes of simultaneous indigenization and Islamization among Muslim communities in Gujarat led the way, followed by Leela Dube's (1969) nuanced ethnography of the Muslims of Kalpeni among the Lakshadweep Islands, who have worked out a compromise between their pre-conversion matrilineal heritage and the patrilineally oriented Arab Islam. In 1972, a special number of *Contribution to Indian Sociology* (issued four years later as a book, see Madan 2001b), carried half a dozen ethnographic and historical papers that highlighted the cultural and historical specificities of Muslim society in Bangladesh, India, Nepal, Pakistan, and Sri Lanka.

(Ahmad 1981: 15). This may be called the 'equilibrium' model of Muslim societies.

The 'equilibrium' model is, of course, descriptive rather than explanatory, and does not answer questions such as what sustains the equilibrium or why fundamentalism is a threat to it. Besides, its stability is contingent upon the absence of any serious disturbances in the wider socio-political environment. It is in conflict with what may be called the 'linear progression', 'syncretism', and 'cyclical' models. Geertz has written about the 'painfully gradual', 'step by step', 'typical mode of Islamization', that perhaps never is complete. As he puts it, 'Islamic conversion is not, as a rule, a sudden total overwhelming illumination but a slow turning towards a new light' (Geertz 1965: 86–87). As a historical statement this is perhaps unassailable, but as an ethnographic statement it is uncharacteristically open ended. Did the Moroccan and Javanese Muslims, about whom Geertz himself has written so insightfully, seem to be awaiting a final moment of complete liberation or enlightenment?

Francis Robinson, a historian, also emphasizes the ever-present ideal of 'perfect' Islam that pulls every Muslim society upwards along 'the gradient of Islamization' (2000: 48)—it may move ahead today and falter tomorrow, but its eyes are always fixed on the ideal. Meanwhile there is tension, not peaceful coexistence. Robinson emphatically rejects Ahmad's 'equilibrium' thesis, because he believes that in cultural settings of the kind that have generally prevailed in India, 'the high Islamic tradition ... steadily [eats] into local custom centred traditions' (2000: 48). Such situations are, therefore, inherently unstable. It is the lack of historical depth in ethnography that, according to Robinson, makes social anthropologists miss the tension and the dynamics.

The argument is at first blush persuasive, but on reflection one wonders how long is long enough for local customs to be wholly absorbed in or displaced by the high tradition. After all the *modus operandi* Ahmad describes has with minor adjustments lasted centuries. The anthropologist describes the sociocultural world as it is, not as it might become. That may be a deficiency in the eyes of some critics, but that is how he or she works.

Ernest Gellner, another anthropologist who has studied Moroccan Islam, provides us with a 'cyclical' model. He begins with David Hume's notion of 'flux and reflux between theism and idolatry'

(Gellner 1981: 7–16), which he paraphrases as 'the oscillation theory of religion' or 'the pendulum swing theory' (Gellner 1969). Combining Hume's formulation, which he considers excessively psychologistic, with Ibn Khaldun's sociologically sensitive idea of the internal rotation between tribalism and urbanism, Gellner offers a model of 'traditional Muslim civilization' (1981: 35). While tribalism was shown by Ibn Khaldun to be promotive of political, social, and civic virtues, urbanism gives rise to civilization and refinement. Tribalism also goes with 'superstition' and urbanism with 'scriptural unitarianism'. There is tension between the two, but it is not disruptive. Gellner maintains that 'the stability and structure of internal rotation' holds until its confrontation with modernity, which 'unhinges the pendulum', purges the superstition, and valorizes 'a true, pristine, pure faith' that is 'fused with ... the burning zeal for a new and juster social order' and even 'with the mystique of Revolution' (1981: 56–62).

Now this is a suggestive though evasive model.[8] In contrast to the passivity of the equilibrium model, and the slow forward crawl with occasional bursts of energy of the gradient model, we have here some dynamism, but no real revolutionary potential (*pace* Gellner). Moreover, there are aspects of it that I find problematic, notably the bland opposition of 'superstition' and 'pure faith'. Gellner's model has, however, found many takers. The Pakistani anthropologist Akbar Ahmed (1986: 3–22) has drawn upon it to argue for a cyclical continuity between the Dara Shikoh–Aurangzeb confrontation in seventeenth century Mughal India and the Bhutto–Zia conflict in Pakistan in more recent times. I am sure the model will also throw some light on the clash between fundamentalist and liberal Islam today. I will not, however, follow this trail here, but explore the potential of a fourth model.

In Asim Roy we have a historian appreciative of the work of anthropologists. He also recognizes the dichotomy of a 'high' (textual, normative, universal) Islam and a 'popular' (contextual, pragmatic, local) domain of Islamic practice (Roy 2005: 32). Conventionally, the

---

[8]Other scholars too, not necessarily influenced by Gellner, have found the idea of cyclical change heuristically useful. See, for example, Geertz (1995: 53–57) on the ideological-cum-political shifts in post-independence Indonesia.

latter is judged in terms of the former and characterized as 'incomplete' or 'degenerate' (Roy 2005: 37), opening the case for reform. Roy rejects both the diagnosis of entities in irresolvable conflict as truth and error and the prognosis of a curative process of homogenization and essentialization (Roy 2005: 58). Such a unilinear view, he rightly argues, grievously neglects both the variety of social structures and the complexity of change that ethnography and history have revealed in abundant measure.

Roy focuses attention more on what happens on the way rather than what might happen at an imagined destination of orthodoxy and orthopraxis. And what happened on the way in Bengal (and doubtless elsewhere) was the emergence of a syncretistic tradition, which, far from being 'spurious', was the outcome of real life choices made by people (Roy 2005: 48). Syncreticism, which is a creative process of 'accommodation and adjustment', that the 'mediators' shaped with a view to achieving their mission at a critical stage of the history of their religious community, is described by Roy as 'a necessary stage in the progress of Islamization' (Roy 2005: 51). Islamization does not, however, mean for him the quest for essentialization or homogenization, or the straight jacket of fundamentalism; liberalism too is a possibility. Islamization is 'only construed to provide an underlying principle of holding a particular Muslim community together in history through change—however loosely and notionally—within a dialectical framework,' said Roy in a personal communication in 2006. His projection of the necessity of Islamization does not foreclose the future possibilities of what I see as a plurality of open-ended situations, short of the abandonment of Islam.

The critical problem thrown up by the four case studies (presented earlier in this chapter) is that of overcoming the vast ethnographic dazzle without surrendering to the twin notions of a single, scriptural Islam and a universal, religiously homogeneous *ummah*. In other words, how may we identify a unifying principle for the internal ideological and behavioural diversities in Muslim societies—a unifying principle other than equilibrium, linear progression, oscillation, or syncreticism—so as to produce a single structure of belief and practice in any Muslim society? For doing this I will revisit Kashmiri Islam.

For the purists and fundamentalists (the latter are different from the former inasmuch as they are as concerned with power, if not more, as they are with scripture), Kashmiri Islam has remained too long in the lap of a Buddhist–Hindu religio-cultural tradition and, therefore, in the limbo of imperfections. In the course of my inquiries and observations among the Muslims of Kashmir, I have found that they literally swear by the Qur'ān, but are unsure of its contents. Whatever they consider right behaviour (like, for instance, not eating freshly cooked food even when it consists only of rice and vegetables from a Hindu home), they *believe* must be in the holy book. It is this uncertainty, which is particularly pronounced among the illiterate, that the fundamentalists exploit, generating a sense of imperfection—even guilt—among the pious. When the notions of orthodoxy and orthopraxis are combined with the promise of political power, we have the classic situation for the rise of a fundamentalist movement.

Muhammad Ashraf Wani, a Kashmiri historian, observes that apart from observing *rozah* (daytime fasting during the month of Ramazān), compliance with the Five Pillars of Islam 'has always remained peripheral to the religious behaviour of Kashmiri Muslims'. He adds that this is true even in 2004–05, although 'considerable religious consciousness has been instilled among them over the past few decades, thanks to the persistent efforts of the revivalists' (Wani 2004: 232–33). Nobody could reasonably argue against the efforts of Kashmiri Muslims themselves to deepen their piety through a fuller adherence to the essentials of belief and practice as given in the scriptural tradition, if they so wish. Whether these essentials are to be defined exclusive of the Kashmiri tradition evolved by the mutually reinforcing exertions of immigrant Sūfī masters and native Rishīs, as the purists and fundamentalists demand, or inclusive of it, is the critical question to be answered.

Is syncretism the answer? Mohammad Ishaq Khan, a senior Kashmiri historian, has cautioned against it, preferring a conceptualization of the relationship of the two traditions in terms of 'convergence' (Khan 1997: 86–96). He argues: 'The "diffusion" of Islamic civilization did not necessarily cause total collapse or disintegration of the local culture; it set in motion such forces as created favourable conditions for the convergence of diverse elements' (Khan 1997: 89).

Khan's concern seems to be that the individuality of the local tradition is likely to get lost in a naïve syncretic (amalgamation, merger) model. Otherwise the difference between syncretism and convergence is, I think, a matter of emphasis only. Roy's notion of a self-consciously constructed *syncretistic* tradition provides an analytically more refined and ethnographically validated alternative model, which could be employed, *mutatis mutandis*, to make sense of the situation in Kashmir and elsewhere too.[9]

I have already indicated that while the equilibrium, linear progression, and cyclical models each captures one aspect or another of the relationship of scriptural (universal) and lived (local) Islams, they do not seem to me to provide a wholly satisfactory interpretive framework for the ethnographic and historical materials considered here. The syncretistic model developed by Roy goes further than the others, but it too does not address the crucial issue of the *relative weight* of the constituent elements of the syncretistic tradition. I may recall here that, clarifying his equilibrium thesis, Ahmad (1981: 12–13) has stressed the need to think in terms of 'levels'. This is a useful lead.

Building upon the various models, and going beyond them, the answer to the question of an appropriate relationship between the two traditions may lie, it seems to me, in invoking the principle of 'hierarchy' as elaborated by Louis Dumont (1980a) in his study of the caste system. Hierarchy is not a method of classification, of constructing typologies of social phenomena, but rather a principle of the integration of opposites—whether universal scriptural Islam and local lived Islams, or the view from above and the view from below

---

[9] As for the relations between Kashmiri Muslims and Hindus, Khan describes the same as 'symbiotic' (2004: 80). I also have argued that, until not so long ago, Kashmiris systematically maintained differing Hindu and Muslim conceptual frameworks within a single society, that they established agreement on the basis of difference (see Madan 1972a). But this situation changed drastically in 1989–91 when the outbreak of militancy in the name of freedom (*azādī*), combined with fundamentalist fervour (*nizām-i Mustafa*), resulted in selective killings of Kashmiri Hindus (the Pandits), rapidly followed by mass migration. Less than 10,000 of the more than 200,000 Pandits survive in the Kashmir Valley (see Madan 2006a: Chapter 7).

(Gellner 1981: 99)—into a meaningful structure or whole.[10] It is then the whole that will illumine our understanding of the inter-related parts, not one part of the other. The whole is integrated but not internally undifferentiated. Hierarchy implies asymmetry, that is, the existence of levels in a manner where there is 'unity' at the 'superior level' and 'distinction' at the inferior level' (Dumont 1980a: 241). The logical and social relationships coincide (see Durkheim and Mauss 1963: 83–84).

It would thus be possible to acknowledge that lived Islam anywhere may be in significant respects not only different from scriptural Islam but even opposed to it. It could yet be argued that lived Islam is included in, or (to use Dumontian phraseology) encompassed by, scriptural Islam, not as an alien *phenomenon* by itself, but in dialectical relation *to* it as a contrary.[11] The relationship between the two may thus be conceptualized as one of *complementary binary opposition*. The universal may no more deny the particular than the particular, the universal. The totality of the religious experience of the Kashmiri Muslims would then turn out to be, first, characterized by a *creative* rather than a *disruptive* internal tension between scriptural injunction and local practice, and, second, *always open to*

---

[10]Gellner's characterization of what the Orientalists do (see Gellner 1981) is rather dated, for the texts that historians use today are of great variety and include accounts of lived Islam. For me here, Gellner's observation provides a succinct entry into the subject of the discussion. Ahmad (1981: 19) writes: 'If the task is a comprehensive understanding of the religious life of Muslims in India, neither the Islamicists' nor the sociologists' or social anthropologists' approach is likely to be wholly adequate.' Eaton (2000: 11) writes: 'Whereas classical Islamicists had asked the question "what can the *text* tell us of the civilization?" a new generation of historians [from the 1960s onward] began asking, "What can the *data* tell us of *societies?*"' In the study of the sociology of Hinduism too, I have argued earlier, it is imperative to combine the book view and the field view (see Chapter Two).

[11]Dumont (1980a: 240) writes:

> The hierarchical relation is, very generally, that between a whole (or set) and an element of this whole (or set): the element belongs to the set and is in this sense consubstantial or identical with it; at the same time, the element is distinct from the set or stands in opposition to it. This is what I mean by 'the encompassing of the contrary'.

Islamization, but never essentially in need of it. How much 'open' depends upon the strength of the local tradition and the character of the wider environment, which together introduce a strong element of contingency into the situation.

When the unlettered but pious Kashmiri Muslim, unable to pray 'properly' because *namāz* must be said in Arabic, stands in a congregation of *namāzī*s, after the prayers have been said, to loudly invoke upon the Prophet blessings based on the Qur'ān and the *Hadīs*, and sings in Kashmiri devotional hymns of praise and prayer in honour of the Prophet and the saints (*n'āt* and *manāqib*)—practices peculiar to Kashmiri Muslims—he or she is a self-certified Muslim. The emphasis is not on adherence to a particular style of prayer, but on the authenticity of spiritual experience, on being, as the Sūfīs put it, 'in the state'. As Khan (2004: 62) has noted, Kashmiri Muslims take pride in calling themselves *ahl-i-itiqād*, *itiqād* being 'both a ... firm conviction that what they believe or what they firmly accept in the mind is true'.

Viewed from such a perspective, lived Islams emerge as varieties of integral religious experience, not as so many cases of incomplete Islamization or degeneration and, therefore, of imperfection. Distinct in content, form and idiom, not wholly but certainly partly, the scriptural and lived Islams are, in any particular place and at any particular time, a hierarchically unified structure of belief and practice. The former is not an imposition upon the latter, which in turn is not a betrayal of or revolt against scriptural Islam. Islam as a world religion will thus be seen as 'the whole' that is (to use Dumont's phraseology again) 'founded on the necessary and hierarchical coexistence of the two opposites' (Dumont 1980a: 43).

Let me then suggest that Islam is one severally, or one *from* many (*e unus pluribum*), just as, according to the foundational doctrine of *tauhid* in Islamic theology, Allah is one ('neither begetter nor begotten', Qur'ān 112), but (Mu'tazilite protestations notwithstanding) has ninety-nine 'beautiful names' (*al-asmā'al-husna*, Qur'ān 7: 179; 17: 110; 59: 22–24), each highlighting an attribute (such as compassion, forgiveness, justice, mercy, majesty, and vengeance) that is contextually meaningful. Likewise, the supposedly religiously homogeneous *ummah*, is, in fact, constituted of diverse peoples and cultures. It will probably always remain so, notwithstanding the undeniable virulence of the contemporary threat of fundamentalism.

If it is denied that the House of Islam (*dār ul-islām*) has many rooms, that the local annals of Islam must be annulled to establish the majesty of universalist Islam, its universality will turn out to be in the long run a chimera. In the meanwhile, the universalistic claims would make Islam a breeding ground for state repression, clerical intolerance, and organized terrorism. Should someone mistakenly seek to justify the inhuman treatment of dissenters, or even delinquents, in the manner of, say, the Taliban zealots, on the ground that the Taliban way also is 'lived' Islam, it would be pertinent to recall that, according to an oft quoted *Hadī*s, 'there are as many paths to god as there are children of Adam' (Nasr 1993: 467). The Great Tradition of Islam itself is, thus, accommodative of pluralism.[12]

An appeal to theology will not, however, suffice for our purpose here. I must, therefore, return to where I began, namely, the affirmation that the sociologist's interest is in what people do rather than in what their traditions say. Put otherwise, sociological questions require historical and sociological, not theological, answers. The question at the beginning of this exercise was whether a world religion such as Islam, with a very large following spread over five continents, could be one or had to be many. Taking five cases of lived Islam (Morocco, Indonesia, the Philippines, Bangladesh, and Kashmir), and briefly examining what some sociologists, cultural anthropologists, and historians have written about them, the conclusion arrived at is that the existence of Islam as a world religion is contingent upon the vibrancy of its many local expressions. These local expressions, however, operate under certain constraints. Like there are certain fundamentals of Islamic belief and practice, there are also certain imperatives of social action that are in our times rooted in the ideal of transcultural human rights, such as the rights to life and liberty within the framework of civil laws.

---

[12]Cf.: The truth is one but the learned state it variously (*ekam sad viprah bahudhāvadanti*) (Rig Veda 1: 164, 46).

Chapter Four

Sikhism:
The Sacred and the Secular

To conquer the mind is to win the world.
—GURU NANAK DEV, Japji 28

One is religious to the extent of one's power.
—SUKHA SINGH, *Gurbilas Davsin Padshai*

*God wanted me to look upon all religions with one eye;
That is why he took away the light from the other.*
—MAHARAJA RANJIT SINGH, in conversation with a Muslim fakir

It is generally agreed that the notion of secularization as a self-consciously articulated theory of social change is relatively recent and of Western origin. The processes of secularization may well be said to be as old as human history. As a modern theory, however, coeval with the rise of modern science and technology, the thesis of secularization bears the imprint of the dialectic of religion and reason or, more precisely, Protestantism and the Enlightenment. In its utopian form, it was put forward as the ideology of secularism, denying any legitimacy to religion in society. Elsewhere (Madan 1997, 2006a), I have underscored the importance of examining the on-going processes of secularization everywhere contextually, that is, in relation to the 'local' religious tradition or traditions. In this chapter, I attempt an examination of the significance of the fact that, in the Sikh religious tradition, an original attitude of qualified world affirmation was in course of time redefined to emphasize the unity of the spiritual and political functions in society, so that what might seem distinct and even contradictory in terms of the Western civilization is here sought to be reconciled. This development within the Sikh religio-political tradition cannot but be of deep interest to students of comparative religion and to theorists of secularization.

SIKHISM AS THIS-WORLDLY ETHIC

Of the great religious traditions of humanity, Sikhism is one of the youngest, being barely 500 years old. Its beginnings and development have been recorded in both oral narratives and literary texts, but these do not always speak with one voice. The fact that the person deemed to be the founder of this religion, Nanak Dev, was literate, as were his nine successors, does not really prove helpful in this regard. Not only are non-Sikh scholars in disagreement over many issues, the Sikhs themselves also have found agreement hard to arrive at.[1] A major difficulty is that, while the historian is sceptical about many details that comprise the tradition because of lack of reliable evidence, the believer considers it self-validated. For the sociologist, while the qualms of the historian seem legitimate, it is tradition that matters, for it moves people and guides their actions. The most crucial illustration of this problem is the status of the biographical narratives called *janam sākhi*, which are anecdotal in character and combine the historian's hard facts with the people's sacred myths (see McLeod

---

[1]Among knowledgeable 'outsiders' we find such sharp disagreements as are illustrated by, for instance, the assertion that the Sikh religious tradition evolved in the direction of creating 'almost a nation' (Eliot 1954: 272) contrasted with the judgement that the Sikhs 'are virtually a caste of the Hindus' (Toynbee 1954: 415). The disagreements among the insiders are equally acute and often on basic issues, such as the meaning of the word 'Sikh' itself. According to Khushwant Singh, the word is 'presumably derived ultimately from the Sanskrit *shishya*, disciple, or *shikshā*, instruction—Pali, *sikkhā*' (1963: 36). While this is the generally accepted view, dissenting views include the following: 'The word "Sikh" ... derives its origin from Pali and means the same as in the great Buddha's Dhammpad—the elect, or in the Sikh parlance, chosen (by God), God's own' (Singh 1978: xxxv; see also Singh 1959: 276).

1976: 20–36). For the Sikh, it is not easily questionable that Nanak was a recipient of divine guidance; and, according to the *Mihārban Janamsākhi*, God gave Nanak a cup of nectar (*amrit*) and ordained that his followers would be redeemed. There is also the question of the authorship of *Bachitar Nātak* and *Dasam Granth*: tradition attributes these works to the last personal guru, Gobind Singh, but modern scholarship is sceptical. The mysteries associated with the origin and development of a religious tradition should cause no surprise, for it is mystery that entails faith.

Given the ambiguities, the sociologist must self-consciously opt for versions of critical events that command general acceptance, and construct a coherent interpretation of the tradition. What follows is such an interpretative effort to examine the place of the sociological notions of secularization and secularism in the Sikh religious tradition.

While for the Sikh believer, this 'new' religious tradition begins with divine revelation, the sociologist must (following Max Weber) seek to supplement 'subjective understanding' (*verstehen*) with 'causal adequacy' as manifest in the relations between relevant historical events. In other words, one must define, if possible, the context for the revelation. Fortunately, it is possible to do so in the case of the Sikh religious tradition: the context for its emergence is provided by the interplay of the political, economic, social, and cultural situations in Punjab in the late fifteenth century.

Ever since the first intrusions of invading Muslim armies in the eleventh century, Punjab had been subjected to much political turmoil and violence. The image of the king had come to be that of a 'butcher',[2] rather than that of the 'protector'. Nanak Dev (1469–1539), a pious, god-loving person of gentle disposition, had felt impelled, after witnessing the brutality of Babar's invasions of north India (in 1524–25), to cry in anguish (Harbans Singh 1966: 5):

> It was Death, disguised as the Mughal that made war on us.
> When there was such slaughter, such groaning,
> Didst Though not feel the pain, O Lord?

---

[2]Nanak Dev, the founder of Sikhism, is said to have lamented: 'This age is a knife, kings are butchers: justice hath taken wings and fled' (Macauliffe 1909: I, xliv).

Nanak's grievance was not only against the invader, but also against native Hindu kings who had abandoned their moral duty of protecting their subjects (who in Hindu political thought are the king's 'children' rather than 'subjects'). While his wail is also a prayer to god to redeem his creatures, implicit in it is a call to man to assume the duty of self-protection—an idea which is in harmony with Nanak's concept of human dignity.

The people among whom Nanak sought to arouse this sense of responsibility were largely the agricultural, artisan, and merchant castes of Punjab; Nanak himself belonged to the Hindu trading caste of Khatris.[3] The former were the economically exploited class. It would be misleading, however, to attribute to him class consciousness in the sociological sense of the term; his references to god as 'magnate' are significant (see Hans 1985: 213). Besides, the people he addressed were enmeshed in religious observances and in the grip of degenerate Brahman priests, who themselves were patronized by Hindu kings—such as those who survived in the hills in the east—and Hindu landlords. Fortunately, the caste system in Punjab (as in Bengal and Kashmir) had already been weakened by the spread of the anti-caste Buddhist religious tradition in north India in the pre-Muslim period. Subsequently, the sociocultural life of the people had, during the medieval period, come under the influence of both the Hindu egalitarian socio-religious movement of *bhakti* ('devotionalism', according to which all are made equal in their love of god) and the pantheistic movement of the Muslim Sūfī orders. The Brahmanical tradition and social organization associated with it were also under pressure from within as a result of the growth (during the fourteenth and fifteenth centuries) of sectarian cults of renouncers (*sannyāsi*s) and occultists (*yogī*s). These three streams of religious thought and practice, Bhakti, Sūfism, and Hatha-yoga, together in synthesis gave rise to the 'Sant' tradition that provided Nanak the materials out of which he produced a reinterpretation for those who chose to become his followers. One may say that Punjab was waiting for Nanak (see Ray 1970: 7–45).

It was in 1499 that Nanak is believed to have given his first message after, he said, god the supreme preceptor (guru), had passed on the holy word (*shabad*) to him. The message was: '*nā koi hindu nā*

---

[3]See Footnote 10.

musalmān' (there is no Hindu and no Muslim).[4] That is, no true followers of the Hindu and Islamic faiths are to be found anywhere any more. Or, alternatively, being a Hindu or a Muslim is meaningless: what matters is that one must be a true devotee of god and realize that the practice of truth is the highest morality: 'Truth above all,/ above truth, truthful conduct (*sachon ore sabh ko/ upar sach achār*) (see Singh 1963: 43). Though the former interpretation has been generally favoured in the Sikh tradition (see Macauliffe 1909: I, 37), the latter seems equally plausible when read alongside other related pronouncements, such as the following: 'Neither the *veda* nor the *kateb* know the mystery.' While the veda comprises the oldest sacred texts of the Hindu religious tradition, the word kateb is used by Sikh theologians to refer to the Torah, the Psalms, the Gospel, and the Qur'ān (see McLeod 1968: 161).

This is not the place, however, to go into the controversial issue of how this religious perspective (it was not yet a tradition) evolved and whether it was more Hindu or Muslim or Buddhist, or an attempted synthesis of Hinduism and Islam.[5] I will rather concentrate on the essentials of the teachings of Nanak Dev,[6] who, in his own lifetime it seems, was known as Bābā rather than Guru. The latter appellation came to be applied to him retrospectively after his death, when the chain of gurus came to be established. Bābās were wandering holy men. The most significant period of his life, 'in terms of his posthumous influence' (McLeod 1968: 230), however, was the twenty years

---

[4]We are on slippery grounds here. Authoritative opinion is certain that these are not Nanak's own words: they are attributed to him in the *Purātan Janamsākhi*. Identical words are traditionally believed to have been an utterance of Kabir (early fifteenth century).

[5]For the argument in favour of a strong Muslim influence, see, for example, Khan 1967. McLeod (1968) has, however, argued against it and contended that a third way, based on the rejection of both Hinduism and Islam, rather than a synthesis of the two, was intended by Nanak. This is also the conclusion at which Grewal ([1969] 1979) arrives at in his study of Nanak. Kapur Singh (1959) has put forward an interesting argument in favour of Buddhist influences.

[6]For accounts of Nanak's teachings I have depended on his own Japji and other sayings (in various English translations). See Khushwant Singh (1963), McLeod (1968), and Ray (1970). Also I have drawn upon notes of interviews I conducted with some educated Sikh gentlemen (including the late Tejeshwar Singh of SAGE Publications) in Delhi in the summer of 1985.

of settled domestic and community life at the village of Kartarpur on the river Ravi. Nanak's thought, like traditional thought generally, was marked by comprehensiveness and consistency: its theology entailed its sociology or, to put it the other way round, its sociology is incomprehensible without reference to its theology.

To begin with Guru Nanak's concept of god, it is clear that his view of the world was theocentric. God is the creator (*kartār*) of everything that exists. It follows that everything is sacred or holy, and the dualistic notion of the religious versus the secular is inadmissible. Man is, however, an easy prey to temptations and readily lapses into immorality.[7] His worst error is egoism or hubris (*haumai*): 'Devoted to pride, I weep in sorrow, saith Nanak. How shall deliverance be obtained?' (Macauliffe 1909: I, 170). It is thus that man becomes separated from his Maker: 'O my Lord, who can comprehend. The excellences! None can recount my sinfulness' (McLeod 1968: 177).

Man is, however, born to be saved. Nanak taught the notion of 'divine commandment' (*hukam*), which entails the idea of divine initiative for the salvation of man: 'Nanak, the True King Himself unites (the believer) with Himself' (McLeod 1968: 175). Although divine initiative comes first, man too must strive for his own salvation. According to Nanak (Singh 1963: 47, n. 41):

The sweat of labour is as beads
Falling by the ploughman as seeds sown
We reap according to our measure.
Some for ourselves to keep, some to others give.

What god intends for man is his *hukam*: this is revealed to man through *shabad* (the holy word) with the guidance of the preceptor (guru) and by meditation on god's name (*nam*): 'For a diseased world the remedy is the Name' (McLeod 1968: 195).

The primacy of Nanak's concern with individual salvation need hardly be emphasized (see Ray 1970: 61); what must not be

---

[7]Nanak warned (Trilochan Singh et al. 1960: 84):

This God-built house of the body,
of which the soul is a tenant, has many doors.
The five temptations that the flesh is heir to
Make daily raids upon it.

overlooked, however, is the fact that he did not teach a selfish concern for one's own salvation alone, but rather the moral responsibility of the true believer for the salvation of fellow human beings as well. According to tradition, Nanak summed up his teaching very simply: *kirt karo, nām japo, vand chakho* (work for your living; abide in meditative recitation of god's name; share what you have with others) (see Singh 1963: 47). The *self* is thus seen in relation to the *divine* and the *social*, so that a withdrawal from either of these relationships must spell one's extinction. It is this combination of piety and practical activity (in the form of worldly labour) which is the essence of Nanak's this-worldliness.

Some Sikh intellectuals find the seeds of secularism in such an ethic of world affirmation. We must be wary, however, about jumping to conclusions. The guru's world affirmation was not absolute but explicitly qualified. As divine creation, the universe is real. He taught: 'Whatever is done by Thee is real: all Thy reflections too are real.' At the same time, he insisted that god alone is 'eternal' and, as such, He is distinct from the universe. What is impermanent is also in a sense false and dangerous since it may turn out to be a snare. Nanak acknowledged the traditional Brahmanical notion of five obstacles to the path of virtue, namely lust (*kāma*), anger (*krodha*), covetousness (*lobha*), attachment to worldly things (*moha*), and egotism (*ahankāra*). Detachment is, therefore, the supreme value (see Grewal [1969] 1979: 267): this-worldliness encompassed by detachment. Borrowing a famous formulation of Weber (1930) about Christian asceticism, we may say that Nanak sought to fashion 'a life in the world, but neither of nor for this world'.

Like the devotees of the Sant tradition, Nanak emphasized that man's ultimate goal should be to merge with god, but unlike some of them he affirmed the worth of man's worldly existence while it lasts, and repudiated the Brahmanical ideal of renunciation as long as it remains confined to external behaviour, like leaving one's home. 'Having renounced the life of the householder (*grihastha*) why go begging at the householder's door?' he asked. 'Of all renunciations, the best is to give up lust, anger and greed' (Jodh Singh 1967: 41). He 'rejected altogether the practice of celibacy and asceticism, of penances and austerities, of pilgrimages and formal religious exercises, worship of images, and the authority of the so-called sacred texts' (Ray 1970: 57). By abandoning both ritualism and occultism, Nanak turned his back on magic and miracles and on the social universe of castes and sects. Instead he extolled the virtues of the company of godly people (*sādh sangat*) which, alongside of the repetition of god's name, absolute truthfulness, contentment, and restraint of the senses, he regarded as the five pathways to union with the divine (see Singh 1963: 42–43). A contentment of the holy assembly or congregation (*sangat*) was the institution of the community kitchen (*guru ka langar*, the guru's kitchen) which dealt a severe blow to Brahmanical notions of purity and pollution and commensal exclusivism. Sitting down to eat together in a single row (*pangat*) was the secular aspect of *sangat*—the physical representation of the moral or spiritual idea of equality, and became a powerful cementing force among Nanak's followers. In short, Nanak held up the ideal of *rāj mein jog* (detachment in the midst of worldly involvements) for his followers to pursue. The way to truth lay for him through the life of a virtuous, but this-worldly, householder.[8]

It is debatable if Nanak thought of himself as the founder of a new religion;[9] he surely would not have wanted to form a new sect. He did, however, want the disciples who had gathered around him to continue to live differently from the others (Hindus, Muslims), and in a state of social and spiritual communion [*āp japo aura nām japāo* (remember god and make the others too remember Him)]. He also named a successor, Lehna (1504–52), whom he renamed

---

[8]Cf. (Talib 1969: 95):

Over the life of the recluse the Guru has exalted the station of the *Grihasti* [householder].... The *Grihasti* is the person fixed amidst moral duty, which he must face and assume even at the cost of suffering. The Guru's meaning is unmistakably clear: our life is circumscribed by material surroundings, yet man must transcend these to affirm spiritual and moral fulfilment.

[9]To call 'the gentle and intense Indian mystic', Nanak, 'the "founder of Sikhism", as is often done, is surely to misconstrue both him and history. He was a devotee (*bhakta*) who ... attacked religious formalized, systematized.... Out of this was born what we call "followerism"' (Smith 1963: 66f.). Toynbee (1960: 9) refers to Nanak as the 'founder' of Sikhism, but adds that Nanak himself would perhaps not have agreed. Most Sikh intellectuals disagree, and reject the notion of the emergence of a 'new religion' as a gradual process that is still in progress.

Angad (literally, 'part of my body') (see Singh 1963: 49). By this single but momentous act, he planted the seeds for the growth of a new religious community, a corporate body such that the distinction between one and the many—whether the gurus over time or the Sikhs at a particular time—was abolished. According to the Sikh religious tradition, Angad and the subsequent eight gurus, though nine different human beings, were but one person and that person was Nanak, who was guided by God, the supreme guru. Therefore, whatever their teachings and actions, these have to be acknowledged to be in essence and indeed in truth Nanak's. The Sikhs have tried thus to overcome the problem of reconciling the teachings and actions of the different gurus. It seems to me, however, that, in the context of the problem set for the present discussion (namely, secularism and secularization) these differences are of critical importance. In fact, they could not but be so, given the changes that took place in the internal composition of the Sikh community and in its socio-political environment over the 150 years or so following Nanak's death.

As stated above, Nanak belonged to a Khatri caste: he was a Bedi. The Khatris were a congeries of castes (*jāti*s, to be precise) comprising the traditional Vaniya (or Baniya) trading and commercial castes, agriculturalists, and artisans. All these communities, unlike the Brahmans and the Kshatriyas (the two highest-ranked castes of priests and warriors, respectively), had a well-developed ethic of work and a market orientation.[10] Expectedly, they often did well by themselves in economic terms (judging by the standards of the medieval period), but they lacked the status of high castes; in fact many of the craftsmen were considered unclean by the two top castes (see Ray 1970: 14). It is they who became the first disciples of Nanak and in large numbers. There was no love lost between him and the Brahmans and the Kshatriyas.

---

[10]All ten of the Sikh gurus were Khatris. The tenth and last, Gobind, was of the Sodhi subcaste. He maintained, however, that both the Bedis and Sodhis were Kshatriyas and, indeed, descended from the lineage of the divine *avatār* Rama of the Hindu religious tradition (see Grewal and Bal [1967] 1987: 109). It may be noted here that, notwithstanding the image of Khatris as traders, some of them are said to have been originally Kshatriyas (see Puri 1988), a category which has long been open to a variety of groups.

The relationship between Guru Nanak and his followers was of mutual advantage. His egalitarian social outlook and ritual-free religious faith offered them release from their relatively low status and the control of the Brahmans. His message made their work respectable as well as profitable. On their part, they not only provided a following for the new guru, but also the material means to operate the quite revolutionary institution of the community kitchen, which provided free food to those followers who needed or wanted to take advantage of the facility. According to a Sikh historian, the Khatri traders found in the teachings of the early gurus 'exactly what they sought and consequently lent their powerful support to the Sikh movement imparting to it the character of an urban or town-based movement'. Subsequently the agricultural classes also came in. 'Their joining the movement was facilitated partly by the hold the commercial classes had on the cultivating classes' (Singh 1969: 3). It was thus that the Sikh innovation became a broad-based social movement of immense potential. Reversing the well-known Weberian argument about the relationship between the Puritan ethic and the spirit of capitalism (see Weber 1930), I would suggest that in Punjab, the market-cum-profit oriented Khatris ensured the success of the religious faith pronounced by Nanak. Their secular outlook converged with Nanak's.

Nanak's choice of Angad as the second guru, instead of one of his sons, in his own life time, is attributed by historians to the former's high spiritual qualities, but some of them also mention that Lehna had a sizable personal following and this may have weighed with the Guru (see Singh 1963: 49). The Sikh community did, in fact, prosper in both numbers and resources under Angad. As a result the institution of the community kitchen (*langar*) became stabilized. He also established the practice of collecting the offerings made by the Sikhs, and there is reason to believe that he may have encouraged the keeping of accounts in the manner of Khatri accountants.[11] He also placed a great emphasis upon physical fitness among his followers who were encouraged to engage in drill, wrestling, and competitive games. He thus planted the seeds of what was to flower into one of

---

[11]Guru Angad evolved the Gurmukhī script using for this purpose basically the script employed by Khatri traders to maintain accounts (see Singh 1978: I, xl). It is obvious that he must have been familiar with account-keeping.

the most deeply ingrained self and other ascribed images of the Sikhs as a people of exceptional valour or, as the British liked to call them, a 'martial race'. By all accounts, Angad was not only a worthy spiritual guru, but also a worldly man and an able organizer of men and institutions. Under his guidance the secular component of Nanak's teaching does indeed seem to have been strengthened.

The size of the following and the resources they commanded had grown so large by the time of Amar Das (1479–1574), the third guru, that special measures for their organization and use had to be taken, and he proved equal to the task. He divided his widespread followers into twenty-two parish-like groups called *manjī*, and placed each *manjī* under an agent, called *masand*, who collected the offerings from the followers and also provided them spiritual guidance. An equal emphasis upon the secular and religious functions of these agents is noteworthy. If a tilting of the balance did occur, it would seem to have been in favour of the secular function.

In this connection, a most noteworthy incident has been preserved in the Sikh tradition. Pointing out that Amar Das 'emphasized the need and sanctity of secular activity among the Sikhs', Gopal Singh writes: 'When Gango, a Khatri, came to see him and asked, "What shall I do to save myself?" the guru replied, "Go and open a bank at Delhi and dwell upon the name of God"' (1978: I, xii). The story may well be apocryphal, but its currency itself is significant. It reminds one of the kind of advice which Puritan pioneers such as Benjamin Franklin gave the newly settled 'pilgrims' in North America (see Weber 1930: 50ff.). It has also been recorded that Amar Das stressed social egalitarianism by insisting that his visitors first eat in the community kitchen before meeting him,[12] and this rule is believed to have been applied even to the Mughal emperor, Akbar, when he visited the Guru. Moreover, though the fare served in his kitchen was rich, Amar Das himself ate frugally and only what he himself earned by his own labour (Singh 1964: 24).

Although asceticism was rejected, austerity was acknowledged as a personal virtue in the lives of these early gurus. At the same time the exhortation to their followers was to strive for worldly

---

[12]*Pehle pangat piche sangat* (first sit down in a row [to eat with others] only then may you sit [with the Guru]).

fortunes. The fourth guru, Ram Das (1534–81), a builder of cities and towns, including Amritsar, which is the holy city most revered by the Sikhs, invited traders from wherever his message could reach to settle down there:

> The Guru asked his Sikhs to help each other in founding business houses and pray for their success. The Sikhs from now on remained no longer small farmers or petty shopkeepers, but went as far as Kabul to buy and sell houses, and become jewelers, embroidery workers, carpenters and masons, bankers and wholesalers. (Singh 1978: I, xii)

With the passing away of Ram Das, the first phase of the evolution of the Sikh community came to an end. During this phase the two most significant factors in the evolutionary process were, first, the unusual personal qualities of the gurus, who combined their spiritual quest with an affirmation of the worth of mundanity in a seamless world view, and second, the social composition of the early followers. These factors were able to operate in unison in relatively well-settled political conditions, particularly during the long and highly tolerant reign of the great Mughal king, Akbar.

Ram Das broke with tradition when he chose his son-in-law as the next guru; the succession thereafter went from father to son while the first three gurus had strictly avoided such choices. Moreover, after Akbar's death the political environment within which the Sikhs had to operate became increasingly hostile, compelling them to abandon their early pacifist ways. Finally, the social composition of the community underwent a radical transformation with the massive infusion of the Jats. In choosing to cope with adverse circumstances from a position of strength and engaging in politics, the Sikh gurus, from now on, contributed to the making of what one may call, borrowing once again the phraseology of Weber (1930: 181), the Sikh 'iron cage'. The Sikhs themselves generally conceive of it as their call of destiny. Increasingly, they became involved with secular power and ultimately sacralized it. More about this is discussed below.

Arjan Mal (1563–1606), fifth in succession, was a great consolidator. Nanak had given the new message for whosoever would listen and bound them in the act and symbolism of the common meal. Angad gave the Sikhs a distinctive script. Amar Das gave them a place of pilgrimage at Goindwal, where he constructed a sacred well (*baolī*). Although this was against the letter and spirit of the teachings of Nanak, it fulfilled the traditional aspirations of the people. Ram Das became the instrument of a miracle, for the tank which he dug out at his new city of Chak Ram Das is believed, by pious Sikhs, to have been filled miraculously by the will of god. Its water is thus no less than *amrit*, the holy water that bestows immortality: hence the renaming of the city as Amritsar, the pool of ambrosia.

Guru Arjan's contributions were a fitting capstone on this edifice. He constructed a temple in the holy tank known as Harmandar Sahib, 'the honoured temple of God' and gave the Sikhs their Holy Book, the Ādi Granth ('the original book'), by committing to writing the prayers, hymns, and sayings of the first four gurus, his own, and those of many Hindu saints and Muslim Sūfīs of the Sant tradition from various parts of the country. The eclecticism has been described as 'an effort to extend the Sikh constituency' (Hans 1985: 215). It may be added here that it was Nanak himself who had started the practice of using his own compositions in prayers or worship (see Grewal [1969] 1979: 284).

Arjan converted the traditional voluntary offering to the guru into an obligatory tithe (*dasvandh*), showing a concern for money obtained by open but somewhat coercive means. This gave a new definition to the relationship of the Sikh guru and his followers. Needless to emphasize, money is a key symbol of a secularized world (see Weber 1930: 174). An indefatigable traveller, Arjan won for the Sikh faith the following of thousands of Jats. By now Sikhs were to be found in many north Indian cities, often as traders. His achievements were recognized widely and he accepted the honoured sobriquet of Sachā Pādshah, 'the true emperor', for himself, signifying the unity of the sacred and the secular functions. He also got involved in contemporary politics and took the side of the rebel prince Khusrau against his father, the emperor Jahangir. This cost Arjan his life, but in the process he gave the Sikhs their first martyr, establishing yet another significant element of the Sikh tradition, namely, the call to martyrdom, which continues to be a powerful motive force in the lives of many Sikhs until today (see Fenech 2000). In fact, the symbolism of martyrdom, which became highly valorized as a result of the killing of the ninth and tenth gurus as also the latter's sons, has been invoked by Sikh fundamentalists in recent years (see Madan 1997: Chapter Three).

I must pause here to explain the significance of the infusion of the Jats into the Sikh fold which was mentioned earlier. Although originally pastoralists in Rajasthan, the Jats had moved into Punjab from the ninth century onward, and established themselves as very hard-working and successful peasant cultivators. Although they had prospered economically, they suffered from a stigmatized identity in relation to caste Hindus:

> With their strong rural base, their martial traditions, their normally impressive physique and their considerable energy the Jats have for many centuries constituted the elite of the Punjab villages. They are also noted for their straightforward manner, for a tremendous generosity, for an insistence upon their right to take revenge, and for their sturdy attachment to the land. (McLeod 1976: 11)

The Khatris were the moneylenders and mentors of the Jats, and the first three Sikh gurus, themselves Khatris, hailed from the Jat country in central Punjab. It was this human component (66 per cent of all Sikhs at the 1881 census) of the burgeoning Sikh heritage which Guru Arjan, who attained martyrdom in 1606, bequeathed to his son with the message 'to sit fully armed on his throne and to maintain an army to the best of his ability' (Field 1914: 19). And Hargobind did exactly as he was told, signifying a major turning point in the continuing redefinition of secularism in the Sikh religious tradition.

THE DOCTRINE OF TWO SWORDS

Hargobind (1595–1644), though only eleven years old when he became the sixth guru of the Sikhs, spoke in the accents of a mature man, according to Sikh oral tradition: 'My *selī* [rosary worn as a necklace by the previous gurus symbolizing their spiritual pursuits] shall be a sword-belt, and my turban shall be adorned with a royal aigrette' (Macauliffe 1909: IV, 2). At his investiture he carried two swords in his sword-belt and explained the significance of his action: '[O]ne to avenge my father, the other to destroy the miracles of Muhammad'

(Narang 1960: 60). In other words, while the one symbolized his temporal power (*mīrī*), the other stood for his spiritual authority (*pīrī*).[13]

Even more portentous was Hargobind's decision to have a new temple erected facing the Harmandar Sahib (but outside the holy tank of Amritsar), which he called the Akāl Takht, 'the Throne of the Immortal God'. Therein he had his own throne built higher than the throne of the Mughal emperor in Delhi. '[I]nstead of chanting hymns of peace, the congregation heard ballads extolling feats of heroism, and, instead of listening to religious discourses, discussed plans of military conquests' (Singh 1963: 63). He asked his agents (*masand*) to fetch him tribute in men, horses, and arms. He raised an army and built a small fortress, Lohgarh (the steel castle), in Amritsar. Hargobind had an ambivalent relationship with the emperor, Jahangir (who had had Hargobind's father tortured to death), suffered imprisonment, and finally during the time of the next emperor, Shahjahan, came into open conflict with the imperial troops on three occasions. The Sikhs acquitted themselves well in these clashes though they also suffered heavy losses (see Singh 1964: 33). By 1634, Hargobind obviously had second thoughts about continued conflict with the imperial power, and withdrew into a quieter way of life in the Himalayan foothills in east Punjab. He stayed there until his death ten years later. Apart from the conflict with the Mughal emperors, he also had to grapple with the organizational problems generated by an expanding and an increasingly heterogeneous following including the Jats and 'superstition-ridden Hindus' (Singh 1963: 66), and even 'criminals and fugitives' (Cunningham [1916] 1955: 50).

What is the significance of 'the call to arms' given by Guru Hargobind in the general context of the evolution of the Sikh

---

[13]It is not clear how exactly Hargobind defined the relationship between spiritual authority and temporal power. His religious tradition had paid little attention to the latter; in fact, Nanak had ridiculed and reviled kings, saying even worms were better, for kings forget god. In this connection the significance of building the Akāl Takht separately, outside the holy tank, may not be minimized. In the comparative context, Dumont (1983b: 15) has observed that the 'logical' relation between the two functions is one of 'hierarchical complementarity with *auctoritas* encompassing *potestas*'.

community, and in terms of the processes of secularization? The established opinion of Sikh scholars themselves flows from their the-oak-tree-in-the-acorn position: 'We do not see any essential difference in the outlook of Guru Hargobind from his predecessors' except perhaps in emphasis which was of course the need of the time' (Gopal Singh 1978: I, xlii). Some non-Sikh historians echo this judgement when they maintain that Hargobind, and later Gobind Singh (the tenth Guru), did not deviate 'from the great ideal of Guru Nanak' by transforming 'a purely pietistic faith and society to a militant and crusading one directed towards temporal ends': they are said to have only elaborated 'in the context of a somewhat different socio-political situation, what Guru Nanak stood for in his own time and space' (Ray 1970: 86). Two inter-related issues of interpretation are involved here: one theological and the other sociological. Sikh hermeneutics has had to reckon with Nanak's admonition, 'fight with no weapons except *shabad* [the holy word]' (Cunningham [1916] 1955: 40), and an explicit formulation on this issue had to await Gobind Singh.

From the sociological point of view, the apparently contextualist approach of scholars such as Gopal Singh and Niharranjan Ray seriously minimizes the significance of both the changing composition of the Sikh community (its internal order) and its relations with the Mughal empire (its external order) and, therefore, provides us with emasculated history. They uncritically echo the traditional Sikh point of view, which discerns even a political dimension to Guru Nanak's concerns, by recalling that he made certain statements about the state and that he too has long been referred to as 'the True King' (Sachā Pādshah). The most authoritative scholarly opinion is best stated by J.S. Grewal, who maintains that 'man's moral commitment is given a clear primacy over his political obligations' in Nanak's teaching (Grewal [1969] 1979: 165)—that 'true sovereignty' according to the Guru was not all political (Grewal [1969] 1979: 166). In other words, society was to be saved by virtuous people and, above all, god, and not by secular power, such as that of kings.

From the specific point of view of the present discussion, therefore, a critical change in the character of secular outlook, and in the process of secularization, must be acknowledged. Nanak's moral this-worldliness, summed up as 'work, worship, and sharing', and faith in divine grace, are from Hargobind's time redefined in terms of temporal power, honour, and revenge. To use a sociologist's phrase, hope has become political (see Martin 1978: 63), and when this happens, the encompassing character of spiritual authority as opposed to temporal power, even if acknowledged, is, in fact, undermined. Writing from the perspective of the historian of religions, Toynbee (1979: 110) has observed:

> While it is manifest in the case of Judaism, Christianity and the Mahayana that a higher religion was being diverted from its mission by being exploited politically, this is not less true, though it may be less obvious, in the case of Islam and Sikhism.

The transformation brought about by Hargobind was radical: its most important characteristic was an emphasis upon the unity of religion and politics, but in a manner that the primacy of the former was weakened. It could also be construed as a process of sacralization, indicative of the elevation of the secular world to a position it had not occupied before: pursuit of power (in the sociological sense of the word) could now pretend to be on par with the religious quest—a thing of value—and even overshadow it. This new world view found its full expression in the words and actions of the tenth and last guru, Gobind Singh, but not before another and a truly glorious martyrdom had taken place.

Hargobind's three immediate successors (his grandson, great-grandson, and son, in that order) are of no particular interest for this discussion, beyond the fact that, though they could not completely withdraw from political involvements, they stressed the pietist–pacific element of the Sikh religious tradition more than its martial fervour. In 1675, Tegh Bahadur, the ninth guru, suffered martyrdom defending the sanctity of a people's religious faith. The efforts of the fundamentalist Mughal emperor, Aurangzeb, to bring Tegh Bahadur, who was widely respected not only by Sikhs, but also by Hindus generally, under the heel were successfully resisted by the saintly Guru until he was executed in Delhi.[14]

---

[14]The importance of the evolving significance of the notion of martyrdom in the Sikh politico-religious tradition is illustrated by Khushwant Singh's translation of a verse attributed to Guru Gobind on the ninth Guru's execution: 'He suffered martyrdom for the sake of this faith' (1963: 74–75). This is not a literal translation.

Gobind Rai (1666–1708) was only nine years old when he was called upon to cremate his father Teg Bahadur's severed head, which had been carried in secrecy to Anandpur (east Punjab). Ever since the retreat of Hargobind into the Shivalik Hills, the Sikh gurus had imbibed the local Hindu cultural and religious ethos. Significant elements of this ethos were the Purānic story of Krishna as a divine incarnation and the cult of Shakti, that is the divinity conceived as 'power' and represented as the goddess. The Hindu concept of power is, of course, total and not to be equated with the notion of political power in the Western civilization. 'The Shakti blended easily with the Jat cultural patterns which had been brought from the plains. The result was a new and powerful synthesis which prepared the Panth [the Sikh community] for a determinative role in the chaotic circumstances of the eighteenth century' (McLeod 1976: 14).

Gobind's upbringing in Patna (in eastern India) and Anandpur took place in a Hindu environment, and he attained considerable knowledge of the Hindu as well as the Sikh religious traditions. He defined his own role almost literally in terms of Hindu scripture. Echoing the Bhagavadgītā, he wrote: 'For this purpose was I born, To uphold righteousness, to protect those worthy and virtuous. To overcome and destroy the evil doers' (Harbans Singh 1966: 176).[15] He, however, repudiated the Hindu idea of *avatār*: 'Whoever calls me the supreme Being shall suffer in hell. Recognise me as God's servant only' (Harbans Singh 1966: 13).

Gobind was obviously deeply impressed by the Hindu cult of the goddess of destruction, and is believed to have written long poems in praise of her: his first composition and only major Punjabi work, 'Var Sri Bhagautiji ki', is based on the Mārkandya Purāna, a Brahmanical text. Subsequently, he wrote a poem in Hindi also, 'Chandī Charitar', honouring the goddess. His designation of the sword as 'Bhagauti', the goddess, recalls the fact that the sword is her symbol in Hindu mythology. He also called god *sarbloh*, 'all steel' (pure steel). The supplicatory prayer, *ardas*, which he composed, begins thus: 'Having

---

[15]Cf. the Bhagavadgītā (IV, 7–8): Whenever righteousness wanes and evil prevails. I go forth from age to age to protect the good, punish the wicked, and re-establish the sovereignty of good.

first remembered the Sword, meditate on Guru Nanak.' Another well-known prayer composed by him concludes with these words (see Harbans Singh 1966: 47):

> Hail! Hail to the creator of the World.
> The Saviour of Creation, my Cherisher,
> Hail to thee, O Sword.

In an earlier composition, 'Shastar Nām Mālā', containing the names of various weapons, Gobind had identified these with divinities and even personified them.

Guru Gobind's inspiration was more his grandfather, Hargobind, than his father, and he waged war against the Mughals. He introduced the notion of *dharmayudda*, 'holy war' or 'war to uphold righteousness', into the Sikh religious tradition, drawing upon, once again, Hindu sources. At the end of his rendering of the story of the Krishna *avatār*, he is believed to have written (see Harbans Singh 1966: 48):

> I have cast into the popular tongue the story of Bhāgvata.
> This I have done with no other purpose, Lord, except to glorify the 'holy war'.

His justification of the theology of the sword (obviously mindful of Nanak's exhortation to his followers to wield no weapon and rely solely on the recitation of god's name) was also conveyed, so it is said, in a message called the 'epistle of victory' (*zafarnāma*), which, tradition has it, he sent to Aurangzeb: '[W]hen all avenues have been explored, all means tried, it is rightful to draw the sword out of the scabbard and wield it with your hand' (see Singh 1963: 78, n. 5). As Khushwant Singh notes: 'It would be idle to pretend that this change of emphasis was purely theological' (1963: 89).

Ultimately, in 1699, Gobind instituted baptism for the Sikhs to constitute a community of the 'pure' (*khālsā*), in deference to god's command, he said. He employed a double-edged sword (*khanda*) to prepare the baptismal water. The baptized Sikh was to call himself Singh (literally, 'lion') in the manner of the Hindu Rajputs (warrior caste) of north India. One of the symbols of an initiated man, he prescribed, should be the sword (*kirpan*), or an emblem of it, which a

Sikh was exhorted to always carry on his person.[16] The emphasis on the sword symbolized the value of valour, and also pointed to a political goal as a part of the religious quest. Grewal and Bal ([1967] 1987: 126) observe: 'More than ever before the activities of Guru Gobind Singh's Sikhs now appeared fraught with political implications, and the stage was set for a deeper conflict with contemporary powers.'

But conflict is never a goal in itself; this could now only be the acquisition of political power—the establishment of a Sikh state. Not long afterwards, the words *rāj karegā Khālsā*, 'the pure (baptized) Sikhs will rule', were added to the daily prayer (*ardas*) by one of his followers. A most significant instrument of the quest for power was to be the band of warriors (*jatha*), modelled on the congregation (*sangat*), bound by codes of conduct (*rahitnāma*). Together these concepts emphasized collective identity and common purpose rather than individual leadership or following. Guru Gobind Singh announced closure of the canon (*gurbānī*) and declared that, after his death, spiritual authority would vest in the Holy Book (Guru Granth Sahib). Temporal power for the furtherance of Sikh secular interests, he declared, would be exercised by the Khālsā (*Guru Panth*), represented at any place and time by five baptized Sikhs.

To say that the significance of Gobind Singh's achievements for the evolution of the Sikh religious tradition and the Sikh community was enormous would be an understatement. The passage from Guru Nanak's pietist and pacifist message of salvation and qualified world affirmation to Guru Gobind's call to his followers to take charge of their destiny as a self-ascribed community, and to take up arms if necessary to achieve their objectives, was the passage from sacralized secularity to secularized religion. Using the criteria developed in an earlier work (Madan 1997: Chapter One), the revolutionary steps taken by the tenth guru could be said to be fundamentalist in

---

[16]The emphasis originally was on the symbolic rather than a real sword; Guru Gobind himself used to wear a miniature sword in his hair. The other related symbols are, as is well known, unshorn hair tied into a knot with a comb placed in it, a steel bracelet worn on the right forearm, and knee-length trousers. Gobind laid down the wearing of unshorn hair as an obligation; the other items are not mentioned in the code of conduct (*rahitnāma*) he had drawn up for the Sikhs (see Khushwant Singh 1953, 1963). For two different and unusual interpretations of the five symbols, see Kapur Singh (1959: 137–54) and Uberoi (1991: 320–32).

orientation. Scripture was concretized (through the closure of the *gurbānī*), and elevated the status of the spiritual guru. The sense of community bonding was greatly strengthened through a variety of measures, including personal and collective names (Singh, Kaur, Khālsā), a ritual of baptism replete with rich symbolism, and a code of conduct. These key elements helped define an exclusive way of life and also provided the basis for cultural critique. Guru Gobind did not hesitate to place power in the centre of the scheme of things. In doing so he was reacting to the situation in which he found himself as the guru of a demoralized following. To the extent to which the situation demanded in his judgement a reshaping of the religious tradition, he responded with vision and vigour. He emerged as a role model for succeeding leaders, but none of them has ever come anywhere near him in achievements (see Madan 1997: Chapter Three).

THE SECULAR STATE OF RANJIT SINGH

The effort to establish a Sikh state succeeded almost immediately after the death (murder) of Guru Gobind Singh in 1708. His chosen successor to carry on the 'holy war'—ironically a Hindu renouncer—felt free to define his own identity. He cast himself in the kingly role, although he said that he was no more than a slave (*bāndā*) of Gobind Singh. Banda Bahadur, 'brave slave' (that was the name he chose for himself), moved swiftly, incited an agrarian uprising, fought Muslim armies, and captured the province of Sirhind from the Mughal governor in 1710, less than two years after Gobind Singh's death. Banda now assumed the title of Pādshah, the emperor, and even issued coins to mark the inauguration of his rule. All this was very short-lived, however, and Banda was executed in 1716. But the consciousness generated by Guru Gobind Singh survived—consciousness of the Khālsā not only as a repository of spiritual knowledge, but also of political will.

Eighty years and more had to pass before a real state was established by a Sikh in 1799, when the eighteen-year-old Ranjit Singh (incidentally a Jat) captured the city of Lahore from three squabbling Sikh sardars who were in control of it (see Singh 1963: 196ff.). A valiant soldier, a shrewd administrator, and a sagacious ruler, Ranjit Singh unified Punjab and adjoining areas under his direct rule, or under other rulers who acknowledged his overall sovereignty and paid tribute to him. Ironically, Ranjit Singh's state was not a Sikh state, but a monarchy, and the prophecy that the Khālsā would rule had not been fulfilled. In fact, it has been asserted that the 'republicanism' of Gobind Singh was 'compromised', 'gradually, progressively and purposely' (Singh 1959: 352), by Ranjit Singh, who assumed the title of Maharaja at a Brahmanical coronation ceremony in 1801. Singh (1963: 360) observes:

> Within a few years after his coronation, he reduced into desuetude the supreme authority of the Sikh polity, the *Gurumata* [the collective will of the community treated as the opinion of the guru], and entrusted the control of the government of his expanding territories to a cabinet of his own choice, in accordance with the ancient Hindu monarchical tradition, [though personally,] he never claimed independence from the *Gurumata*.

We have here an important concept, namely, the secular state, which was new in the evolution of the Sikh religious tradition: a gulf was created—a wall erected—between the polity and the personal religious faith of the ruler. Ranjit Singh's first act on entering Lahore had been to 'pay homage' at two of the city's mosques associated with its Muslim rulers (see Singh 1963: 197). He preserved in a broadly defined policy of non-discrimination towards all communities by personally celebrating their religious festivals, and by proclaiming the equality of all citizens before the law (Singh 1963: 203). Although such pluralism could not be said to be alien to the Sikh religious tradition,[17] it did entail serious compromises: the

---

[17]Gobind wrote in his 'Akal Utsat' (Harbans Singh 1966: 3):

Recognise all mankind, whether Hindus or Muslims, as one.
The same Lord is the Creator and Nourisher of all.
Recognise no distinctions among them.
The monastery and the mosque are the same.
So are the Hindu worship and the Muslim prayer.
Man are all one.

He is said to have echoed the Qur'ān (109: 3), and said to a Muslim *qāzī* (judge): 'Your religion is good for you and our religion for us.' A modern Sikh commentator calls this a 'strange twist' to Guru Nanak's mission (Hans 1985: 218).

notion of the Khālsā as the repository of political power (*Guru Panth*) was one of the casualties.

'The factor which contributed most to Ranjit Singh's success,' writes Khushwant Singh, 'was his respect for all faiths.' He further points out that 'Ranjit Singh's court reflected the secular pattern of his state' and that 'there were no forced conversions' in his time. 'This attitude won the loyalty of all his subjects' (1963: 294–95). But, and as already pointed out above, other Sikh historians contest this judgement on one crucial point: according to them Ranjit Singh's secularism was against the Sikh religious tradition (see Singh 1959: 284–387), for it destroyed the hierarchical unity (in the Dumontion sense, see Footnote 11 in Chapter Three) of spiritual authority and temporal power. Contemporary historians also have been somewhat sceptical about his fair treatment of Muslims. Nevertheless, Ranjit Singh may well be considered a precursor of the secularism of Jawaharlal Nehru and the Constitution of the Republic of India. Nehruvian secularism, however, is an anathema to those who claim to speak in the name of the Sikh religious tradition (see Madan 1997: Chapters Three and Eight).

Ranjit Singh died in 1839, and the kingdom he had built collapsed in 1846, creating a situation in which the Sikhs, shorn of political power, sought refuge in their religious faith, but found it much diluted. The 'iron cage' of worldly involvements had gradually confined the faith too narrowly. Like the Muslims who, in a similar situation of loss of political power, had earlier turned to the 'purification' of their religious life (see Madan 1997: Chapter Four), the Sikhs too sought solace in reviving the orthopraxis that went hand in hand with their orthodoxy. This involved, among other things, reassertion of the supreme position of the guru, elimination of those elements of Hindu ritualism which had reasserted their sway in the everyday life of the Sikhs and, freeing of the Sikh temples from the control of priests who were not baptized Sikhs. The socio-political concomitant of these moves was the redefinition of Sikh identity in the negative slogan 'We are not Hindus' necessitated not only by the inner urge for reform, but also the external pressure exercised by the revivalist Hindu Arya Samaj (Madan 1997: Chapter Seven). Religion thus became a 'sign' of distinction between Sikhs and Hindus, and was reduced to being its own 'shadow' (to borrow a formulation from Dumont 1970b: 91).[18]

Though the Gurdwara Act of 1925, the control of the temples passed into the hands of a democratically elected body, namely the Shiromani Gurdwara Prabandhak Committee (SGPC), and the political movement against British imperialism and Hindu cultural hegemony was taken charge of by the exclusively Sikh political party, Akali Dal (see Khushwant Singh 1966: 193–216). Although the Sikhs were nearly unanimous in relation to their religious goals, they found themselves divided politically. Events that could be seen as a reassertion of Sikh republicanism also carried in them the seeds of disruptive politics. The partition of the subcontinent in 1947 was a deadly blow to the Sikh community, which found itself driven out of areas that had been its home since the very beginning. The sense of political grievance deepened with the passage of time, and the Akalis repudiated any notion of the separation of religion and politics and the state that political analysts derived from the Constitution of India. This repudiation became the basis for the demand for a Sikh homeland (see Nayar 1966 and Harbans Singh 1983: 343ff.).

Simultaneously with these political developments, large landowners, mainly Hindus but also Sikhs, became the principal beneficiaries of the successful Green Revolution in Punjab, and expanding opportunities in industrial enterprise and urban professions. As worldwide opportunities for secular success beckoned, the Sikhs responded enthusiastically, but at a price, namely, the increasing 'incidence of apostasy': '[T]he sense of belonging to the Sikh community requires both the belief in the teaching of the *Ādi Granth* and the observance

---

[18]For a different interpretation of the events of the second half of the nineteenth century, see Oberoi 1994. He questions the thesis of the cultural decline of Sikhs, and regards the same as a construction of the British and the new elites who spearheaded the Singh Sabhas. While Oberoi pays due attention to the opportunities that the British rulers generated (and not in the armed services alone), I think he plays down the impact of the collapse of the kingdom bequeathed to the Sikhs (indeed all Punjabis) by Ranjit Singh. There is a strong similarity between this situation and the downfall of the Mughal empire in the early eighteenth century. In both cases, many community leaders linked loss of power to a decline in the quality of the religious life, and initiated corrective steps along both the cultural and political routes (see Madan 1997: Chapter Three).

of the Khalsa tradition initiated by Guru Gobind Singh' (Khushwant Singh 1966: 303). In the circumstances, it seems that the Sikh faith will survive only if it is enforced by the state, and this could only be done by a Sikh state (see Khushwant Singh 1966: 305).

The most serious threat to religious faith is modernization, which includes secularization in the sense of a restricted role for religion in the life of the individual, but the Sikhs with their this-worldly tradition are unlikely to turn their back on the modern world. If this indeed be so, then it is only to be expected that 'fundamentalism', which often is an expression of a guilty conscience, will in one form or another characterize pockets of Sikh public life for quite some time to come. In the eye of the orthodox, the three values of 'work, worship, and sharing' have been displaced by 'parasitism, godlessness, and selfishness' in the lives of many apparently successful and modernized Sikhs. Hence the call, 'Be good Sikhs', given by the fundamentalists (see Madan 1997: Chapter Three).

❖

To conclude I will say, in this chapter I have been concerned with an examination of the Sikh religious tradition with a view to finding out what it teaches us about the patterns and processes of secularization. This is a particularly worthwhile exercise in view of the assertion of many Sikh scholars that, while their religious faith postulates the unity of religion and politics, it is at the same time a 'secular religion'. In fact it has been argued that 'this comingling of motifs [spiritual authority and royal power] makes for a certain secularization of faith in Sikhism' (Singh 1973: 22), so that confidence is expressed that 'the Sikh faith has an in-built mechanism that can absorb successfully the essential spirit of secularism' (Samundari 1973: 6).

The foregoing discussion suggests that there are three possible meanings of secularism within the Sikh religious tradition, and a fourth one outside it, but affecting Sikh life today. Each connotation derives from a particular pattern of secularization, which in turn is causally linked to certain, antecedent critical events in a manner observed elsewhere (see Martin 1978). These are: (i) world affirmation or 'mundanity', (ii) the unity of religion and politics and, therefore, of the gurdwara and the state, (iii) religious pluralism and the separation of religion and politics, and (iv) a narrowing of the role of religion in society. Of these, the first meaning does not by itself entail the second: in fact, and as noted by a number of Sikh scholars, the merger of functions 'ultimately weakened the original religious impulse' (Singh 1973: 22). As for the third and fourth patterns of secularization, it is obvious that they are at variance and even in conflict with the first and the second, and have been, therefore, rejected by orthodox Sikhs.

In the context of inter-religious comparison, it is obvious that confident theories of modernization notwithstanding a hiatus exists. The 'translation' of ideas from one civilizational setting to another, even after the 'transfer' or related institutions (most notably the 'modern' state) has formally been achieved, is not easy. India's major religious traditions—Hinduism, Islam, and Sikhism—do not provide the kind of idiom which the Christian tradition, before and after Luther, did for secularization in its European manifestations. And yet it is these that until recently used to be, and still are by some diehard secularists, recommended as universally valid. Needless to add, idioms are only part of the story, the part on which the foregoing discussion has focused. Idioms go with institutions and may even evolve from the latter. The sociological perspective is committed to the importance of institutions, but their consideration is not a part of this discussion.

Chapter Five

Gandhi and Weber:
The Work Ethic, Capitalism, and Conscience

[H]e who renounces earns a thousand-fold.
—GANDHI, 'Anasaktiyoga'

That economics is untrue which ignores or disregards moral values.
—GANDHI, Presidential Address to Belgaum Congress, 1924

Only a small portion of existing concrete reality is coloured by our value-conditioned interest and it alone is significant to us.
—MAX WEBER, '"Objectivity" in Social Science'

Certainly all historical experience confirms the truth—that man would not have attained the possible unless time and again he had reached out for the impossible. But to do that a man must be a leader, and not only a leader but a hero as well, in a very sober sense of the word.
—MAX WEBER, 'Politics as Vocation'

In the preceding four chapters, I have tried to highlight some conceptual and methodological issues in the study of India's cultural traditions with specific reference to what generally are called religious ideas, values, and attitudes. Continuing in the same vein, I focus my attention in this chapter on religious ethics and on the cross-cultural dichotomy of instrumental and ultimate values. I begin with a brief reference to how Mrinal Miri, a distinguished Indian philosopher, approaches this problem, and then, following him, engage with Mahatma Gandhi and Max Weber. The attraction of proceeding thus lies in that it brings intercultural comparison into the discussion. The comparative perspective was, of course, introduced in the chapters on Indian secularism and Islam; I will return to it in Chapters Eight and Nine in my discussion of Louis Dumont's work.

ULTIMATE AND INSTRUMENTAL VALUES

One of the abiding themes of Mrinal Miri's work is his concern with the exploration of the significance of being a 'person'. This is, of course, one of the constitutive themes of sociological inquiry (see, for example, Carrithers et al. 1985), which is my own area of research and study, just as it is of philosophical reflection, Professor Miri's speciality (for an innovative discussion of the subject, see Wollheim 1984). To be a person means, sociologically, being more than an individual; it connotes one's situatedness within a collectivity of individuals, held together by common values, purposes, and procedures, which are to a very large extent externally given, that is, socially defined and controlled by shared norms, customs, and laws. One's personhood, the fact of togetherness, is also defined by the instrumental (economic, political) and value (moral) choices that one makes, for no one comes wholly moulded out of the crucibles of custom or by the tyranny of tradition. Conformists generally outnumber the innovators, but the latter are never wholly absent. What, then, is it to be a moral agent? And why should one be moral at all? Needless to emphasize, these are questions that have ontological, epistemological, and ethical dimensions, and have long engaged the philosophers. Liberal sociologists generally have, however, abstained from telling people how to live; this is particularly true of those who derive their inspiration from Max Weber (1864–1920) rather than Émile Durkheim (1855–1917).

For a philosopher like Miri, these (and other related questions) may well lead to a multi-stranded engagement with the thought of Mahatma Gandhi (1869–1948), more precisely with Gandhi's deep concern for the preservation of autonomy of the individual, conceived as a moral agent, in the face of the threatening presence of the 'modern' state (with its violence) and 'modern' industrial civilization (with its mass production technologies and the devaluation of the human being) no less than the unreasonable demands of tradition. In an important essay on Gandhi's conception of moral life in the context of plurality of religions, Miri (2003: 118–28) sets out to examine the notion of 'humanism', which he arguably locates in the ambit of 'Western modernity'. But then 'humanism stands in close but extremely uneasy relationship with another pervasive feature of modernity: modern Western epistemology, dominated by ... the "ideology" of natural science' (Miri 2003: 119).

This ideology produces, Miri notes, what Max Weber called the 'disenchantment of the world' (Weber 1948b: 129–56), that is, its being brought under the regime of reason alone. In other words, 'there are no mysterious incalculable forces' and 'one can, in principle, master all things by calculation ... [by] technical means and calculation' (Weber 1948b: 159). Weber considered this turn in the history of Western civilization inevitable *and* regrettable. He wrote (1948b: 155):

> The fate of our times is characterized by rationalization and, above all, by the 'disenchantment of the world'. Precisely the ultimate and most sublime values have retreated from public life into the transcendental realm of mystic life or into the brotherliness of direct and personal human relations.

In the light of Weber's insights, Miri (2003: 119) detects a major problem characteristic of the predicament of modern man:

> Since the world revealed by our rational—scientific—epistemic gaze is not a world in terms of [ultimate] values, what might be called a dharmic world, the humanist values must be articulated in the language of rights and not in the language of ontological commitment.

For such a language of commitment, Miri recommends we should turn to Gandhi, whose 'pre-modern or traditional' approach flows from 'the unqualified conviction that our existence is spiritually grounded' (2003: 122). In Gandhi's thought, 'we have an alternative epistemology—an epistemology which can be termed the epistemology of *ahimsa* or love—one that accounts for the possibility of self-knowledge which is also, at the same time, knowledge of moral truths' (Miri 2003: 127).

In this chapter, I make an attempt briefly to highlight some significant convergences between Gandhi and Weber's perspectives on the conflict between ultimate and instrumental values that lies at the very core of modern life. More specifically, I discuss their views on the notions of the work ethic, capitalism, and conscience. A more detailed and intensive discussion must await another occasion.

GANDHI'S CONCEPTION OF WORK AS DUTY

The years 1908–09 were of immense importance in the spiritual and intellectual development of Mahatma Gandhi. In the midst of a wide range of professional, political, and social activities, he read voraciously and, by his own acknowledgement, experienced an enormous inner turmoil, a kind of enlightenment. He read the Bhagavadgītā, the Bible, and the Qur'ān, and also select works of a number of Western thinkers including Edward Carpenter's *Civilization: Its Cause and Cure*, John Ruskin's *Unto This Last*, and Leo Tolstoy's *The Kingdom of God is within You*. He was inspired by the scriptures and stirred by the other works.

Gandhi wrote in his autobiography that he 'discovered' some of his 'deepest convictions' reflected in Ruskin's book, so much so indeed that it made him 'transform' his life ([1927] 1940: 224). Thus, he found in it a welcome valorization of, first, the 'good of all', placing it above the 'good of the individual', and, second, 'the life of labour'. In Tolstoy's *The Kingdom of God is within You*, which Gandhi wrote 'overwhelmed' him, he found additionally a welcome emphasis on the importance of an inner strength rooted in 'profound morality' and utter 'truthfulness', and a reflection of his own conviction in the superiority of non-violent passive resistance to evil (Gandhi [1927] 1940: 102). Both these thinkers and others too were deeply disturbed, Gandhi thought, by the manner in which Western civilization had moved away from its Christian moorings, seduced by industrial technology and dominated by the power and violence of the modern state.

These critical perspectives found urgent expression in Gandhi's writings, particularly in his own critique of the materialist, industrial civilization in his *Hind Swaraj*, which was written in Gujarati over ten days late in 1909 (during a voyage that brought him back to South Africa from England). The Gujarati text was published in 1909 itself (exactly a hundred years ago), and the English version, *Indian Home Rule*, the following year. Addressing the core issue of the true character of what could rightly be called 'civilization', he argued that it must consist in the attempt to rise above material welfare, the quest of which is an endless and, therefore, essentially unsuccessful chase (see Gandhi 1997: 37). Going beyond the demands of bodily well-being, civilization must give first priority to the 'performance of duty' and 'observance of morality'. Civilization must mean simply but fundamentally 'good conduct' (*sudhāro* in Gujarati), so defined by values that are spiritual and, therefore, universal.

The idea of performance of one's duty within a moral framework, undertaken willingly and in full awareness, is absolutely fundamental to Gandhi's conception of what it is to be human. Put otherwise, it is work ethic that defines our humanity. For him, the propensity to work is ingrained in human beings. Self-incurred abstinence from work is a vice. Leisure is a physical necessity, but only within limits, for it is natural to experience fatigue in both intellectual and physical work. In this context, he accorded priority to physical over intellectual work. The most concrete expression of such a work ethic is 'bread labour', which, Gandhi wrote, literally means 'labour for *roti*'. He called it a 'divine law' and acknowledged in many scriptures (Gandhi 1971: 149). Time and again, he equated work with worship—drawing upon the Benedictine aphorism, *laborare est orare* (Gandhi 1969: 164)—and, indeed, with god himself. 'To a people famishing and idle, the only acceptable form in which God dare appear is work and promise of food as wages. God created man to work for his food, and said that those who ate without work were thieves' (Gandhi 1966b: 289). The reference here is to the Bhagavadgītā: '[H]e who eats without offering sacrifice eats stolen food' (Gandhi 1971: 149).

The Bhagavadgītā was, of course, of fundamental significance in the making of Gandhi's moral vision: he called it his 'spiritual reference book' (Desai 1946: 126). He acknowledged that he found the ideas of bread labour and work ethic in it even before reading Ruskin and Tolstoy (Gandhi 1969: 159). It may be in order, therefore, to highlight here very briefly some of the core ideas of the third chapter of the Bhagavadgītā to which Gandhi drew attention (Gandhi 1969: 159). Work (*karma*) is rooted in human nature (*guna*) and is essential for both personal (physical) survival and for public good. Understood thus, work is no less than a sacrificial offering (*yajna*): it is other-oriented rather than self-oriented. The self, of course, may not be disregarded, but the good of others must come first. Work is, therefore, a moral imperative, undertaken in a spirit of detachment (*anāsakti*) for the well-being of others, particularly the oppressed, and for the preservation of the social order (*loka samgraha*). While the performance of chosen or allotted work is to be wholly detached from any idea of personal gain or enjoyment of the fruits of action (*nishkāma karma*), it must be characterized by total dedication.

Inspired by his own religious tradition (more precisely, by his often original interpretations of it), and by his reading of the works of certain non-Indian scholars, Gandhi evolved a clear notion of a work ethic. Its key elements, it seems to me, are: self-reliance; 'bread labour'; a balancing of physical and mental activities; limitation of personal wants (contentment) without loss of dignity; and a blending of self-interest and altruism. All these ideas coloured Gandhi's thinking generally, including his economic thought. Proclaiming '[t]hat economics is untrue which ignores or disregards moral values' (see Dasgupta 1996: 25), Gandhi maintained that all economic choices (for example, what to produce and by what means, what to consume and how much) are contextualized (culturally and socially specific) moral choices. 'Desire for fruit is the only universal prohibition' (see Desai 1946: 134).

WEBER ON THE PROTESTANT ETHIC

Gandhi's work ethic reminds one of Max Weber's discussion of the Protestant ethic (Weber 1930). Between 1904 and 1905, Weber published three essays on the emergence of what he called 'the spirit of capitalism' in the West (see Weber 1930). He traced its beginnings in large part to the religious anxiety that their faith in predestination generated among pious Puritans regarding their fate: was it damnation or salvation? In the hope of receiving some intimation about the same in the pursuit of secular activities, they led ascetic but active lives, seeking success in their economic pursuits, making profits, and using their savings more for expanding their enterprises than for consumption, and, thus, accumulating the surpluses that are essential for the growth of capitalism. Weber wrote: '[W]here capitalistic acquisition is rationally pursued [in terms of well-defined goals], the corresponding action is adjusted to calculations in terms of capital' (Weber 1930: 18). Capital (or wealth), it must be noted, is in itself value neutral. What one does with it and why is what ultimately matters. Is one a 'capitalistic adventurer' (Weber 1930: 20), or does one have certain deeper concerns (for example, about redemption) and higher objectives? In respect of the Puritans Weber wrote about, namely, the Calvinists, it has been said that they sought salvation through an inner-worldly asceticism, and found Mammon, an unintended consequence. To quote Weber (1930: 53):

> The summum bonum of this ethic, the earning of more and more money combined with the strict avoidance of all spontaneous enjoyment of life, is above all completely devoid of eudaemonistic, not to say hedonistic, admixture. It is thought of so purely as an end in itself, that from the point of view of happiness of, or utility to, the single individual, it appears entirely transcendental and irrational.

Modern, Western capitalism, Weber clarified, is characterized by rational, market-oriented organization of industry and free labour, and separation of the domains of domesticity and business, and is supported by technological inputs and formal legal and administrative procedures (Weber 1930: 21–25). Its ideological basis was the Calvinist doctrine of a theocentric world, created by God for His own glory, within which the individual must dedicate himself to work for the achievement of god's purpose. In such a world, work is to be pursued in a disciplined and rational manner, not for its material gains as such or personal enjoyment, but as duty unto god or, in Gandhi's words, as sacrifice (an offering to god incarnate Krishna). As in Gandhi's formulations, although in a significantly distinctive manner, there is in Weber's formulation of the Puritan's predicament of utter loneliness no option except the selfless performance of one's duty, which must be deemed as self-rewarding.

By the twentieth century, capitalism had emerged, Weber noted, as an external milieu, a coercive force that drove individuals and groups in the West mindlessly forward, and became the core of a new industrial, capitalist civilization. The 'care for external goods', he wrote, was to have rested on 'the saint's shoulders' like 'a light cloak, which can be thrown aside any moment'. But it had fatefully become in due course 'an iron cage' from which there was no escape, but from which religious asceticism itself had, perhaps, finally escaped. Indeed, the drive to 'economic acquisition' would not end, he warned, 'until the last ton of fossilized coal is burnt' (Weber 1930: 181). Weber elaborated his prognosis by once again emphasizing that 'the pursuit of wealth, stripped of its religious and ethical meaning tends to become associated with purely mundane passions, which often actually give it the character of sport' (Weber 1930: 182). In conclusion, he castigates those self-important busy bodies ('specialists without spirit, sensualists without heart'), who 'imagine' that they have 'attained a level of civilization never before achieved': 'the idea of duty in one's calling prowls about in our lives like the ghost of dead religious beliefs' (Weber 1930: 182). These profound value judgements, deeply thought-out and intensely felt, expressed with stunning simplicity, could well have come from the pages of *Hind Swaraj*.

GANDHI AND WEBER ON THE WESTERN CIVILIZATION AND CAPITALISM

Gandhi too wrote about this same civilization and its lust for material goods in *Hind Swaraj*, warning that: 'Those who are intoxicated by modern civilization are not likely to write against it' (1997: 35). But he had no doubt that a civilization, which measured 'progress' by the ability to multiply human needs without limitation and then strove to meet them through technological innovation and machine production, reducing workmen to the condition 'worse than that of beasts' was to be 'shunned'. In such a civilization, unbridled greed overtakes genuine needs, and technical efficiency replaces absolute values; rational restraint, morality, and religion are ignored. Needless to emphasize that when Gandhi discusses labour-saving technological devices, consumerism, and so on, he is talking about the capitalist mode of production. In 1947, about a year before his death, he had observed that, although never many in number, 'capitalists have employed machine-power regardless of the interests of the common man and that is why our condition has deteriorated today'.

Therefore, he advised, that: 'We should be as cheerful in using machines as a doctor is in prescribing poisonous medicines' (Gandhi 1983: 249).[1]

Elaborating the contrast between the indulgent (consumerist) characteristic of capitalist society and self-control (limitation of wants), Gandhi drew pointed attention to the consequences of modern medical interventions which, in his judgement, encourage bodily appetites and weaken the mind (Gandhi 1997: 63). 'Medicine does often benumb the soul of the patient,' he wrote (1997: 63, fn. 118). The mind/soul–body relationship as conceptualized by Gandhi may be called hierarchical, so that the mind/soul encompasses the body: this combination ensures total well-being. If the body is elevated above the mind/soul, however, the normal hierarchical order is reversed, a confusion of values ensues, and this spells disaster.

These ideas are indeed very similar to Weber's on the subject of the technical (that is external) control of human life. Focusing pointedly on 'modern medicine' as a 'practical technology' that enables the prolongation of life, often against the wishes of the patient and his or her relatives, Weber concludes:

> [W]hether life is worth while living and when—this question is not asked by medicine. Natural science gives us an answer to the question of what we must do if we wish to master life technically. It leaves quite aside, or assumes for its purposes, whether

---

[1]Dasgupta (1996: 81–82) comments helpfully:

Gandhi's reading of the trend of technology has something in common with that of Karl Marx. Marx, too, believed that industrial capitalism had an inherent tendency to become increasingly capital-intensive ... and this led in the long run both to the substitution of competition by monopoly and to increasing misery of the masses of working people. However, Marx believed this process to be historically self-correcting for it would lead to society becoming divided into warring classes ... and ultimately to the overthrow of capitalism and the rise of a different kind of society in which the means of production would be held in common. Gandhi's vision was very different. He wanted to avoid the evils of the industrial system by avoiding industrialization itself.

we should or do wish to master life technically and whether it ultimately makes sense to do so. (1948b: 144)

Once again, it is a question of values. Both Gandhi and Weber are conscious, in Gandhi's terms, of the peril of the confusion of values and loss of autonomy, and in Weber's terms, of the substitution of instrumental values for ultimate values and the onset of 'meaninglessness' as an inescapable dimension of the retreat of ultimate values from the public domain.

'Civilization is not an incurable disease' however, Gandhi wrote (1997: 38), contradicting Carpenter. A significant difference between Gandhi and Weber is that, although both were pessimistic about the fate of Western civilization, Gandhi rejected the notion of historical inevitability in the affairs of humanity at large and, therefore, was unlike Weber, who was convinced of the irreversibility of rationalization as a historical process, an optimist. 'Pessimism is never normative to *Hind Swaraj*' (Parel 1997: xlv).

As noted earlier above, Weber wrote of the 'cloak' that could have been 'thrown aside' from one's 'shoulders' had it not become crippling armour. This immediately recalls to one's mind Gandhi's take on non-possession, *aparigraha*, for example, in a crucial speech at the Guildhouse Church in London on 23 September 1931. Once he had realized the significance of this ideal, he said, he began the process of discarding possessions immediately; although doing so was not easy at first, he persevered. And, then, he said: 'I can say a great burden fell off my shoulders', because the 'possession of anything' is 'a troublesome thing'. But why? Gandhi's answer was: 'Civilization, in the real sense of the term' consisted not in the multiplication of wants, but in their 'deliberate and voluntary, restriction': 'the only thing that can be possessed by all is non-possession'. Such an attitude alone, he maintained, can make one truly altruistic and increase one's 'capacity for service' (see Iyer 1986: 381–91). For Gandhi the ideal of service, *sevā*, was a matter of both social responsibility and good conscience. It led him to the ideal of universal love which he shared with Tolstoy, and of which Miri (2003) reminds us.

For the realization of the ideal of *sevā*, which is the same as complete non-egoistic identification with the welfare and, indeed, the suffering of others,[2] Gandhi considered absolute truthfulness, non-violence, non-possession, and so on, as essential credentials of the *satyāgrahī*. One particularly notable expression of such a relationship was Gandhi's notion of trusteeship. The owners of honestly acquired wealth, having acquired the same with the help of others (for example, labour), must consider it, not in terms of absolute ownership, but as capital held in trust on behalf of those others and of society at large (see Ganguli 1973: 271; see also Dasgupta 1996: Chapter 6). Capital in itself is value neutral, it was noted above in the context of the Puritan ethic discussed by Weber; what bestows value (or 'disvalue') on it is how and for what purpose it is used, for egoistic self-aggrandizement violently, or for self-less common good non-violently.

Capital, in Gandhi's judgement, should be regarded and utilized as a positive social resource; to get rid of its owners violently 'would be to kill the goose that laid the golden eggs' (quoted in Dasgupta 1993: 151). The point rather was to recognize that, 'although we are all born equal ... [and] have a right to equal opportunities, nevertheless we have not all the same abilities'; society must not 'lose the gifts of a man who knows how to accumulate wealth' (Dasgupta 1993: 153). For the capitalist to utilize his special abilities and to voluntarily see himself as a trustee, he needs to have a deep sense of moral responsibility, of conscience, which indeed is what Tolstoy's 'kingdom of God' within oneself was all about.

Writing in 1942, Gandhi observed: '[E]arn wealth if you want but like Jamnalalji [Bajaj[3]], all your earnings should be fair earnings ...

---

[2]We may recall here the opening verse of one of Gandhi's very favourite hymns, the one by Narsi Mehta: *Vaishnav janato téné kahiyé jé pīr parāyī jānī ré/ para dukhé upkār karé jo mana abhimān na ānī ré* (They alone may be called godly who know the pain of others as their own/ and alleviate their suffering without taking pride in doing so).

[3]Jamnalal Bajaj, businessman, mill-owner, and 'freedom fighter', was a devoted follower of Gandhi. Nanda (1990: 310–11) writes:

> Under Gandhi's influence he [Bajaj] became increasingly conscious of the indissoluble link between ends and means.... [In a] will executed in 1921, he assigned three-fourths of his estate to objects approved by Gandhi and expressed a wish that after his death his business should be wound up, or conducted on a restricted scale.

for the good of the people' (Gandhi 1979: 312). As in Weber's thinking, so in Gandhi's too, wealth in itself is value neutral; what really matters is what one does with it. In his own pithy words: 'One rupee can purchase for us poison or nectar' (Desai 1946: 130). Moreover, for Gandhi, affirmation of such supreme values as *sevā* and trusteeship did not yet absolve one of the imperative of moral means: good ends do not justify bad means. This maxim finds interesting echoes in Weber's thought, but the convergence may not be readily perceived.

GANDHI AND WEBER ON POLITICS AND ETHICS

Let me elaborate on this convergence. It is, of course, well known that Gandhi subscribed to the holistic view of social action. No area of activity, least of all politics, could be considered exempt from moral imperatives. For him, politics was the *yuga dharma* of our time, that is the most appropriate means of serving social purposes in the modern age. The orientation had to be wholly altruistic. One is reminded of Weber's crucial distinction between living 'for' politics and living 'off' politics:

> He who lives 'for' politics makes politics his life, in an internal sense. Either he enjoys the naked possession of the power he exerts, or he nourishes his inner balance and self-feeling by the consciousness that his life has *meaning* in the service of a 'cause'. (Weber 1948c: 84)

The notion of 'cause' well represents, I think, Gandhi's ideas of *sevā* and *dharma* or moral duty. And, of course, Gandhi did not carve out separate arenas of action for politics and *dharma*.

Obviously, given the deep-seated modes of dualism in Western thought, one could hardly expect to find such holism in Weber. In fact, he wrote: 'He who seeks the salvation of the soul, of his own and of others, should not seek it along the avenues of politics, for the quite different tasks of politics can only be solved by violence' (Weber 1948c: 126). Pursuantly, he made an important distinction between the ethic of assuming responsibility for the consequences of one's actions, which is what should guide one in politics, and the ethic of ultimate ends or moral conviction (we might say, conscience), which leads one to higher goals, notably the recovery or creation of values that enable one to overcome in one's personal life the disenchantment of the world.

A politician must pre-eminently have, Weber contended, three qualities, namely: (i) 'passion'; (ii) 'a feeling of responsibility'; and (iii) 'a sense of proportion' (Weber 1948c: 115). All these three qualities can be illustrated by reference to Gandhi's public life. By 'passion' Weber meant, it seems to me, the ability to sincerely attend to a public cause with absolute intensity, and this is what characterized, for example, Gandhi's efforts on behalf of the Untouchables or Harijans (as the Dalits were then called). The notion of 'responsibility', that is, answerability for the foreseeable consequences of one's actions, may indeed be said to have guided Gandhi when he, for instance, immediately suspended the Civil Disobedience Movement in 1922 following the clash in Chauri Chaura between a group of protestors and some policemen, ending in the latter being burnt to death. He took the blame upon himself, and even undertook a penitential fast (see Nanda 1981: 231–37). Finally, 'a sense of proportion' can be illustrated by recalling that Gandhi maintained that although the ideal was 'equal' distribution of wealth, he was practical enough to concede that one would have to settle for 'equitable' distribution.

The framework for the operation of the ethic of responsibility in Weber's discussion is political action. The ethic of ultimate ends or conviction obviously transcends this arena in Weber's but not in Gandhi's judgement. Weber himself was, however, uncomfortable with this dichotomy, although he had set it up. 'If one makes any concession at all to the principle that the end justifies means, it is not possible to bring an ethic of ultimate ends and an ethic of responsibility under one roof or to decree ethically which ends should justify which means' (Weber 1948c: 122). The two types of ethics are, he concluded, 'not absolute constructs but rather supplements', and 'only in unison' do they 'constitute a genuine man—a man who *can* have the "calling for politics"' (Weber 1948c: 127). Was not Gandhi such a man, for he allowed no 'concession'? He asserted emphatically that it 'is a great mistake' to argue that 'there is no connection between the means and the end' (1997: 81). He *never* abandoned this fundamental position. Thus: 'There is no wall of separation between means and ends.... This is a proposition that admits no exception' (*Young India*, 17 July 1924, quoted in Bose 1948: 36).

As a public figure, Gandhi was an excellent exemplar of the ethic of responsibility as Weber defined it. But ultimately he grounded *all* his actions not in scriptural authority, public opinion, or pragmatism, but in what he called his 'inner voice', 'the deepest within me'. To put it in Luther's words cited by Weber: 'Here I stand; I can do no other' (1948c: 127).[4] The traditional terms for this inner conviction or compulsion are *ātmanah tushti, priyam ātmanah, priyam icchitām,* and so on, that is personal satisfaction or conscience. It is considered one of the signs or sources of *dharma,* moral conduct, in authoritative texts such as the *Manusmriti* (see *Manusmriti* 2.12 in Olivelle 2004).

Weber was deeply interested in the comparative study of the ethical traditions of the West, on the one hand, and India and China, on the other. He mistakenly considered Brahmanical ethics completely situational, lacking in any absolutes beyond the notion of traditionally defined social (*varna*) obligations, for there is *sādhārna dharma* applicable to all. Within this framework, however, there is a conflict between action that takes consequences into consideration, represented by Arjuna's stand at the beginning of the Mahābhārata war (why fight merely for the sake of a kingdom if this involves the killing of kith and kin, even of one's gurus, and general destruction?) and socially sanctioned obligations (it is the Kshatriya's duty to fight for his honour and for royal power), which is Krishna's position. Weber was aware of this conflict, and pointed out that Krishna had had the final word (Weber 1958: 180–91).[5]

---

[4] Aron's gloss of Weber's position is worth quoting for it describes Gandhi's position too: 'The ethic of conviction is the morality that urges each of us to act according to his feelings ["inner voice"] without explicit or implicit reference to the consequences. The example of the absolute pacifist will illustrate the point' (1967: 210).

[5] Needless to add, we have here one of the central problems of moral philosophy to which thinkers have returned time and again. Thus, Amartya Sen (2000: 480–82) has come down on the side of Arjuna: '[O]ne must take responsibility for the consequences of one's actions and choices, and ... this responsibility cannot be obliterated by any pointer to a consequence-independent duty or obligation' (Sen 2000: 482). Having said this, Sen elaborates: '[T]he epic *Mahabharata* ... gives both sides much room to develop their respective arguments, with the evident presumption that this is an argument in which there are two reasonable sides' (Sen 2000: 482). In fact, Arjuna had willingly opted for war as the legitimate means of regaining the lost kingdom and the hesitation on the battlefield was, as he admitted, the result of moral confusion. And Krishna too emphasized on occasion the importance of taking consequences into account (see Matilal 1989: 1–19).

There is a third moral position in the Mahābhārata, that of Yudhishthira, who, outraged by the repeated recourse to expediency and transgression of moral values throughout the fratricidal war, regarded conscience a higher guide to moral action than either the concern for consequences (responsibility), or for social obligation irrespective of the consequences (*jāti dharma*). The true inheritor of Yudhishthira's mantle in twentieth-century India was, it has been suggested (see Zaehner 1962: 224–53), Gandhi. He wrote: 'To me God is Truth and Love; *God is ethics and morality*.... God is conscience' (quoted in Zaehner 1962: 226). His rejection of the acquisitive society (and by implication of Western capitalism) also was for him a matter of conscience, or of the ethic of ultimate ends, as Weber would have put it. The appeal to one's conscience entails the unremitting exercise of critical self examination, which was an inalienable part of Gandhi's life, in the hope of self-knowledge. And 'self-knowledge', Miri has told us (as I said in the very beginning of this chapter), is also 'knowledge of moral truths'.[6]

---

[6]The convergences and contrasts between Gandhi's and Weber's positions on ethical questions need to be explored in greater depth than has been possible here. At places in their writings, and as I have hinted earlier, even their choice of critical words and phrases (for example, cloak, burden on shoulders, roof, wall) is strikingly similar. More importantly, in the writings I have cited, they draw on the same sources at least twice, using them similarly as well as dissimilarly. I have already mentioned Tolstoy's influence on both of them (see Green 1978). Let me mention here the second source, namely, the *Sermon on the Mount*, which Gandhi read in London in 1889–90. He wrote in his autobiography ([1927] 1940: 51):

> [T]he Sermon on the Mount ... went straight to my heart. I compared it with the *Gita*. The verses, 'But I say unto you, that ye resist not evil; but whosoever shall smite thee on thy right cheek, turn to him the other side also. And if any man take away thy coat let him have thy cloak too', delighted me beyond measure....

> Compare the sincerity and simplicity of the foregoing with the nuanced formulation of Weber: 'What man will take upon himself the attempt to "refute scientifically" the ethic of the Sermon on the Mount? For instance, the sentence, "resist no evil", or the image of turning the other cheek?' (1948b: 148). But then: 'Except for a saint it is an ethic of indignity. This is it: one must be saintly in everything, at least in intention, one must live like Jesus, the apostles, St. Francis, and their like' (1948b: 119). Their like in our times? Gandhi?

Part II

SOCIOLOGICAL TRADITIONS: EXEMPLARS, INTERPRETERS

> As one traces the evolution of sociology from school to school, true theoretical alternatives appear. Problems are posed, new theories are instituted. The relations of theory and method have to be rethought again and again.
>
> —DON MARTINDALE, *The Nature and Types of Sociological Theory*

Methodological pluralism is a well-recognized characteristic of sociological thought everywhere. Raymond Aron, the French sociologist, once wrote about 'two typical schools' of sociology (in the West), the 'Marxist' and the 'American', in Volume I of *Main Currents in Sociological Thought* (1967). Similarly, British political philosopher W.G. Runciman identified 'four traditions' of British sociology, namely, 'the evolutionary, the politico-economic, the ethnographic and the administrative reformist' (see his *Sociology in Its Place and Other Essays*, 1970).

India is no exception to this general tendency, and a number of approaches, mostly borrowed or adapted, have been in vogue. In this part of the book, the focus is on the making of some of these traditions. I open with an account of Radhakamal Mukerjee's remarkable intellectual journey from his conception of comparative economics to a sociology of values via institutional economics and social ecology. This is followed by a discussion of the search for synthesis in the sociology of D.P. Mukerji, one of the founders of the discipline in India, and of the trajectory of his work from the general to the specific. M.N. Srinivas's explicit espousal of empiricism, already discussed in the chapter on Hinduism (in Part One), is carried forward to suggest that he implicitly recognized the possibility of genuine insights derived from personal experience supplemented by moral imagination. A dialogic approach, combining the view from 'within' with that from 'without', is taken up for discussion in the next two chapters dealing with Louis Dumont's work and the journal *Contributions to Indian Sociology* which he founded, and I, with the support of some colleagues, continued. It is argued that his methodological persuasions have resulted in a multiplicity of alternative approaches being explored by both his critics and those who acknowledge the positive aspects of his approach and his use of the comparative method. The Epilogue is an attempt to look at my own work as a sociologist and cultural anthropologist, and acknowledge the influences that have shaped it.

Chapter Six

Radhakamal Mukerjee and His Contemporaries

Each individual, by virtue of his inclinations, has a right to principles which do not destroy his individuality.
—GOETHE, Conversation with J.D. Falk

[T]he task of sociology [is] to combat the tyranny of economics.
—RADHAKAMAL MUKERJEE, *The Institutional Theory of Economics*

A true general theory of society is the corpus of theories, laws, and explanations of social sciences; it is a body of integrated and coordinated knowledge relating to society as a whole. For society is not divisible. Only the social sciences for the sake of analysis and specialization are fractionalized.
—RADHAKAMAL MUKERJEE, 'Faiths and Influences'

TOWARDS AN INTERDISCIPLINARY APPROACH

Radhakamal Mukerjee (1889–1968) may truly be regarded as the *primus inter pares* among the founding fathers of sociology in India. Although his early work was devoted to the formulation of a specific programme of 'Indian' economics, and a genuinely universal economic science constructed from the building blocks of 'regional' economics, it was this endeavour itself in which lay the seeds of his sociology. It is remarkable that at quite a young age, when he was still in his twenties, he had a clear conception of the scope and method of an interdisciplinary social science, embracing economics, sociology, political science, and social philosophy.

Now, where did the roots of Mukerjee's interdisciplinary approach lie? Fortunately, we can answer this question fairly accurately, for he wrote a short autobiographical essay when he was sixty-six (Mukerjee 1956), and an autobiography towards the end of his life, which was published posthumously (Mukerjee 1997). He read English literature, history, and philosophy as an undergraduate at the prestigious Presidency College in Calcutta in the years immediately after the upsurge of nationalist fervour in Bengal, following the partition of the province in 1905. The idea that he should study 'for the country and the nation' took possession of him, and he opted for an M.A. in economics, the subject, which he believed, 'could provide the scientific and adequate answers to the grave national issues of Indian misery, exploitation and subjection' (Mukerjee 1997: 66).

As it turned out, he was one among the first group of students to obtain the Master's degree in economics and sociology at Calcutta University in 1910; the combined course had been introduced there two years earlier at the initiative of its famous and visionary vice chancellor, Asutosh Mukerjee. Mukerjee recalls: 'Somehow an integrated study of the social sciences, of Economics, Political Science, Social Philosophy and Sociology stimulated in me the desire and striving to envisage man, society and civilization as wholes that defeat any compartmentalization and its aims' (1997: 68). He read voraciously the works of the intellectuals of the late nineteenth and early twentieth centuries in Bengal, who were the makers or flowers of the Bengal Renaissance (see Dasgupta 2010; Kopf 1969), such as Bankim Chandra Chatterjee, Romesh Chandra Dutt, Ishwar Chandra Vidyasagar, Bipin Chandra Pal, Aurobindo Ghose, and Rabindranath Tagore. Also, he heard Ananda Coomaraswamy, the Sri Lankan art historian, lecture in Calcutta: 'Indian humanity, he stressed eloquently, was as much impoverished by aesthetic and spiritual subjection as by economic and political slavery' (Mukerjee 1997: 86). He read Western social thinkers, such as Adam Smith, Comte, Marx, Mill, Hobhouse, Giddings, and Ross—the Europeans in English translation—and imbibed their 'broad humanism'. Nationalism provided the framework within which holism and humanism were established as the bedrock of Mukerjee's intellectual quest.

Among the senior academics of his own time who influenced Mukerjee most, two names stand out most luminously: Brajendra Nath Seal (1864–1938) and Patrick Geddes (1854–1932), the former taught philosophy at Calcutta University, and the latter, sociology and civics at Bombay. Seal would have inherited his interest in sociology from his father, who was a follower of Auguste Comte, as many other Bengali intellectuals of the time were (Forbes 1975). He lectured on what he called 'comparative sociology' at Calcutta in 1917. Three years later (in 1921), he became the vice chancellor of Mysore University, where he introduced the subject at the undergraduate level with the help of A.R. Wadia, who, we have been told, 'regarded sociology as "applied philosophy"' (Mukherjee 1977: 32–33). Seal's interest in sociology and also in statistics as tools of social analysis did not, it has been said, find many takers, but he obviously influenced such enthusiastic young minds as Radhakamal Mukerjee and P.C. Mahalanobis; the latter, originally a physicist, won even greater international recognition as a statistician than Mukerjee did as an economist or sociologist. Mukerjee describes Seal as a 'legend in intellectual Bengal', venerated widely for his 'encyclopaedic knowledge'. He acknowledges that it was from Seal he learned to appreciate the 'comparative method in the study of civilization' and in the 'study of economic and political institutions', binging out 'the multilinear character of human social evolution in different regions and cultures' (Mukerjee 1997: 87–88).

Besides Seal, Mukerjee acknowledges deep indebtedness to Patrick Geddes whom he first met in Calcutta in 1914 and 1915, at the very beginning of the latter's sojourn in India. Geddes was a senior Scottish academic, who had been invited to give four public lectures in Bombay (Munshi 2007: 172); he travelled to other cities too, including Lucknow and Calcutta, where he lectured at academic institutions. Mukerjee had just begun his teaching career as an economist at Krishnath College in his hometown of Berhampore in north Bengal. It seems that a close and enduring relationship between the two men took shape. In his autobiography, Mukerjee remembers Geddes as 'one of the greatest minds' he encountered in his life (Mukerjee 1997: 96), a judgement shared by some other leading scholars, such as Lewis Munford (see Munshi 2007: 175). Geddes, who had taught botany and zoology in the UK, and had researched the mutual relationship of spatial and social dimensions of life, was made professor of Sociology at Bombay University in 1919, and retired from there in 1924, but he had already helped two of his brightest students, G.S. Ghurye and N.A. Thooti, to get scholarships for postgraduate studies in sociology in England. More about Ghurye is discussed below.

Altogether, it has been said, 'Geddes' influence on sociologists in India remains negligible' (Munshi 2007: 174–75). Mukerjee was obviously an exception, for he acknowledges Geddes as 'a major influence': it was from him that, Mukerjee says, he learned the significance of 'social mapping and charting', 'regional planning', and the interplay of 'Place-Work-Folk', or 'Environment-Function-Organism', and the importance also of the notion of 'energy' to sociology from which the concepts of 'manpower and manday' were derived. Geddes, on his part, wrote the introduction to Mukerjee's first book, *The Foundations of Indian Economics* (1916), which was published in 1916 when he was just twenty-seven years old, commending Mukerjee's plea for the revitalization of the village community.

From Berhampore, Mukerjee went to Lahore in 1917 to give a set of special lectures on Indian economics at the Punjab University, a subdiscipline that was largely his creation and rejected by orthodox economists. Under this arrangement, he lectured in many places including Delhi, where Mahatma Gandhi chaired his presentation on 'Agriculture and Industrialism' at St. Stephen's College (Mukerjee 1997: 122–23). The same year, Mukerjee returned to Calcutta as a regular lecturer in economics at the University, and taught, besides economics, sociology and political philosophy (Mukerjee 1956: 9). In his inaugural address, he 'emphasized the essential need of Regional Economics without which ... General Economics ... [could not] be formulated' (Mukerjee 1997: 124). Sociology entered into his enunciation of the scope of Indian economics through his emphasis on the 'region' as the appropriate unit of study, conceived as a geographical, biological, economic, social, and cultural complex. This led to his emphasis on the study of ground reality from interdisciplinary and comparative perspectives.

MUKERJEE AT LUCKNOW UNIVERSITY

In 1921, Mukerjee was appointed as one of the first two professors at the newly established University of Lucknow (the other was

Birbal Sahni, who was to become a world renowned paleobotanist). He had an offer from the University of Bombay also (Geddes must have recommended him), but preferred Lucknow presumably because it afforded him the opportunity of not only building a new department in conformity with his own idea of a regionally located and sociologically informed discipline of economics, but also influencing the structure of the teaching of social sciences generally. Thus, he suggested the inclusion of political science in the curriculum (Mukerjee 1997: 181–82). Mukerjee succeeded in having his department called the Department of Economics and Sociology from 'the very day the university started to work' (Mukerjee 1956: 10). It survived as such until 1955 when a separate Department of Sociology was created (ironically under his watch as vice chancellor: he felt powerless in the face of the unstoppable push towards specialization, but tried to make a virtue of it; see Mukerjee 1997: 185).

In his inaugural address at Lucknow, delivered on 8 August 1921, Mukerjee called for 'a new school of economic thought and research', which would be free from 'barren abstractions' through a concentration on the 'local problems of peasants in the fields, the labourers of the factories, and the artisans of the cottages' (Mukerjee 1997: 151). A year later, in an address to the University Sociological Society, which he helped establish, Mukerjee pointed out the importance of 'historical and comparative methods' in the study of regional and cultural differences; in tune with the understandings of those times, he called for 'a greater knowledge of race psychology and of diverse social schemes and standards of peoples'. He further observed that, 'climate and regional factors ... [lay] behind two standards of utilization of land in the world—the South East Asiatic standard of rice cultivation, hand labour, and largely non-flesh diet, and the Western standard based upon wheat cultivation, work animals, and agricultural machinery', resulting in 'contrasted social types and social relations, viz. the communal-conservative and [the] individualistic-liberal' (Mukerjee 1997: 152). I may clarify that the word 'communal' had not then the negative connotation it acquired later; it was a synonym for 'communitarian'. What we have in these very brief observations is an outline of the scope and methodology of institutional economics or economic sociology: the scope, social morphology, and social dynamics; the methodology, empiricism, and comparison.[1]

Even as he was giving shape to it, Mukerjee attempted to communicate his integrated approach to economics through his lectures. He wrote (1997: 119–20):

> In the early years of my own teaching I deeply felt the necessity of relating economic theories and doctrines not only to economic history [history of economic thought] but also to the concrete social and economic environment and to the crying issue of economic disintegration and economic recovery. I, therefore, began a thorough empirical study of economic conditions in the Indian villages and towns in order to correct the distortion of Western deductive-abstract theorizing and formulation in the class room.[2]

In his first book, *The Foundations of Indian Economics* (1916)[3], Mukerjee had already called for rehabilitation of the traditional

---

[1]Needless to say, in these perspectives, we find echoes of the views of the founding fathers of sociology in the West. Thus, Auguste Comte (1798–1857) also found the key to diversities of social morphology in differences of race, climate, and political action, and outlined the scope of sociology in terms of 'statics' (social structure or order) and 'dynamics' (social change or progress). Herbert Spencer (1820–1903) looked upon social life as the continuous striving for adjustment between the social or internal environment and the external or natural environment. In his view, human society was characterized by a stable internal arrangement of social units, which was not, however, unchanging, but was subject to a differentiating evolutionary process. I do not have the space here to explore in reasonable detail the roots of Radhakamal's ideas in classical sociology. Similarly, one could explore the roots of Mukerjee's economic ideas and moral sentiments in classical economics—in the writings of Adam Smith and John Stuart Mill, for instance—but that is a major undertaking for disciplinary historians.

[2]Already in 1919 he had (in a lecture on 'The Foundations of Indian Sociology' at Madurai) lamented the consequences of Western industrialism in India in the form of 'the disintegrated village and the sordid, overcrowded city'. To attend to them, 'the future economic superstructure' would have to be built 'on the bedrock of our characteristic economic habits and institutions, our village system and agrarian economy, and the means and methods of our traditional city-planning and organisation' (Mukerjee 1956: 9–10).

[3]There is some uncertainty about the exact year of publication of some of Mukerjee's books. I have tried to be as accurate as possible, but all the doubtful entries are marked with an asterisk in the references at the end of the book.

organic village (cooperative socioeconomic system, a balancing of agriculture and industry, small-scale and large-scale industrial production, production and distribution, and so on). Almost immediately it attracted adverse criticism from his contemporaries. For instance, Brij Narain, an economist based in Lahore, where Mukerjee had given lectures on Indian economics, characterized his description of the Indian village and industrialism, and of the Hindu ideal of limitations of wants, 'idealistic', and even factually inaccurate. He warned: 'The lesson that history teaches us is that, so long as a country has remained a predominantly agricultural country, it has remained poor and in a lower stage of civilization as compared with manufacturing countries' ([1919] 2009: 62). Sixty years later, Bhabatosh Datta of Presidency College, Calcutta, considered *The Foundations of Indian Economics* Mukerjee's 'most significant work', notwithstanding 'a romantic picture of the Indian rural economic life' (1978: 28–31) in its pages. It was 'more detailed than anything comparable', and distinguished by the manner in which the role of caste and religious beliefs in the rural economy was brought out, much beyond 'what a mere economist could have given', and comparable with 'the best work on sociology in his time' (Datta 1978: 29).

The shaping of an adequate, socially specific economic science is what Mukerjee talked about in his lectures at Lucknow University. We get a fair idea of his interdisciplinary approach from *Borderlands of Economics* (1925), which comprised the substances of these lectures over about five years. The topics treated included economic behaviourism, the anthropological and institutional perspectives on economic activity, the 'anti-intellectualism' of economics and the need for its humanization, and the relevance to economics of biology, geography, ecology, sociology, psychoanalysis, ethics, and even physics. In the forward-looking, optimistic concluding paragraph of the book, Mukerjee (1925: 270) wrote:

> The acquisive and possessive impulses which have been so much exaggerated in the last few decades will be duly limited in vital modes of association, and the separation between the intrinsic or final and instrumental or economic ends, which has threatened to

corrode social life, will warp no longer the feeling and judgement of peoples.[4]

INSTITUTIONAL ECONOMICS

The first major statement of Mukerjee's evolving theoretical position was presented by him in the first volume of his *Principles of Comparative Economics* published in 1922. A core principle of his thinking was that the psychological basis of the economic science—namely, a 'hedonistic calculus on the balance of pleasure and plain, of which the single aim is to secure the greatest happiness at the least cost of painful effort' (Mukerjee 1922: 59)— was outmoded. He drew attention to other psychological factors, which are socially determined and include, notably, family values and social sympathies. What factors are valorized in a particular place and time is historically contingent. An example he gave was the contrast between the attempt to realize 'social instincts ... through the super-imposition of the State' on 'individualistic justice and individual self-expression' as in the West, and their given character in the East, where 'the community or group is already an integral part of the individual personality, and the economic unit is not the individual as individual, but the individual as community or, if you please, the community in the individual' (Mukerjee 1922: 74–75). Cultural values and social arrangements are held forth as significant in the evolution of economic stages and types (Mukerjee 1922: Chapter XI). From such perspectives, it

---

[4]It may be recalled that Max Weber (1864–1920) had already written in a similar vein at the beginning of the century in his seminal studies of capitalism, but his writings in German were not available to Mukerjee, for they had not yet been translated into English (Weber 1930). I mention the convergence of views between the two scholars only to draw attention, first, to the radicalism of Mukerjee's approach to the task of doing economics and his ethical concerns, and, second, to his optimism about the future of humanity, in contrast to Weber's resignation to a kind of historical inevitability in a modernizing (rationalizing) world. Mukerjee never let go of this optimism, but to sustain it he turned increasingly to religious faith, a path that Weber did not take (see Chapter Five).

was but to be expected that the prevalent economic theories would be found flawed because they 'depended solely on physical and psychological conditions of a certain type, or "stereotype", and hence [were] endowed with an absolute and inviolable character' (Mukerjee 1922: 207). It was this absolutism that Mukerjee questioned in *Principles of Comparative Economics*.

The book was read widely and has long been recognized as a classic. It was this book that made Melville Herskovits, who shaped the discipline of economic anthropology, acknowledge Mukerjee as a pioneer in the field (Herskovits 1952: 23). The economist-turned-anthropologist, Raymond Firth, noted Mukerjee's plea for a comparative approach involving Western and 'non-Western economic forms', but doubted that economists would be convinced (Firth 1951: 126–27).

To sum up, the comparative method Mukerjee advocated was based on a critique of the seemingly logical and rational assumptions of classical and neoclassical economics, which marginalized cultural and social institutions, and also, in the case of India, its recent colonial past. He emphasized specification against generalization and valorized the community, with its values of sharing and solidarity, above the self-oriented, profit-maximizing individual. His methodological position attracted criticism from Indian economists, who believed that economic behaviour everywhere had to be analysed in universalist terms, for the motivations that drive it are rooted in human nature and cut across cultural differences. Sociology at this point of Mukerjee's thinking was, it seems to me, a perspective, a contextualizing methodology for economic analysis and not, perhaps, yet a subject that claimed his exclusive attention.

During the 1930s, Mukerjee brought his thinking and writing on the scope and significance of 'the economic science' to a conclusion with the publication of *The Institutional Theory of Economics* (1940). The book went beyond the work of orthodox institutionalists and even John Commons's (1934) pioneering work on the subject. Writing about the social sciences generally, Mukerjee observed that the core problem was that of providing an adequate understanding of 'the relations between the individual and society, and their reciprocal relations to the environment' (1940: 5).

As for economics as such, he wrote that only a multidimensional, interdisciplinary approach, at once empirical and normative, would help 'bridge the gap between economic theory and economic policy' (Mukerjee 1940: 10). He further argued against the tendency to reduce key economic processes, such as 'the exchange process' to 'some ultimate determinants like marginal desiredness'; instead, he called for their consideration 'as expressions of man's manifold instincts, habits and interests, derived not from rationality but largely from his social and institutional influences' (Mukerjee 1940: 33). Regrettably, however, economics had proceeded from the time of its founders (notably Adam Smith) along a narrowing path in the hands of neoclassical economists like Robbins (1932) as being concerned with 'an abstract aspect of social behaviour' regarding 'the disposal of scarce means' (Mukerjee 1940: 2). Behind 'the positivistic approach' of Robbins and others of that ilk, Mukerjee wrote, 'lurks the social atomism of British liberals and utilitarians' (1940: 59).

Again and over again, Mukerjee enunciated what he considered the basic principle of sound economic analysis. Thus: 'No choice in the economic field can be appropriate or "rational" which is inconsistent with human norms and values in political, familial and other fields of man's institutional life' (Mukerjee 1940: 65). And again: 'Without a theory of institutions, economists are prone to assume a single framework of laws and customs within which individuals and groups "rationally" carry on their economic activity' (Mukerjee 1940: 193). In this manner, economics would have to achieve 'a new realism' by aligning with 'the other social sciences dealing with different phases of social life, and by its integration into the master science, sociology' (Mukerjee 1940: 66). In fact, Mukerjee called upon sociology '*to combat the tyranny of economics*' (1940: 318, emphasis added). This obviously was a plea for the restoration of the community in the social sciences which had been fabricated around the notion of the individual. The fight, Mukerjee wrote, was 'against the "economic imperative", which the autonomy of modern economics decrees', and added that 'we have now to stress the categorical imperative of the realm of moral values and the "cultural imperative" of the entire realm of ethical and social values' (Mukerjee 1940: 318). The scope, or (should one say?) responsibility, of sociology as the study of social values as much as of economic interests was thus clearly laid out.[5]

SOCIAL ECOLOGY

During the 1920s and 1930s, one line of argument that Mukerjee developed—and which I have just briefly outlined—proceeded from economic regionalism to comparative economics and institutionalism, and, eventually, to sociology. Another that developed simultaneously of which the first intimations are present in *Borderlands of Economics* (1925), led from economic regionalism to the notion of regional balance, which he developed in several pioneering studies

---

[5]Somewhere in the book, Mukerjee uses the expression 'dismal determinism' to castigate the work of the economists of his time, presumably echoing Thomas Carlyle's characterization of economics as the 'dismal science'. A recent, radical critique of the fundamental assumptions of economics (bearing on individualism, 'rational' self-interest, the normative character of the market, and the ideal of the nation state) by the Harvard economist Stephen Marglin (2008), carries the title of *The Dismal Science*; the subtitle is *How Thinking like an Economist Undermines the Community*. Mukerjee devoted considerable attention to what he called the contrasting ideal types (in the Weberian sense of the term) of market-based 'modern capitalism' and 'communalism', the latter being a community-based economy, such as that of precolonial India (Mukerjee 1940: 213–32; 1997: 128f.). Marglin did not know of Mukerjee's work until I drew his attention to it early in 2009. In a somewhat different vein, Nobel Laureate Joseph Stiglitz has pointed out that, the West has created:

> [A] society in which we do not act together as a community to address our common needs, partly because rugged individualism and market fundamentalism have eroded any sense of community and have led to rampant exploitation of unwary and unprotected individuals and to an increasing social divide. (Stiglitz 2010: 275)

And, of course, Louis Dumont (1970a) has persuasively argued that 'the genesis and triumph of economic ideology' (his use of 'ideology' rather than 'science' is no small matter) represents the late entry, in the late eighteenth century, of the category 'the economy' and of individualism and egalitarianism into Western thought in a manner that valorizes relations between people and things at the cost of relations between themselves: the individual with his possessions as opposed to the ensemble of social relations.

(Mukerjee 1926, 1938a). Conceptualizing the region as a dynamic 'field' or 'configuration', he stressed the interplay of naturally given environment and culture, which tends towards 'balance' or 'equilibrium', 'shifting the life-balance now in favour of man, now against him'. Further, he wrote: 'Perhaps the most important contribution of ecology is the idea of the region as an intricate network of interrelations. The region exhibits a complex pattern of adaptation between the environmental factors and the plant and animal communities including human societies' (Mukerjee 1938a: 1–2).

These studies culminated in the first ever systematic, theoretical study on social ecology (Mukerjee 1945a; see also Quinn 1956: 267–73). He clarifies by saying that social ecology, as he conceived it, had to go beyond 'human *individual* adjustments to the environment' (the field of human ecology), and embrace 'the adjustments of man's *social* structures and functions, of the processes of interaction between region, occupation and society—the sociological equivalent of environment, function and organism [Geddes's framework, see above]—out of which arise all social phenomena' (Mukerjee 1945a: viii). Unlike American pioneers in the field of ecological studies such as Robert Park, Mukerjee emphatically includes the role of culture in the making of ecological relations. 'Culture is the guardian,' Mukerjee wrote (1945a: 339), 'that assumes not merely a true balance between different parts of institutional life, but also between man's material and non-material social equipment and his region.' Just as culture is inconceivably independent of the environment, the latter too is shaped (or distorted) by the former.

Treating social status and social mobility as the key constitutive ideas of sociology, 'the moving threads weaving the texture of social relationships and behaviours and institutional patterns in the fly-shuttle of ecological space and time' (Mukerjee 1945a: 78), Mukerjee argued that 'what is position in ecological space, status is in social space' (1945a: 159). Further, he observed (1945a: 159–60):

> It is the task of sociology to determine the nature of the status system, investigate the nature of various groupings and institutions where individuals interact in the various dominant, subordinate and co-ordinate relations, and ascertain the value and symbol systems by which rank or any social position (status) is assigned by the community.

Social status and social mobility thus are, respectively, the morphological (or structural) and dynamic (or organizational) dimensions of society.

Here we receive from Mukerjee a broad definition of the scope of sociology as an empirical, positive science going beyond the watchdog conception, as it were, proposed in *The Institutional Theory of Economics* (1940). The focus now is on social integration, very much in the manner of the French sociological tradition, according to which social space is a constructed, symbolic, moral space. While mindful (like Robert Park) of the usefulness of the exact (quantifiable) approach of social ecology, Mukerjee never abandons his social ameliorative and ethical concerns, which finally lead him to the sociology of values, his final sociological testament. Regionalism, for Mukerjee, was more than a descriptive device; it was a practical strategy as well. 'Regional planning,' he insisted, 'would not accept only the pecuniary valuation of technology and economy but [also] recognize human values as the ultimate product of the human adjustment' (Mukerjee 1940: 317). As the philosopher Samuel Hart (1956: 175) puts it: 'Mukerjee does not write as a cool spectator of human values and disvalues. He shares with all great men the noble, creative vision of a better and more dignified humanity.'

THE SOCIOLOGY OF VALUES

Mukerjee's last two major sociological works, *The Social Structure of Values* (1949) and *The Dynamics of Morals* (1951), are products of vast scholarship, an idealistic empiricism that rejects the fact-value dichotomy, and a humanism which is grounded in the biopsychic unity of humankind, but respects cultural differences. The point of departure is the explicit declaration that: 'The problem of social values is the core of social theory', and the call to sociology to 'develop a central theory of norms and values as basic units in the description and explanation of social relationships and behaviour' (Mukerjee 1949: 6). It is important to note that Mukerjee writes of 'social values', that is, not values which may be deemed to have descended from high above, but values that arise from patterns of social interaction, which themselves are guided by value judgements.

Such a perspective immediately faces the problem of cultural relativism, which Mukerjee sought to overcome by invoking a continuum of extensions and ascensions, as it were. Put otherwise, the local extends into the global and the unity of civilizations is the destiny of humankind. In this search, as in much else, Mukerjee remained under the abiding influence of Brajendranath Seal, who had defined 'the meaning of progress in history' as 'a confluence of many streams, bringing together conflicting cultures, conflicting national values and ideals' (1924: 2). Such a quest may well seem more of an imperative today, when we read and hear so much about 'the clash of civilizations' (Huntington 1997), but is not just for that reason easily realizable. Mukerjee never worked out vigorously the notion of unity, leaving one with the apprehension that it was no more than a rather arbitrary process of selection and collection, not a dialectical or, if you wish, transcendental, perspective. Similarly, while the social surely is in some sense moral, when the moral is raised to the level that is called 'cosmic', as Mukerjee does—'[s]ocial relations obtain their true meaning, zest and direction from the sense of the worth of humanity and of the cosmos' (Mukerjee 1956: 20)—one comes close to adopting a mystical perspective. His attraction to mysticism as the highest form of religious experience is something Mukerjee acknowledges explicitly in many of his writings, beginning with *The Theory and Art of Mysticism* (1938b) and ending with his autobiography, *India: The Dawn of a New Era: An Autobiography* (1997).

Mukerjee (1949: 107) formulates the notion of continua of levels in the following words:

> Neither human goals and interests conceived biologically or economically grovel on the earth; nor ideals or norms live in paradise. All cooperate and interpenetrate in real life, in concrete human relations achieving the eternal, the rational and the universal on the earth here and now.

He fails to make it clear how exactly the 'interpenetration' takes place. In other words, and as A.K. Saran (1958: 1017–21) rightly points out, he introduces the notion of levels, but evades the problem of interlevel communication and integration that this generates. Limitations of space and my competence preclude further discussion of this major methodological issue, which actually is a metaphysical issue.

Let me, then, only illustrate Mukerjee's handling of the problem by briefly outlining his typology of social groupings—a subject of central concern to sociology—and their value dimensions. Four types of group, namely: (i) crowd, (ii) interest–association, (iii) society, and (iv) commonalty are identified. The corresponding nature of social interaction (group participation) is: (i) instinctive-motor, non-moral; (ii) emotional–rational, a-moral; (iii) emotional–rational, moral; and (iv) ideological–mystical, transmoral. And the corresponding ethical norms are: (i) for the crowd, none; (ii) for interest-association, reciprocity; (iii) for society, equity and justice; and (iv) for commonalty, love, equality, and solidarity. Needless to add, this typology, which is far more elaborate than what I have outlined here (see Mukerjee 1949: Chapter IV), combines the sociological and psychological perspectives in a manner characteristic of all of Mukerjee's work. And it also leads him away from sociology (as this subject is generally understood and practiced) towards a mystical view of human sociality. In his own words, 'values, then, reach their highest power and most comprehensive sharing as these come under the protection and direction of religion and art' (Mukerjee 1949: 398).

To the best of my knowledge, no sociologist in India or anywhere else has developed the sociology of values in the manner indicated by Mukerjee, although many, including Karl Mannheim (in a prepublication comment printed on the jacket of the book), have recognized both the importance of the task and appreciated his efforts to engage with it. As an institutional economist and a sociologist, Mukerjee remains a solitary figure. If some economists today have reservations about the direction their subject has taken, such as the Nobel Laureate Joseph Stiglitz and Stephen Marglin (see Footnote 5 in this chapter), they do so without any awareness of Mukerjee's pioneering efforts. It is his work as a social ecologist that has perhaps survived the best, and that is so because of the grave prospect of environmental degradation with which the whole of humankind is faced today, rather than any general recognition of his intellectual innovativeness (see Guha 1994: 11–12).[6]

MUKERJEE'S CONTEMPORARIES

What I have said so far places Radhakamal Mukerjee in the centre of the scene in the making of sociology in India in the second quarter of the twentieth century, from the year of his appointment as professor of economics and sociology at the University of Lucknow in 1921 until his retirement in 1951. He was, of course, a towering figure during this critical, formulational period recognized as such in India and in the West. But he was not the only 'pioneer' (to borrow the term from Ramkrishna Mukherjee 1977), there were others too, not many, but not insignificant, most notably Benoy Kumar Sarkar (1887–1949) at Calcutta University, G.S. Ghurye (1893–1983) at

---

[6]A recent, very short, but positive assessment comes from a development economist, J. Krishnamurty, who writes, among other things: 'Today, Mukerjee is widely regarded as a pioneer of environmental economics, as indeed of several other topics. In his work he developed interdisciplinary approaches, focused on institutional factors, and extended the boundaries of whatever subject he took up' (2009: 155).

A similar appreciation of Mukerjee's work by a sociologist has not come to my notice. Srinivas and Panini (1973) devoted just about 300 words to him in their long essay on the development of sociology and social anthropology in India: they obviously did not know his work well, or D.P. Mukerji's for that matter (see Footnote 6 in Chapter Seven). I wrote to Professor Srinivas about the inadequacies and factual errors of the article when it came out; he wrote back saying he would look into the matter, but nothing happened thereafter by way of correction and elaboration. Most significantly, a recent comprehensive volume on the founders of sociology and social anthropology in India (Uberoi et al. 2007), which has chapters on Geddes, Ghurye, Sarkar, and Mukerji, lacks any discussion of Mukerjee's contributions except some stray references in two chapters. Uberoi informs me that, having already asked me to do an essay on D.P. Mukerji, she and her colleagues did not know of anyone to ask to write on Mukerjee. In any case, she adds, Mukerjee seemed to have receded from the horizon of today's generation of sociologists. I may recall that Ramachandara Guha (1994), who describes himself as a historian, acknowledges Mukerjee's pioneering contributions to social ecology.

Bombay University, and D.P. Mukerji (1894–1961) at Lucknow University. Limitations of space preclude detailed discussion.

Let me, then, begin with D.P. Mukerji. (To avoid confusion, I will refer to Mukerjee by his first name, Radhakamal, and to Mukerji by his initials, DP, in this part of the chapter.) He was Radhakamal's choice as his principal colleague in the building of the Department at Lucknow, and was brought in as a lecturer in 1922. They had many significant things in common, including their sociocultural background in Calcutta, training in history and economics (DP had M.A. degrees in both subjects, and one presumes he too attended the sociology classes that Mukerjee had), and the interdisciplinary approach to the study of social sciences. They both argued that the scope of the social sciences in India should be rooted in the specificities of Indian culture, which for Radhakamal meant upper-caste Hindu culture, and for DP, a 'synthetic' Hindu–Muslim culture that began to be shaped in the medieval period, but whose evolution was distorted by the colonial intrusions. Within this composite culture the Hindu elements remained salient (Mukerji [1942] 1948).[7]

The convergences of viewpoint were more than matched by differences. For Radhakamal, the social was embedded in the cosmic; consequently, his robust empiricism was in the ultimate analysis tempered by intuitive understandings. As already noted, he was a deeply religious person. In contrast, DP was an agnostic, and dialectical materialism and the historically situated human agent were for him the sources of the dynamics of human history. He resisted being

---

[7]More interesting, and even daring, was Mukerjee's decision to bring in D.N. Majumdar in 1928. One of the first M.A.s in anthropology from Calcutta University, he was considered a promising researcher. To justify his appointment, Mukerjee convinced the vice chancellor that, in a country like India, the study of non-monetized economic transactions was imperative. Accordingly, Majumdar was appointed as lecturer in 'primitive economics', which embraced hunting and food gathering tribes, shifting cultivators, village artisans, craftsmen, and the like. To fulfil his full share of teaching responsibilities, Majumdar once told me, he had also been assigned a course of lectures on monetary economics. This was made good sense within the recommended comparative perspective. By the 1940s, the number of M.A. courses in sociology had been increased to three and of anthropology to two, and a number of M.A. and Ph.D. dissertations in these subjects were written.

labelled as a Marxist, conceding no more than being a 'Marxologist'. Empirical research uninformed by a sense of history and deductive reason, he maintained, could only by superficial. Unlike Radhakamal, he never engaged in fieldwork or survey research, but concentrated on exercises in conceptual clarification and historical interpretations. It is not hard to imagine that the two men, so different temperamentally and in their methodological orientation, gradually drifted apart, and DP created his own space. His influence extended well beyond the academe and extended to 'progressive' (so-called) circles; its mainstay was talk. He was a great teacher and a much admired conversationist. To quote Ramkrishna Mukherjee, 'he wrote less, talked more, and left an indelible impression on his students, colleagues and contemporary Indian intellectuals' (1977: 35). It is not surprising that Radhakamal makes no mention of DP or D.N. Majumdar in his autobiography. DP did, however, occasionally refer bibliographically to Radhakamal's work in his earlier studies (see, for example, Mukerji 1924: Bibliography, iv; [1942] 1948: 217, 225).

Deferring a fuller discussion of DP's work to Chapter Seven, it may be briefly noted here that he wrote five books in English and a considerable number of essays, some of which were collected in three volumes, of which the last, *Diversities* (1958), is the most important.[8] His first two books, *Personality and the Social Sciences* (1924) and *Basic Concepts in Sociology* (1932), are exercises in conceptual clarification, more a conversation with himself than with others, about the nature of sociology. There is no engagement here with Indian social reality. His third, and, I think, most important book, *Modern Indian Culture* ([1942] 1948), is all about the dynamics of Indian culture during the medieval and colonial periods. It is an exercise in historical sociology, marked by observations such as this: 'It was through the assimilation and conflict of such forces ["Buddhism, Islam, Western commerce and culture"] that Indian culture became what it is today, neither Hindu, nor Islamic, neither a replica of the

---

[8]He also wrote in Bengali, but as he himself ruefully noted, those who read him in English generally could not read Bengali, and those who read him in Bengali did not read him in English (Mukerji 1958: vii)! Let me, then, turn to his books in English to merely indicate the scope of his work. I will be very brief: somewhat more detailed discussions are available elsewhere (see Madan 1977a, 1994c, 2007a, 2009).

Western modes of thought nor a purely Asiatic product' (Mukerji [1942] 1948: 1). It discusses religion ('the mystical outlook' of the people rather than scriptural religiosity), economic processes and the emergence of a mimetic middle class in the nineteenth century, social mobility as a result of 'modern' (that is, Western) education, the impact of an emerging, post-feudal class structure on literature, and the sociology of Indian music and the fine arts. Modern Indian culture is called an 'artifice of an unreal class structure', not an organic growth (like the middle classes in Europe). 'How this artifice has worked is the story of this book,' says Mukerji ([1942] 1948: viii).

Modern Indian Culture is a unique work, a product of thinking about modern Indian society from a Marxian, or (shall we say?) Marxological, perspective without yielding to the idea that the non-material aspects of society are merely superstructure, determined by the system of economic relations (the mode of production conceived of as the base), without any substance of their own. It is a book that retains its relevance in terms of the issues it address (for example, the Hindu–Muslim divide and the formation of the middle classes) and the manner in which it does so.[9] I may briefly add here that Radhakamal also was interested in the formation of classes under the auspices of colonialism and had himself been involved in the trade union movement, but his perspective was liberal humanist. His *The Indian Working Class* (1945b) was the first book of its kind, based more on fieldwork and personal experience than on secondary data.[10]

Of all of DP's last writings, none has, perhaps, attracted more attention, both appreciative and critical, than his presidential ad-

---

[9]Two specialized monographs also may be mentioned; his study on Tagore, whom he knew personally (Mukerji [1943] 1972), and the 'small booklet' on Indian music (Mukerji 2002). He explicitly called his approach sociological. His discussions of Indian Music (in *Modern Indian Culture* and the two books just mentioned) were, as far as I know, the first ever sociological studies of the subject ever attempted. With the arrival of ethnomusicology, the situation has, of course, changed since then. DP also authored two books on music in Bengali: one of them, *Sur O Sangati*, comprises correspondence between him and Tagore, no one less, and is, perhaps, the only book the poet coauthored with anybody (Munshi 2009a: 22).

[10]On a personal note, I may mention that when I passed my M.A. examination, qualifying for a university research scholarship, Mukerjee suggested I do a Ph.D. on the basis of fieldwork among factory workers in Kanpur.

dress to the First All-India Sociological Conference at Dehra Dun in 1955. Acclaiming the synthetic perspective of sociology, and arguing for an engagement with real life problems, he observed (1958: 229):

> Sociology has a floor and a ceiling, like any other science; but its speciality consists in its floor being the ground-floor of all types of social disciplines, and in its ceiling remaining open to the sky. Neglect of the social base often leads to arid abstractions, as in recent economics.

He was, however, quick to warn against 'the jungle of the so-called empirical social research monographs', and clarified that the 'social base' or 'ground' lies in 'social traditions', which are not static: 'Traditions do change' (Mukerji 1958: 237). His was not, therefore, a call for traditionalism, which he explicitly rejected (Mukerji 1958: 241), contrary to what some critics have alleged. DP, in fact, asserted that 'the knowledge of social traditions shows the way to break them with the least social cost, if that is necessary or inevitable' (1958: 231). More emphatically, he said: '[S]ociology should *ultimately* show the way out of the social system by analyzing the process of transformation', keeping in mind all the while that 'the thing changing is more real and objective than change per se' (Mukerji 1958: 240, 241).

It is clear that in DP's conception, the sociology of India would have to identify its own subject matter, and accordingly devise its own methodology. Is that something anybody today would find difficult to accept? I recognize, however, that there is a disconcerting aspect of DP's argument the way he constructs it, namely, his explicit privileging of the Brahmanical Hinduism of Sanskrit texts in his discussion of tradition: for instance, in his notion *sampradāya paramparā* (Mukerji 1958: 236), and most notably in his insistence on the knowledge of Sanskrit as a requirement for Indian sociologists (Mukerji 1954: 237). This concern (or discomfort) persists, notwithstanding the strong disclaimer that his emphasis on the 'normative orientation' of the group as against '"voluntaristic" individual action' is equally true of all the 'religio-cultural traditions of India' (Mukerji 1954: 234), or his later modification regarding his position on Sanskrit by making room for, besides Sanskrit, 'any such language in which the traditions have been embodied as symbols' (Mukerji 1958: 233).

Everything considered, Radhakamal and DP were two very different kinds of sociologists—temperamentally, intellectually, and ideologically. I know that it is a commonplace to speak of 'the Lucknow School of Sociology' (see, for example, Joshi 1986), but there is no solid evidence for it. The former was basically an economist by education and even temperamentally (interested in addressing practical problems such as poverty and exploitation), who turned full time to sociology via social ecology, and finally to epistemological and metaphysical questions. By contrast, DP, a historian first and then an economist and sociologist, began with general, conceptual clarifications in his adopted field of sociology, and then turned to the concrete problems of making sense of contemporary history and the making of a modern India, distinctively Indian but not insular. In this regard, he considered Tagore the greatest exemplar, perhaps more than Gandhi himself. In a tribute to G.S. Ghurye on his sixtieth birthday, DP hailed him as 'the only Indian sociologist' among 'sociologists in India' (1954: 237). This was, of course, a comment as much on Radhakamal's recent, theoretical, sociological writings (for example, his general theory of values) as on Ghurye's corpus, which was, in terms of its substantive content, concrete although broad in scope, and had its roots in the study of the Brahmanical textual traditions. Did DP not see the danger of such a preoccupation?

❖

Let me then turn to Ghurye, who was four years younger than Mukerjee. Sanskrit was in the family (they were Brahmans), and he studied it at college. A perusal of *Manusmriti*, he writes in his autobiography (Ghurye 1973: 37), aroused his interest in the study of social institutions like marriage, and led him to sociology and cultural anthropology. He applied for the sociology scholarship which the government announced (there was another in economics), and was selected on the recommendation of Patrick Geddes who interviewed him. Unlike Mukerjee, Ghurye was far from being enthusiastic about Geddes: 'I could get nothing more out of [his lectures] than that place created or dictated work and moulded the people who in their turn conditioned their own work, and both in the process modified the place' (Ghurye 1973: 38). You will recall that, this same idea had seized Mukerjee, as it were, and led him to develop the discipline of social ecology. Ghurye chose to go to the London School of Economics to work with L.T. Hobhouse, a social evolutionist, but moved on to Cambridge where he came under the deep influence of the psychologist-turned-anthropologist, W.H.R. Rivers, known in his time as a leading exponent of 'cultural diffusionism' because he had 'come to the conclusion that the anthropological approach to Sociology was the most appropriate one' (Ghurye 1973: 45). This included, of course, fieldwork. After earning his doctorate, he returned to Bombay in 1924 where he was appointed as reader and head at the University. He became a professor ten years later. Gradually, he built there the first fully fledged, independent department of sociology in India.

One of the research papers Ghurye prepared in fulfilment of the requirements of a doctoral degree in anthropology at Cambridge was on 'the ethnic theory of caste'. He expanded this to produce his most famous work *Caste and Race in India* ([1932] 1969), a classic in its own right, and a worthy successor to S.V. Ketkar's ([1909] 1979) book on caste, which was the first study of the subject by an Indian scholar. No major work on caste published after Ghurye's book, including Dumont's (1970a) and Dirks's (2002), but, strangely, excluding Bayly's (1999), fails to draw upon Ghurye's conclusions. Although he did not wholly accept the earlier theses of the racial origin of caste, he did consider the institution an evolving product of the interplay of caste and Brahmanical ritualistic ideology. His focus on changes during British rule (he maintained that occupational castes were their creation) and on the internal structure of caste (caste, subcaste) were seminal contributions.

After three later editions, with a changed title (class and occupation in place of race), the original title was finally restored in the fifth edition (in 1969). Apart from its substantive conclusions, the book was notable for its deft interweaving of Sanskrit textual materials and the different kinds of information generated during the colonial period. In subsequent work, for instance the ethnography of the Mahadev Kolis (Ghurye [1957] 1963), he also drew upon fieldwork. Arguably, he was the doyen of Indian sociologists from the 1930s onwards over the next three decades. Mukerjee's identity as a scholar suffered from his interdisciplinary studies: economists had no use for his sociology and sociologists were not even qualified to judge his economies, which, needless to emphasize, is very ironical.

Ghurye wrote an autobiography (1973), Pramanick (1994), a book on his work, and Upadhya (2007), an excellent essay. I do not, therefore, have to go further into his published work, which was as voluminous and as varied in range as Mukerjee's. Like Mukerjee, he remained deeply imbued with traditional Brahmanical perspectives; often, as in his work on the status of Indian tribal communities ([1943] 1963), or on social tensions (1968), Ghurye vehemently asserted what could only be called a strident Hindu point of view. Upadhya (2007: 215) succinctly captures this aspect of Ghurye's sociology: 'He believed that Hinduism is at the centre of India's civilizational unity and that at the core of Hinduism are Brahmanical ideas and values that are essential for the integration of society.' One does not find a similar political concern in Mukerjee's work, which, as I noted earlier, is characterized by a quest, largely unsuccessful, for intercivilizational synthesis.

I may also note here that Ghurye and Mukerjee did not discuss each other's work, of which they could not possibly have been unaware. There is a reference to Mukerjee in Ghurye's autobiography: it is about their relative standing at the International Sociological Association, and intended to show Mukerjee in a bad light (Ghurye 1973: 131). Mukerjee was far more well-read in Western scholarly traditions (economic, sociological, and philosophical) than Ghurye, whose main strength lay in, as already stated above, his command over Sanskrit and his scholarship in classical texts in that language.[11] Unlike Mukerjee who cited from the work of American, British, and European (particularly French and German) social scientists, Ghurye showed

---

[11] It should be noted, however, that Ghurye wrote an appreciative essay on Comte, citing the authority of those like Alfred Weber and A.N. Whitehead who held him in high regard, and castigating those, like F.A. Hayek, who criticized him and also those, like Bertrand Russell, who just ignored him. Ghurye himself considered 'the law of three stages of knowledge' and the 'hierarchy of sciences' of fundamental importance. He concludes: 'Comte's positive philosophy was intended precisely to be the History and Philosophy of Sciences' (Ghurye 1957: 28). What I find of greater interest is that Ghurye used the occasion to pay 'homage' to Comte on the centenary of his death to write about the 'Indian contribution to sociology of knowledge', namely, the many vedic and post-vedic '*vidyā*s', all the way down to the Purānas and *itihāsa* (historical) texts (Ghurye 1957: 29–70).

little familiarity with them. Referring to the rich body of Western scholarship in the sociology of religion, Pramanick (1994: 144) comments: '[W]here does Ghurye fit in this theoretical world? Perhaps nowhere.'

Ghurye's historical approach, coloured by the narrow diffusionist theory of the early twentieth century[12] (in contrast to Mukerjee's generalizing, theoretical perspectives and his quest for a universalistic society theory) did occasionally lead him to inquire into the cultural linkages between Europe and India (see Ghurye 1948, 1955), but the core of his scholarly work was centred in India.[13] This was his second strength: take out his magnum opus on caste and his contribution will be largely shorn of its continued interest. Some of his empirical work, notably the study of *sadhu*s (Ghurye [1953] 1964) had an all-India focus, but some of it was confined to western India and the city of Bombay (now Mumbai).

In the development of sociological studies of Indian society and culture, and in the institutionalization of the sociological profession, Ghurye's contributions, including the work of his students inspired or, at least, encouraged, by him have been more significant than Mukerjee's. None of the latter's sociology students achieved the eminence of scholars like Iravati Karve, A.R. Desai, and M.N. Srinivas. Besides, Ghurye achieved much more in the establishment of a professional association (Indian Sociological Society) and its journal (*Sociological Bulletin*) than Mukerjee ever attempted or did (a journal he founded did not survive long).

❖

To sum up, Radhakamal Mukerjee, D.P. Mukerji, and G.S. Ghurye contributed significantly in diverse but complementary ways to the establishment of sociology as an academic discipline in India. At the beginning of the section on Mukerjee's contemporaries, the first person I named was Benoy Kumar Sarkar, and his contribution, which

---

[12] On Ghurye's almost unthinking and exclusive commitment to Rivers and diffusionism, Pramanick writes: 'Ghurye was not a functionalist. Marxism did not have any influence on him. The Parsonian theory of social action appeared to him to be a false abstraction. And Ghurye did not have any knowledge of Max Weber either' (1994: 225). He admitted as much to Pramanick.

[13] It is likely that it was Ghurye's interest in the 'Egyptian affinities of Indian funerary practices' that made him advise Srinivas to do fieldwork among the Coorgis to study their 'burial practices' (Ghurye 1973; Srinivas 2002: 667).

was idiosyncratic in several respects, also must be recognized. Mukerjee and Sarkar were very close friends during their college and university years; in fact, Mukerjee, in his autobiography, describes Sarkar as one of the 'influences' intellectually, and also emotionally (see Mukerjee 1956: 6; 1997: 61, 92), but as the years rolled by, distances grew between them. There is hardly any evidence of mutual influence in their published work, notwithstanding many areas of common interest.

Sarkar was consumed by nationalistic fervour; besides, a wanderlust drove him to Europe, the USA, and the Far East, where he spent over ten years (1914–25). He had a hungry mind too and learnt French, German, and Italian. He read sociologists such as Comte, Durkheim, Tönnies, Weber, and Pareto in the languages in which they wrote, and he wrote about them. Sarkar's informed engagement with the work of Western sociologists, irrespective of the merit of his evaluations, is a unique chapter in the history of sociology in India. Only a few other sociologists have attempted to do the same, such as A.K. Saran (see, for example, Saran 1963, 1971), and J.P.S. Uberoi (1978, 1984), but it may be noted that neither of them have the command over European languages that Sarkar did, nor the experience of extended living abroad.

Sarkar's overriding passion was to bring out the intense, thisworldly concerns of India's intellectual traditions because it was their alleged absence that had been regarded by Western scholars as the main reason for India's 'backwardness'. As he put it: 'The transcendental and other-worldly aspects of Hindu life and thought have been made too much of' (Sarkar [1937] 1985: 6). In this respect, he was dismissive of Weber's work on Indian religions. Arguing against Weber, he wrote that 'religion was a social force in Hindu culture only in the sense in which it is used by Durkheim': to wit, 'society is in every region and age essentially religious' (Sarkar [1937] 1985: 22). He insisted on the similarity between the 'rationalism' of the Protestant ethic, as analysed by Weber, and what he identified as the unbroken tradition of materialism in the Hindu tradition. Sarkar borrowed the term 'positive' from Comte's 'positivism' and reshaped it to describe the Hindu tradition in what is, perhaps, his best known book, *The Positive Background of Hindu Sociology* ([1937] 1985).

The book is a detailed (irritatingly prolix), introductory discussion of the classical Brahmanical text, *Shukranīti*, which, he asserted, was a sociological work; hence, the use of the term 'Hindu

Sociology'. What interested him most was that the ancient Dharmashāstra, Arthashāstra, and Nitishāstra texts were, in his opinion, 'non-transcendental and non-mystical'; in other words, they contained 'secular, worldly, materialistic, and "positive" elements of [the] Hindu social economy' (Sarkar [1937] 1985: 5, 15–17, 56, and elsewhere). He assiduously sought for earlier parallels in the Brahmanical, Buddhist, and Jaina traditions of Western ideologies of power (economic and political) to conclude that 'materialism first, materialism second, and materialism always has been the foundation and the background of Hindu civilization for six thousand years [sic] from Mohenjo Daro to the age of Rāmkrishna-Vivekānanda' (Sarkar [1937] 1985: 635). Bhattacharya (1990: 419) in his comprehensive study of Sarkar's work observes:

> The entire gamut of Sarkar's indological and sociological studies has been pervaded by a quest for the sources of a possible rejuvenation of the Indian (Hindu) culture in its past so that it could draw its sustenance from its tradition for facing up to the challenge of the industrially and scientifically advanced nations of the west.

For Sarkar, as for Ghurye, vedic knowledge was a living source of philosophical wisdom and practical knowledge. In fact, there is more in common between Sarkar and Ghurye than between Sarkar and Mukerjee. All three had wide and varied interests, and wrote voluminously on, besides sociological themes as such, art, eroticism, literature, and so on. But even less than Mukerjee, Sarkar is no longer a live influence. Chatterji (2007: 106–31) thinks that Sarkar's contributions are at best 'a footnote in the history of Indian sociology' (2007: 106), and Bhattacharya (1990) laments that he has been neglected even by the Bengalis.

Both, however, survive, as Chatterji and Bhattacharya attest in the case of Sarkar, for their historical interest: they throw light on the critical interplay between the shaping of the social sciences and the making of national consciousness in India in the late nineteenth and early twentieth centuries. This is, of course, also true, although not exactly in the same manner, of the work of D.P. Mukerji and G.S. Ghurye. All four were not only the founders of sociology in India, but also contributed significantly to the making of a modern social consciousness, without losing a sense of roots, however. Mukerjee recalls in his autobiography that he and other like-minded young intellectual (notably, Sarkar) realized early that 'Indian recovery and reconstruction must proceed as much on educational and social planes as on political lines' (1997: 92).

A FINAL COMMENT

Times change. Every age, it has been well said, is defined by the way it copes with the challenges it faces. Today, we the sociologists of India, are still, or should be, the rooted bearers of a modern consciousness, but the content of this consciousness, and our sense of rootedness—the two are mutually entailed: the one makes no sense without the other—is inevitably different. In this chapter, honouring the contributions of Radhakamal Mukerjee, I have concentrated on bringing out the range of interests and the flow, as it were, of his thought, for these are so little remembered today. Limitations of space have precluded detailed evaluation. First things, surely, must come first. Let me then confine myself to recalling what Mukerjee's ablest pupil and sternest critic, A.K. Saran said: 'In his intellectual career Dr. Mukerjee has tried to meet the challenge of the West almost in all forms in which it has come', but without noteworthy success because he 'is not a deep thinker' (1958: 1018, 1020). I have quoted rather heavily from his writings in the hope that doing so will give the readers of his essay some idea of Mukerjee's vast erudition and a flavour of his style, which does not actually invite emulation, but was characteristic of him—rather hurried, repetitive, verbose, and replete with cross-disciplinary citations.

Let me conclude by saying that it is not my intention to suggest that, today, we live off the fruits of the work of Mukerjee and his contemporaries. But it is important to know what interested and moved our founding parents. Beyond that, our strivings have to be our own, of the twenty-first century. While deprivation, disease, and illiteracy and other Millennium Development Goals are still with us, we face new problems too, which we share with the rest of the world. Double-edged technological innovations, environmental degradation, globalization, identity concerns in the setting of unprecedented movement of peoples across countries (as refugees fleeing political persecution or as migrants in search of a better life), and religious resurgence (as personal piety or politically motivated religiosity) are some of these new challenges. What do we, as sociologists, have to say about them? That is the constitutive question of sociology today, everywhere.

Chapter Seven

D.P. Mukerji:
Towards a Historical Sociology

I was trained to think in large terms. It made me ... search for the wood behind the trees.

The value of Indian traditions lies in the ability of their conserving forces to put a break on hasty passage. Adjustment is the end product of the dialectical connection between the two. Meanwhile [there] is tension.

—D.P. MUKERJI, *Diversities*

In this chapter, I discuss the work of Dhurjati Prasad Mukerji (1894–1961), one of the founders of sociology in South Asia (who has already been introduced in Chapter Six). I will first try briefly to locate him in his intellectual settings in Calcutta (now Kolkata) and in Lucknow. I will then recall, again briefly, my personal memories of him as a teacher in the last years of his academic pursuits at the University of Lucknow in the early 1950s. Finally, I will discuss at some length his contributions as a scholar with particular reference to his later work (the early 1940s onwards) in which the search for synthesis in both the unfolding of the historical process and the most fruitful way of its study was highly salient. It was his considered judgement, I think, that the most creative way to 'read' history was to focus on the dialectic embedded in it and investigate it from an interdisciplinary perspective (combining history, economics, psychology, and sociology).

I

The Settings: Calcutta and Lucknow

The Bengali intelligentsia of the 1890s—the decade of D.P. Mukerji's birth—were participants in a new phase of the renaissance that had been ushered in earlier in the century by the leaders of a nascent middle class, from among whom Rammohan Roy (1772–1833) is the most celebrated and even considered by many the father of modern India. Among the defining characteristics of this new awareness one could mention, first, a fine-tuned receptivity towards the ethical precepts of Christianity and the intellectual, literary, and artistic achievements of the West, and then, in a kind of 'second movement', a resurgent, redefined Hinduism alongside a rediscovered Sanskrit literary tradition. More than any others, perhaps, Rabindranath Tagore (1861–1941) and Swami Vivekananda (1863–1902) compelled attention, and not among intellectuals alone. After the turn of the century came the partition of Bengal in 1905 and the Swadeshi movement (1905–08) (see Ray 1984). The latter, and an upgraded Calcutta University under the dynamic leadership of Ashutosh Mookerji with provision for postgraduate studies, were the critical components of the intellectual setting in which D.P. Mukerji's generation completed its higher studies.

DP (henceforth I will refer to him, as he was most widely known by his initials) was born on 5 October 1894 in a Brahmin, middle-class family that had a fairly long tradition of intellectual pursuits. After his 'Entrance' examination, he tried several combinations of subjects, including the natural sciences, the latter being preferred by the brightest students of those days. One such student, Satyen Bose, who was to become a famous physicist, later recalled DP as a warm and friendly fellow student, a gifted conversationist, and a lover of books and Indian music (see his introductory note in Mukerji [1943] 1972). In the event, DP took Master's degrees in history and economics, the latter with distinction.

DP opted for a career in teaching which began at Bangabasi College, Calcutta. He also began to write and publish in both Bengali and English, and soon acquired a reputation as a brilliant, young man with broad intellectual interests and sound critical judgement. As

Satyen Bose recalled, 'his critical appreciation and his judgement on the aesthetics of music were held in high regard by all'. He published in *Sabuj Patra* and *Parichaya*, two influential Bengali magazines, and his writings attracted the notice of Rabindranath Tagore, Pramatha Chaudhury (founder editor of *Sabuj Patra*), and the novelist Saratchandra Chatterji. He wrote not only on music and literary topics, but also on such themes as democracy, capitalism, and anti-intellectualism (see Munshi 2009b). Sociology those days, DP used to tell us (in the early 1950s), was often mistaken by the general reading public for social reform, socialism, or sanitized sex *à la* Marie Stopes (author of the best selling *Married Love*)! And this in spite of the fact that already, in the late nineteenth century, many Calcutta intellectuals honoured Auguste Comte at an annual festival: Bankim Chandra Chattopadhyay (1838–1894) for one was familiar with both his and Herbert Spencer's views (see Kopf 1969).

A studio portrait of DP of around this time (the early 1920s) shows him seated in a large cane chair, dressed in a Western-style suit and shoes, with a stiff collar shirt and necktie. A felt hat rests on a small pile of books on the nearby ornate table. His facial expression already has the intensity that I was to become familiar with thirty years later.

DP joined the newly founded University of Lucknow as a lecturer in economics and sociology in 1922 at the invitation of Radhakamal Mukerjee, who obviously expected the former to help him in shaping the interdisciplinary approach to research in and teaching of economics. This promise was not, as already discussed in Chapter Six, realized, at least in the manner Mukerjee anticipated.

II

D.P. Mukerji as a Teacher

D.P. Mukerji's career as an intellectual included, most prominently, his contributions as a teacher. In fact, there would be a general agreement among those who knew him personally (as students, colleagues, or friends), and who had also read his written work, that he had a much greater and abiding influence on others through the spoken rather than the written word. The freedom that the classroom, the coffee house, or the drawing room gave him to explore ideas and elicit responses was naturally not available via the printed page. Moreover, the quality of his writing was uneven, and not all that he wrote could be expected to survive long.

When I became his student, DP was already in his late fifties (see Madan 2009). Lean in build, intense in expression, and elegant in appearance (long-sleeved white cotton shirts, the tails tucked in, and white trousers in summer; suits or tweeds in the winter; *dhoti–kurta* always at home), he cut an elegant figure. He usually began his classroom lecture on a formal note (he spoke very gently, at times in whispers), but would soon spice it with stories, insightful observations, fascinating asides, and witticisms. One could never be wholly sure what DP would speak about on a particular day—the topic addressed on the previous lecture day, a book he had read since then (he literally devoured books, pencil in hand, at an incredible pace), a concert he had been to or a movie he had seen the previous evening, or a news item in the morning's papers. There was a significant continuity, he seemed to want to tell us, between the classroom and the world outside. If one did not explore this relationship, one was a born loser, and unsuited to the scholarly life. DP did not wholly disown the ivory tower, for he valued the view from afar, but deprecated insularity.

DP took an interest in our political views, in the books we read and the music we heard (the Lata phenomenon had just begun and he was amused!), in the clothes we wore (it took him long to reconcile to the bush shirt), and so on. His emphasis upon aesthetic values elevated them to the level of the ethical. The students who joined him in the quest for knowledge and the making of a meaningful life became a personal concern to him, as scholars-in-the-making and as human beings. He aroused their intellectual curiosity, guided their reading, stimulated their thinking, and watched over them with care and even affection. DP once told me that the best thing about being a teacher was to see eager eyes brighten and young minds blossom. I discovered many years after his death that the well known bookseller of Lucknow, Ram Advani, had offered to let me buy books on credit when I was still a student without an income, because, as he told me, DP had suggested that he do so. I can recall many other similar acts of personal kindness.

What matters more, perhaps, is that DP conveyed to his students the judgement that the life of scholarship and intellectual questing was a life of daring, and indeed a life very much worth living. It was socially useful no less than personally satisfying. It was a life for the sceptical and the restless, not for the contented and the lazy. The life of the intellectual was honourable and intellectuals were the very salt of life. DP had himself once been persuaded to step outside 'the grove of Academe', but had not found the experience particularly exhilarating. In 1938, he had been prevailed upon to become Director of Information to the government after the Congress had formed the ministry in (as it was then) the United Provinces. He was reputed to have discharged his duties with rare ability and distinction. Among his noteworthy initiatives was the establishment of the Bureau of Economics and Statistics. He quit three years later, as soon as the Congress relinquished office, and returned to the university, happy to be back where he truly belonged. His only other involvement with the government was the membership of the Uttar Pradesh Labour Enquiry Committee in 1947.

DP's reputation as a teacher was not confined to the students of economics and sociology, but was generally acknowledged at the university level. His lectures on the history of economic and social thought, and on historical sociology ('culture and civilization'), were particularly appreciated during the days of my studentship. Outside the curricula, his radio talks and newspaper articles covered the graphic arts, music, cinema, literature, and politics. I remember two erudite lectures on the social foundations of epic poetry, and impromptu discussions of many new books (including Carr's *New Society*, Sorokin's *Social Philosophies of an Age of Crisis*, Hauser's *Social History of Art*, and Nirad Chaudhuri's *The Autobiography of an Unknown Indian*), and films (such as *The Death of a Salesman*, *Snakepit*, and *Rashomon*). I also remember many articles in the *National Herald* ranging from a discussion of Nehru's personality (the type that prefers 'merger' to 'emergence') to a lament on state-organized cultural 'shows', and an appreciation of Faiyaz Khan's *gayaki* (musical style).

I have heard DP criticized for having been a dilettante, a non-serious amateur. I guess his dilettantism may be admitted, but it would have to be acknowledged as a love of the fine arts and a thirst for knowledge that had range and purpose. It would take wide reading and a discriminating mind, not to mention the rare art of conversation, to make a dilettante of DP's calibre. About his conversations, his colleague, S.K. Narain (of the Department of English) described them in an obituary as 'rich and varied and wise and scintillatingly brilliant'. Ashok Mitra recalls DP's 'wit' and 'magnetism', and how he would tease curious visitors from Calcutta, saying that their interest in him was a part of their sightseeing in Lucknow (see Avasthi 1997: 261)!

After twenty-odd years as a lecturer, DP was made a reader in 1945. Those days, Indian universities followed the principle of a single professor in the department. In 1949, Acharya Narendra Deva, the vice chancellor, broke with this tradition when he bestowed a personal professorship on DP—a gesture that was widely hailed in the university and amidst intellectuals in the city. Today's university teachers will find it hard to believe that it was only when DP became a professor at the age of fifty-five that he was allotted an office room to himself—'life space!' he called it in gentle glee. The writing desk in the room, he proudly said, had come as a gift from his devoted student, A.K. Saran, who was by then his colleague.

Compared to Radhakamal Mukerjee, DP was hardly known outside India. While Mukerjee travelled abroad fairly frequently for conferences and lectures, particularly to Europe, England, and the USA, DP's first overseas trip came as late as in 1952 when he visited the USSR. The following year he went to the Netherlands as a visiting professor at the Institute of Social Sciences at the invitation of the well-known Dutch anthropologist Professor Hofstra. Retirement at the Lucknow University was due in 1954. Dr Zakir Hussain, vice chancellor of Aligarh Muslim University (AMU) and an economist (he later became the President of India), invited him to AMU as professor of economics for as long as he wished to stay there. Intellectuals of DP's calibre, Zakir Hussain let it be known, enriched the quality of intellectual and social life at a university by their presence, for the presence of such persons never was a mere physical fact. DP accepted the invitation without great enthusiasm, for his life had been a rich tale of two cities, Calcutta and Lucknow, both famous for their differently crafted cultural traditions. In Lucknow, DP's admirers felt deeply deprived: his long-time friend M. Chalapathi Rau, editor of the *National Herald* and no mean intellectual himself, spoke for virtually everybody when he asked why Lucknow was letting Aligarh 'take away one of its glories'?

As it turned out, DP's stay at Aligarh lasted only a couple of years. In 1956, his persistent problem of a sore throat was diagnosed as cancer. He underwent major surgery in Switzerland which saved his life, but left him physically and mentally shattered. A skilled Zurich surgeon saved his life and voice, but DP never again could talk long or loudly. For a man who relied heavily on the spoken word, this was a cruel blow. He continued at Aligarh for three more years, and then retired to live in Dehra Dun (where he had made his last major public appearance at the Sociological Conference in 1955) in the summers and in Calcutta in the winters, with occasional visits to Lucknow. It was in Lucknow that I last met him in the spring of 1961, at the home of his younger colleague and former student, V.B. Singh. The scene was familiar: friends and colleagues sat out in the lawn in a circle to talk with him. He made me sit by his side so that I might hear him better. (He knew I had a hearing problem.) Everything was as it used to be, but he was not what he used to be.

DP's last piece of writing was a short memoir of his colleague and friend, D.N. Majumdar, who had died suddenly in 1960. He prepared it at my request for inclusion in a memorial volume. He wrote to me that the piece was shorter than he would have wished: 'You wanted me to do it. But it could not be long. As you know, I am too ill for all that' (Mukerji 1962). Like everything else that DP ever wrote, this memoir too was in longhand, and he had such a fine handwriting. Exactly four months later, he died in Calcutta on 5 December 1961. As A.K. Saran (1962a) noted in an obituary, DP died of physical exhaustion and intellectual loneliness.

III

D.P. Mukerji as Scholar–Author

There are two misconceptions about DP and I would like to comment on these. The first and more common of these is that midway in his intellectual career he became a Marxist, but was never able to master the theory and method of Marxism; or that he *was* a Marxist. Second, he has been described as *basically* a Hindu intellectual, a conservative who was only superficially modern.

Aware of the first characterization, but scornful of it, DP used to jestingly say that the most that he could be described as was a 'Marxologist'! He had discovered Marx (and Hegel) fairly early, but at no stage was he an uncritical Marxist. His deepest interest was in the Marxian method (see Mukerji 1945) rather than in any dogmas. In a short paper entitled 'A Word to Indian Marxists', included in his *Views and Counterviews* (1946: 166), he had warned that the 'unhistorically minded' young Marxist ran the risk of ending up as a 'fascist', and Marxism itself could 'lose its effectiveness in a maze of slogans'. Nevertheless, it would not be misleading to say that DP did indeed favour Marxism in various ways, ranging from a theoretic emphasis upon the economic factor ('mode of production') in the making of culture to an elevation of practice to the status of a test of theory, and that this preference is prominent in his later works. It was a close but not altogether comfortable embrace.

As for his being a Hindu, he was of course a Brahman by birth and upbringing, and not apologetic about it. He retained a lifelong interest in classical Indian thought, which he considered essentially dynamic. '*Charaiveti, charaiveti*' (Forward, forward!) from the *Aitareya Brahmana;* was one of his favourite aphorisms. In the making of the mosaics of medieval and modern Indian cultures, he considered the centrality of Hindu contributions a historical fact. By becoming a part of the pattern, however, it had ceased to be exclusive. (More about this is mentioned below.) As for Brahmanical religious beliefs and rituals, he rejected these quite early in his own life. Actually, he took a broadly Marxist view of religion as an epiphenomenon, but castigated Indian textbook Marxists for their failure to examine closely the reasons why religion is the social force that it apparently is in India. (As is well known, Marx himself had posed a similar question to Engels.)

At the same time, DP rejected what he considered a Western fiction, namely, that the Indian mind was 'annexed and possessed' by religion (see Mukerji [1942] 1948: 6). The Chārvāka theses on states of consciousness being purely physical fascinated him. It could be that DP failed to squarely face the difficulties that his triple loyalty produced; his Brahmanical intellectualism, liberal humanism, and Marxist praxis could not be built into a single, rigorously worked-out theoretical framework. As in the work of Radhakamal Mukerjee, DP's quest for synthesis remained elusive. And he was aware of this, perhaps more acutely than he cared to let others know.

Being an intellectual meant two things to DP. First, discovering the sources and potentialities of social reality in the dialectic of tradition and modernity, and, second, developing an integrated personality through the pursuit of knowledge. Indian sociologists, in his opinion, suffered from a lack of interest in history and philosophy and in the dynamism and meaningfulness of social life. In his presidential address to the first Indian Sociological Conference (in 1955), he had complained: 'As an Indian, I find it impossible to discover any life-meaning in the jungle of the so-called empirical social research monographs' (Mukerji 1958: 231). Western sociological theory generally, and its then fashionable Parsonian version in particular, did not satisfy him because of its overweening accent on the 'individual' or the 'actor-situation'. Paying attention to specificities in a general framework of understanding was a first principle that he derived primarily from Marx and from Weber too. He developed this methodological point in an important essay on the Marxist method of historical interpretation (Mukerji 1945).

Early Works: The Nature of Social Science

Let me now turn to DP's major published works. It is interesting to note that he considered his first two books, *Personality and the Social Sciences* (1924) and *Basic Concepts in Sociology* (1932), 'personal documents'—the early fruits of his endeavour to formulate an adequate concept of social science. The first book, he avowed, was written with 'the sole purpose' of clarifying his 'attitude towards systematized knowledge of society and life in general'. For this purpose, he organized his ideas around the notion of 'personality'. He took up the position that the abstract individual would be a narrow focus of social science theorization: a holistic, psycho-sociological approach was imperative. It was this 'synthesis of the double process of individuality [individuation?] and the socialization of the uniqueness of individual life, this perfect unity' that he called 'personality' (Mukerji 1924: ii). It remained a core concept in his thinking. Towards the end of his life he returned to its clarification when he distinguished the holistic idea of *purusha* from the Western notion of the individual (*vyakti*). The relationship of *purusha* and society free of the tension that characterizes the relationship of the individual and the group was, DP maintained, the key to the understanding of Indian society in terms of tradition (Mukerji 1958: 235; see also Munshi 2009b: 44–50).

At the very beginning of his intellectual career DP committed himself to a view of knowledge and of the knower. Knowledge was not, as he put it, mere 'matter-of-factness', but ultimately, after taking the empirical datum and the scientific method for its study into account, philosophic (Mukerji 1932: iv–v). Economics (he used to tell us thirty years later) had to be rooted in concrete social reality, that is, it had to be sociological; sociology had to take full cognizance of cultural specificity, that is, it had to be historical; history had to rise above a narrow concern with the triviality of bygone events through the incorporation in it of a vision of the future, that is, it had to be philosophical. Given such an enterprise, it is obvious that the knower had to be a daring adventurer with a large vision rather than a timid seeker of the safety of specialization. He pointedly asked in the mid-forties (Mukerji 1946: 11):

> We talk of India's vivisection, but what about the vivisection of knowledge which has been going on all these years in the name of learning, scholarship and specialization? A 'subject' has been cut off from knowledge, knowledge has been excised from life, and life has been amputated from living social conditions. It is really high time for Sociology to come to its own. It may not offer the Truth. Truth is the concern of mystics and philosophers. Meanwhile, we may as well be occupied with the discipline which is most truthful to the wholeness and the dynamics of the objective human reality.

Basic Concepts in Sociology, a product of DP's engagement with Western social thought, discusses the notions of 'progress', 'equality', 'social forces', and 'social control'. His exposition of these concepts is marked by both a positive attitude to the Western liberal outlook as also a lack of ease with the prevailing sociological theories, which he considered excessively ethnocentric and mechanistic. DP emphasized the importance of the comparative cultural perspectives and of the historical situatedness of social reality: 'It may be urged against the above point of view that every systematic body of knowledge assumes all these. But when we assume, we forget' (Mukerji 1932: xvi). Above all, he stressed the role of reason ('Practical and Speculative Reason')—the intellectual ability to deduce or infer—as the primary source of knowledge. Moreover, knowledge was, he believed, 'most intimately related to better living as the

Greeks realized and others forgot.... The only justification of these pages is to help to the best of one's ability in this installation of Reason in the heart of the subject' (Mukerji 1932: xvi). The ultimate objective was not merely understanding, but 'the development of Personality' (Mukerji 1932: x).

Rejecting the evolutionist notion of 'progress' as a natural phenomenon, DP stressed the element of 'purpose' in the life of human beings. Development is not growth, he maintained, but the broader process of the unfolding of potentialities (in this he followed Hegel and Marx though he did not say so explicitly), and added that the 'emergence of values and their dynamic character' must receive adequate consideration (Mukerji 1932: 9). He further wrote (Mukerji 1932: 15):

> Progress can best be understood as a problem covering the whole field of human endeavour. It has a direction in time. It has various means and tactics of development. Fundamentally, it is a problem of balance of values. The scope of the problem is as wide as human society, and as deep as human personality. In so far as human values arise only in contact with human consciousness at its different levels, the problem of progress has unique reference to the changing individual living in a particular region at a particular time in association with other individuals who share with him certain common customs, beliefs, traditions, and possibly a common temperament.

It seems to me permissible to derive from the foregoing statement the conclusion that 'modernization' was the special form which 'progress' took for peoples of the Third World in the second half of the twentieth century. If this is granted, then the following ideas need to be pondered (Mukerji 1932: 29–30):

> Progress ... is ... a movement of freedom.... What is of vital significance is that our time-adjustments should be made in such a way that we should be free from the necessity of remaining in social contact for every moment of our life. This is an important condition of progress. In leisure alone can man conquer the tyranny of time, by investing it with a meaning, a direction, a memory and a purpose. Obstacles to leisure, including the demands of a hectic social life, often mistaken for progress, must be removed

in order that the inner personality of man may get the opportunity for development. This is why the Hindu philosopher wisely insists on the daily hour of contemplation, and after a certain age, a well-marked period of retirement from the turmoil of life. The bustle of modern civilization is growing apace and the need for retirement is becoming greater.

This passage has a contemporary ring, and it is very relevant. If we paraphrase it, using words and phrases that we are more familiar with today, we get a succinct reference to the unthinking craving for and the human costs of modernization, including alienation, to the values of individual freedom and human dignity, and to social commitment. For DP, progress was, as I have already quoted him saying, a problem of balancing of values; and so is modernization. When we introduce values into our discourse and the rationalist perspective that he recommended will have it in no other way, we are faced with the problem of the hierarchy of values, that is, with the quest for ultimate or fundamental values. For these DP turned to the Upanishads, to *shantam*, *shivam*, *advaitam*, that is, harmony, welfare, unity:

> The first is the principle of harmony which sustains the universe amidst all its incessant change, movements and conflicts. The second is the principle of co-ordination in the social environment. The third gives expression to the unity which transcends all the diverse forms of states, behaviours and conflicts, and permeates thought and action with ineffable joy.... On this view, progress ultimately depends on the development of personality by a conscious realization of the principles of Harmony, Welfare and Unity. (Mukerji 1932: 35)

This appeal to Vedanta, while discussing the Western notion of progress, is a disconcerting characteristic of DP's thought throughout. He sought to legitimize it by calling it 'synthesis', which itself he described as a characteristic of the historical process, the third stage of the dialectical triad. He thus evaded, it seems to me, a closer examination of the nature and validity of synthesis. Its existence was assumed and self-validating. One's disappointment and criticism of DP's position is not on the ground of the civilizational source of this trinity of values, but on the ground that harmony, welfare, and unity are too vague and esoteric as they make their elusive appearance in his discourse; and he does not show how they may be integrated with such values of the West as are embodied in its industrial civilization. On the positive side, however, it must be added that DP's preoccupation with ultimate values should be assessed in the light of his deep distrust of the installation of science as the redeemer of mankind and of scientific method (based on a narrow empiricism and exclusive reliance on inductive inference) as the redeemer of the social sciences.

DP, it would seem, was always deeply sensitive to the social environment around him. To the extent that the society in which he lived the life of a scholar was undergoing change, there was a discernible shift in his intellectual concerns also, and he was conscious of this. He even wrote about it later: 'In my view, the thing changing is more real and objective than change per se' (Mukerji 1958: 241). He was a very sensitive person, and many of those who knew him intimately will recall how a turn in events—whether of the university, the city, the country, or the world—would cast a gloom on him or bring him genuine joy. He had an incredible capacity for intense subjective experience: it perhaps killed him in the end. (One of his favourite books was Goethe's *Werther*.) In all his writings he addressed himself to his contemporaries: he had an unstated contempt for those who write for posterity with an eye on personal fame and some kind of immortality, and I think he was right in this attitude. As R.G. Collingwood wrote in his famous autobiography, good writers always write for their contemporaries (1970: 39).

It would seem that what DP was most conscious of in his earlier writings was the need to establish links between the traditional culture of which he was a proud though critical inheritor and the modern liberal education of which he was a critical though admiring product. The two—Indian culture and modern education—could not stay apart without each becoming impoverished—as indeed had been happening, and, therefore, had to be synthesized in the life of the people in general and of the middle classes and intellectuals in particular. In this respect, DP was a characteristic product of his times. He was attracted by the image of the future which the West held out to traditional societies and, at the same time, he was attached to his own tradition, the basis of which was the Hindu heritage. The need to defend what he regarded as the essential values of this tradition thus became a compelling concern, particularly in his later writings.

Dualities never ceased to interest DP, and he always sought to resolve the conflict implicit in persistent dualism through transcendence. This transcendence was to him what history was all about—or ought to be. But history was not for him a tablet already inscribed, once for all, and for each and every people. Hence, his early criticism that, in the hands of Trotsky, Lenin, and Bukharin, Marx's materialist interpretation of history had degenerated into 'pure dialectic' (Mukerji 1932: 184). This criticism was repeated by him again and again. In 1945, he complained that the Marxists had made the 'laws of dialectics' behave like the 'laws of Karma—predetermining every fact, event and human behaviour in its course; or else, they are held forth as a moral justification for what is commonly described as opportunism' (Mukerji 1945: 18).

For DP historiography was meaningless unless it was recognized that the decision to 'write history' entailed the decision to 'act history' (Mukerji 1945: 46). And history was being enacted in India in the 1930s, if it ever was during DP's lifetime, by the middle classes and, under their leadership, by the masses. What they were doing increasingly bothered him, for history had not only to be enacted, but to be enacted right. The question of values could not be evaded. The middle classes whose intellectual life was his concern in his earlier work were also his concern in his later work, but now it was their politics that absorbed him. In this respect, DP's concern avowedly with himself was in fact sociological, for he believed that no man is an island unto himself, but embedded not merely in his class, but also in his total sociocultural environment. The focus was on modern Indian culture and the canvas naturally was the whole of India.

Modern Indian Culture

The year 1942 saw the publication of *Modern Indian Culture: A Sociological Study*. A second revised edition was completed in 1947, the year of independence, but also of partition. It was written under the impending shadow of the partition of India; inquiry and anguish are the moods of the book. The problem, as he saw it, was first to explain why the calamity of communal division had befallen India, and then to use this knowledge to shape a better future. Sociology had to be the interlocutor of history and it was no mean role; indeed it was an obligation. His analysis led him to the conclusion that a distortion had entered into the long-established course of Indian history and crippled it. The happening responsible for this was British rule. But let me first quote DP's succinct statement of the character of modern Indian culture ([1942] 1948: 1):

> As a social and historical process ... Indian culture represents certain common traditions that have given rise to a number of general attitudes. The major influences in their shaping have been Buddhism, Islam, and Western commerce and culture. It was through the assimilation and conflict of such varying forces that Indian culture became what it is today, neither Hindu nor Islamic, neither a replica of the Western modes of living and thought nor a purely Asiatic product.

In this historical process, synthesis had been the dominant organizing principle and the Hindu, the Buddhist, and the Muslim had together shaped a world view in which, according to DP, 'the fact of Being was of lasting significance'. This meant that there had developed an indifference to 'the transient and the sensate' and a preoccupation with the subordination of 'the little self' to and ultimately its dissolution in 'the Supreme Reality' (Mukerji [1942] 1948: 2). This world view DP called 'the mystical outlook'. He maintained that Islam could have on its arrival in India shaken Hindu society in its very roots, but Buddhism served as a cushion. Buddhism itself had failed to tear the Hindu society asunder and had succeeded only in rendering it more elastic. Muslim rule was an economically progressive force, but, on the whole, it brought about only a variation in the already existent socioeconomic structure (Mukerji [1942] 1948: 65–67), and provided no real alternatives to native economic and political systems: 'The Muslims just reigned, but seldom ruled' (Mukerji [1942] 1948: 24).

British rule, however, did prove to be a real turning point in as much as it succeeded in changing the relations of production, or to use DP's own words, 'the very basis of the Indian social economy' ([1942] 1948: 24). New interests in land and commerce were generated, a new pattern of education was introduced, and physical and occupational mobility received a strong impetus. Overshadowing all these developments, however, was the liquidation of an established middle class and 'the emergence of a spurious middle class'

> ... who do not play any truly historical part in the socio-economic evolution of the country, remain distant from the rest of the people in professional isolation or as rent receivers, and are divorced from the realities of social and economic life.... Their ignorance of the background of Indian culture is profound.... Their pride in culture is in inverse proportion to its lack of social content. (Mukerji [1942] 1948: 25)

It was this middle class which helped in the consolidation of British rule in India, but later challenged it successfully; it was also the same middle class which brought about the partition of the country. Its rootlessness made it a 'counterfeit class' and, therefore, its handiwork (whether in the domain of education and culture, in the political arena, or in the field of economic enterprise) had inevitably something of the same spurious quality: 'The politics and the culture of a subject country,' DP wrote, 'cannot be separated from each other' ([1942] 1948: 207). To expect such an 'elite' to lead an independent India along the path of genuine modernization, DP asserted with remarkable prescience, would be unrealistic. He wanted that before they could be expected to remake India, modernize it, the elite themselves must be remade. And he wrote a forthright, if not easy, prescription for them: '[C]onscious adjustment to Indian traditions and symbols' (Mukerji [1942] 1948: 215), for 'culture cannot be "made" from scratch' (Mukerji [1942] 1948: 214).

It is important to understand why he made this particular recommendation, why he wanted the withdrawal of foreign rule to be accompanied by a withdrawal into the self which, let me hasten to add, was quite different from a withdrawal into the past or plain inaction. DP was not only *not* a revivalist, he was keenly aware of the imminent possibility of revivalism and its fatal consequences. He noted that it would be the form that political hatred disguised as civil hatred would take after independence. But he was not hopeless, for he fondly believed that revivalism could be combated by giving salience to economic interests through a 'material programme' that would cut across communal exclusiveness. He envisaged India's emancipation from the negative violence of the constrictive primordial loyalties of religion and the caste through the emergence of class consciousness (Mukerji [1942] 1948: 216). He was silent on class conflict, however, and his critics may justifiably accuse him of not seeing his analysis through to its logical conclusion. His optimism was the sanguine hope of an Indian liberal intellectual rather than the fiery conviction of a Marxist revolutionary.

In any case, we know today, half a century after DP's expression of faith on this score, that class does not displace caste in India. Nor do they coexist in compartments: they combine but they do not fuse. DP's vision of a peaceful, progressive India born out of the 'union' of diverse elements, of distinctive regional cultures, rather than out of the type of 'unity' that the British imposed from above (Mukerji [1942] 1948: 216), however, remains eminently valid even today. The accommodation of various kinds of conflicting loyalties within a national framework, rather than national integration, is the right strategy for the new African and Asian states faced with cultural pluralism, and they are finding it to be both feasible and advantageous. We all know how Pakistan broke up in 1971 (for an excellent, recent analysis, see Shaikh 2009).

DP's plea for a reorientation of tradition was, then, of a positive nature—an essential condition for moving forward, restoring historical dynamism, and re-forging the broken chain of the sociocultural process of synthesis. Employing Franklin Giddings's classification of traditions into primary, secondary, and tertiary (Mukerji [1942] 1948: 34), he suggested that by the time of the British arrival, Hindus and Muslims had yet not achieved a full synthesis of traditions at all levels of social existence. There was a greater measure of agreement between them regarding the utilization and appropriation of natural resources and, to a lesser extent, in respect of aesthetic and religious traditions. In the tertiary traditions of conceptual thought, however, differences survived prominently.

It was into this situation that the British moved, blundering their way into India, and gave Indian history a severe jolt. As generally believed, and DP concurred, they destroyed indigenous merchant capital and the rural economy, pushed through a land settlement based on alien concepts of profit and property, and established a socially useless educational system. Such opportunities as they did create could not be fully utilized, DP said, for they cut across India's traditions, and 'because the methods of their imposition spoilt the substance of the need for new life' (Mukerji [1942] 1948: 206).

The Making of Indian History

At this point it seems pertinent to point out that, while DP followed Marx closely in his conception of history and in his characterization of British rule as uprooting, he differed significantly not only with Marx's assessment of the positive consequences of this rule, but also with his negative assessment of the pre-British traditions.

It will be recalled that Marx had in his articles on British rule in India asserted that India had a long past, but 'no history at all, at least no known history' (Marx and Engels 1959: 31), that its social conditions had 'remained unaltered since its remotest antiquity', that it was 'the British intruder who broke up the Indian handloom and destroyed the spinning-wheel', that it was 'British steam and science' which 'uprooted, over the whole surface of Hindustan, the union between agriculture and manufacturing industry'. Marx had listed England's crimes in India and proceeded to point out that she had become 'the unconscious tool of history whose actions would ultimately result in a 'fundamental revolution'. He had said: 'England had to fulfil a double mission in India: one destructive and the other regenerating—the annihilation of old Asiatic society, and the laying of the material foundations of Western society in India' (Marx and Engels 1959: 31). Thus, for Marx, as for so many others since his time, including Indian intellectuals of various shades of opinion, the modernization of India had to be its Westernization.

As has already been stated above, DP was intellectually and emotionally opposed to such a view about India's past and future, whether it came from Marx or from liberal bourgeois historians. He refused to be ashamed of or apologetic about India's past. The statement of his position was unambiguous:

> Our attitude is one of humility towards the given fund. But it is also an awareness of the need, the utter need, of recreating the given and making it flow. The given of India is very much in ourselves. And we want to make something worthwhile out of it....
> (Mukerji 1945: 11)

Indian history could not be made by outsiders: it had to be enacted by Indians. In this endeavour they had to be not only firm of purpose but also clear-headed. DP wrote (1945: 46):

> Our sole interest is to write and to act Indian History. Action means making; it has a starting point—this specificity called India; or if that be too vague, this specificity of the contact between India and England or the West. Making involves changing, which in turn requires (a) a scientific study of the tendencies which make up this specificity, and (b) a deep understanding of the Crisis [which marks the beginning no less than the end of an epoch]. In all these matters, the Marxian method ... is likely to be more useful than other methods. If it is not, it can be discarded. After all, the object survives.

'Specificity' and 'crisis' are the key words in this passage: the former points to the importance of the encounter of traditions and the latter to its consequences. When one speaks of tradition or of 'Marxist specification', one means, in DP's words, 'the comparative obduracy of a culture-pattern'. He expected the Marxist approach to be grounded in the specificity of Indian history (Mukerji 1945: 45; 1946: 162ff.), as indeed Marx himself had done by focusing on capitalism, the dominant institution of Western society in his time. Marx, it will be said, was interested in precipitating the crises of contradictory class interests in capitalist society (Mukerji 1945: 37). DP, too, was interested in movement, in the release of the arrested historical process, in the relation between tradition and modernity. He asked for a sociology which would 'show the way out of the social system by analysing the process of transformation' (Mukerji 1958: 240). This could be done by focusing first on tradition and only then on change.

The first task for us, therefore, is to study the social traditions to which we have been born and in which we have had our being. This task includes the study of the changes in traditions by internal and external pressures. The latter are mostly economic. Unless the economic force is extraordinarily strong—and it is that only when the modes of production are altered—traditions survive by adjustments. The capacity for adjustment is the measure of the vitality of traditions. One can have a full measure of this vitality only by immediate experience. Thus, it is that I give top priority to the understanding (in Dilthey's sense) of traditions even for the study of their changes. In other words, the study of Indian traditions should precede the socialist interpretations of changes in Indian traditions in terms of economic forces (Mukerji 1958: 232).

This brings me to the last phase of DP's work. Before I turn to it, however, I should mention that Louis Dumont has drawn our attention to an unresolved problem in DP's sociology. He points out that 'recognition of the absence of the individual [in the modern Western sense] in traditional India' obliges one to 'admit with others that India has no history', for 'history and the individual are inseparable'; it follows that 'Indian civilization [is] ... unhistorical by definition' (Dumont 1967c: 239). Viewed from this perspective, DP's impatience with the Marxist position regarding India's lack of history is difficult to understand. It is also rather surprising that having emphasized the importance of the group as against the individual in the Indian tradition and of religious values also, he should have opted for a Marxist solution to the problems of Indian historiography (see Dumont 1967c: 231). DP hovered between Indian tradition and Marxism, apparently, but not really perhaps, without much strain. His adherence to Marxist solutions to intellectual and practical problems gained in salience in his later work, which was also characterized by a heightened concern with tradition. His was a classic case of the 'opposed self': in W. B. Yeats's words, 'Myself wars on myself'.

Modernization: Genuine or Spurious?

For DP the history of India was not the history of her particular form of class struggle because she had experienced none worth the name. The place of philosophy and religion was dominant in the history, and it was fundamentally a long-drawn exercise in cultural synthesis. For him 'Indian history was Indian culture' (1958: 123). India's recent woes, namely, communal hatred and partition, had been the result of the arrested assimilation of Islamic values (Mukerji 1958: 163); he believed that 'history halts unless it is pushed' (Mukerji 1958: 39). In other words, people make their own history, although (as Marx pointed out) not always as they please.

The national movement had generated much moral fervour, but, DP complained, it had been anti-intellectual. Not only had there been much unthinking borrowing from the West, there had also emerged a hiatus between theory and practice as a result of which thought had become impoverished and action ineffectual. Given his concern for intellectual and artistic creativity, it is not surprising that he should have concluded: 'politics has ruined our culture' (Mukerji 1958: 190).

What was worse, there were no signs of this schism being healed in the years immediately after independence. When planning arrived as state policy in the early 1950s, DP expressed his concern, for instance in an important 1953 paper on 'Man' and 'Plan' in India (1958: 30–76), that a clear concept of the new man and a systematic design of the new society were nowhere in evidence. As the years passed by, he came to formulate a negative judgement about the endeavour to build a new India, and also diagnosed the cause of the rampant intellectual sloth. He said in 1955: 'I have seen how our progressive groups have failed in the field of intellect, and hence also in economic and political action, chiefly on account of their ignorance of and unrootedness in India's social reality' (Mukerji 1958: 240).

The issue at stake was India's modernization. DP's essential stand on this was that there could be no genuine modernization through imitation. A people could not abandon their own cultural heritage and yet succeed in internalizing the historical experience of other peoples; they could only be ready to be taken over. He feared cultural imperialism more than any other. The only valid approach, according to him, was that which characterized the efforts of men like Rammohan Roy and Rabindranath Tagore, who tried to make 'the main currents of western thought and action ... run through the Indian bed to remove its choking weeds in order that the ancient stream might flow' (Mukerji 1958: 33).

DP formulated this view of the dialectic between tradition and modernity several years before independence, in his study of Tagore published in 1943, in which he wrote ([1943] 1972: 50):

> The influence of the West upon Tagore was great ... but it should not be exaggerated: it only collaborated with one vital strand of the traditional, the strand that Ram Mohan and Tagore's father ... rewove for Tagore's generation. Now, all

these traditional values Tagore was perpetually exploiting but never more than when he felt the need to expand, to rise, to go deeper, and be fresher. At each such stage in the evolution of his prose, poetry, drama, music and of his personality we find Tagore drawing upon some basic reservoir of the soil, of the people, of the spirit and emerging with a capacity for larger investment....[1]

This crucial passage holds the key to DP's views on the nature and dynamics of modernization. It emerges as a historical process which is at once an expansion, an elevation, a deepening and a revitalization—in short, a larger investment—of traditional values and cultural patterns, and not a total departure from them, resulting from the interplay of the traditional and the modern. DP would have agreed with Michael Oakeshott, I think, that the principle of tradition 'is a principle of continuity' (Oakeshott 1962: 128).[2] From this perspective, tradition is a condition of, rather than an obstacle to, modernization; it gives us the freedom to choose between alternatives and evolve a cultural pattern which cannot but be a synthesis of the old and the new. New values and institutions must have a soil in which to take root and from which to imbibe character. Modernity

---

[1]DP drew an interesting and significant contrast between Bankim Chandra Chatterjee and Rabindranath Tagore. He wrote:

[Bankim] was a path-finder and a first class intellect that had absorbed the then current thought of England. His grounding in Indian thought was weak at first; when it was surer... [it] ended in his plea for a neo-Hindu resurgence. Like Michael Madhusudan Dutta, Bankim the artist remained a divided being. Tagore was more lucky. *His saturation with Indian tradition was deeper; hence he could more easily assimilate a bigger dose of Western thought.* (Mukerji [1943] 1972: 75–76, emphasis added)

[2]Marx, it will be recalled, had written (in 1853) of the 'melancholy' and the 'misery' of the Hindu arising out of the 'loss of his old world' and his separation from 'ancient traditions' (Marx and Engels 1959: 16). The task at hand was to make the vital currents flow. That this could be done by re-establishing meaningful links with the past would have been emphasized, however, only by an Indian such as DP. I suspect DP would have sympathized with Oakeshott's assertion that the changes a tradition 'undergoes are potential within it' (1962: 128).

must, therefore, be defined in relation to, and not in denial of, tradition.[3] Conflict is only the intermediate stage in the dialectical triad: the movement is towards *coincidentia oppositorum*. Needless to emphasize, the foregoing argument is in accordance with the Marxist dialectic which sees relations as determined by one another and, therefore, bases a 'proper' understanding of them on such a relationship.

Synthesis of the opposites is not, however, a historical inevitability. It is not a gift given to a people unasked or merely for the asking: they must strive for it self-consciously, for '[c]ulture is an affair of total consciousness' (Mukerji 1958: 189), it is a 'dynamic social process, and not another name for traditionalism' (Mukerji 1958: 101–02). History for DP was a 'going concern' (1945: 19), and the value of the Marxist approach to the making of history lay in that it would help to generate 'historical conviction' (1958: 56), and thus act as a spur to fully awakened endeavour. The alternative to self-conscious choice-making is mindless imitation and loss of autonomy and, therefore, dehumanization, though he did not put it quite in these words.

Self-consciousness, then, is the first condition, or form, of modernization. Its content, one gathers from DP's writings of the 1950s,

---

[3]Many contemporary thinkers have expressed similar views. For example, Popper writes (1963: 122):

I do not think we could ever free ourselves entirely from the bonds of tradition. The so-called freeing is really a change from one tradition to another. But we can free ourselves from the taboos of tradition; and we can do that not only by rejecting it, but also by critically accepting it. We free ourselves from the taboo if we think about it, and if we ask ourselves whether we should accept it or reject it.

Shils puts it somewhat differently (1975: 203–04):

One of the major problems which confronts us in the analysis of tradition is the fusion of originality and traditionality. T.S. Eliot's essay, 'Tradition and Individual Talent', in *The Sacred Wood*, said very little more than that these two elements coexist and that originality works within the framework of traditionality. It adds and modifies, while accepting much. In any case, even though it rejects or disregards much of what it confronts in the particular sphere of its own creation, it accepts very much of what is inherited in the context of the creation. It takes its point of departure from the 'given' and goes forward from there, correcting, improving, transforming.

consists of nationalism, democracy, the utilization of science and technology for harnessing nature, planning for social and economic development, and the cultivation of rationality. The typical modern man is the engineer, social and technical (Mukerji 1958: 39–40). DP believed that these forces were becoming ascendant:

> This is a bare historical fact. To transmute that fact into a value, the first requisite is to have active faith in the historicity of that fact.... The second requisite is social action ... to push ... consciously, deliberately, collectively, into the next historical phase. The value of Indian traditions lies in the ability of their conserving forces to put a brake on hasty passage. Adjustment is the end-product of the dialectical connection between the two. Meanwhile [there] is tension. And tension is not merely interesting as a subject of research; if it leads up to a higher stage, it is also desirable. The higher stage is where personality is integrated through a planned, socially directed, collective endeavour for historically understood ends, which means ... a socialist order. Tensions will not cease there. It is not the peace of the grave. Only alienation from nature, work and man will stop in the arduous course of such high and strenuous endeavours. (Mukerji 1958: 76)

In view of this clear expression of faith (it is that, and not a demonstration or anticipation of the inevitable, if it could be possible), it is not surprising that he should have told Indian sociologists (in 1955) that their 'first task' was the study of 'social traditions' (Mukerji 1958: 232), and should have reminded them that traditions grow through conflict (see Chapter Seven: 137–39).

It is in the context of this emphasis on tradition that DP's specific recommendation for the study of Mahatma Gandhi's views on machines and technology, before going ahead with 'large scale technological development' (Mukerji 1958: 225), was made. It was no small matter that from the Gandhian perspective, which stressed the values of wantlessness, non-exploitation, and non-possession, the very notions of economic development and under-development could be questioned (Mukerji 1958: 206). But this was perhaps only a gesture (a response to a poser), for DP maintained that Gandhi had failed to indicate how to absorb 'the new social forces which the West had released' (Mukerji 1958: 35). Moreover, 'the type of new society enveloped in the vulgarized notion of Rama-rajya was not only non-historical but anti-historical' (Mukerji 1958: 38). But he was also convinced that Gandhian insistence on traditional values might help to save India from the kind of evils (for example, scientism and consumerism) to which the West had fallen prey (Mukerji 1958: 227).

The failure to clearly define the terms and rigorously examine the process of synthesis, already noted earlier, reappears here again and indeed repeatedly in DP's work. In fact, he himself recognized this when he described his life to A.K. Saran as 'a series of reluctances' (Saran 1962a: 169). As Saran notes, DP 'did not wish to face the dilemma entailed by a steadfast recognition of this truth', that the three world views—Vedanta, Western liberalism, and Marxism—which all beckoned to him 'do not mix'.[4] One wonders what DP's autobiography would have been like.

Theories of Modernization

I hope to have shown in this necessarily brief discussion that, despite understandable differences in emphasis, there is on the whole a remarkable consistency in DP's views on the nature of modernization. Not that consistency is always a virtue, but in this case it happens to be true. Genuine modernization, according to him, has to be distinguished from the spurious product and the clue lies in its historicity. The presentation of the argument is clear, but it is not always thorough and complete, and may be attacked from more than one vantage point.

Saran (1965), for instance, has pointed out that DP does not subject the socialist order itself to analysis and takes its benign character on trust, that he fails to realize that a technology-oriented society cannot easily be non-exploitative and not anti-man, that the traditional and modern worldviews are rooted in different conceptions of time, that traditional ideas cannot be activated by human effort alone, that given our choice of development goals we cannot escape Westernization, and so forth. It seems to me that DP's principal problem was that he let the obvious heuristic value of the

---

[4] It may be noted though that in his earlier writings DP had shown a greater wariness regarding the possibility of combining Marxism with Hindu tradition. Referring to the 'forceful sanity' of the 'exchange of rights and obligations' on which Hindu society was organized, he had written (1932: 136): '[B]efore Communism can be introduced, national memory will have to be smudged, and new habits acquired. There is practically nothing in the traditions on which the new habits of living under an impersonal class-control can take root.'

dialectical approach overwhelm him and failed to probe deeply enough into the multidimensional and, indeed, dynamically integrated character of empirical reality. He fused the method and the datum.

I want to suggest, however, that DP's approach had certain advantages compared to those others that were current in modernization studies of his time. An examination of those modernization theories is outside the scope of this discussion; I will, therefore, make only a rather sweeping generalization about them. They seemed to fall into two very broad categories. There were, first, what one may call the 'big bang' theories of modernization, according to which tradition and modernity were mutually exclusive, bipolar phenomena. This entailed the further view that before one could change anything at all, one had to change everything. This view is, however, unfashionable now, and to that extent sociology has moved forward.

Second, there were what we may call the 'steady state' theories of modernization, according to which modernization was a gradual, piecemeal process, involving compartmentalization of life and living; it was not through displacement but juxtaposition that modernization proceeded. As a description of empirical reality, the latter approach was, and is, perhaps acceptable, but it creates a serious problem of understanding, for it in effect dispenses with all values except modernity, which is defined vaguely with reference to what has happened elsewhere—industrialization, bureaucratization, democratization, and so on—and almost abandons holism.

By this latter view, one is committed to the completion of the agenda of modernization, as it were, and hence the boredom, the weariness, and the frustration one sees signs of everywhere. The gap between the 'modernized' and the 'modernizing', it is obvious, will never be closed. No wonder, then, that social scientists already speak of the infinite transition—an endless pause—in which traditional societies find themselves trapped. Moreover, both sociology and history teach us, if they teach us anything at all, that there always is a residue, that there always will be traditional and modern elements in the cultural life of a people, at all times and in all places.

The virtue of a dialectical approach such as DP advocated would seem to be that it reveals the spuriousness of some of the issues that the other approaches give rise to. At the same time, it may well be criticized as an evasion of other basic issues. I might add, though, that it does provide us with a suggestive notion, one which we may call 'generative tradition', and also a framework for the evaluation of ongoing processes. All this of course needs elaboration, but the present chapter is not the place for such an undertaking. Suffice it to say, the notion of generative tradition involves a conception of 'structural' time more significantly than it does that of 'chronological' time. 'Structural' time implies, as many anthropologists have shown, a working out of the potentialities of an institution. Institutions have a duration in 'real' time, but this is the surface view; they also have a deeper duration which is not readily perceived because of the transformations they undergo.

IV

Concluding Comments

Looking back at the published corpus of Radhakamal Mukerjee and D.P. Mukerji, we have to note that it has all but disappeared from the sociology curricula of Indian universities and even from the libraries. Most of their books are out of print. Moreover, most of the Indian universities offering sociology courses were established after the death of these two scholars. Three of DP's books (*Modern Indian Culture, Diversities*, and *An Introduction to Indian Music*) were, however, reissued in 2002, but I doubt this is a result of any serious revival of interest in his contributions. It would not be incorrect to say that Mukerjee's work, despite its many shortcomings, has left a deeper mark than DP's. As already noted in Chapter Six, as a pioneer, Mukerjee was a man in a great hurry, who wrote a great deal on a wide variety of subjects, but did not go deeply into anyone of them. He did, however, contribute to laying the foundations of a number of new fields of study, including economic anthropology, institutional economics, social ecology, the sociology of values, and socioeconomic studies of rural life and the Indian working class. DP's scholarly output was, by comparison, meagre. He wrote regularly in the newspapers and periodicals, notably *National Herald* and *The Economic Weekly* (the editorial of the inaugural issue of the latter publication was, if I remember correctly, from his pen) on subjects that were usually only of topical interest.

As far as I know, there is no book-length study of the contributions of either scholar.⁵ A festschrift in honour of Mukerjee (see Singh 1956) bears witness to his work being relatively well known, particularly in the USA. Among others, Pitrim Sorokin, Talcott Parsons, Carl Zimmerman, Emory Bogardes, and Manuel Gottlieb contributed papers to it. Two memorial volumes dedicated to DP (see Avasthi 1997; Singh and Singh 1967) are more an expression of respect than a discussion of his work. It is noteworthy that the Avasthi volume contains a number of tributes to DP as a teacher and lover of books. Several essays or discussions, published in the latter book and elsewhere, have been devoted to aspects of DP's work (see Joshi 1986; Madan 1977a, 1994b; Mukherjee 1965; Nagendra 1997; Saran 1965), but an extended evaluation is yet awaited. I understand that the considerable body of DP's published work in Bengali has fared better; at least some of it is in print, and some essays have recently been translated into English (see Munshi 2009b). His Bengali writings include, notably, an early work on social distance, a volume comprising correspondence with Tagore about literature and music, and a fiction trilogy in which he employed the stream of consciousness technique, apparently for the first time in Bengali literature. What I do know is that there is no one among Indian sociologists today who can put us in mind of D.P. Mukerji. The times have changed and, doubtless, Indian sociology too has moved forward. I only wish there was better informed and critically nuanced appreciation of what the founders strove for and achieved.⁶

---

⁵D.N. Majumdar, the third member of the Lucknow 'trinity', has fared no better. Only one of his books, which is an undergraduate-level text (see Majumdar and Madan 1956), is in print. At a birth centenary conference held in Lucknow in 2003, under the auspices of the Ethnographic and Folk Culture Society (of which he was the founder in 1947), several speakers recalled their close association with him, but no paper devoted to an assessment of his scholarly work was presented. Majumdar's lasting contribution, it seems is the journal *The Eastern Anthropologist*, which is now in its fifty-fourth year of publication.

⁶Actually, there has been quite some misrepresentation of DP's work. Nearly every statement in the two paragraphs devoted to it in a fairly long essay (Srinivas and Panini 1973, reproduced in Srinivas 2002a), is either factually incorrect or otherwise misleading. It is indeed surprising that the authors should suggest that DP 'viewed the process of change under British rule as similar to changes under earlier alien rulers [*sic*]' or that they should think he changed his views about 'synthesis' in his later writings. His concern with the cultural 'specificity' of India is misrepresented as an emphasis on 'uniqueness'. Even his name is misspelled (Mukherjee instead of Mukerji)!

Chapter Eight

M.N. Srinivas: Empiricism and Imagination

The effort really to see and really to represent is no idle business....
—HENRY JAMES, *The Art of the Novel*

[F]iction never lies; it reveals the writer totally.
—V.S. NAIPAUL, in Patrick French, *The World Is What It Is*

[Sociology] has oscillated between a scientific orientation which has led it to ape the natural sciences and a hermeneutic attitude which has shifted the discipline towards the realm of literature.
—WOLF LEPENIES, *Between Literature and Sciences*

INTRODUCTORY REMARKS

In this chapter written as a contribution to a forthcoming Festschrift (edited by Shail Mayaram and Ravi Sundaram) in honour of Ashis Nandy, I provide a comparative reading of M.N. Srinivas's ethnographic writings and two short stories, the first of which was published at an early stage in his career as a social anthropologist, and the second, nearly half a century later. Nandy admired Srinivas's work and, perhaps, more than it, his company and conversations with him. In a comment on a published observation of mine on Srinivas's *The Remembered Village* (1976), Nandy asked if my placing the book alongside certain celebrated works of fiction about everyday life in Karnataka was

[A]n admission that Srinivas, by crossing the barriers between literature and the social sciences, has only enriched the latter? Or, [was it] a homage to the creativity that, when forcibly distanced from hard empiricism, reaches paradoxically a higher order of empiricism? (Nandy 2001b: 22)

❖

Srinivas, the foremost social anthropologist of village India in his time, lived virtually all his life in cities, except a year of fieldwork (1948) in a Karnataka village. He was born in Mysore in 1916 and died in Bangalore in 1999. In between, he lived in a number of cities including Armidale (in Australia), Baroda (for eight years), Berkeley, Bombay (now Mumbai), Chicago, Delhi (for about a dozen years), Manchester, Oxford, Palo Alto (in the USA), and Singapore. Eventually, in 1973, he moved to Bangalore in his home state, which had also been his anthropological stamping ground (present-day Karnataka includes Coorg and the former princely state of Mysore). As far as I know, except for an essay on Bangalore (Srinivas 1996), Srinivas never wrote about any of the cities or houses he lived in. There is a very brief mention in one place of the 'bungalow' (Srinivas 1995) at 14 Cavalry Lane on the Delhi University campus in which the Srinivases lived for many years, of the flowering and fruit trees he and Rukmini Srinivas planted there, and of the birds and squirrels that lived in them.

More significantly, perhaps, he never wrote negatively about city life or nostalgically about village life. Even so, and as Nandy (2001b) has persuasively observed, for urban, educated Indians of earlier generations (such as Gandhi, Satyajit Ray, and Srinivas), the village was an abiding element of their moral imagination. What Nandy has written about himself is also true of Srinivas: '[I] ... am not the offspring of village India. Nor [am I someone] who finds the tinsel glitter of the city an immoral, seductive presence. [I am] a child of modern India ...' (Nandy 1995: ix). Nandy believes that this is no longer true, that the village has receded from the moral imagination of the urban, educated Indian.

In Bangalore, the Srinivases built themselves a home and called it Arekere. Thinking it to be a common noun, I asked him for its meaning. He told me that Arekere was the name of his ancestral village, from where his parents had migrated to the not-too-distant city of Mysore. On my first visit to Arekere (in 1978 or 1979), he fondly showed me the main house door of traditional design, which, he said, had been obtained from his ancestral village. I wondered whether Arekere, the house, in spite of its concreteness of brick, cement, and steel, was an imagined village. Did the gestures of naming the house and obtaining the door from the ancestral village convey a longing for roots, and a romantic rejection of the city and embracing of the village? Arekere must have been largely similar to Rampura, the village he made famous in *The Remembered Village*, as the two villages are quite close to each other, and neither is far from the city of Mysore.[1]

Srinivas has left us many descriptions of Rampura—its landscape, its fields and ponds and trees, its seasons, its people and animals. He even describes the homestead he lived in—the village headman's 'bullock house'—with its sights and sounds, and smells which were not pleasant. He was usually quite busy there, and the villagers were friendly to him, but living there did often get upon his nerves, and he would readily escape to Mysore, only 22 miles from Rampura, for a few days.

Srinivas recalls: 'It was pleasant to get back to electric lights, piped water, good food, and above all privacy. It was delightful to walk around without having to be asking questions and making notes.' His Rampura friends were not welcome while he was away in Mysore, 'a refugee from the village'. His selfishness made him feel guilty when he went back there; he tried to be 'extra nice', invited them to have 'snacks and coffee', and gave 'small gifts to some of them' (1976: 33). Srinivas's reputation as a champion of fieldwork lay somewhere away from 'home' notwithstanding, I wonder whether he really enjoyed it himself.

It is, therefore, unlikely that his Rampura experience would ever have persuaded him to turn his back on city life or name his Bangalore home Arekere. The tension between the real and the imagined may have been more pronounced in the case of Srinivas's

---

[1]Arindam Chakrabarti has pointed out to me that, in the phraseology of Sanskrit case grammar, Arekere, the house, could be said to have been Srinivas's *locative* home (where you live), *oblative* home (where you are from), and *accusative* home (where you wish to arrive at). This is an interesting insight.

last home, but it was presumably present wherever he lived. Tradition and modernity, perhaps, always wrestled for his soul (as they did in the case of D.P. Mukerji, see Chapter Seven). If only one would have thought of asking him about it in his lifetime, one could have perhaps constructed some fascinating narratives of Srinivas's real and imagined homes, meaning by home more than the house of residence, and including in it the larger setting, whether of the village or the city.

What one still can do is to explore the theme of imagined homes and worlds in Srinivas's writings, in the considerable body of his ethnographic work and the two short stories that he gave us. Did he write others which he did not, however, publish? Perhaps he did, like the one he mentioned in a late essay (Srinivas 2002a: 595).[2] We do not know. I made several attempts (in personal conversations and through correspondences) to draw him out on the subject of his fictional writings, but never succeeded. He always was evasive, even shy about it, and made it seem as if the stories really did not matter. Not long before his death, when he was finalizing an anthology of his writings, I proposed to him formally through his publisher (OUP) to include the two stories, but he did not do so. This was, I think, a pity because not only do the stories have considerable literary merit, they

---

[2] Actually this would have been a very remarkable story. It seems that he wrote it in the early 1940s; in any case it was then that he gave it to Raja Rao (the famous author of *Kanthapura* and other works of fiction) to read. Srinivas recalls that the story was based on an actual happening. A poor, old, Mysorean Sanskrit scholar, who had 'spent several years in Benaras compiling a dictionary of Vedic words', had had the misfortune to see his efforts literally end in ashes: his manuscript had 'caught fire accidentally'. The story, called 'Old Man of the Books', had described 'how the old man reconciled himself to the destruction of his life work' (Srinivas 2002a: 595).

How indeed? Alas! We do not know, because Srinivas did not publish the story. The tragic end of many years of hard work obviously had not brought the narrator of the story the unexpected and rich rewards that came to Srinivas himself when he lost his processed fieldnotes: many readers, including the novelist U.R. Ananthamurthy (see Nandy 2001b: 11) and the social anthropologist Scarlett Epstein (1976), have called *The Remembered Village* his best work, indeed a classic. Surprisingly, Srinivas did not mention the old man's woes in it, nor comment on how the one accident uncannily foretold the other. Indeed, and as far as I know, it was only in 1998, a year before his death, that he revealed the existence of the story. Srinivas the writer of stories was, it seems to me, an intriguingly reticent person.

also are significant in relation to the thematic foci of his ethnographic corpus and his outlook on life. In what follows, I will try to bring out this significance.

THE POETICS OF ETHNOGRAPHY

To begin, let me briefly revisit an old question: What kind of a text is an ethnographic text? This question lay at the heart of the realization in the second half of the nineteenth century that the traveller's tale, the missionary's account, or the colonial administrator's report, its detail notwithstanding, yet was not systematic and objective enough for the 'scientific' understanding of non-Western peoples, or the comparative study of human cultures. The anthropologist needed to gather his or her own data, from informants brought over to the deck of the ship or the verandah of a white man's house, or, best of all, by living among the 'natives', learning to speak their language, observing what all they did, and seeking to find out how they themselves made sense of it. This way of doing anthropology was, of course, called participant observation, and Malinowski was its first famous exemplar. Years later, Jarvie (1964) called it 'the revolution in anthropology'. The 'final goal', Malinowski wrote at the very beginning of *Argonauts of the Western Pacific* ([1922] 1953), was 'to grasp the native's point of view, his relation to life, to realize *his* vision of *his* world'. Perhaps also, 'through realizing human nature in a shape very distant and foreign to us, we shall have some light shed on our own' ([1922] 1953: 25).

I would like to suggest that what is of crucial importance in the two statements about the goal of anthropology is encapsulated in the verb 'realize'. What is it to realize something? What is the nature of 'realization'? And what is needed to arrive at it? According to the dictionaries, to realize means to become so fully aware of something, or a situation, as to be able to claim a clear understanding of it. The basis of understanding is factual, but no truly *great* ethnographic work acquired its greatness from its factual content alone. Besides facts, one of course needs a theoretical framework, a roadmap as it were, to meaningfully chart one's course through the plethora of facts. But even this combination of fact and theory is not enough. What is additionally needed is *imagination*, the ability to rise above the factual base to form a holistic image of social reality, or, in other words, to arrive at a comprehensive understanding of it to capture its eidos. Every sensitive anthropologist is aware of this goal, but not everyone is able to bring it off.

Moreover and interestingly, Malinowski sought to bind the ethnographer and his reader in a bond of shared imagination, or, to put it in other words, make them accomplices in the act of creation. At the very beginning of the classic monograph, he invites the reader to '[i]magine yourself suddenly set down ... alone on a tropical beach close to a native village, while the launch or dinghy which has brought you sails away out of sight' ([1922] 1953: 4). He thus highlights the ideal of total immersion in the life of the people to be studied, far away from one's own world. The ultimate objective, as he reminds the reader in the concluding chapter, is 'the study of the native in his outlook on things, his *Weltanschauung*, the breath of life and reality which he breathes and by which he lives' ([1922] 1953: 517). Malinowski concludes that, for the members of a culture, it is all a matter of 'a definite vision of the world, a definite zest of life' ([1922] 1953: 517). The coming together of the native's *vision* and the ethnographer's *imagination* creates the moment of comprehension.

The lure of imagination would seem to have been an abiding one during Malinowski's three expeditions to the Trobriand Islands, from 1914 to 1918, and in diverse ways. An entry in his diary in 1918 is noteworthy. He wrote:

> I sat on the bench for a while.... I thought about the stars, the sea, the enormous emptiness of the universe in which man is lost; the moments when you merge with objective reality, when a drama of the universe ceases to be a *stage* and becomes a performance—these are the moments of *nirvana*. (Malinowski 1967: 120)

One might add that among the major influences on Malinowski's craft as a social anthropologist were a novelist and a classical scholar. 'Malinowski saw the key to an authentic ethnographic rhetoric in the literary imagination of Conrad and Frazer' (Thornton 1985: 13).

Among British anthropologists of the next generation, Evans-Pritchard was by common consent the greatest in terms of the broad range and depth of insight of his work. He too affirmed the importance of 'intuitive powers' and 'imaginative insight' and 'literary skill' in the making of a truly successful ethnographer, besides the basic requirements of 'intellectual ability', 'technical training', and 'the right kind of temperament'. He regretted, however, that these qualities were 'rare' and hard to cultivate. Indeed, he added, one needs to have 'a touch of genius' (Evans-Pritchard 1951a: 82).

The idea of the merger of perspectives, of the external and the internal, should have a particular appeal to Indian readers. Let me, then, turn to two Indian perspectives on fieldwork. If anyone deserves to be called the father of Indian ethnography, it is Sarat Chandra Roy (1871–1942); a lawyer by training, his professional work had brought him into contact with the tribal peoples of Bihar (see Dasgupta 2007). In an article published in *Man* towards the end of his life, he observed:

> [The] objective methods of investigation of cultural data have to be helped out, not only by historical imagination and a background of historical and geographical facts, but also by a subjective process of self-forgetting absorption or meditation (*dhyana*) and intuition born of sympathetic immersion in, and self-identification with, the society under investigation. (Roy 1938: 146)

Now, *dhyāna* is more than meditation: it is, according to the dictionaries, the act of mental projection (of the attributes of a deity, for instance), an imaginative act; Roy would have been aware of this connotation also.

In this insightful statement, Roy suggested that an authentic understanding of a society is possible only when a body of objectively observed and empathetically contextualized facts is brought to life through deep reflection and the exercise of historical imagination. I should think that historical imagination here connotes the capacity to not only consider the past of institutions, but also to visualize their future. In other words, good ethnography needs more than fieldwork notes for it to be written, it also—in fact more importantly—needs a sort of genius and inspiration. This is, of course, also true of good fiction, which, as the Victorian novelist George Eliot once observed, is the 'exercise of a veracious imagination in historical picturing' (Berger 1977: 217). I will not go here into the arguable claim that the birth of the novel in the West anticipated the emergence of sociology (see Lepenies 1988), or that it was itself an outcome of the diminishing appeal of mythology in the post-Enlightenment West (as Lévi-Strauss somewhere suggests).

Having cited Malinowski, Evans-Pritchard, and Roy on the foundations of good ethnography in the dialectic of observed reality and its imaginative representation, let me move forward a generation and note what Srinivas had to say on the subject. Writing in the mid-1960s, when his fieldwork days were long over, he wrote (Srinivas 1967b: 156):

> Successful field work involves not only the sociologist's painstaking collection of a vast amount of the minutae of ethnography, but also his exercising his powers of empathy to understand what it is to be a member of the community that is being studied. In this respect, the sociologist is like a novelist who must of necessity get under the skin of the different characters he is writing about.... Needless to say, this involves not only his [the ethnographer's] intellect but his emotions as well.

The agreement between Malinowski, Evans-Pritchard, Roy, and Srinivas is remarkable. All four subscribed to social realism inasmuch as they believed that the facts of social life have an existence independent of the ethnographer, and are available to observation from outside. The facts of social life comprise what people believe, what people do, and what sense they make of it all. It is the task of the ethnographer to independently establish connections between beliefs and behaviour, and to render them and the internal understandings of everyday life sociologically intelligible. To do this, all four exemplars clearly maintained, the ethnographer needs more than a capacity for careful, observation: he (or she) must have a theoretical framework and, besides, the imagination to capture the people's vision of life. He (or she) has to make explicit what may be implicit or only dimly perceived by them.

Geertz puts it well when he describes the quest of the anthropologist in a double pun:

> On the literal level, it [the phrase 'after the fact'] means looking for facts ... on the first turning it means ex-post interpretation, the main way (perhaps the only way) one can come to terms with the sorts of lived-forward, understood backward phenomena

anthropologists are condemned to deal with [remember Kierkegaard]. On the second (and even more problematical) turning, it means the post-positivist critique of empirical realism, the move away from simple correspondence theories of truth and knowledge which makes the very term 'fact' a delicate matter. (Geertz 1995: 167f.)

In brief, ethnographic narratives are not merely descriptive, mirror images of social reality: they are interpretive and, thus, constructs of the mind.

SRINIVAS'S ETHNOGRAPHY: A BRIEF OUTLINE

In his first published book (Srinivas 1942), Srinivas wrote about family and marriage among clean caste Hindus (Brahmans and others) of what was then the princely state of Mysore. Data for it had been collected in 1937–38 from published sources, including government reports and works of fiction, and during a brief period of fieldwork in a village. The character of Hindu society being what traditionally it has been, he devoted quite some attention to the family as a site for the performance of rituals: puberty rites, marriage rites, birth of children and their naming rites, and celebratory and periodical rites, including fasts and festivals (see Chapter Two).

In continuation of this focus on the interweaving of kinship, marriage, and religion, Srinivas presented a theoretically grounded discussion of religion and society among the Coorgs, fieldwork for which had been conducted in 1940 and, perhaps, in 1941. The first product of this had been a very long (two-volume), descriptive Ph.D. dissertation at the University of Bombay. The same material was reworked at Oxford for another doctoral degree and later published as a monograph (Srinivas 1952), which is widely considered a classic. Besides what he called ritual complexes ('wholes made up of several individual ritual acts'), he also entered the domain of beliefs, notably those of ritual purity and pollution. Taking a Radcliffe-Brownian view, he examined the functional role of ritual in the maintenance of social solidarity (see 'Foreword' by Radcliffe-Brown in Srinivas 1952: vi).

Coming to Srinivas's third monographic study, it is devoted to a comprehensive description of a multicaste Karnataka village, which he called Rampura, first in a number of masterly articles and then in the book *The Remembered Village* (1976). The circumstances in which this book was written, and which gave it its title, are well-known among anthropologists and Indianists generally. To recall very briefly, Srinivas lost the processed version of his fieldnotes, painstakingly accumulated over nearly twenty years, when his study at the Center for Advanced Study in the Behavioral Sciences at Stanford was destroyed by arsonists. His sense of shock and irreparable loss was, understandably, immense. Among those who helped him to see a road ahead, which he took, was the well-known anthropologist Sol Tax. Srinivas has provided a gist of their conversation two days after the arson. Tax told him that:

> While the loss of my processed data was indeed a disaster, I should not forget that my colleagues valued my study not only because of the new material it provided on Indian rural life but because it was I who had done the fieldwork. *My mind, and my entire personality, had been involved in that experience, and what did I remember of it? I should try to do a book on Rampura based solely on memory. Indeed, I should forget that I had made any field notes.* (Srinivas 1976: xii, emphasis added)

The original fieldnotes were actually safe and still available, but Srinivas decided to refer to them only very sparingly. This was indeed a challenge to exercise not only the capacity to remember and recall, but also to one's imagination. It may be noted here that the first of the two epigraphs of the book, obviously chosen with great care, reads: '[The anthropologist has] to be also a novelist able to evoke the life of a society.' The author of this insightful observation is Marcel Mauss. As for the thematic foci of the book, these include the economy (which had received no attention in the two earlier monographs), the family and the household, intercaste relations, class and factions, and, of course (although rather surprisingly briefly), religion.

The special character of the book as a work of ethnography based on intensive fieldwork, which is also a work of imagination, since it is primarily though not exclusively based on memory, has been widely discussed. This is not the place to go into the details of that discussion. Suffice it to recall that some commentators have stressed the solid factual core of the book. Thus, Mayer (1978) has asked if Srinivas could really be said to have written from memory, as he had already published many important articles on the basis of his fieldnotes which he still possessed. Others have wondered if Srinivas had, as Nakane (1978) put it, 'maximized' his memory, leading to a picture of rural life which was more like a painting than a photograph, a work of imagination.

In my introduction to a review symposium (Madan 1978), I wrote about the likely appeal of *The Remembered Village* among the general reading public. These readers would, I observed, find telling similarities between Srinivas's book and such widely admired novels of rural life in Karnataka as Raja Rao's *Kanthapura* (1938) and U.R. Ananthamurthy's *Samskara* (1976). I then suggested that *The Remembered Village*, perhaps, belongs more with the novels of Srinivas's famous friend, R.K. Narayan. It has, for instance, the same emphasis on characterization and the evocation of the scenic in everyday life, and the same delectable sense of humour as in Narayan's well-loved novels and stories about life in the imagined town of Malgudi. It was this comment that Nandy picked up to pose the question on the different orders of empiricism quoted at the beginning of the present chapter.

Articles based on fieldwork in Rampura were mentioned earlier in the chapter. Srinivas published a large number of them during his long innings as an author. In the last year of his life, 1999 (he of course did not know that it would be the last), he selected forty essays for publication as a single volume. His classification of the contents of the book into eight parts is a noteworthy reiteration of his interests. The headings are: village studies, caste and social structure, gender, religion, cultural and social change, sociology and social anthropology, method, and autobiographical essays (Srinivas 2002a). The chosen essays are thematically focused, methodologically simple but rigorous, and felicitously written. Articles such as the ones on Sanskritization, dominant caste, and the social system of a Karnataka village, were milestones not only in his career as a social anthropologist, but also in the sociology of India.

What Srinivas wrote *about* in his monographs and the articles found highly condensed and imaginative expression in two short stories, and I turn to these now.

THE STORIES

As already noted, Srinivas published only two short stories. When I read the second of these stories, I asked him if there were more; he referred me to an earlier one, which, he said, was virtually lost in a defunct magazine. I actually got to read this one too when it reappeared in 1997. Originally, it had been published in 1941 in the inaugural number of *Indian Thought*, announced as a quarterly journal, which did not, however, complete even the first year, owing to, perhaps, the difficult wartime conditions. R.K. Narayan, the novelist, was the editor. Srinivas (he was twenty-five then) contributed a short story and an account of a bus ride from Mysore to Mercara in Coorg: he was exploring the possibilities of fieldwork there (Srinivas 1997).[3]

The story, 'The Legend on the Wall' is about an evening in Kirnelli, 'a small, sleepy village on the banks of the Hemavati.' The unidentified narrator is standing at the *ghat*, in front of an old, decaying temple which is guarded, as it were, by a huge sacred *peepul* tree. The setting sun

> ... stood poised over the Hemavati like a flaming disc.... Glow worms twinkled like gems in the hedge on the other bank. The world ... waited in a hushed silence to receive the goddess of night. And in harmony with the hour the temple bell rang.

The narrator is in a thoughtful mood and goes down the steps to sit on one of them, 'just as the evening sky gives itself up to any colour that chooses to splash itself on it'. He had seen, every time he visited the village, something written on the temple wall to the right of the entrance door, which was no longer legible and partly covered by lichen.

Soon his thoughts are interrupted by the temple priest, who has come out of the temple and, standing by his side, grumbles that the

---

[3] 'The Road to Mercara' is about as long as 'The Legend on the Wall', and reads like a story with its humourous tidbits about fellow passengers, including a thieving boy and a Mercara Rajput bragging about his hunting prowess. Srinivas mentions the anticipated fear of loneliness during fieldwork and his nostalgia (already!) for 'the crowded and brilliant life that flows through the veins of Bombay. I hungered for it. Solitude and loneliness are attractive to those who don't know either, I told myself'.

temple cobra has failed to make its appearance to accept the weekly ritual offering of milk. Wishing to get rid of the intruder, the narrator says caustically that the snake may have died, for they do die. The priest dismisses the narrator's blasphemous thought, telling him that the *nag* had first appeared 'one night thousands of years ago, at the bidding of Iswara', and has ever since made its weekly appearance except whenever a Holeya untouchable pollutes the holy precincts of the temple by being around.

The priest then unfolds the story. In those ancient times, the area was a kingdom and Holeyas were village watchmen whose duties included the sounding of warning in the event of any external, aggressive intruders. One day, when the noon-time sun was at its blazing worst, Kencha, the chief watchman, espied what looked like the advance team of an army. Tired after a night-long vigil though he was, the dutiful Kencha took off and ran as fast as he could to convey the bad news to the authorities concerned. By the time he reached Kirnelli, he was almost dropping dead with fatigue and thirst. As he approached the Brahman well, he knew only too well that no Holeya may ever dare to pollute it by drawing water from it: that was the time-honoured custom. And yet, deeply tormented by thirst, he broke the taboo: he picked up a small vessel left at the well by a Brahmin woman and drank off the water in it. He had called her, hoping she would mercifully agree to pour some water for him, into his cupped palms perhaps, but she had not heard him. And now, as he was quenching his thirst, she came out and, seeing him drinking from her pot, shrieked. Alerted, the men in the house came out too, only to be outraged by what she told them about the act of desecration.

Kencha was again running, with the angry Brahmans in hot pursuit; one of them even hurled a brick at him. He realized that, if he ran fast enough, he could hide in the temple precincts where he would be safe. He managed to enter, but 'fell prostrate before the inner door'. Kencha had now defiled the temple too, but, traditionally, a temple was a sanctuary, and no one could be abused there, not even a Holeya. As soon as one of the chasing Brahmans reached the outer wall, he heard a groan, and he leaped in over the wall. 'He was just in time to see the tail of the temple *nag*, disappearing into a hole in the wall. The divine *nag* had punished Kencha.' But the dying Kencha did manage to say that he had seen a horde of invaders, and begged the news be conveyed to the village chief. He did his allotted duty.

And ever since, the priest tells the visitor, our narrator, the *nag* refuses the weekly milk offering if a Holeya happens to come around. 'The *nag* is sure to kill the sinful Holeya who dared to come near the temple even though he may climb and hide himself in the tallest tower on the earth.' He concludes with a question: 'Did you see a Holeya?'

The visitor is greatly angered, but knows that the priest is a prisoner of an unchanging, narrow, hateful tradition. He then confides in the reader:

> As I walked I wondered how the Brahman would feel if he learnt the fact that he had been all along talking to a Holeya or rather a Holeya in khaki, a Bachelor of Arts, and the Assistant Superintendent of Police in Kundur State. The strength of his belief would only increase, because the *nag* chose to keep away. He would dip many times in the icy cold Hemavati to wash away the contamination of sitting by the side of a *Holeya*.

❖

The second short story, titled 'The Image Maker', was published in *The Illustrated Weekly of India* in 1988. The narrator is a pious temple priest, Thimma, of the village of Kodagahalli in Karnataka, and the events he describes are of the 1940s and later. The author of the story who recounts Thimma's tale is, as Thimma describes him, a 'book-learned man' who has travelled all over the world. He is, one may surmise, Srinivas, and the story may well have been constructed around actual events. We have no such clue to the origin of the first story.

Like the earlier story, this one too invokes the spirit of the evening, when there still were 'a few minutes of twilight before total darkness descended on the village'. It is a common, pan-Indian, Brahmanical belief that the moments that are neither of the day nor of the night—*sandhyākālah* in Sanskrit—are, obviously, outside normal time, they are liminal. They are portentous and, perhaps, an appropriate time for revealing old secrets, as they are for prayers. The listener of Thimma's narrative is startled to hear from the 'deeply religious' priest of the Ganapati temple—Ganapati is, of course, the remover of obstacles and promoter of success in work—that 'there was a time ... long ago' when he did not 'believe in God'. And he proceeds to tell a story, rather like the temple priest of the first story.

Thimma had grown up in Kodagahalli, a potter's only son and not a very skilled apprentice. The father was the only artisan of his caste there, and made 'pots, pans, lamps and tiles for the villagers, and each family gave him in return some paddy and straw during the big harvest' in the winter. This arrangement of intercaste relations, found virtually all over India, has been well-documented by many ethnographers including Srinivas, under the general name of the *jajmani* system. The potter's wife, 'a byword for hard work and cheerfulness', was a loving mother to Thimma. Unfortunately, she died suddenly during a cholera epidemic when he was only twelve, leaving both father and son desolate. Thimma had prayed hard for her recovery to the local Madeshwara, and even to the distant 'powerful deity at Tirupati', but to no avail. It was then that he had lost his faith in god. 'Why did he allow my mother to die? Why didn't he save her?'

The potter's work suffered as, in the midst of his bereavement, he had also to attend to household chores, since Thimma was no good at them. Forced by circumstances, he remarried, taking a young widow from another village as his wife. Stepmother and stepson 'disliked each other from the beginning'. She made him work hard and did not give him enough to eat. Soon, she succeeded in convincing her husband that Thimma was a worthless drone, spoiled by his mother. These family quarrels often ended in Thimma getting beaten, sometimes mercilessly. The thrashing with a rope was so severe one night that it raised welts on his body. Thimma ran away from home very early next morning before anyone else was awake, and walked all the way to the nearby city of Mysore.

As good luck would have it, the covered verandah of the house in which Thimma took shelter, was that of a childless Brahman couple; the husband was a maker of sacred images. Finding him frightened and famished, and hearing his tale of woe, they took pity on him. They offered him food, shelter, and a small monthly stipend in return for domestic help. The specialist artisan showed him his collection of multicoloured images of gods and goddesses which he had made for sale in the market. Whatever he had learnt of the craft in his own home now came handy to Thimma. Soon bonds of affection flowered between the three of them.

Thimma could now occasionally risk expressing opinions on serious matters, such as those of faith. One day he asked the *puja*-performing old man 'how he could regard anything he made with his own hands' as god. The image maker quietly told him: 'You are right and wrong. Yes, human hands make images, but who made human beings?' And the images, particularly those of the auspicious Ganapati, continued to be made by them, and they sold well. Thimma recalls:

> I took great delight in making Ganapatis. Men were such fools. The idea of a deity with a human being's body crowned with an elephant's head, riding a field rat, with a cobra tied round his potbelly to prevent the food from bursting, amused me. Could folly do worse than call this God and worship it?

And then came the twist of fate. Sent for shopping to a market, Thimma was recognized there by an old neighbour from Kodagahalli, although he had been away seven years. He learnt that his stepmother had eloped with a trader, 'and this had been a blow to his [father's] manhood'. Humiliated and lonely, he had begun to pine for his son. His health had broken down, and he had died recently. Hearing all this, Thimma was stricken by grief and guilt. Then there was the house and the piece of paddy land to claim. His foster parents appreciated his dilemma and agreed to his going back to the village. They assured him, however, that he would always be welcome to come back to them; after all he had been a son to them.

Kodagahalli welcomed the prodigal son. Thimma resumed the ancestral work of a potter, but he also made small Ganapati images. He made them beautiful and they sold fast at the weekly village market. He prospered, and his fame as a competent image maker spread to other villages. One day, the headman of the village of Hundi arrived in Kodagahalli to order an eight-foot tall Ganapati image. The 'louts' of another village had made fun of the people of Hundi at the last annual Ganapati festival because their Ganapati image, brought to the sacred Kaveri for immersion, was smaller than the four-foot Ganapati of the taunters! Thimma refused, protesting that he knew nothing about the making of such large images. Not willing to be easily spurned, the visiting headman sought the help of the local counterpart. The latter brought into his efforts of persuasion such considerations as village pride and intervillage solidarity. He promised all help to Thimma, including relief from his routine obligations as village potter.

Reluctantly, Thimma and his assistant set to work, experimenting with materials, including a bamboo framework for the image, specially ordered from the caste of basket makers, and the finest clays for the body. His headman kept an anxious eye on the progress of his work from a shapeless mass of materials to the completed image, just in time for the festival. 'It is a wonderful piece of work, Thimma, your best. I like it so much that I want to keep it in our own village but it has to go to Hundi.' The Hundi headman also came to see the image for himself, and seeing it, exclaimed: 'It is beautiful. It appears as though the deity himself has inspired you. We will give you 500 rupees for it.'

News of the marvellous image spread fast, and droves of villagers came with appropriate offerings of fruits and flowers to look at it. The next day the image would be taken to Hundi in a truck; it was too big for a bullock cart. At night, when 'the sky beyond was clear, with a crescent moon and stars' and 'the air heavy with the smell of flowers, incense and camphor', the tired Thimma felt 'pleased' with his handiwork, 'but the thought that Ganapati would go out of the village ... disturbed [him] vaguely'. Had dedicated and intense work of many days produced a deep attachment? Or, perhaps, unknown to himself, had work come close to becoming worship?

He and his assistant decided to have a final, lingering look at the image, lanterns in their hands. Somehow, Ganapati was stern, rather than smiling as Thimma had intended to make him. Where and why had he gone wrong, he wondered? As he was thinking about all this, he 'suddenly felt the image wink at [him] with the left eye'. Taken aback, he wondered if he was losing his mind. Taking a closer look, he 'thought that the left corner of the eyelid had come down a bit, concealing that part of the eye'. But, then, 'How could a lifeless image wink?' A miracle had happened before his own eyes—opened them, as it were! He decided that he would not let the image be taken away.

The next morning, Thimma lied to everybody concerned that Ganapati had appeared to him in a dream overnight, and told him that he wished to stay in Kodagahalli. The headman, who himself had secretly wished to retain the image in the village, agreed that Ganapati's wishes must be obeyed. He pleaded with the headman of Hundi to allow the image to stay where it was, and promised him that the people of Hundi would always have 'the right of making the first offerings' at the annual festival.

Everything settled satisfactorily, the Kodagahalli headman confided in Thimma: 'I didn't want to raise this point when the Hundi headman was here, but the image's left eye seems to be partially closed. It was not like that yesterday—both eyes were fully open.' Struck as if by a 'thunderbolt', Thimma decided there and then to devote the rest of his life 'to the service of Ganapati'. He donated all his property; the headman raised the necessary resources, and a temple came up for Ganapati to stay in. Thimma became the God's priest; his loss of faith had been a temporary aberration. But Thimma wondered why Ganapati had mischievously chosen to wink at him, make fun of him, rather than employ some more solemn gesture to cure him of his 'sinfulness'. When the listener of his narrative commented that it was not given to 'mere men to know the ways of God', Thimma 'nodded assent'.

CONCLUDING REFLECTIONS

What is the significance of the two stories for our appreciation of Srinivas's ethnographic studies? And what do they tell us about his personality? The larger issue of the relationship of ethnography and literature provides the setting for this chapter, but it is not its main focus.

Both stories evoke traditional south Indian Brahmanical culture with its rituals and devotions, its notions of purity and pollution, auspiciousness and inauspiciousness, its sacred spaces, such as temples, wells, and river *ghat*s, and sacred objects like trees and man-made images, its metaphysical notions of fate and grace, and its affirmation of the place of miracles in everyday life. Both stories construct for us village society in terms of caste, based on the foundational opposition between the Brahman and the Untouchable and including the presence of intermediate castes, such as the artisans and craftsmen. They look inwards within a caste or subcaste (*jāti*) at intrafamily relations. And they look outwards at village honour and solidarity, intervillage cooperation and rivalries, and the never-too-distant city.

Alongside the evocation of tradition, the story about the Brahman and the Holeya highlights upward mobility among the depressed castes, facilitated by modern education and non-traditional forms of governance, including formally trained and recruited police personnel in place of traditional hereditary watchmen. It replaces fate (*karma*) by human agency. In short, the themes that I identified earlier in this chapter as central to Srinivas's ethnographic corpus are present in the stories in condensed but clearly articulated terms—not all the themes, of course, but certainly most of the major ones.

Is that all? Are the stories merely summaries of the ethnographic works? I do not think so. The first observation I have in this regard is that they frame the formal writings and, in fact, the first story even anticipates them. It appeared in 1941, a year before the Mysore book, at the very beginning of Srinivas's career as a social anthropologist. It is remarkable how well it foretells Srinivas's abiding interest in caste and social mobility, in addition to rituals and the family, which were the focus of the Mysore book. For forty-odd years, he studied these aspects of the Hindu society. In course of time, the impact of urbanization on rural India also entered into this work, as it does into the second story. The latter, published forty-seven years later, is a reminder, as it were, that everything of significance about village life has been said in the two stories.

Something more must be taken note of: the stories have moral concerns that I do not find in the ethnography, and an aesthetic quality that shines in some parts of *The Remembered Village*, but is not present in the Coorg and Mysore monographs. When the sun sets on the village of Kirnelli, where the first story is located, it also sets on decadent aspects of Brahmanical culture. The arrival of the Holeya in khaki is a moral statement by Srinivas no less than by the rebel narrator. The sun is bound to rise again, but it never does so every day in exactly the same place along the horizon.

All is not dross, however, in traditional culture. There is a charm in its enchanted character, and in the miracles that bring happiness to the believers. Am I imagining too much when I see in the venomous cobra and its appearances and disappearances a symbol of the dark side of Brahmanical culture—'dark' because it valorizes a set of values that denies the equal moral worth of all human beings—and in the auspicious (traditionally so considered) Ganapati its sunny side? It is relevant in this regard to remember that Srinivas himself was a believing Brahman. Indeed, in an article published in a major, English language newspaper, he affirmed that the principle of 'the fraternity of all human beings', irrespective of racial, ethnic, religious, caste, and class identities, was 'logically' derived from 'the idea of God as creator', rather than from the 'philosophy' of 'secular humanism' (Srinivas 1993). The article was considered a scandal by many of his rationalist friends and professional colleagues, but he stood his ground.

In this connection, I would particularly like to draw attention to the character and significance of the narrative voices in the two stories. In 'The Legend on the Wall', these are of the two arch antagonists of the traditional Hindu world, the Brahman and the 'Untouchable', representing the complementary binary opposition of the principles of ritual purity and pollution. This is one of the two axes along which social life is structured, the other is power. As already stated, the author, Srinivas, stands behind the Holeya, it seems to me, for human dignity and social equality; or, in other words, for achieved rather than ascribed status. We are presented here with a glimpse of a secularizing world.

In 'The Image Maker' also there are two antagonistic narrative voices, but they belong to the same person at two different, critical moments in his life. He recalls his *loss of received faith* through the application of reason to a personal experience, namely, unanswered prayers. He then recalls the moment of his *recovery of faith* through the personal experience of a miracle, which he considers *real* in the deepest possible sense and truly transformative. Reason had lost to faith. The author also stands for faith by acknowledging the inscrutability of divine interventions in human affairs. Srinivas affirms that there is more in this world than meets the secularist eye. This does not mean, however, that he abandoned the secularist position of the first story; rather he drew attention to the inherent limitations of secularism as a worldview, to the inborn frailties of the demon of cold reason.

The stories are significant, I suggest, and not incidental items in Srinivas's bibliography. They reveal a subtle aesthetic sensibility and an acute moral imagination. Through the medium of fiction, Srinivas said things that he did not through his ethnography, perhaps, because, he thought he should not do so, wary of the alleged snare of value judgements, aware of modernity's rejection of the miraculous, and devoted to the idea of ethnography as objective description of observed reality. It is amusing to recall here that Radcliffe-Brown, his Oxford mentor, had advised him not to waste his 'scientific talents' on such intellectual pursuits as the interpretation of 'culture patterns' in the manner of Ruth Benedict (Srinivas 2002b: 672) to which he had felt drawn! The two short stories are, I believe, testimony to

Srinivas's literary abilities, which remained mute, however, most of his life.

Let me suggest, then, that the stories are, implicitly, a critique of ethnography's naive realism, where it exists (as, for instance, in Radcliff-Brown's notion of 'social structure', which informed Srinivas's 1952 study of Coorgi rituals), its pretensions of comprehensiveness, which are common, and its stance of value neutrality, which often is superficial. This does not, of course, imply that works of fiction are superior to ethnographic accounts; I am only suggesting that the two genres, while significantly different, have more to tell each other than one might think at first blush. The boundaries between them will survive, but to make a rigid division between the two (as the imagined versus the real) is surely to deny the ethnographer the benefit of a source of insights that good literature surely is. Indeed, the division diminishes both genres.

Besides, did the stories reveal Srinivas's humane personality and his evolving moral sensibility more fully (if not 'totally' as V.S. Naipaul suggests fiction does) than his ethnography? Do the stories have an authenticity that is more significant than the truthfulness that most ethnographers aspire to? Are real worlds illumined by imagined worlds in ways that they never can be self-illumined? And is this, then, what Ashis Nandy meant when he wrote of creative writing, such as Srinivas's *The Remembered Village*, attaining 'paradoxically a higher order of empiricism' (see p. 175)? The answer to these questions is, I think, best given in the affirmative. And, maybe, instead of providing an answer to Nandy's question, we should ask him a counter-question: Is he really suggesting the possibility of 'transempirical' understanding?[4]

---

[4] I do not wish to engage here with the postmodernist idea that traditional ethnographic narratives are inevitably partial, since every ethnographer has a viewpoint, and also tends to arrogate authority to her or his work. They are in that sense 'half-truths' and 'fictions'. As Clifford puts it: 'Even the best ethnographic texts—serious, true fictions—are systems, or economies, of truth' (1986: 7). This does not mean, however, that 'ethnography is "only literature"' (Clifford 1986: 26). The value of this insight, and others like it, has been diminished by overkill. But that is another story.

Chapter Nine

Louis Dumont:
The Man and His Work

The principle is simply that all human institutions are meaningful.... To discover their meaning is only a matter of toil and unblinkered attention.
—LOUIS DUMONT, in T.N. Madan (ed.), *Way of Life*

The death of Louis Dumont in November 1988 removed from the world of twentieth-century anthropology one of its towering figures, one who dared to enlarge the scope of the subject beyond the confines of localized fieldwork among 'other peoples'—preliterate tribes and peasants—to include the comparison of civilizations in which 'we ourselves' are involved. His own focus was on India and the West. His exemplary studies were based on methodologies that he devised for the study of particular societies and for intercivilizational comparison, and these are of universal applicability.

Grandson of a painter and son of an engineer, Dumont combined in his way of looking at the world the qualities of both vocations, namely, creative imagination and an abiding interest in the concrete. The first principles underlying his scholarly endeavour were the acknowledgement of the meaningfulness of social institutions (besides their functional utility) and the indispensability of holism (in the sense that 'parts' find their meaning in relation to the 'whole', which is to be considered higher than or superior to any of its elements) in their interpretation. As for comparison, he believed, together with other structuralists, that the deeper the differences between two cultures, or to put it in other words, the more distant the view

(Lévi-Strauss's [1983] *Le regard eloigne*), the greater the likelihood that comparing them will yield significant understandings of both.

Dumont's approach to the study of Indian society, first articulated in the 1950s, marked a significant departure from the prevailing preoccupation with the study of behavioural patterns and their explanation in the functionalist mode. He was interested in the ideas of people no less than in their material culture and social institutions. Moreover, he underscored the importance of ideologies, which he defined as the fundamental ideas and values held in common by a group of people—at the highest level, by a society. But, he maintained, ideology does not tell us everything about a society that is significant: it must, therefore, be confronted with social action. His approach encountered more criticism, perhaps, than unqualified acceptance; but virtually every serious scholar who contributed to the sociology of India in the second half of the twentieth century, including Dumont's severest critics, acknowledged the seminal and abiding importance of his work (see Madan 1982a and Khare [2006] 2009). While Indianists have in recent years moved away significantly from Dumont's intellectual concerns and methods, his work on Western society has received greater and more appreciative attention than before (see, for example, Celtel 2005; Parkin 2003).

❖

Dumont began his academic career in the mid-1930s under the guidance of Marcel Mauss, leading sociologist and Sanskritist. World War II interrupted his studies, but not entirely. He enlisted in the war, was taken prisoner of war, and was detained in a factory on the outskirts of Hamburg. There he studied German. Before long he began to teach himself Sanskrit, and this effort lasted a whole year. He then had a chance meeting with Professor Schubring, a specialist on Jain studies, thanks to the connivance of a sentry, and received formal instruction in the language. Back home in 1945, at the end of the war, he returned to the Musée des Arts et Traditions Populaires (ATP), where he had worked earlier in a non-academic position. Here he was engaged in a research project on French furniture and undertook the study of a folk festival, the Tarascon, about which he later wrote a monograph, *La Tarasque: Essai de description d'un fait local d'un point de vue ethnographique* (1951). Already, in this study,

Dumont's eye for ethnographic detail and his holistic approach (the local Tarascon was studied in relation to Mediterranean Christianity) are in evidence. Around this time he also carried forward his interest in India, generated by Mauss's teaching, and took lessons in Hindi and Tamil at the École des Langues Orientales, and studied the available ethnography of south India. Among his patrons were the comparativist Georges Dumézil and the Indologist Louis Renou.

Dumont spent the years 1949 and 1950 in Tamil Nadu studying the Pramalai Kallar who stand somewhere in the middle of the ranking order in the regional caste system. It is interesting to note that he chose to focus on south India because, he believed, it was the encounter of the Aryan-speaking people from the north with the southern Dravidians that had been responsible for the genesis of post-Vedic Hinduism and the sociocultural configuration of classical India. In the later years, he considered these ideas 'primitive' and excessively 'culturological', and blamed the scholarly climate of the times for his interest in them. Moreover, studies of Dravidian culture were relatively less common, and it seemed a good idea to choose a non-Brahman caste as the point of entry into this underexplored domain.

Based on intensive fieldwork and methodical study of literary sources, two important monographs, *Hierarchy and Marriage Alliance in South India* and *Une Sous-caste de l'Inde du sud: Organisation sociale et religion des Pramalai Kallar*, were published in 1957 (see Dumont 1957a, 1957b). The first is one of the richest ethnographic accounts of India ever published. Regrettably, an English version took long to prepare because of the length of the work and Dumont's insistence on the absolute accuracy of translation. It was finally published in 1986, thirty years after the original French edition. (I will write more about this below.)

Hierarchy and Marriage Alliance was written in English and is dedicated to Claude Lévi-Strauss. Dumont had read in manuscript the chapters on India of *Les structures eléméntaries de la parenté* (Lévi-Strauss 1949), and maintained that his familiarity with Lévi-Strauss's analysis of prescriptive/preferential forms of marriage provided him with just the right approach to the interpretation of the data he collected. He was, thus, able to show how the socalled cross-cousin marriage is not episodic in character, but actually generates an enduring bond, or 'alliance', between two patrilineages. This means in effect that a man of a particular lineage 'X' shall marry his mother's brother's daughter from lineage 'Y', just as his father had done before him and his son would do after him. Dumont once told me that Lévi-Strauss's reaction to the pre-publication version of this monograph, though positive, was restrained; but E.E. Evans-Pritchard, who confessed his inability to fully follow the argument, had been most encouraging. Dumont had known Lévi-Strauss since the mid-1930s (when he had assisted the latter with the processing of his South American fieldwork notes), but apparently they never came very close to each other. Ironically, Lévi-Strauss publicly regretted in a published interview (in the early 1990s, if I remember right) the distance between them when both had most of their work behind them.

Dumont returned home from India in 1951, and was back at ATP and his furniture studies. A year later he succeeded M.N. Srinivas as lecturer in Indian sociology at Oxford University. There, he developed a close relationship with Evans-Pritchard and came to appreciate the importance of the perspective from outside the society under study, so that writing a social anthropological account meant 'translating' the culture studied into the language of one's own culture, employing the sociological idiom for the purpose. One is reminded of Lévi-Strauss's felicitous characterization of anthropology as 'a conversation of man with man' (1967: 20). The five years at Oxford, he told me many years later, had completed his education and gifted him a 'stereoscopic vision'. They certainly were of critical importance in the formulation of Dumont's methodology for the study of the Indian civilization. And it was mostly at Oxford that *Une sous-caste* and *Hierarchy and Marriage Alliance* were written.

In 1955, Dumont returned to Paris to take up a research professorship at the École Pratique des Hautes Études (renamed as École des Hautes Études en Sciences Sociales in 1975). In the inaugural lecture he gave there, he declared that the sociology of India must lie at the 'confluence of Sociology and Indology' (Dumont and Pocock 1957: 7). The method was dialectical in the sense that although Indology may provide points of departure, the principles derived from it were to be confronted with what the people actually did (their observable meaningful behaviour). He himself characterized it as a combination of the views from 'within' and 'without', yielding understanding at a higher level. An English version of this programmatic text was published jointly with David Pocock in 1957 in the first number of *Contributions to Indian Sociology*, of which they were the founding editors. During the following ten years, Dumont published in this periodical a number of searching studies on a broad range of themes including the village community, caste, marriage, kingship, renunciation, and nationalism. The refinement of conceptual and methodological issues in these essays attracted wide attention among Indianists, and generated vigorous debates (see Chapter Ten and Khare [2006] 2009).

It was an affirmation of his (and Pocock's) openness to debate that some of the critical responses (notably F.G. Bailey's) were published in the pages of *Contributions* itself. Pocock opted out of editorial responsibility in 1964, but Dumont kept the journal going for another three years before closing publication in 1966. His essays in *Contributions* were experimental and a preparation for something larger and of greater importance: a general work on society in India. This work was anticipated in three lectures which Dumont delivered in 1962 at the Centre for Culture and Civilization at the Venetian Institute of the Orient, dealing with the themes of society, religion, thought, history, and contemporary change. They were published in 1964 in Paris under the title of *La civilization indienne et nous: Esquisse de sociologie comparée*. (An Italian version came out a year later; the small book was, however, never translated into English.) But I am getting ahead of the narrative: we must stay a little while longer with the 1950s.

Dumont spent fifteen months in 1957–58 in a village of eastern Uttar Pradesh (Gorakhpur district). Although the duration of fieldwork was not much shorter than in Tamil Nadu, north India did not capture him as the south had. He had found the landscape flat and dusty, he once complained to me, the climate trying, the cultural area complex ('too many castes in the village!'), and the people rather uninteresting, quite unlike the sharp and intelligent Tamils ('geniuses'). He told me in 1982 that he had already forgotten the dialect spoken in the village, but that he would remember Tamil until the last day of his life. The fieldwork, however, contributed to his interest in inter-regional comparison and he published searching analyses of marriage and kinship terminology (Dumont 1983a), and of the Brahmanical notion of ritual 'debt' within the category of *sapinda* or lineal ancestors (Dumont 1980b). He pointed out that in both the north and the south, a major consideration in the making of marriage, whether between strangers as in the north, or kin/affines as in the south, was the protection or, if possible, enhancement of social status and family prestige. The principle of hierarchy was, he asserted, pan-Indian: it gave expression to a civilizational unity.

The presence of castes everywhere, he said in 1955 (Dumont and Pocock 1957), was a token of the cultural unity and distinctiveness of India. From 1951, Dumont lectured and wrote about caste. The ripe fruit of this pedagogic-cum-research endeavour was his magnum opus, *Homo Hierarchicus* (in French originally [1966a] and in English in 1970 [1970a]), which was for several decades the most widely discussed work on the subject—a recognized major classic translated into many languages, but, ironically, not as yet into any Indian language. He argued that the sociological interpretation of caste, which must be taken seriously as a civilizational scheme or mode, and not treated as a product of 'degeneracy', should begin with carefully chosen first principles that Indians themselves have evolved; the imposition of conceptual categories drawn from Western (or any other) civilization must be avoided. Dumont focused on the notion of ritual purity derived from both the textual tradition and ethnography. He maintained that various crucial aspects of the caste system—marriage rules, food regimes, hereditary occupational roles, and so on—can be derived from 'the necessary and hierarchical coexistence' of purity and its opposite, impurity.

By his interpretation, caste was different from other forms of social stratification because of the 'disjunction' of ritual status and secular (politico-economic) power within the same social system. The latter, though opposed in principle to the former is contained in or encompassed by it. He called this 'encompassing–encompassed' relationship of the whole and the part 'hierarchy', and distinguished the latter from simple ranking or inequality. The task, according to Dumont, was to 'typify' caste in terms of civilizational specificities, and learn from it: not to classify it and reduce it to a mere type within a familiar social taxonomy. 'India of caste,' he wrote, 'teaches' people in the West 'hierarchy, and this is no little lesson' (1970b: 164).

Hierarchy is not so much an attribute of social organization in India as it is a method of dealing with intergroup relations (including difference) in a manner that resolves conflict through inclusion rather than confrontation or exclusion—through a grammar of values rather than the exercise of power ('domination resting only on itself'). From this perspective even the so-called 'fifth category', the *panchama*, is part of the social system and not outside or excluded from it. When power is elevated to the status of value, Dumont warned, we end up with totalitarianism. Moreover, the theory of hierarchy admits the possibility of reversal when we move from the level of principles (structural homogeneity) to that of practice (ethnographic diversity). Hence the importance of mutual interrogation between the two levels. Status would like to deny power, but it exists as an aspect of intergroup relations. Power 'pretends' to be the equal of status in Indian society, but is so only (as Dumont puts it) in a 'shamefaced' manner.

The subordination of the political and economic criteria of social stratification to that of ritual status in Dumont's model, however, plays down the significance of social change in colonial and contemporary times. Did not caste lose its political significance as late as in the eighteenth and nineteenth centuries? As for what has been happening in the twentieth century, although Dumont explicitly recognized the emergence of intercaste competitiveness in the politico-economic domain ('juxtaposition of substances') in place of a structure of interdependence (organic solidarity) as a departure from tradition, he regarded this as behavioural change, rather than a radical transformation of the system as a whole at the level of values or principles. Moreover, empirical change without an ideological backup could only be precarious. In fact, Dumont maintained that caste as a system of relations of a particular kind exists or does not exist; it does not change.

For his critics the foregoing view of holism was overly intellectualist, even Platonic, and certainly one of the most problematic aspects of Dumont's methodology. For him, I presume, his analysis was an exercise in deductive logic (working out the implications of first principles): the question of revision, much less updating, did not therefore arise. *Homo Hierarchicus* was a complete, theoretical work that helped us understand the vast body of available ethnographic data on caste. Now, models are not true or false: they explain more or less, and must be judged in terms of the principle of parsimony (the fewer the explanatory variables, the better) and their explanatory power. The question then is not whether Dumont is right or wrong, but first, whether his argument is intelligible and internally consistent (in my understanding of it, it is both), and second, what it is that we have learnt from his studies of the Indian civilization. The latter question is still being debated.

❖

After the publication of *Homo Hierarchicus*, it was (in his own words) *homo aequalis*, representing Europe and the West generally that beckoned to him. It was India that helped him problematize the West. The individualism of the West and its sub-theme of egalitarianism are best understood, Dumont maintained, in the light of holism and hierarchy. Not only was the 'individualist configuration' of the West to be compared with the Indian configuration (not at too superficial a level of ethnographic description, but in terms of the underlying principles), particular expressions of individualism within the Western setting were also to be compared to deepen understanding. The intellectual tools shaped in the Indian forge were now to be applied to the understanding of another civilization.

The results of the studies of the ideological presuppositions of Western civilization or, more precisely, of the ideology of individualism, were published in the form of a book followed by a number of essays that were later collected in two volumes. All three works came out in English and French versions.

From Mandeville to Marx: The Genesis and Triumph of Economic Ideology (1977)—the French title was *Homo aequalis I: Genèse et épanouissement de l'idéologie économique* (1977)—argued that speaking the language of relations (which a structuralist must), the transition from tradition to modernity in Europe occurred when, among other changes, the primacy of the relationship of persons to one another (holism) was displaced by the primacy of the relationship of persons to things, conceived as property (individualism). This development ultimately freed economics from the constraints of both morality and politics—as evidenced in Locke's treatises on government, Mandeville's fable of the bees, and Adam Smith's theory of value. Restating the transformation in terms of the determinative character of material conditions of life (infrastructure) in the context of relations between persons, society, and consciousness (superstructure), Dumont analysed the development of Marx's thought to show how, eventually, economics came to supersede politics. Indeed, a similar hierarchical relationship was shown to be present in Locke's work also. Dumont called this 'the modern revolution in values', and maintained that it was the central problem in the comparison of societies.

The second book *Essays on Individualism: Modern Ideology in Anthropological Perspective* (1986b) continued the examination of the modern ideology. The centre of attention was not the individual as an empirically given sense-datum, for such individuals are present in all societies, but on the elevation of the individual to the status of value. Individualism was presented as the global ideology of modern society. The Brahmanical ideology of renunciation also valorizes the individual, but the renouncer is located by choice outside the world of caste and family ties, although not wholly detached from it: he looks back at it as a reformer. The modern ideology by contrast affirms the secular world and promotes voluntaristic action or praxis in relation to the latter from within it. The primacy of the economic category and individualism are mutually entailed. As in the first book, the focus is on ideas and values (the essay 'On Value', included in the volume, is one of the finest that Dumont ever wrote), not as fixed entities or substances, but as hierarchical configurations of relations.

While tracing the history of individualism in Europe from its Christian beginnings (individual outside the world) to its modern expressions (individual in the world), Dumont introduced a further refinement, namely, the presence of national variants of modern ideology. The third and last book in the series, *German Ideology: From France to Germany and Back* (1994), develops this theme. The focus is on the German variant. He explains that the beginnings of the divergence are traceable to the distinctiveness of the German version of the Enlightenment compared to the Western (French), for it was religious rather than secularist. The 'estrangement' was expressed through an extraordinary intellectual and artistic blossoming in Germany between 1770 and 1830, marked by the growth of community consciousness defined culturally.

An essential but apparently contradictory accompaniment of these developments was the ideal of 'self-cultivation' (*Bildung*). Thus, the combination of community holism and self-cultivating individualism was the 'idiosyncratic formula of German ideology'. One 'is a man through his being a German', but the Frenchman thinks of himself as 'a man by nature and a Frenchman by accident'. The

Enlightenment in its secular expression and the Revolution are the formative forces in France; Lutheran Pietism and the Reformation, in Germany. In its German version, individualism emerges as a cultural category par excellence, distanced from the socio-political domain which is crucial in France. But the political category is not wholly absent: the belief that the German state had a vocation to dominate the world takes care of that.

The situation is complex, and the German–French contrast has ontological and epistemological significances; indeed, its ethical dimension may not be denied. Underlying it is a question of immense philosophical import. This is how Dumont puts it:

> How, without contradiction, can we acknowledge the diversity of cultures and at the same time maintain the universal idea of truth-value? I think it can be done by resorting to a ... complex model ... where truth-value would figure as a 'regulative idea', in the Kantian sense. (Dumont 1994: 34)

Such an exercise is not, however, taken up in the book. Indeed, it ends with a rhetorical question:

> That these two countries, each bound to its idiosyncrasy, are impervious to that of their neighbour, should not cause surprise. But is it not somewhat pathetic to see each of them neutralize its own experience in order to salvage the ideological framework in terms of which the country has been wont to think of itself and the world over a great length of time? (Dumont 1994: 235)

❖

I first met Louis Dumont in 1954 (or was it 1955?) when he gave a lecture on marriage alliance in south India in the Department of Anthropology at the University of Lucknow, where I had just begun my teaching and research career. I had seen his early papers on the subject of his talk. The first of these (incidentally also his first publication on India) had been published in 1950 in *The Eastern Anthropologist*, which was edited by D.N. Majumdar at the Department (see Dumont 1950). Two other papers had appeared in *Man* in 1953 (Dumont 1953a, 1953b). I had found all three papers quite 'technical' and difficult to grasp. His lecture was helpful in making me understand a little better what he was doing. I was particularly interested as, at that time, I was considering the possibility of a study of marriage and kinship among the Pandit Brahmans of rural Kashmir. The question I asked during the discussion that followed Dumont's lecture perhaps made some sense (I do not remember what it was), for he not only responded to it verbally, but also gave me an off-print of his *Man* paper. As already stated, this was difficult to follow, given the prevailing state of thinking on marriage and kinship. As we know, Radcliffe-Brown was puzzled by it: he could not figure out how mother's brother and sister's son, in the setting of cross-cousin marriage, were to be regarded as primarily affines and marriage itself, as an enduring alliance among affines rather than marriage between blood relatives (see Dumont 1983a: 18–23). In the event, my fieldwork among the Pandits (1957–58) was not at all influenced by Dumont's ideas or approach. My teachers at the Lucknow and Australian National Universities were all thoroughgoing functionalists.

I saw the first issue of *Contributions* in Canberra in 1958, and was quite struck by Dumont's call for the cross-fertilization of Indology and sociology, particularly so because my ANU teachers had warned me against involvement with textual materials, which was described by one of them (Derek Freeman) as the 'besetting fault' of Indian anthropologists. It was only on my return to Lucknow in 1959 (after completing the writing of my doctoral dissertation) that I really sat down to carefully read Dumont's inaugural lecture and the other essays, including the one on kinship. I was greatly attracted to the new approach proposed, and became a watchful reader of *Contributions*.

Dumont's essay on renunciation in India's religions, which came out in 1960, with its key notion of the dialogue of the man-in-the-world and the renouncer, impressed me enormously: it made me realize clearly that what was missing in my account of Pandit family and kinship was any discussion of the ideology of the householder. I eventually wrote a paper on it, after more inquiries in the field, in 1976 (Madan 1981b). During 1962–63, I spent a year at the School of Oriental and African Studies in London, and became acquainted at first hand with F.G. Bailey's severe criticism of Dumont's approach. Although I had reservations of my own about the latter, I thought that it was Dumont rather than Bailey who had more to offer to Indianists.

In 1964, when I was teaching in the Department of Social Anthropology at Karnatak University in Dharwad (in south India), I hesitantly wrote to Dumont about my appreciation and doubts. To my surprise and delight, he responded promptly and asked me to prepare an article spelling out the reservations. I was diffident, but sent him a short paper in 1965; this was included by him as the lead article in the final (1966) issue of *Contributions*. The same issue also carried an article of his own in which he responded pointedly to my observations alongside his reply to other critics. He acknowledged that his approach could be seen as eclectic ('positive-cum-subjective'), but contended that the viability of the view from outside could not possibly be doubted. He drew attention to the analytical studies published in *Contributions* (Nos 1–8), and observed that 'duality or tension' was 'the condition *sine qua non* of social anthropology'. I appreciated that Dumont had conceded that the 'implications' of the approach advocated by him 'should be more fully worked out', for that was what I had suggested.

During our 1964 exchange of letters, I had expressed regret that *Contributions* was going to cease publication: this had been announced by him. I urged him to reconsider his decision. He may have been told the same by others. His reply was forthright: If I and others were concerned, why did we not take responsibility for a successor journal? As for him, he had had his say on the methodology of the sociology of India and was engaged in other, more substantive, studies. A three-cornered correspondence between Dumont, Adrian Mayer, and me followed; soon afterwards Bailey and Pocock were also involved in the consultation. The plans for a successor journal matured rapidly through 1965. Meanwhile, I took up a faculty position at IEG, Delhi. Thanks to the strong support of M.N. Srinivas, the Institute agreed to sponsor the journal. Dumont agreed to the use of the title, *Contributions to Indian Sociology*, with the addition of the words 'New Series'. He also gave his consent to becoming one of the editorial advisers. The new *Contributions* was announced and welcomed by Dumont himself in the last number (1966) of the original series. It began publication in 1967 (see Chapter Ten).

After 1954, I had met Dumont a second time early in 1957, when our paths crossed in Lucknow, but only fleetingly. It was only late in the summer of 1968 that our first extended meetings took place in Delhi. He had read my book *Family and Kinship: A Study of the*

Pandits of Rural Kashmir (1965) and reviewed it favourably in *Annales* (in 1968). He wrote to me that he had taken it up for discussion at his seminar. The first issue of *Contributions* (New Series, or NS) also had reached him, and he was rather pleased with it. His assessment of it (conveyed in a letter of March 1968) was: 'honourable and substantial'. He promised all the support that he could possibly give us. We talked of much else including his Centre for Indian Studies at the École and, of course, Lévi-Strauss—the man and his work.

From then onward, we remained in regular correspondence and met many times over the next three decades, in Delhi, Paris, Cambridge (MA), and New York, and at the Dumonts's country home in Chalo (outside Paris). It had also been a great pleasure for my wife Uma and me to have come to know Suzanne Tardieu Dumont, who herself worked at the Musée des Arts et Traditions Popularies, and published an excellent volume on the movable furniture (almirahs, chests, sideboards, and so on) of the Normandy area. I had met Dumont's first wife, Jennie, a few times, but did not quite get to know her well. She died in 1977.

The publication in 1970 of the English translation of *Homo Hierarchicus* offered an excellent opportunity for further discussion of Dumont's approach and its substantial analytical and interpretative results. Accordingly, I decided to organize a review symposium on the book for publication in *Contributions*. Dumont readily agreed to contribute to it. A similar suggestion reached him soon afterwards from Sol Tax, editor of *Current Anthropology*, but he advised against a second discussion. Ten scholars from England, France, Germany, India, the Netherlands, and the USA contributed to the symposium. Dumont wrote a considered response (see Dumont 1971), clarifying the notion of hierarchy.

One of my own main observations was in line with my 1966 paper (see Madan 1966a) in which I had raised the problem of the most satisfactory manner of integrating the views from 'within' and 'without'. The particular form this question had taken in *Homo Hierarchicus* was reflected in what I described as the unusual design of the book, with a main and a supplementary text. The former had been constructed theoretically and deductively, and the latter empirically (derived from ethnography, Dumont's own and that of many others), and comprised a considerable body of elucidatory notes.

Ascertaining the extent of consonance between the model and the observed social reality seemed to be, I wrote, a secondary concern, resulting in a 'devaluation of the ethnographic datum'.

Responding to this observation rather briefly, and in the specific context of contemporary social change, Dumont observed that development was essentially an individualistic rather than a social category and, hence, it was not surprising that the theoretical stance of *Homo Hierarchicus* should seem unhelpful to me. He elaborated his argument more directly in the preface to the complete (revised) English edition of the book (1980a xxii–xxiii): he emphasized that, in his considered judgement, the textual duality or tension that I had detected did not in fact exist, for he had 'always given the final word to observed reality'. This was confirmed by the fact, he wrote, that he had not suppressed the difficulties that the argument encountered from the data. The devaluation of the ethnographic datum that I had complained about was present, he wrote, but only relatively, as a result of 'hierarchization of traits'.

I found this a welcome clarification, but my doubts were not completely stilled. Thus, in the chapter on Dumont's work in *Pathways* (Madan 1994c), I pointed out that one would hardly want to disagree that all that is observed is not equally significant; the problem lay with the manner in which a particular criterion of hierarchization emerged as self-certified and all-encompassing in character. In short, Dumont and I never quite stopped talking about *Homo Hierarchicus*.

In 1978, I assumed the office of the Member-Secretary (chief executive officer) of the Indian Council of Social Science Research (ICSSR). One of the very first things I undertook was the activation of social science collaboration between the Council and the Maison des Sciences de l'Homme (MSH) in Paris. I proposed to Clemens Heller, the administrateur of MSH, and he agreed that selected French works in the social and human sciences, which presented a distinctive point of view, should be translated into English. The Maison would take the responsibility for the translation and the Council, for publication. The first book in the series that we chose was *Une sous caste*. Dumont gave his consent and Michael Moffatt, who himself had done fieldwork in Tamil Nadu and published a monograph which derived its key ideas about the nature of the caste system from Dumont's work (Moffatt 1979), agreed to supervise a professional translator. Dumont himself made the final revision. It took long—Dumont was not easily satisfied—but the work was done. *A South Indian Subcaste* was released in Delhi in 1986 (see Dumont 1986a) at a function at the French embassy's cultural affairs division by Iqbal Narain, the new Member-Secretary of ICSSR.

In 1980, I anticipated that Dumont would be turning seventy-five the following year and that this event would happily coincide with the twenty-fifth year of publication of *Contributions* as a continuing journal (original and New Series). Accordingly, I decided to put together a Festschrift in his honour. The response to my proposal from Indian, American, British, and European scholars whom I invited to write was enthusiastic. I chose the broad theme of the goals and the value orientations of life (*purushārtha*). Most of the essays received were of outstanding quality and, together, made a splendid work and worthy tribute. Published as the silver jubilee volume of *Contributions* (1981) and as a book, *Way of Life: King, Householder, Renouncer: Essays in Honour of Louis Dumont* (1982a), the Festschrift was presented to him at a well-attended function at IEG, Delhi, in January 1982. His presence in India along with his wife, Suzanne, was a coincidence: they were on a private visit ('It is the last, a farewell!' he confided in me), but I persuaded him to come to the function. Responding to the brief discussion on aspects of his work, to the salutatory speeches, and to the presentation of the volume by M.S.A. Rao (at that time the doyen of the sociologists of Delhi), Dumont said, among other things that, in recent years, he had virtually abandoned the field of Indian studies. By itself, the decision seemed perfectly defensible to him, but on a visit to India, the aspect of 'human relationships' acquired an unanticipated salience, and his decision became, in his own eyes, 'difficult to justify'.

A second Festschrift, *Différences, Valuers, Hiérarchie* edited by Jean-Claude Galey (1984), and containing a contribution by, among others, Lévi-Strauss, came out two years later. There were other honours too: invited lectures, medals, prizes, honorary doctorates (Chicago, Lausanne), membership of learned societies, and the coveted selection as a Chevalier de la Legion d'Honneur (1987).

❖

My image of Louis Dumont is of a person who was resolutely single-minded in the pursuit of the life of the intellect. It consumed him, but he enjoyed it too. In the last years of his life, however, Louis told me more than once, in personal conversations and in letters, that he found his work excessively exacting. Writing in April 1991, he rather humourously touched on the topic of ageing, which, he said

> ... means turning inwards and perceiving more and more dimly the outside. Everything slows down, so that I was happy delivering a month ago the manuscript of my next book to the publisher. It is about Germany (and France) and the interplay of cultures. It will be the last one, so that I feel relieved, as on holiday for good!

Yes, I thought: 'Why should the aged eagle spread its wings?' But Louis was not really retiring.

The last time, we met him (my wife Uma and I were guests at a lunch [along with Jean-Claude and Penelope Galey, and Thomas Trautman and his wife] in the Dumonts country home in Chalo in the summer of 1993). Louis, looking fit and well, spoke animatedly about various things including the ideas of 'nation' and 'nationalism' with special reference to France. He seemed concerned about contemporary developments. By 1997, he had some reflections to offer and (Galey informed me) presented these at three seminars that summer. Later in the year, he mentioned in a letter the frustration of slow progress. So much so indeed that, I suspected, he almost welcomed an occasional distraction as respite. Louis had written to me in early 1997, acknowledging receipt of my book *Modern Myths, Locked Minds* (Madan 1997): 'Your book landed here, enticing me to a promising journey. Very uncautiously, I did embark, and I am not yet back home, but have discovered new landscapes.'

Throughout his intellectual career, Louis was fully conscious of the importance of what he was doing (the questions posed, the answers attempted). He was distrustful of 'system builders' (his phrase) and inflated egos, however, and played down the significance of individual achievement. For him genuine intellectual advancement came from collective endeavour. In this respect also he was a holist: one scholar's work may be better than another's, but the collective corpus is superior to both. Louis thrived in the company of likeminded people, but would retreat into a shell when he found communication and sharing of ideas difficult. This led some colleagues to complain of his arrogance and intolerance, but that was, I think, a misunderstanding. He was, on the whole, a reticent person, even shy, and preferred the research colloquium to the classroom.

Louis was generous to his younger colleagues and students, but expected single-minded devotion to work in a measure that sometimes became burdensome. This often led to the rupture of relations. Incidentally, he once pointed out to me, rather plaintively, I think, that he had never had an Indian student. On another occasion, he turned down my request to review a book in *Contributions* on the ground that his review would be negative—he considered it a wrong-headed work—but the author had as good a right as anyone else to build a career. Louis explained that while he was engaged in the production of *Contributions* he considered it an obligation to write against tendencies that he considered wrong, but after the closure of the journal, he would like to be less outspoken.

In his letters to me, Louis graciously expressed appreciation of even such small things as editorial suggestions for the finalization of some of his essays. In May 1993, the University of Paris X (Nanterre) made me a docteur honoris causa (thanks to the initiative of Oliver Herrenschmidt and the support of Eric de Dampiere and other friends). Louis did not come to the ceremony ('I feel more and more inadequate in that sort of situation,' he wrote to me), but subsequently came to know that I had acknowledged my deep intellectual debt to him in my acceptance speech, which was sent to him. He wrote (in July 1993): 'Once again, congratulations! Personally, I did not expect to be celebrated in that sort of way. Of course, I know your integrity and your kindness. Yet there is something unreal about all this.'

In 1991, I informed him about the excellent arrangements that I had been able to make to hand over editorial responsibility for *Contributions* to a small group of able colleagues. And I thanked him for his advice and encouragement over the years. His reply (in April 1991) was typically generous, recognizing individual contribution but emphasizing collective gain:

> Actually it is not enough to congratulate you for having successfully conducted the publication for 25 years. In all justice we should be able to [accord you a formal recognition of some kind] for such a rare performance and such a distinguished service to the profession.... You are too kind to me; I do not deserve to be

thanked, for I did just nothing. I certainly won't presume to give an estimate of what has been achieved in these 25 years of *Contributions*, and it is entirely your work.

I could not have asked for more. Louis was similarly forthright in his appreciation of whatever he liked of my scholarly work. For example, my discussion of the dialectic of ethnic and national boundaries in the emergence of Bangladesh (Madan 1972b) and of the structural implications of marriage among the Pandits of rural Kashmir (Madan 1975b), or my exploratory essay, 'Secularism in its Place' (Madan 1987b). About the latter he wrote (in March 1988):

> I enjoyed it, it is very clear and elegantly written, well thought-out and deeply felt. I agree with probably each and every statement in it. But in the end I am left with a kind of (philistine) question, 'Where do we go from here?'... I should need to take up again the thread of my speculations on communalism, etc. The problem is daunting.

But Louis did not like everything that I sent him, and frankly expressed disagreement.

He usually did so gently, but chided me on one occasion for the loose use of words resulting in the conflation of 'dominance' and 'deference'! He found my lectures *Culture and Development* (1983a) of little interest. The strongest criticism that I am able to recall is in a letter of August 1982. Commenting on my essay on the ideology of the householder, which I contributed to *Way of Life* (the Festschrift in his honour), which he liked, he protested my lack of discrimination in quoting from his essay on renunciation. His observations, he wrote, were 'a preliminary sociological mapping of a huge country, without immediate contact, for of course the Kallar had nothing to say on such topics' and I 'embarrassed' him by failing to distinguish between 'lace' and 'coarse fabric'.

I find the forgoing comment interesting for several reasons. First and foremost, Louis's unrelenting self-appraisal, modifying or discarding conclusions that in his judgement had not stood the test of time. A good example of this attitude was his published exchanges with Sylvia Vatuk on aspects of Hindi kinship terminology and the subsequent re-analysis that he published in *Contributions* (Madan 1975b). When Patricia Uberoi wanted to reproduce his paper on marriage in India (Madan 1966a) in a book of readings, he wrote to me in July 1992: 'I cannot allow reproduction of something that I repudiated as false. Against this no historiographical or pedagogic consideration can prevail. No compromise is possible.' Eventually, he agreed to the reproduction of excerpts from the paper on the condition that the impugned parts were omitted and his reservations noted by the editor. Louis was indeed an exemplar in such matters.

Second, I find the 'lace and coarse fabric' contrast interesting because of the choice of metaphors, reiterating his image of himself as an artisan at work, to which Jean-Claude Galey also has drawn pointed attention in his perceptive contribution to *Way of Life* (1982a: 11). Finally, and somewhat ironically, we have in Louis's statement his candid confession that, when it came to certainty regarding what counts in everyday life in India, he did not know the Brahmans well, only the Kallar. He took the same position when I sent him the first draft of a paper on auspiciousness and purity for his comment. He replied (in January 1981): 'I am afraid I do not understand much of such things, perhaps because I am not conversant with really Brahmanical ideas and because the Kallar are little concerned with astrology etc. Surely you are right to stress time....'

Louis's complete identification with his work created difficulties in his relations with other academics because he did not easily separate the personal from the professional dimensions of social relationships. He was quick to take offence, felt cross all too readily perhaps, but if convinced of the sincerity of the critic, he was eagerly responsive. I felt more than somewhat embarrassed to read in the preface to the 1980 edition of *Homo Hierarchicus* that Louis regarded me as a commentator whose good faith was not in question, for this implied that this doubt did exist in his mind in respect of some other critics. He, of course, proceeded to forcefully reject my characterization of the book as comprising two parallel texts—a point mentioned above—but only after affirming the existence of a bond of friendship between us (Dumont 1980a: xxii).

Louis's impatience with his critics arose partly, I think, from the tendency of most reviewers to mix praise and blame in a casual manner. Given his own serious and methodical approach, he perhaps expected every responsible reviewer to attach relative weights to the pluses and minuses of a work to arrive at a clear overall assessment. I recall how angry he was with Edmund Leach's reviews of

Homo Hierarchicus (in Dumont 1971 and elsewhere) because of the discontinuity between very high praise and careless criticism. As the years rolled by, other books followed, and the critics went about their work in their usual contrary way; Louis stopped teaching excepting occasionally. One of the last occasions on which he wrote to me on such a matter concerned an article by David Rudner assessing his work on Dravidian kinship (*Contributions* 24, 1990). The author had used the word 'inquest' in the title. Louis was annoyed. He wrote to me (in April 1991): 'Am I a malefactor to be subjected to an "inquest"? Why such hostility? Is it there in place of solid argument? ... It is a relief to turn away from such inanities. The apple trees in my valley are in full bloom.'

The demeanour of aloofness noticed by many people was a mask that enabled Louis to keep this emotions, positive as well as negative, under wraps. But he did drop guard occasionally, and revealed a capacity for a multitude of feelings. I have a letter of October 1975 in which he confessed to a sense of sadness that, he wrote, overcame him every year on the onset of the autumn, 'as if the past summer was the last one' of one's life. I may add that it was the house in Chalo with its indoor spaces, outdoor wine cellar, walk ways, trees, birds, and so on, and above all calm tranquility that perhaps made the autumnal return to the smaller apartment in Paris more than somewhat unwelcome to him.

The Dumonts, Louis and Suzanne, came to Harvard University on a short visit in November 1984. My wife and I were there, and they came to our apartment. It was a lovely autumn day, and Louis was cheerful. As he and Suzanne settled down on a divan, I managed to get a picture just when Louis had put his arm round her. It came out a beautiful snapshot, and I sent a copy to Paris. Obviously delighted, but confessing a measure of embarrassment, he wrote: 'You showed too much of our intimacy!'

Louis had, in fact, a finely tuned sense of the appropriate that was wholly genuine. In 1985, at one of our meetings in Paris, he asked me about how my two children were doing in their studies. On hearing that our daughter was in the last year of her Master's course in sociology, he asked if she had a copy of *Homo Hierarchicus*. When I said that we indeed had a copy at home—in fact the one that he had given to me—he responded that she should have one of her own!

He got out a fresh copy from his bookshelves, and after writing 'For Vandana', paused and observed: 'I can hardly say "with love" to an Indian girl!' He then wrote, 'with blessings'. This was, according to the Indian norms of etiquette, the most appropriate inscription, and it was most sincerely meant.

Louis was not only well-conversant with many a fine point of Indian culture, he also appreciated aspects of it. For example, Carnatic (south Indian) music. On a visit to Paris in May 1993, I gave him an audio cassette featuring the great maestro V. Doreswamy Iyenger playing the *veena*. Sometime later, he wrote to me that he had just heard it and it had moved him deeply:

> I was literally transported. It was as if one of the recitals I had heard long ago at the house of my friends, the Wolfs, in Madras was going on. There were perhaps differences, but the miracle was that it was the same nevertheless. India was there, to breathe, almost to touch. I must refrain from commenting further: too much is there, and too little judgement: your gift has opened the sluices....

Louis did indeed feel strongly attached to Tamil Nadu, its people, and its culture. In one of his letters he wrote of his 'Tamil patriotism' which was sometimes hurt by the failings of Tamils (such as the failure to build library resources, the topic of the letter); in another, he wrote how his 'Tamil blood' boiled on reading about Sri Lankan ethnic killings.

In early 1995, my wife and I visited the Nataraja temple in Chidambaram. On the drive back to Chennai, I persuaded the driver to leave the main road and pass through some villages. We hoped to see an image or two of Aiyannar, the village protective deity, about whom Louis has written a superb essay. We did not succeed, but we did manage to see something quite similar, and I photographed it. In due course, a copy went to Louis. He wrote back (in April 1995):

> You can hardly imagine how deeply that photo touched—and touches—me. Probably the light—or is it the presence of two small terra cotta horses and of the tall human figure sitting on a platform, a strongly evocative profile that moved me in an extraordinary way? It suggests that I have remained attached to that land, which your photo makes immediately recognizable, to an

extent I am not conscious of. There are of course some reasons for this, but perhaps also the work done, the energy spent, ties one to a place. The picture will remain near me.

There is another picture that remains near us in our home in Delhi. It is a floral design for wallpaper, crayon on paper, done a hundred years ago by Victor Emile Dumont, who was renowned for such designs (and for cartoons that were used by the weavers of northern India to make cashmere cloth for export to Europe). Louis gave it to us in 1982, fondly calling it 'Grandfather's flower!' He added: 'It is one of the very last left with me, and there will be no more Dumonts left in our line after I am gone.' But there is a Dumont who still lives in the memories of the people who were privileged to be his friends. And, of course, he lives in his works.[1]

---

[1] This chapter is based on Louis Dumont's published works; two interviews with him, one by Jean-Claude Galey (1982) and the other by Christian Delacampagne (see Dumont 1981); his letters to me and our conversations during the period 1964–98; and my own earlier writings. While quoting from his letters, I have omitted the dates, indicating only the month and the year. Textual sources have been clearly identified wherever this seemed necessary, but page numbers have not always been included. To save the text from cluttering, I have refrained from citing sources for occasional keywords or phrases drawn from his published works. Further details may be looked up in the list of references at the end of the book.

Chapter Ten

Contributions to Indian Sociology: Towards Methodological Pluralism

All knowledge of cultural reality ... is always knowledge from particular points of view.

—MAX WEBER, ' "Objectivity" in Social Science'

In Chapter Nine, I presented an intellectual profile of Louis Dumont. Among his other ventures, I discussed the journal *Contributions to Indian Sociology*. In this chapter, I will consider the character and significance of this journal in some detail.[1] Unavoidably, there is

---

[1] This chapter is a revised and extended version of the keynote address delivered at the seminar to mark the fiftieth anniversary of *Contributions* held at IEG on 6 December 2007, during the Institute's own golden jubilee year. I am grateful to the editors, Amita Baviskar and Nandini Sundar, for their invitation to speak at the seminar. Needless to add, they are in no way responsible for its contents.

I would also like to place on record the Institute's deepest appreciation of the collaboration of the publishers: Asia Publishing House for two years (1967–68); Vikas for fourteen (1969–82); and since then SAGE Publications India Pvt. Ltd. Dharma Kumar and I offered our respective journals, *Indian Economic and Social History Review* and *Contributions*, to Tejeshwar Singh in 1982, and with SAGE they have stayed. Singh was present at the seminar, and I was able to personally thank him. Sadly, he died a week later, suddenly and prematurely.

Editorial support has been provided over the years by a number of colleagues, among whom I would like to particularly thank Esha Béteille, Aradhya Bhardwaj, Shernawaz Billimoria (now Sherna Banerji), and Meenakshi Thapan at IEG, R.K. Jain and Ritu Menon at Vikas, and Omita Goyal at SAGE. *Contributions* (NS) has indeed been the kind of collective endeavour that Louis Dumont so dearly valued and commended.

some repetition here of both information and argument from the previous chapter: the original versions of both were written as self-contained essays. I have allowed the repetitiveness to remain in the interest of letting each chapter stand on its own.

I try to answer three questions. First, with what objective did Louis Dumont (situated in Paris) in association with David Pocock (his successor as lecturer in Indian sociology at Oxford) launch *Contributions to Indian Sociology* as an annual publication in 1957? Second, why did he bring the periodical publication to a close in 1966? And third, what led some of us to start a new series in the following year (1967)? These are questions to which factual answers can be given. Apart from mentioning the significance of *Contributions* for my own work, I do not make any attempt to evaluate Dumont's project, and refrain from both praise and criticism or agreement and disagreement. Before we may do any of this, it is imperative that we get the facts of the case right. I do, however, go beyond a mere narration of facts, and clarify certain issues about which serious misunderstandings are regrettably widespread.

I begin in the first section of the chapter with a discussion of Dumont's theoretical orientation from which he derived the approach he recommended for the study of Indian civilization and the societies that comprise it. In the second section, I focus on the contents of the nine numbers of *Contributions* that came out between 1957 and 1966. I conclude this section with the reasons for the closure of the original series. In the third section, I write briefly about the considerations that led to the decision to continue the publication of *Contributions* as a new series with redefined objectives. Some remarks are also made about the editorial steering of the course of the journal since 1967. The chapter concludes with a few remarks about recent developments and future prospects.

I

Dumont's Approach to the Study of Indian Society

The narrative begins in 1957 during which year Dumont's monographs on the Pramalai Kallar and marriage alliance in south India and the first number of *Contributions* were published. This surely was a coincidence; *Une sous-caste de l'Inde du sud* (Dumont 1957b, 1986a) was published by Mouton in Paris, *Hierarchy and Marriage Alliance in South Indian Kinship* (1957a), by the Royal Anthropological Institute in London, and *Contributions to Indian Sociology* (Dumont and Pocock 1957), again by Mouton in Paris. Publication of the three works in the same year is, however, significant as it helps to underscore the internal unity of Dumont's work. The evaluation of these publications—in fact of Dumont's entire oeuvre—title by title, independently of one another, which is what most commentators and critics have done, is sure to lead one astray. The holistic approach that he recommended for the study of social facts—the parts become intelligible when seen in relation to the whole—applies to his published works also.

The focus of Dumont's inquiries broadens from the local in the Pramalai Kallar book to the regional in the marriage alliance monograph, to the subcontinental-civilizational, programmatically in *Contributions* and concretely although in a rather limited way in the first of these publications. The relationship of the local and the civilizational is stated very briefly in the latter work (1957b, 1986a). The objective, he writes, is 'to treat the group [subcaste] as a microcosm in which the elements of the macrocosm would be seen in their living relations' (Dumont 1986a: 2). The logic of the procedure lies in the fact that 'the "civilization" in which a caste participates is also present within it' (Dumont 1986a: 3).

The progression from the local/folk to the subcontinental/civilizational helped Dumont to constitute the civilizational unity of India, which *for him* was an empirical fact, and not merely an ideological construction. It should be added here that the two south Indian works were the product of two years of sustained fieldwork in Tamil Nadu (1949–51), conducted through the medium of Tamil. The shorter and more technical discussion of 'marriage alliance' partly grew out of the consideration of preferential forms of marriage in the larger ethnographic study (Dumont 1986a: 196–215). Partly it was grounded in Lévi-Strauss's ([1949] 1969) classic work on the elementary structures of kinship. The three works together comprise an interrelated oeuvre; they are not a mere assemblage of texts. A common theoretical orientation runs through them, and binds them together methodologically. Ten years later, in the introduction to *Homo Hierarchicus* (1967a), Dumont wrote: '[I]t is not enough to say that I owe everything, or almost everything to the French tradition in sociology' (Dumont 1980a: xv).

The French tradition that he invokes is not the exclusively empiricist, positivist Comtean tradition, but the one that derives from Émile Durkheim and his circle. It is a perspective which is sociologistic, that is anti-reductionist and holistic. Social reality, Durkheim argued, comprises social facts in their double aspect of being 'things' and subjectively apprehended, internally meaningful, 'collective representations' (Durkheim 1938, 1953). The final, most considered definition of *représentations collectives* is to be found in his most mature work, *The Elementary Forms of Religious Life* ([1915] 1995). They are, in Fields succinct words, 'shared mental constructs with the help of which human beings collectively view themselves, each other and the natural world' (see Durkheim [1915] 1995: xviii).

From Durkheim's *magnum opus* we learn that collective representations signify 'the world of ideas and feelings that morally unify the group', and that, '[e]ach civilization has its ordered system of concepts which characterizes it' (Durkheim [1915] 1995: 273, 437). Indeed, 'in all its aspects and at every moment of its history, social life [anywhere] is only possible thanks to a vast symbolism' (Durkheim [1915] 1995: 233). Collective representations obviously are more significant in traditional, group-oriented societies than in modern, individual centred ones. Anomie sets in when they are severely weakened.

Dumont received Durkheim's teaching through personal association with Marcel Mauss (Durkheim's nephew and most distinguished pupil), whose influence upon him, Dumont recalled late in his life, was 'conversion-like' (see Galey 1982: 6f.). He also acknowledged his indebtedness to the works of other scholars of the circle, notably the studies of caste by Bouglé (1908) and Hocart (1938), which together are the subject of the second number of *Contributions* (in 1958). These scholars extended Durkheim's comparative sociology to include in it the study of Indian civilization, relying primarily on Sanskrit textual sources, but including, in the case of Hocart, fieldwork in Sri Lanka. It is important to note that these scholars (including, besides Mauss, Bouglé, and Hocart, Hertz, Mus, and Dumézil) were comparativists with knowledge of Indological texts; they were not Indologists. Their interest was in general categories (or theoretical concepts) in the exploration of the character of human society, such as gift exchange (Mauss 1970) and sacrifice (Hubert and Mauss 1964).

In the shaping of Dumont's theoretical orientation, Mauss is, of course, the most significant influence. His 1930 essay on civilizational analysis (Mauss [1930] 2004) is cited by Dumont in the lead essay in the inaugural number of *Contributions* (Dumont and Pocock 1957: 11). For Mauss, civilizations comprise cultural phenomena—'ideas, practices, products'—which have individuality (distinctive character) and physical boundaries within which they embrace several societies. This last point is emphasized by Dumont (Dumont and Pocock 1957: 11) and we must not lose sight of the emphasis. Pursuantly, he approvingly recalls Mauss's criticism of Rivers for failing to recognize that the Todas were embedded in the larger Indian civilization (Dumont and Pocock 1957: 8).

Simultaneously, Dumont noted in *A South Indian Subcaste* (1986a: 5):

> Indian tribes themselves cannot without risk be considered strangers to [the Indian] civilization. This fact has two consequences. On the one hand it requires important changes of method compared to those used in the monographic study of simpler societies. On the other it allows a sociological grasp of the civilization itself ... anthropology ceases to juxtapose itself to Indology, in order rather to combine with it.

In Dumont's judgement, the fact that the Pramalai Kallar subscribed to, among other ideas, the notions of ritual purity and pollution meant that they were participants in a subcontinental, civilizational ethos (Dumont 1986a: 461–64).

In the leading essay of the inaugural number of *Contributions*, 'For a Sociology of India', which had been delivered two years earlier as the inaugural lecture, Chair of Sociology of India at the École Pratique des Hautes Études (6th Section) in Paris, Dumont maintained: 'It should be obvious, *in principle*, that a Sociology of India [as a "whole", a civilization] lies at the point of confluence of Sociology and Indology' (see Dumont and Pocock 1957: 7, emphasis added). The qualifying words 'in principle' are important as they make room for a certain flexibility to accommodate contextual differences and local traditions. Dogmatism is eschewed.

Dumont contrasted the proposed approach with the prevailing preoccupation of anthropologists studying India (as a geographical region) with supposedly isolated tribal communities, and observed: 'The great mass of the Indian population did not interest them but only those primitive "reserves" which it was hoped would throw valuable light upon the history of the settlement and culture of the subcontinent' (Dumont and Pocock 1957: 8). He praised Srinivas's (1952) Coorg study for breaking with the earlier tradition inasmuch as it looked beyond the local in the discussion of Hinduism to 'the implications of the existence of a common [subcontinental] civilization' (Dumont and Pocock 1957: 2).

The emphasis on collective representations and the inclusion of Indology as source material implies, Dumont writes in the Kallar book, that avoiding 'arbitrary' (and therefore 'dangerous') ideas, 'we must take pains not to introduce any concept whatsoever into the description which is not, either that of the people themselves, or shown necessary by direct analysis of the material, even if it is not present in the consciousness of those concerned' (1957b: 347). Needless to recall here that the idea of 'collective consciousness' also is derived from Durkheim, who regarded it as the soil, as it were, in which 'collective representations' are grounded (see Durkheim 1953: 18, [1915] 1995: 232).

Transcending narrow ethnography, Dumont said in the inaugural number of *Contributions* (Dumont and Pocock 1957: 11f.):

> [M]odern social anthropology has made a serious contribution to ... [the] definition [of social facts à la Durkheim, 'things' as well as 'collective representations'] in its insistence that the observer see things from within (as integrated in the society which he studies) and from without ...[,]

that is, from the perspectives of his own culture and of his discipline. Dumont proceeds to clarify: 'Fundamental ideas literally "go without saying".... Only their corollaries are explicit. The caste system for example appears as a perfectly coherent theory once one adds the necessary but implicit links to the principles that the people themselves give' (Dumont and Pocock 1957: 12). In the apparently complicated matter of matrilateral cross-cousin marriage in a patrilineal society which the Tamils practice, Dumont observed that what he learnt from the people emerged as a meaningful whole when considered in the light of Lévi-Strauss's theories (see Galey 1982: 17).

In structuralist language, this would mean bringing above the level of consciousness that which is below it, making manifest what is latent. This also is a Maussian imperative. Dumont approvingly quotes Mauss: 'A sociological explanation is finished [completed] when one has seen what it is that people believe and think, and who are the people who believe and think that' (Dumont 1980a: 13). Hocart too had been quoted earlier to the same effect: '[L]earn from the people themselves which modes of thinking we have the right to apply and which we should reject' (Dumont and Pocock 1957: 11).

What I have described above surely cannot be called in all fairness an Indological approach. Sanskrit texts are not treated as the sole source of information, nor are they elevated to the level of final authority. The texts are to be mined, as it were, for ideas, like the local cultural traditions usually are, but these ideas have to be confronted with the lived reality. 'Ideology', Dumont writes, 'does not tell us everything about a society' (1966b: 22), just as observed behaviour without reference to ideas and values—'collective representations'—that underlie them will remain incomprehensible in a deeper sense.

Both perspectives—the textual and the contextual—leave unexplained 'residues'. Dumont affirms that it was his years at Oxford as lecturer in Indian Sociology (in succession to M.N. Srinivas, 1951–55), which exposed him to fieldwork-based British social anthropology at its best, and brought him the gift of 'the second eye which helped [him] develop a sort of stereoscopic vision' (see Galey 1982: 18). His initiation into the field of Indian studies had been as a student of languages (Sanskrit and Tamil), but first-hand contact with India was as a fieldworker in Tamil Nadu which, it may be repeated, lasted two years (1949–50). Ultimately, no culture is comprehensible, according to Dumont, outside the framework of intercultural or intercivilizational comparison: '[D]ifferent cultures can be made to communicate within a single man's [anthropologist's] experience. Duality, or tension, is here the *sine qua non* of social anthropology or, if one likes, of a sociology of a deeper kind' (1966b: 23).

Responding to my criticism that in *Homo Hierarchicus* data about observed behaviour had been subordinated to the deductive argument (Madan 1971: 4), Dumont stated:

> I must protest energetically; the 'model' [I had characterized 'Homo Hierarchicus' as a model (Madan 1971: 9), contrasting it with Mandelbaum's (1970) portrait of society in India based on a careful summing up of the extant ethnographic literature] is given

in order to account for 'contemporary social reality' entirely in the perspective of social anthropology. If another model does it more economically, this one must be rejected.... *I have always given the last word to observed reality*, as indeed Madan acknowledges at several points. (Dumont 1980a: xxii, emphasis added)

In the article 'For a Sociology of India' in *Contributions* 1, Dumont had drawn attention to what he characterized as the 'infancy' of the sociology of India, and offered to his professional colleagues, to quote his own words again, 'one clear orientation among others', adding that 'others may define it in a quite different manner' (Dumont and Pocock 1957: 22). This orientation, I have tried to show, is dialectical, confronting ideology with behaviour and vice versa; it repudiates methodological exclusivism; it is open to further field research and clarification of the theoretical argument, and is not dogmatic. Nor indeed is it exclusively Indological, as many critics including Béteille (2003: 44) assert, or 'the book-view' of Indian society as Deshpande (2003: 15) alleges. It is true that in *Homo Hierarchicus*, which is the only source that Béteille cites, 'the fundamental opposition' of ritual purity and pollution is derived from 'normative literature' (Manu and others), but Dumont does not construct an abstract (metaphysical) system on its basis: he rather employs it to provide an interpretation of empirically observable intercaste relations—of, as he puts it, the disjunction of status and power (see Dumont 1980a: 212ff. et passim). It is indeed ironic that someone who modestly claimed the acquisition of 'a second eye' through his 'second training' with Evans-Pritchard after the initial apprenticeship with Mauss, and consequently a 'stereoscopic vision', should yet be judged to be but one-eyed, a proponent of the Indological approach and the book view of Indian society through the medium of *Contributions*.[2]

---

[2]In view of the rejection by Saran (1962b) of Dumont's methodology, it is indeed puzzling that Béteille (2003: 44) should in one sweeping sentence group them together as purveyors of the Indological as against the historical approach. He refers to differences between them, but does not specify what these are. Saran could be called a 'traditionalist' in the mould of A.K. Coomaraswamy and Mircea Eliade (see Saran 1958), but not an Indologist or Sanskritist. In the early 1950s, when I was a student at the University of Lucknow, he used to discuss the theories of the likes of Marx, Weber, and G.H. Mead, and draw heavily upon C.S. Pierce and the early Wittgenstein in his lectures on the theory of language (see, for example, Saran 1963, 2003). I know of no publication of Saran's that could be called Indological.

So much then, about the theoretical orientation that was presented to the students of Indian society by Dumont in 1957 in the three works published that year, but particularly in the inaugural number of *Contributions*. The orientation was further clarified in a set of lectures published five years later (Dumont 1962) and in subsequent numbers of *Contributions*, and then brought to fruition in *Homo Hierarchicus* (1967a, 1980a). The concept of hierarchy (and derivatively, of hierarchization) had already been introduced in the marriage alliance study (Dumont 1957a) in the familiar sense of social gradation, but its elaboration into a refined notion of the 'encompassing' of the contrary came only later (see, for example, Dumont 1967a, 1971). I will not follow that trail here; I will instead turn to the nine numbers of *Contributions*, original series, to examine the approach to the study of Indian society advocated there.

II

Contributions to Indian Sociology

Not only was Dumont's theoretical orientation derived from Durkheim, the character of *Contributions* also owed much to *L'Année Sociologique*, which Durkheim founded in 1896 with the assistance of Marcel Mauss, his nephew and most distinguished pupil (like Dumont was to establish *Contributions* in collaboration with Pocock). In the first issue of this journal, which came out in 1898, Durkheim outlined editorially its general perspective. He had been an admiring student of Fustel de Coulanges, and it is not at all surprising that he considered historical scholarship within a comparative framework the foundation of his new venture. He wrote: 'As soon as history takes on the character of a comparative discipline, it becomes indistinguishable from sociology. Sociology, in turn, not only cannot do without history but it needs historians who are, at the same time, sociologists' (see Wolff 1960: 343). It is this insight which underlies, I think, Dumont's formulation of the complementarity of Indology and sociology in the sociological study of India. As for the format of the contents of *L'Année Sociologique*, Durkheim mentioned a 'first part ... for original papers', focused and methodological. 'The second and largest part [was to be] dedicated to analyses and bibliographical notes' (Wolff 1960: 344). These observations by Durkheim also indeed described *Contributions to Indian Sociology* when it made its first appearance.

Nine annual numbers of *Contributions* came out between 1957 and 1966. There was no issue in 1963. A leaflet accompanying the first number described it as 'an irregular publication devoted to the progress of Indian sociology', offering 'a distinct point of view' for colleagues to 'agree and disagree with', so that 'a clarification of aims and methods may be effected' (quoted in 'Announcement' in *Contributions* IX). The inaugural issue, under the joint editorship of Dumont and Pocock, opened with, as already mentioned, a revised version of Dumont's 1955 inaugural lecture with the title of 'For a Sociology of India', in lieu of an editorial. Besides, there were two analytical articles; one reviewed two collections of village studies—the ones edited by Marriott (1955b) and Srinivas ([1955] 1960)—and the other was devoted to Karve's (1953) pioneering work on kinship organization in India. All three contributions were unsigned to emphasize, as Dumont clarified later (see Galey 1982: 19), the collaborative character of the enterprise; moreover, the word 'contributions' in the title of the periodical was chosen to highlight this character. The next two numbers were similar in format, devoted to caste (1958: Number II) and religion (1959: Number III), respectively. I believe that the discussion of the two collections of papers on village studies was first written by Pocock, and the critique of Karve's book, by Dumont. They went over each other's drafts to produce the final, jointly authored but unsigned texts.

The third number also carried a critical review of the first number by Bailey, who complained that the editors had 'come near to defining "sociology" out of existence' (Bailey 1959: 88). He clarified: 'To the Indologist what is unique in India is his interest. The comparative sociologist, on the other hand, wants to find out what India has in common with other societies.' Rhetorically, Bailey asked, 'is there an Indian chemistry' (Bailey 1959: 97)? His position was clearly reminiscent of the late nineteenth century *Methodenstreit* in Germany.

The debate had been joined; it was about the character of sociological knowledge and about an appropriate methodology for the study of society in India. The antagonists were sociological functionalists and French structuralists, or, we might say in Dumont's own words, 'classifiers' and 'typifiers' (Dumont 1967b). Over the following years, Dumont held his ground on this epistemological issue, looking upon 'difference', or, in Lévi-Strauss's (1985) phrase, 'the view from afar', as a richer source of insights and understanding than a focus on similarities. Dumont's studies of Indian civilization helped him, he claimed, problematize Western civilization. Thus, he wrote, 'the India of caste and *varna* teaches us hierarchy, and this is no little lesson' (1966b: 30; see also Madan 2006b: Chapter 12). As for the rather acerbic question about Indian chemistry posed by Bailey, Dumont conceded: '[W]e should have been more circumspect and preferred to talk of the "Sociology of India"' (1966b: 23, fn. 9), instead of Indian sociology.

Number IV (1960) onwards, *Contributions* looked more like a regular journal, with signed articles by the editors and other contributors, but the presence of Dumont remained strong in its pages. The last three numbers were edited by Dumont alone; Pocock's absence on fieldwork in India was given as the reason. Presumably, they had ceased to be like-minded; Pocock confirmed this to me in 1964. The editorial in Number IV mentions 'warm encouragement and detailed discussion' by reviewers (p. 7). It emphasized that the editors were 'concerned with what happens in India in relation with methods of study and comparison within and without India' (p. 9).

Not counting some minor pieces of correspondence and commentary, forty-five articles were published in *Contributions*. Of these three were editorials (two by Dumont and one by him and Pocock), one was an obituary (of a young scholar, Bernard Pignéd, by Dumont), and three were excerpts from classic works, one each by Bouglé, Hocart, and Tocqueville—the former two on caste and the latter on individualism. Ten articles were devoted to what I would call considerations of methodology or theory; of these Dumont wrote four by himself and two (including a rejoinder to Bailey) together with Pocock, and Pocock wrote two. Bailey and I wrote the remaining two.

Coming to substantive articles, twenty-eight in number, these may be divided into two categories (following Durkheim's scheme for *L'Année Sociologique*), namely, original articles and discussions of published works. The original articles may be further broadly classified as ethnography, discussions of ethnography, Indology, or modern history. Of the six articles devoted to ethnography, three are by Dumont, and are based on two years of fieldwork in Tamil Nadu and fifteen months (1957–58) in Uttar Pradesh. The remaining three are, one each, by F.G. Bailey, Christoph von Fürer-Haimendorf, and Bernard Pignéd. Indological articles, four in number, include Dumont's two seminal essays on renunciation in Indian religions and on kingship in ancient India, and an essay each by Madeleine Biardeau and Robert Lingat—the former based on the Upanishads, the latter on Manu. Modern history also accounts for four papers: three by Dumont, including one on the conceptualization of the village community during the colonial period, another on nationalism and communalism in the first half of the twentieth century, and the third on the theme of individualism in the West.[3] There is also a paper by Daniel Thorner on Marx on India. Another two—one by Dumont on individualism in India and the other by J.D.M. Derrett on the Hindu joint family—bridge Indology and modern history. Actually the last three numbers of *Contributions* (Numbers VII to IX) are devoted to 'modern history'; this is indicated on the contents page of each number.

As for discussions of ethnographic literature (Durkheim's 'analyses and bibliographical notes'), there are twelve of these—eight by Dumont, two by Dumont and Pocock, and two by Pocock. We thus see that Dumont authored individually or jointly with Pocock, three editorials and six methodological pieces. Besides, he contributed three ethnographic studies, two Indological essays, three historical exercises, ten book discussion papers, and an obituary—a total of twenty-nine out of forty-five contributions, or more than half. It may be asserted that the numbers I have given conceal the 'fact' that the overall methodological thrust of *Contributions* was Indological. That, I think, would not be quite fair. Objectively speaking, *Contributions* maintained a balance between ethnography, history, and Indology,

---

[3] I may also draw attention here to another major paper of Dumont (1976) on the colonial period. Even so, it is arguable that his understanding of the sources (both historical and Indological) was perhaps flawed. Thus, Dirks (2002: 54–59) makes a plausible case for the separation ('disjunction') of status and power being not traditional, but a consequence of the colonial intervention. Olivelle (1998) is even more persuasive when he points out that there is little evidence in the *dharma* literature of any direct (causal) relation between states or degrees of ritual purity and caste hierarchy. These issues, important though they are, do not concern me here.

which indeed was the stated intention. (For ready reference, the foregoing breakdown of the contents of the nine members of the original series is presented in Table 10.1.) What is undeniable is the fact that the mode of interpretation developed by Dumont in the pages of *Contributions* (1957–66) eventually led him to produce in *Homo Hierarchicus* (1967a), notwithstanding some discussion of recent developments, a synchronic (that is timeless, ahistorical) model of the caste system. I said so in the review symposium on the book (Madan 1971: 12), but he did not respond to this characterization.

I now come to the closure of the original series. In the inaugural number of *Contributions* (1957), the editors wrote that they were offering 'a general perspective and starting point', which they hoped 'some of [their] colleagues may choose to consider' (p. 7). In the editorial to the fourth number (1960), they again wrote about 'a general perspective' which they had presented together (p. 7), and promised three more numbers. They added: 'Later on, apart from our own effort, the future of the publication will depend upon the attitude of others'; further, they affirmed that 'no development [was] ruled out' from the 'basis' they had provided (p. 11). A cryptic, boxed announcement on the contents page of Number VII (1964) read: '*Contributions* VIII is likely to be the last of the series'. In the event, there were nine numbers in all as, it was stated in Number VIII, all of the accumulated matter could not be accommodated in one issue.

In the editorial in the last number (1966b), entitled 'A Farewell', Dumont referred to the 'aloofness' of others: '[W]hat appears to us as basic has not appeared so to most of our colleagues' (p. 7). There is unconcealed disappointment here, but also a hint of achievement: '[W]e have realized our stated intention in the measure of our ability. This is why the present Editor feels no compulsion to carry on beyond the point where, he thinks, the burden can be laid down without demerit' (p. 8). More than a dozen years later, in 1979, he could afford some wry humour: 'In some quarters, the first three numbers of *Contributions* were taken almost as a kind of defamatory publication.' He further observed that the kind of 'radical questioning of the presuppositions in force [presented in the early issues of *Contributions*], in the manner of *L'Année Sociologique*' was simply not welcome for nobody wanted to 'modify' his or her own position and, therefore, 'with very few exceptions, abstained from participating in the discussion' (see Galey 1982: 19).

Table 10.1: *Summary of Contents—CIS I to IX (1957–66)*

	Editorials	Method-ological/ Theoretical Essays	Originals: Ethno-graphic	Originals: Indologi-cal	Originals: His-torical	Originals: Indologi-cal Historical	Originals: Excerpts from Texts	Analyses of Ethno-graphic Materials and Texts	Others	Total
I (1957)		LD–DFP						LD–DFP: 2		3
II (1958)							Hocart Bouglé	LD		3
III (1959)		Bailey	LD					LD: 6 review articles		8
IV (1960)		LD–DFP	Haimendorf	LD				DFP		5
V (1961)		LD; DFP	Bailey; LD							4
VI (1962)			Pignéde	Lingat LD		Derrett		DFP	LD: Obituary	6
VII (1964)		LD; DFP			LD					4
VIII (1965)	LD	LD		Biardeau	LD	LD		LD		6
IX (1966)	LD	LD; Madan	LD		Thoner LD		Tocqueville			6
Total	3	10	6	4	4	2	3	12	1	45
LD/LD–DFP	2/1	4/2	3	2	3	1	–	8/2	1	24/5

Note: LD refers to Louis Dumont, while DFP refers to David F. Pocock.

It may be noted here parenthetically that both *L'Année Sociologique* and *Contributions to Indian Sociology* were actually experimental periodicals for the presentation and discussion of sociological ideas by various authors using the comparative method and seeking new perspectives. Both journals were, perhaps not surprisingly, short lived. *L'Année Sociologique* (first published in 1898) discontinued publication in 1913 owing to World War I. In 1923–24, Marcel Mauss, comparativist and Sanskritist (whose celebrated essay on the nature and function of sacrifice, jointly written with Henri Hubert on the basis of, among others, Vedic sources, appeared in the inaugural issue of the journal, pp. 29–138), began a second series to carry forward the earlier initiative. Durkheim had died in 1917. It did not, however, survive long; the circle that gave the original series its vitality had been depleted. *Contributions* never became the organ of a 'school', but fortunately, the New Series has had a longer life—so far.

Turning back to *Contributions*, and as I have mentioned, Bailey had forthrightly attacked the perspective offered and so had Saran (1962b), although for almost the diametrically opposite reasons. Dumont (1960, 1966b) responded to both. Many others had been privately critical. Srinivas told me in 1966 that he found the 'evangelical zeal' of the journal editors 'insufferable', but, on the whole, he was positive about *Contributions*. He had been hailed as a path maker in both *A South Indian Subcaste* (Dumont 1957b: 2) and in the leading essay in the inaugural number of the journal (Dumont and Pocock 1957: 8); in fact, his Coorgs book (Srinivas 1952) was acclaimed in the third number as a 'classic' and discussed at considerable length (Dumont 1959: 9–35). Marriott (1969) obviously found the perspective offered interesting, but he did not say so in print until he reviewed the original (French) edition of *Homo Hierarchicus*, which he considered in some respects a disappointing climb down. (For Dumont's response, see Dumont 1971.)

III

The New Series

I now turn to my third and last question: Why the New Series? As already stated (see pp. 205ff.) I discovered *Contributions* in 1958, the second year of its publication, when I was working on my doctoral dissertation in the Anthropology and Sociology department of the ANU. The department, started a few years earlier by S.F. Nadel who came over from England, was at that time one of the most distinguished outposts of British social anthropology. I had wanted to do a fieldwork-based study of kinship values and had sent a research proposal to Nadel, who had accepted me as a student, and recommended me for the award of an ANU scholarship in 1955, but I never was able to get a detailed feedback from him as he died suddenly early in 1956 before my arrival in Canberra (see the Epilogue, pp. 249ff.). The idea had been scotched, however, by the redoubtable Edmund Leach (then at Cambridge) while on a visit to ANU to consider the invitation to succeed Nadel. He told me that, as a structural-functionalist, the subject of values bothered him, and asserted that it made better sense to focus on interests, for kinship was after all an idiom for the articulation of interests. I followed his advice after it was endorsed by both my supervisors, W.E.H. Stanner and Derek Freeman, themselves Ph.D.s from London and Cambridge, respectively. Thus, my attention was pointedly focused on people's verbal and non-verbal behaviour during my fieldwork. Ideas and values were treated with scepticism, against my own earlier inclinations. The first two issues of *Contributions* were very welcome to me like a breath of fresh air for the stress these placed on the significance of the ideas of the people, but it was too late for me to change course. I kept in touch with the journal, however, and avidly read each number when it arrived.

The fourth number (1960) reached me in 1964 in Dharwar, where I was a middle-level faculty member at the Karnatak University. I was really disappointed to read the announcement about the impending closure of *Contributions*, and wrote to Dumont to reconsider his decision. To convince him about the seriousness of my interest, I included in my letter both appreciation and some sceptical remarks about the approach advocated in the journal. Although I had met him twice at Lucknow University during my student days, I had never corresponded with him. To my pleasant surprise, Dumont responded promptly, saying two things. The decision to discontinue publication of the periodical was irrevocable. If I believed that *Contributions* had been a significant intervention in the sociology of India, I should join with like-minded scholars and continue the exploration of alternative approaches to the study of society in India. As for my doubts about his and Pocock's approach, I should prepare a note in somewhat greater detail, and he would publish the critique along with a response. It was thus that the last issue of *Contributions* opened with my short article (Madan 1966a) and concluded with a major restatement by Dumont of his position, which included a response to my observations (Dumont 1966b).

Obviously some other colleagues also (whose identity he did not reveal) had 'expressed concern', as Dumont stated in his editorial in Number IX, 'and even offered help towards its continuation' (p. 7). His suggestion to us all was, as he put it in the said editorial, to form a 'board of editors' and bring out a journal 'more representative of the speciality as a whole' (p. 8). It seems that the only person who actually accepted his advice (or challenge) was me. I requested Dumont that the new journal be allowed to be called *Contributions to Indian Sociology*. As he noted in the editorial of Number IX, he agreed to this, but insisted that the words 'New Series' should be used to distinguish the new venture from the earlier one.

The correspondence between us in the summer of 1964 had set me thinking. Informal discussions with Adrian Mayer (of the School of Oriental and African Studies, London) early in 1965 (in Patna at a conference and then in Dharwar at the Karnatak University) resulted in the decision to go ahead. Acknowledging Dumont's emphasis on collective action, we decided to constitute an editorial board consisting of, besides ourselves, David Pocock (Oxford) and Edward Harper (Seattle). To underscore our openness to the projection of a multiplicity of approaches, and the international character of the effort, we invited, besides Louis Dumont himself, F.G. Bailey (Sussex), S.C. Dube (Sagar), Milton Singer (Chicago), and M.N. Srinivas (Delhi) to become editorial advisers. It cannot be judged to be anything else but a tribute to the original *Contributions* that every single person we approached accepted our invitation to help.

The New Series finally became a viable possibility when P.N. Dhar, Director of IEG, where I had moved in 1966, agreed to sponsor the journal, and Samuel Israel, principal editor at Asia Publishing House, accepted the responsibility for publication without subsidy. *Contributions* (NS) was announced in the last number of the original series by Dumont in the editorial (somewhat sentimentally, he wrote, '*Contributions* is no more. Long live *Contributions* (NS) in the service of the sociology of India!'), and separately in an announcement which I had written. The objective of the New Series was stated modestly and very briefly as the promotion of the sociology of India through the publication of articles, communications, and so on, that were grounded in ethnography *and* theoretically self-conscious.

In my article in the last issue of *Contributions* I had written:

> The Indian practitioner of sociology has been content to live the life of an intellectual imitator: he has assiduously sought to apply techniques learnt from English and American books to obtain answers to questions mostly suggested by the content of Western sociology. (Madan 1966a: 10)

I thought *Contributions* would be an excellent forum to try to remedy these deficiencies, and to do more.

Accordingly, I set out in 1966 itself to look for papers. Two friends, Harold Gould and Ralph Nicholas, and a former student, R.S. Khare, provided the three long papers that, alongside a short note by me, entitled 'For a Sociology of India: Some Clarifications' (Madan 1967: 90–93), comprised the first number of the New Series. I worked as the principal editor of *Contributions* (NS) for twenty-five years (1967–91), a very long time indeed for shouldering such a responsibility. The beginnings were cautious, but progress in terms of submissions and sales was steady. The title surely was the richest asset; international editorial and advisory support was the other. The journal became biannual in 1975.

It surely is for others, not me, to judge how sound the foundations then laid were. I may, however, draw attention here to a few editorial initiatives which, perhaps, helped to bestow a distinctive identity on *Contributions* (NS). Before I proceed, I should mention that Harper left the editorial team in 1970 owing to serious health problems (which ultimately led to his premature death); his place was taken by Harold Gould. Subsequently, local support in Delhi was strengthened immensely in 1975 when Veena Das (Delhi University) and Satish Saberwal (Jawaharlal Nehru University) joined the editorial team. Saberwal later introduced book reviews into the journal on a regular basis.

Perhaps the very first initiative I should mention followed from the fact that the editorial team was in full agreement with Dumont that the New Series should not confine itself with the articulation of any particular methodological position, but rather provide a forum to interested scholars to explore diverse theoretical orientations. To underscore that this indeed was the intention, the first number concluded with (as I have already stated) a note entitled 'For a Sociology of India' (Madan 1967: 90–93), to keep alive the debate that was generated by Dumont's initial formulations under this title and published as the leading article in *Contributions* I (Dumont and Pocock 1957: 7–22; see also Madan 1966a: 9–16). Thereafter, every volume of *Contributions* (NS) during the next twenty-five years concluded with an article, usually invited and short, under the same title ('For a Sociology of India') and devoted to the discussion of the scope and character of the speciality. In the process a variety of perspectives was put forward, many of them critical of Dumont's position.

Another early initiative was a review symposium on Dumont's *Homo Hierarchicus* which formed the bulk of the fifth number/volume (1971). At that time, *Contributions* (NS) did not carry book reviews. Two other review symposia, one on Srinivas's *The Remembered Village* (1978: 12, 1) and the other on the work of two distinguished Sri Lankan anthropologists Gananath Obeyesekere and Stanley Tambiah (1987: 21, 1) were very successful.

As editorial work proceeded apace, I became aware of three criticisms based on assessments of the character of the original series. I was asked by several colleagues whether *Contributions* (NS) was going to be a journal devoted to the study of Hindu society, Indological in orientation, and neglectful of urban India. Overlooking the unreasonableness of this criticism, I decided to respond positively. Pursuantly, a special number each was devoted to the Muslim communities of South Asia (1972: 6), historical movements in late nineteenth and twentieth century India (1974: 8), and processes and institutions in urban India (1977: 11, 1). The editorial responsibility for the urban India number was taken up by Saberwal (1978), who had actually come forward with the idea of such a volume. It may be added here that the Muslim communities' number was welcomed widely, and was issued as a hardcover volume in 1976 (Madan 1976a). Its appearance persuaded many students of Muslim societies in South Asia to submit papers for consideration, resulting in two enlarged editions of the first volume (Madan 1995, 2001b).

The editorial practice of producing special, thematically focused numbers was thus established. By 1991 (when I retired from the editorship), two more such special numbers were brought out, one edited by Veena Das, one of my coeditors, (1985: 19, 1; see Das 1986) and the other by McKim Marriott, a guest editor (1989: 23, 1; see Marriott 1990). The former focused on 'texts' of various kinds, ranging from the Purāṇas to government records, as a source and medium of the social construction of reality. The latter number was structured around Marriott's own influential work directed towards the making of a sociology of Hindu society in terms of indigenous categories of thought. More special numbers/volumes have been published since then. In view of the positive reception of the hardcover edition of the Muslim communities' number, subsequent special numbers also (with one exception) have been issued in similar editions.

Finally, I would like to mention here a major undertaking, namely, the putting together of a special volume (1981a: 15, 1 & 2) as a Festschrift to honour Louis Dumont on his seventieth birthday in 1981, which was also the twenty-fifth year after his launching of *Contributions* in 1957. It was later published as a book (Madan 1982a). With contributions from an international galaxy of scholars (social anthropologists, historians, Indologists, and philosophers), the volume addressed the traditional conceptions of the alternative 'ways of life' represented by three exemplars, namely, the king, the householder, and the renouncer. I wrote a concluding commentary on the significance of Dumont's approach (Madan 1981a: 403–18).

In an editorial in the last issue that I edited (1991: 25, 2), I wrote that working for *Contributions* (NS) had been 'a unique experience' from which I had 'learnt a great deal', and which I had also enjoyed deeply (p. 190). It was gratifying that a gracious contributor to the same issue of the journal should have referred to my labours as 'twenty-five year *tapasyā* at the editorial desk' (Parry 1991: 207).

IV

Concluding Remarks

The reception *Contributions* has had at the hands of an international readership encourages me to believe that what has been achieved over more than half a century by the original and the New Series has indeed been a most significant intervention in the making of the sociology of India. Dumont's contribution to this endeavour was, of course, foundational. The founding editors of the New Series were urged by him to chart their own course. Thereafter, not once during the twenty-five years of my editorship (1967–91) did he tell us what to do, but never withheld cooperation when the same was sought. In 1970, he readily agreed to my proposal for a review symposium on *Homo Hierarchicus*, and responded to the evaluations and criticisms of the contributors (Dumont 1971: 58–78). On more than one occasion, we published articles critical of his work after clearance by referees, but only once did he mildly express annoyance in a personal letter to me (see p. 214 for reference to Louis's letter written to me in April 1991 expressing annoyance to Rudner's use of the word 'inquest' in the title of his article) because he considered the criticism (of aspects of his work on Dravidian kinship) ill informed.

Those who came in as editors after the first team retired in 1991— namely, Veena Das, Ramchandra Guha, Dipankar Gupta, and Patricia Uberoi—have made *Contributions* what it is today—wider in scope than before and more contemporary in outlook. Uberoi had, in fact, joined the earlier editorial team as book review editor in 1988. In 1999, *Contributions* became a triannual. Guha and Das retired from the editorship when, one after the other, they left Delhi to pursue their academic careers elsewhere. Satish Deshpande came in as reviews editor in 1986.

During the fifteen years from 1992 to 2006, the editors attempted to strengthen the foundations of international 'dialogue' and the dialectic of theory and ethnography that had already been laid in the preceding years. They also sought to promote 'the new pluralism of paradigms now available within the social sciences' (see Das et al. 1992). One of the means employed to achieve these goals was the production of special volumes, each under the editorship of one or more of the editors or guest editors or of both types of editors. The themes covered were social reform, sexuality, and the state (1995: 29, 1 & 2); tradition, pluralism, and identity (1998: 32, 2); industrial labour (1999: 33, 1 & 2), visual practices and ideologies in modern India (2002: 36, 1 & 2); migration, modernity, and social transformation (2003: 37, 1 & 2); and contemporary expressions of caste (2004: 38, 1 & 2). These themes bear witness to the responsiveness of *Contributions* (NS) to new intellectual interests, methodological approaches, and professional challenges, contrary to the observation of some readers that Dumont's influence on the journal has precluded a broadening of its scope and the neglect of the historical approach (see, for example, Thapan and Lardinois 2006: 16).

Criticism such as the foregoing reflects a rather superficial reading of what has been published in *Contributions* (NS) over the years. The current team of editors—Amita Baviskar, Veena Naregal, and Nandini Sundar—who took over editorial responsibility in 2007, present a careful, factual assessment. They note that, although the articles published during 1967–91 were mostly about 'Hinduism, marriage-family kinship, and caste, in that order, followed by comments on the Sociology of India', the impression that the journal had long remained 'under the shadow of Dumont' is misleading. They note the emergence of engagements with 'the diversity of social contexts to be found on the subcontinent and a willingness to look beyond the confines of "village India"' (Baviskar et al. 2007: 1).

Further, the editors observe:

> Some early and interesting initiatives were taken in the study of science, domestic architecture and space, law, institutions, conflict and violence. New approaches and areas of research were consolidated in the form of special issues.... A turn towards history began in 1979 and has had some continuing impact, especially in the study of kingship and the state. (Baviskar et al. 2007: 2)

Looking forward into the near future, the editors wrote: 'Much of the direction that *Contributions* takes ... will depend upon the way ... sociology and anthropology respond to the new challenges of our times. For our part, however, we wish to flag an interest in bringing both passion and polemics to the journal.' They committed themselves to the promotion of 'civilized and informal sociological disagreement on approaches, methods and substantive issues of research and pedagogy' (Baviskar et al. 2007: 3). This is indeed the best way forward.

On an earlier occasion, I wrote in *Contributions* that 'the sociology of India moves forward dialectically', one theoretical viewpoint interrogating another. While 'a multiplicity ... of such viewpoints is a fact and not unwelcome in principle', I emphasized the importance *and* problematic character of 'communication'. I also drew attention to the danger of confusion arising from that 'most hopeless condition of atomization' about which Dumont and Pocock (1960: 82) had cautioned us. 'The establishment of a common ground for discussion, therefore, remains as important a task now as it has been in the past and as difficult as Dumont says he found it' (Madan 1982: 417). I am sure the value of *Contributions* will continue to lie in large measure in its being a forum for discussions of the kind the present editors are looking for and the maturation of the sociology of India requires.

Epilogue

Engagements and Passages—
An Exercise in Reflexivity

> [F]rom the shore
> I push'd, and struck the oars, and struck again
> In cadence, and my little Boat mov'd ...
> —WORDSWORTH, *The Prelude*

> Why cannot an anthropologist treat his own life as an ethnographic field and study it?
> —M.N. SRINIVAS, *Collected Essays*

> [O]ur beginnings never know our ends.
> —HAROLD PINTER, The 2005 Nobel Prize Lecture

THE BEGINNINGS

Long engagements interspersed with winding, cross-disciplinary passages seem to have characterized my career as a cultural anthropologist and sociologist over the last fifty-odd years. Chance and choice, contingency and design, both have shaped it.

During my childhood years of study in Srinagar (Kashmir), first with tutors at home and then in school (Standards IX and X), English (language and literature) and History interested me most from among the subjects we were taught. Interest in English was aroused early by my father's explicitly stated, enormous respect for the language as a mode of nuanced expression, and his efforts through conversation rather than formal instruction to make me proficient in it (see Madan 2010: 191). This interest was later nourished by my brother (ten years older than me), who began his M.A. studies in English when I was in the tenth standard at school.

As for History, I owe my interest in it to one of my home tutors, who made it sound like a string of stories. He was particularly interested in military engagements, and drew sketches of battle plans (Alexander's crossing of the Jhelum, the battles of Panipat, Plassey, and Arcot). Those were the early years of World War II, and he expressed great admiration for Hitler's 'military genius'. Later, at school, one of my teachers, who had studied ancient Indian History for his M.A., noticed my interest in the subject and encouraged it: he loaned me his copy of Radhakumud Mookerjee's [1928] 1972 book on Asoka and also a book of the political maps of India over two millennia. Around the same time, I read with avid interest a book in my father's collection, *Great Men of India*, which had individually authored chapters on ancient and medieval kings, statesmen of modern India, writers, scientists, industrialists, and others.

When I entered college, the choice of three subjects, besides the compulsory English, was open to me, and I wanted to concentrate on History, which I would have had to combine with Economics and a classical language (Persian or Sanskrit). Unfortunately, these classical languages were looked down upon as poor choices, lacking both academic value and practical utility. My father knew both languages, but he did not speak up for them. So, I ended up choosing what most of my friends did and what my elder brother had done earlier, namely, Mathematics and the Natural Sciences. I did not like this combination and fared poorly at the examinations. Two years later, I had to take only two subjects, besides English (in which I opted for the honours course). By then Economics had begun to interest me (some of my friends studied it), but instead of History, I chose Political Science, which was a new offering at the college. Political Theory seemed to go well with Economic Theory; there was no comparable course in History. Quite readily, I jettisoned History!

Another two years went by, and I had to choose a subject for postgraduate studies. Although my performance at the examinations had been outstanding in English and Political Science, I decided to go in for an M.A. in Economics in which I had not done so well. Economics seemed the right subject in those early days of independence; there was much talk of planning. My Economics professor heartily approved of this decision, but was dismayed to learn that I wanted to enroll at the University of Lucknow (where my brother had preceded me). He considered the interdisciplinary character of the Economics courses there a dilution of the subject and the architect of the same, Radhakamal Mukerjee, a poor economist. I may learn other things there, he warned me, but I would not learn any real Economics. But to Lucknow I went, and it was there that my academic career began at the turn of the middle of the (twentieth) century.

INTRODUCTION TO ANTHROPOLOGY AND SOCIOLOGY

The Department of Economics and Sociology had been established at the University of Lucknow in 1921 under the headship of Radhakamal Mukerjee (1889–1978), who had persuaded the authorities concerned to have combined courses in the two disciplines. Over the following decades, he had expanded further the scope of economic studies (research and teaching) in the department by including courses on cultural anthropology (see Chapter Six and Madan forthcoming).

When I enrolled as an M.A. student, compulsory courses in the first year included Micro- and Macro-economics, Institutional Economics, Demography, Ecology, and Sociology. Besides, there was an optional course, and the choice was between a couple of economics papers and Cultural Anthropology. I had never heard of the latter subject and consulted a dictionary, which described it as the comparative study of races and cultures. That sounded interesting. The faculty member who taught the subject was D.N. Majumdar (1903–60), a hugely popular teacher, I learnt, with a Cambridge Ph.D., who was a Fellow of the National Institute of Sciences. I was impressed (see Madan 1994c), and chose Cultural Anthropology. The beginnings of a career in Cultural Anthropology and Sociology could hardly have been more fortuitous and uncertain. Within a year, I turned my back on Economics when, in the second year, I chose the Sociology–Anthropology group of courses instead of the pure Economics group.

History of social thought, theories of values, culture and civilization, and general anthropology (including some topics in physical anthropology, but mainly the history of ethnological theory) were the compulsory courses. For the optional paper, I chose 'Labour', which was more Economics, but also some Sociology, because one of the two teachers who taught it was D.P. Mukerji (1894–1961), a famous sociologist who was considered one of the luminaries of the University of Lucknow (see Madan 2007b and Chapter Seven).

Mukerji also guided us through an intensive study of Toynbee's theory of civilizations, besides lecturing on the founding fathers of Sociology (Durkheim, Marx, Pareto, Weber). Toynbee fascinated me: he took me back to history, on the grand scale, and comparative literature, and opened to me the immense attraction of understanding through comparison. I read selectively from the first six volumes of *A Study of History*, which were then available, but studied very closely D.C. Somervell's excellent summary of the same (Toynbee 1947). Stressing the importance of History, Mukerji maintained that a sociological understanding of social institutions and processes was dependent upon their contextualization in a space-time ('where-when') framework, that is their history. And historical understanding in turn was dependent upon a sense of direction and values or, put otherwise, a philosophy of history, such as dialectical materialism.

While the course on culture and civilization focused on literate cultures, ethnological theory (A.L. Kroeber, Robert Lowie, Bronislaw Malinowski, Ruth Benedict, Margaret Mead, Franz Boas), taught by Majumdar, extended the scope of our studies to bring 'primitive' society into focus. For theory, we read the contributions of American and British anthropologists; our prescribed or suggested readings in ethnography introduced us to the tribal societies of India through monographic studies by, besides Majumdar himself, S.C. Roy, Verrier Elwin, and others. The two courses, namely, 'Culture and Civilization' and 'Ethnological Theory', were obviously complementary. Together, they seemed to embrace all of humanity and to be an invitation to consider everyday life worthy of serious study, concretely rather than in the abstract.

The two teachers were, however, methodologically suspect in each other's eyes. Mukerji's interest in 'theory' seemed rather vague and airy to Majumdar; the latter's empiricism was judged to be much too narrow by the former. Majumdar held to the position that *legitimate* theorization in the social sciences was nothing more than generalization from observed facts. Logical deduction from initial assumptions was a procedure alien to him. For him, the range of ways of life ('cultures') among peoples of the world was as 'real' as, say, the distribution of blood groups among them. One had to ensure that ethnographic data were reliable in the sense of being verifiable, and their analysis was rigorous and guided by appropriate theory, which, for him, was functionalism informed by cultural and social evolution.

By the time I completed my M.A. (in 1951), it was obvious to me that research and teaching were to be my vocation, and not civil service as I had earlier fancied. (I had even registered for a diploma course in Public Administration at the University, but did not pursue it seriously.) Mukerjee informed me that I was eligible for a university scholarship for research, and recommended a problem in the area of the sociology of labour, which had long been one of his own major interests. It was quite common those days for a university teacher to 'assign topics' to his students. Majumdar also said that he could get me a government research scholarship (with higher remuneration), but I would have to work on some aspect of tribal social structure, with the focus on what he liked to call their 'rehabilitation'; the word development had not yet gained currency. Mukerji, aware of my interest in historical sociology, and in Toynbee in particular, suggested that I consider working on Toynbee's 'method', or lack of it, by examining his use of sources on the Indic civilization. I wanted to work with him, and I wanted to be self-supporting. After some vacillation, I settled for doctoral work with Majumdar without wholly abandoning other scholarly interests. Mukerji continued to guide my reading, and led me to the work of historians like Burckhardt, Carr, Collingwod, and Croce, and sociologists like Mumford and Sorokin (see Chapter Seven).

I may briefly mention here that, besides Mukerji and Majumdar, we were taught by Radhakamal Mukerjee (social structure of values, psycho-social genesis of morals) and A.K. Saran (1922–2003) (symbolic interactionism). Mukerjee's lectures were based on his own books and tended to be dull; Saran, a stern critic of positivism, was simply inaccessible to me. I learnt to appreciate his vast scholarship only later, although I never could embrace his metaphysics (see Madan forthcoming).

During my early years at Lucknow University, I had the opportunity to hear, besides my teachers, a number of distinguished visiting scholars including A. Aiyappan, N.K. Bose, Louis Dumont, Irawati Karve, S.F. Nadel, and M.N. Srinivas. The subject of Srinivas's talk (winter of 1954–55) was fieldwork, and he spoke about the qualities of a good fieldworker, emphasizing, above all, total commitment. Not only must the fieldworker be a genuine participant observer, he said, but also consider his relationship with the community he chooses to study as more than a strategy for data collection, a moral responsibility. He went so far as to suggest that the best fieldworkers are single individuals without family obligations. It is worth recalling here that Srinivas himself did his fieldwork among the Coorgs and in the village of Rampura in Karnataka before he got married.

Srinivas also stressed in his talk the importance of fidelity to facts. The importance of memory and imagination that are a distinguishing feature of his book, *The Remembered Village* (1976), were not, of course, anticipated in his talk (see Chapter Eight). Actually, the discussion that followed his presentation was marked by a sharply stated difference of opinion between him and A.K. Saran on the issue of positivism in the social sciences. For Srinivas, Sociology was at its best when it was grounded in observable data in the manner of Social Anthropology. In fact, he considered a distinction between the two domains to be a colonial hangover. Saran's commitment was above all to a metaphysical perspective on social reality.

I would also like to mention the powerful impact N.K. Bose made upon some of us when he spent a day with the students of the University of Lucknow in the winter of 1950. He lectured on caste in modern Bengal, on temple architecture in Orissa, and finally on Gandhi. The range of his interests seemed wide like D.P. Mukerji's, but while the latter was a social theorist, Bose was, first and foremost, a fieldworker and a man interested in practical affairs. There was something earthy about him in the best possible sense of the term, which attracted me.

It was apparent from Bose's first and second talks that, for him, observation was a broad-based and wide-ranging engagement with social phenomena (caste, temple architecture), which was not to be bound by a narrowly conceived rulebook. A great deal of what he told us about changes in the caste system was based on his own day-to-day interaction with people than fieldwork in some village or town. In contrast, his work on Orissan temples was obviously based upon carefully planned and painstaking research, carried out practically single-handed. And when he spoke about Gandhi, he spoke more as a social activist with a deep moral concern for human suffering than as a social scientist interested in the forms of social life. In our day with Bose, social anthropology was presented to us as a part of our own lives, not a study of other cultures. The objective and the subjective were both accommodated in his method.

THE QUEST FOR OBJECTIVITY

Anthropology, I had learnt from Majumdar, was the study of 'primitive societies', of cultures other than the literate and the industrial. The so-called tribes of India were what Indian anthropologists had studied. It was inexpensive and convenient to do fieldwork within the country, and there was no dearth of tribal people. He had done so himself, in Chota Nagpur (Bihar), Mirzapur (Uttar Pradesh), Jaunsar Bawar (Uttar Pradesh), and elsewhere, studying communities such as the Ho, Tharu, and Khasa.

Conscious of my inadequacy and even awkwardness in relating to strangers and cultivating social relationships, arising partly from advancing signs of impairment of hearing (owing to otosclerosis) and also perhaps attracted to Mukerji's emphasis on the importance of general, if not explicitly stated theoretical issues, I asked Majumdar if fieldwork among tribal people was an essential requirement of a programme of doctoral studies in Anthropology. He said that, strictly speaking, it was not, for the limited purpose of preparing a dissertation, but one could not hope to make a professional career out of Anthropology without it. Accordingly, it was agreed that the subject of my dissertation would be the 'rehabilitation' of Indian tribes, and the data for it would be drawn from published sources of various kinds, including anthropological monographs and government reports. At that time the critique of development as a destroyer of cultural pluralism had not yet emerged, nor had the idea that the 'other' was, in fact, constituted by the anthropological method itself. Development from above was then considered a moral obligation rather than arrogance, and the 'other' cultures were considered essentially backward and in need of help or rehabilitation.

About a year later, I joined a group of M.A. students who were being taken to Ranchi (Bihar) for a two-week 'field trip' as part of their training in Anthropology. It turned out to be a depressing experience for me. Not that the Oraons appeared to be culturally very different from the Hindu villagers of the same area. What upset me was our own behaviour. Everybody in our group, I found, was asking the villagers questions about their family and economic life, religious beliefs, and similar matters of significance, without any regard for their feelings or convenience. My shyness crippled me, but I did manage to take photographs of an old woman's funeral procession and cremation, without first seeking anybody's permission to do so. As we came away from the village, I had the uncomfortable feeling that there was something improper about such field trips. This feeling was accentuated by the fact that one of the girl students in our group had cried at the cremation, but no one else had shown any emotion. A year-long stay in the field by an anthropologist working on his own would be, I thought, far from the kind of 'assault' in which we had been engaged. Nevertheless, a strong feeling that anthropological fieldwork was in a certain sense degrading to the unwilling subjects of observation, a violation of their personal life by strangers, took firm hold of me. This feeling was, perhaps, partly a cover for my own incapacity for fieldwork among strangers.

Gradually, almost imperceptibly, it occurred to me that a solution to the problem probably lay in studying my own community, the Pandits of the Kashmir Valley, though not my own family circle and kindred, or any other such grouping in the city of Srinagar where I had grown up. Years later I wrote: 'It is clear to me now, though it was not then, that I was transforming the familiar into the unfamiliar by the decision to relate to it as an anthropologist' (1975a: 134).

Early in 1955, S.F. Nadel visited Lucknow during a lecture tour. I took the opportunity to discuss my fieldwork problem with him. He told me that he could see no objection to an Indian studying aspects of the caste or community of his birth. He stressed the importance of training in formal anthropological research which, he thought, should help one to overcome the limitations of subjective bias. He also emphasized the importance and advantages of a good command over the 'native tongue' to anthropological research, particularly in the study of kinship and religion, and pointed out that being a native speaker would give one a head start in fieldwork. He had written about the importance of language competence in fieldwork in *The Foundations of Social Anthropology* (1952), which had impressed me enormously as a work on methodology like which there was no other available then. Not that it was an easy book to read, but I studied it closely.

Soon afterwards, I discontinued work on my dissertation on the 'rehabilitation' of Indian tribes. Majumdar, who had by then himself initiated a research project in non-tribal village near Lucknow (see Majumdar 1958), agreed that I could write a dissertation on the basis of fieldwork among the Pandits of rural Kashmir. Accordingly I sent a proposal to Nadel at ANU for the study of 'kinship values': Radhakamal Mukerjee's lectures and his book, *The Social Structure of Values* (1949), may have had a deeper impact on me than I was conscious of at that time. He had laid considerable stress on family relationships and their underlying values of love, sharing, and solidarity.

ANU awarded me a scholarship in the summer of 1955. I could never find out what Nadel actually thought of my research proposal, for he died early in 1956 before my arrival in Canberra. I had been apprehensive that he might not approve of the theme I had suggested. There was no evidence of such an interest in his own published work. My confidence had been somewhat shaken by A.K. Saran, who had summarily rejected the idea of a study of values through fieldwork. My clarification that what I intended was to find out, through close observation, the norms and values that were not merely verbalized by people, but could be shown to have actually influenced choices and behaviour in real life situations, left him totally unconvinced. This was, of course, in tune with his known opposition to positivism and to the idea of a social science.

An unexpected development may be mentioned here. In the summer of 1954, Majumdar asked me to write down my lectures on social anthropology to undergraduate students of the university for possible publication. I did this very reluctantly over a period of about eight months, and handed over the scripts to him, as he asked, every week. The lectures were based on available textbooks, some basic works, and a considerable number of ethnographic studies of Indian tribes. After going over the scripts, Majumdar suggested some revisions, which I made. He then sent the typescript to Asia Publishing House. *An Introduction to Social Anthropology* came out under our joint names early in 1956, a couple of months before my departure for Australia. Fifty-odd years later, the book is still in print in the original English and a Hindi translation.

My career as an author thus began not by my own choice, but that of one of my teachers. I might add that reviewers were uniformly kind to the book. Robert Redfield wrote in the *American Anthropologist* of the freshness he found in its pages of the encounter between Western anthropological theories and Indian ethnographic data. He recommended it as a *vade mecum* for Indian students. Today, the book, elementary in character and severely dated, is an embarrassment to me, but the demand for it from students persists.

After my arrival in Canberra, the first person to discuss my proposal with me at considerable length was Edmund Leach, who was on a short visit to ANU. He had been invited to consider if he would like to succeed Nadel as the professor. He told me in a typically forthright manner that, given his structural-functional approach, the focus of my proposed research worried him. He said that I would be making a serious mistake if I got involved in a theme so vague and so difficult to handle as 'values', and advised a focus on 'objective facts'. What mattered most in peasant kinship systems in South Asia was, he asserted, that 'people had land and they had maternal uncles'. This was obviously his way of saying that the two most significant factors governing kinship relations and family life were the ownership and inheritance of property, notably land, and the disputes that arose over it among agnatically related kin who were the offspring of different mothers in an extended family. He advised me to collect case studies of family disputes and subject them to careful analysis, so that the existence of cultural norms may be demonstrated, and to avoid getting bogged down in 'an ideal, value-governed, mythical state of existence'.

Leach thus raised doubts about the study of kinship values, as had Saran earlier, but for the very opposite reasons. His advice, as I understood it, was to leave alone the people's notions of ideal behaviour, and to adopt a statistical concept of customary or normative behaviour: to study people's behaviour itself—that is, the objective reality—rather than their ideas about it, which were subjective formulations of objective reality, often no more than distortions and rationalizations. One could trace this distrust of what people say or affirm to the many excellent demonstrations of the gap between word and deed that abounded in ethnographical literature, beginning with Malinowski's famous monographs on the Trobriand Islanders.

Although rather disappointed by Leach's rejection of the proposed focus of my research, I was greatly relieved that he had not objected to my studying the Pandits, my own people. He had not raised a question which I had feared he might, namely, how I could ensure that my research among my own people would be marked by scientific objectivity, as required by orthodoxy. I partially revised my research plan on the lines suggested by Leach.

The question of objectivity was not, however, absent in the discussions I had with various faculty members on my proposed fieldwork in Kashmir. One of them, Derek Freeman (1916–2001), already well known for his masterly studies of the Iban of Sarawak (see Appell and Madan 1988), cautioned me repeatedly to steer clear of Indological texts, and not get carried away by people's ideas about their culture and society. He called giving too much attention to such texts and ideas 'the besetting fault' of the work of Indian anthropologists on Hindu society. The anthropologist should, they all said or implied, draw his or her conclusions directly from observed behaviour, guided by well-established fieldwork techniques. The Department stocked copies of the venerable *Notes and Queries on Anthropology*, and I too equipped myself with one. I should add here that, besides Freeman, another faculty member, W.E.H. Stanner (1905–81) was my co-supervisor. No two persons could have been more unlike each other than these two men. Freeman's conception of the role of supervisor was directional; Stanner seemed more interested in helping me find my own way, as it were (see Barwick et al. 1985). My friendship with them both lasted until the very end of their lives.

We understand the import of such exhortations much better today than I was capable of doing then. My advisers emphasized that, in today's language, Indians were not to be trusted to produce objective and reliable ethnography about themselves without the benefit of modern social science perspectives. Even when trained in them, they had to be careful about not losing their objectivity by being overwhelmed ('beset') by native categories of thought. The few books that I carried with me to the Kashmir village where I went for fieldwork were what were then considered exemplary anthropological studies of marriage and kinship, notably the Nuer and Tallensi books by E.E. Evans-Pritchard (1951b) and Meyer Fortes (1949), respectively. Halfway through fieldwork, I felt the need for an authoritative work in Hindu law, and obtained one (by mail), but that was as far as

I went. Irawati Karve's *Kinship Organization in India* (1953), which I had read carefully was not with me in the field, for I had read it carefully and was not very interested in kinship terminologies like she obviously was. On the whole, I thought I had the dangers of subjective bias and a book view of society well under control, notwithstanding the fact that my Pandit villagers had lots of ideas about the character of their family life.

In fact, they had not merely stray ideas, but a coherent and well-articulated ideology of the householder. I assembled this ideology from both statements made directly by informants in reply to my questions and observations on all sorts of topics which reflected the ideology. But eventually, on my return to Canberra, I did not include a discussion of it in my dissertation. My focus was on observed behaviour, which would have been fine but for the fact that my notion of what constituted 'behaviour' was rather narrow. Thus, I failed to collect sufficient materials on Sanskritic rituals, such as initiation, marriage, and the rites addressed to manes because I believed that the quest would soon lead me to the forbidden texts. Caution about presuming that what is given in the texts is also to be found, and in the same form in real life would have been in order. A total avoidance of the texts other than the book on Hindu law, however, was a mistake that I made, but nobody told me that I was doing so. I did not then realize that being objective requires paying attention to the subjective point of view, in other words native 'texts' (oral or written), or first-order interpretations, or whatever one may call them.

A DIALECTICAL PERSPECTIVE

Early in 1959, when I was nearing the completion of the writing of my dissertation, I read the English translation of a lecture, 'For a Sociology of India' (Dumont and Pocock 1957), by Louis Dumont (1911–88) which had been earlier delivered (in French) in Paris in 1955. The approach advocated by him, attaching equal importance to Indology and social anthropology in the making of the sociology of India, reopened for me the whole issue of the place of the ideas of the people in anthropological fieldwork and the ethnographic narrative. I have already discussed this passage from one perspective to another in Chapters Nine and Ten, but would like to briefly recapitulate it here.

Dumont's argument seemed clear and convincing to me. It should suffice to recall here that, after affirming that the study of any civilization is ultimately inspired by 'the endeavour to constitute an adequate idea of mankind' (Dumont and Pocock 1957: 9), he observed that 'modern social anthropology had made a significant contribution' to the definition of social facts as things and as collective representations through 'its insistence that the observer sees things from within (as integrated in the society which he studies) and from without'. Following Evans-Pritchard, Dumont described 'the movement from one point of view to the other as an effort of translation', but cautioned that 'in this task it is not sufficient to translate the indigenous words, for it frequently happens that the ideas which they express are related to each other by more fundamental ideas even though these are unexpressed' (Dumont and Pocock 1957: 11–12).

Dumont's perspective was welcome to me as it pointed to a seemingly satisfactory way out of the alleged conflict between anthropological and native understandings of the social reality: not by privileging the former and devaluing (and even excluding) the latter, but through a confrontation of the two. To the extent to which my dissertation had considerably relied on the Kashmiri Pandits' own conceptions of kinship, marriage, and the family (see Madan 1965), I felt vindicated. At the same time it was obvious that, in the absence of a solid theoretical position (such as I now found in Dumont's statement), I had not proceeded systematically, not far enough. I attempted to do so later in a number of essays (written between 1976 and 1985, see Madan 1987a), which included one on the ideology of the Pandit householder. By then the role of ideas and ideologies in social life, and in anthropology, had begun to receive serious attention. Also, behaviouristic conceptions of culture were being replaced by symbolic ones that emphasized meaning and significance. In some of these essays I turned to notable works of fiction in various Indian languages for insights on aspects of everyday life not easily accessible to the outside observer. With the arrival of the novel on my anthropological desk, I had finally put behind me an *exclusive* social science conception of the discipline. Needless to add, I had never abandoned literature, but it had been driven, as it were, into the privacy of my after-work hours (see introduction in Madan 1987a and Chapter Eight).

Dumont's approach came under attack from F.G. Bailey soon after the publication of the English version of the 1955 lecture. Bailey restated the orthodox behaviourist position and advocated evasion of the ideas of the people, 'supposing they have any ideas which is not always the case' (1959: 90). He dismissed Dumont's approach as 'culturological' and stuck in the intuitive understanding of the unique. This was serious distortion. There were a few others who joined the debate, including A.K. Saran, who refused to grant Dumont the privilege of the ground he claimed to stand on. He wrote magisterially: '[S]ocial reality *qua* social reality has no "outside"... the only outside is interpretation in terms of an alien culture' (1962b: 68). The conflict between 'scientific objectivity', so-called, and 'subjective understanding' was presented in a particularly uncompromising form in these criticisms.

Having followed the debate with interest, I tried to formulate my own response to it. I made the following two points, among others. While recognizing the significance of the dialectic of the views from within and without, I complained that Dumont weakened his argument by asserting that the sociologist shares the external point of view with the natural scientist. I wrote:

> I am not sure that such a point of view exists.... If it did, it should have been possible for us to study social life through observation unaided by communication with the observed people.... [W]hen the sociologist allows 'the principles that people themselves give'... to enter his analysis and explanation, he surrenders a truly external position. (Madan 1966a: 12)

In response, Dumont argued that if the external point of view had not existed, there would have been no social anthropology, but conceded that the approach advocated by him 'might rather be called positive-cum-subjective' and reasserted: 'Duality, or tension is ... the condition *sine qua non* of social anthropology, or, if one likes, sociology of a deeper kind' (Dumont 1966b: 22–23).

Although I may not have stated my position very clearly, what I was trying to suggest was that, beyond a point, a stark opposition between scientific objectivity (howsoever defined) and 'subjective understanding' is sterile: it produces the kinds of negative extremism exemplified by Bailey's and Saran's comments cited above. As social anthropologists, we were concerned with the 'concrete' and the 'particular'; to adequately describe and interpret the same, and provide causal explanations when doing so seems appropriate and possible, we need 'abstract' and 'general' concepts. It cannot be otherwise in the human sciences, and I am quite comfortable with this middle position.

MUTUAL INTERPRETATION OF CULTURES

As my anthropological–sociological studies continued, the opposition between objectivity and subjectivity ceased to worry me. I also questioned the requirement of the personal study of an alien culture on the part of every anthropologist. What seemed crucial to me was bridging the gap, or, conversely, creating it, between the observer and the observed. I described fieldwork as the feat of 'living intimately with strangers' (Madan 1975a). It would have been more meaningful to call if the effort of 'living strangely with intimates', which was what I had done during my fieldwork among the Pandits of rural Kashmir. The anthropologist studying his own culture, I wrote, 'is an insider who takes up the posture of an outsider, by virtue of his training as an anthropologist or a sociologist, and looks at his own culture, hoping to be surprised. If he is, only then may he achieve new understanding' (Madan 1975a: 149).

Subsequently (Madan 1982b), I moved a step further, and argued that anthropology was best conceived, not as the study of 'other' cultures, but as 'the mutual interpretation of cultures', and that we must adhere firmly to the notion that anthropology resides in this nexus, that it is a kind of knowledge—a form of consciousness—which arises from the encounter of cultures in the mind of the anthropologist. What an observer learns about an alien society's observable modes of behaviour will not yield anthropological understanding unless he or she is able to grasp, in the first place, the subjective purposes and meanings that make these modes of behaviour significant to the people concerned. But the knowledge about one's own beliefs and rituals which an informant may impart to the investigator is not anthropological either. In other words, anthropological knowledge is not to be discovered, but generated by confronting, first, what people say with what they do, and, then, confronting the view from within with the view from without. The influence of Dumont's teaching is explicit.

The anthropologist's task, I argued, is to establish 'a synthesis between the introversion of self-understanding and the extraversion of the scientific method' (Madan 1982b: 7). It was thus that I arrived at the conclusion that Anthropology was, perhaps, best defined as the mutual interpretation of cultures: learning about one's own culture from the other cultures one studies, just as one uses insights derived from one's cultural experience—one's personal anthropology—as well as knowledge of ethnography to make sense of the cultures one writes about. Writing as a creative rather than merely recording activity, was soon going to attract a great deal of attention. Naïve realism and an uncritical mirror theory of knowledge were under attack. There was a great deal of overkill in some of these writings, but there was a hard core of genuine criticism of the orthodoxy, which fitted well with my views developed over the years.

In a later paper written in 1985 (Madan 1990), I briefly discussed the images of India in the work of some prominent American anthropologists, from Alfred Kroeber to McKim Marriott, to conclude that all of them seemed to be grounded in empirical reality: what distinguished them from one another was the perspective of each. Echoing James Clifford (1986), I called these representations partial, that is, committed and incomplete, and added that this did not mean though that someone has to piece them together and render them complete. Their utility lay in their being what they were and in their mutual contestation. The assessment of the truth value of anthropological images thus turns out to be not merely a question of information about the present situation or historical roots of institutions, or of future possibilities, but also a debate about appropriate perspectives. Such debates are, of course, notoriously inconclusive. One clear guideline though is that the perspective which enables us to understand more of the facts on the ground economically and in an internally consistent manner, and does not claim exhaustiveness, is to be preferred to those that lack coherence and lay claims to monopoly over truth.

I returned to the theme of the character of anthropological knowledge one last time in the introductory chapter to my book *Non-renunciation: Themes and Interpretations of Hindu Culture* (1987a). Writing about first-order interpretations which a people provide when questioned about their culture, I suggested that, while the interpretations fabricated by the people themselves may seem adequate and explicit to them, they usually are opaque to the outsider, which is what the social anthropologist is, in one sense or another: if not born in another society, his training as an anthropologist teaches him to turn a skeptical eye at everything that seem familiar. 'Interpretation thus involves the social anthropologist in a process of unfolding or unraveling what are at first riddles to him, by working out their implications: ... it is a search for significance and structure' (Madan 1987a: 7–8).

Just as the internal interpretations one encounters in the course of fieldwork are several, I continued, the external interpreters also may be many, each capturing a particular facet of social reality, a particular cultural theme, and providing a comparative or general perspective on it. To say this is not to surrender to solipsism, but to affirm the legitimacy and value of pluralism. The illusions of completeness and permanence that an ethnographic text creates are useful, each in its own way, but the interpretive endeavour knows no finality. As the questions change—and this happens for a variety of reasons ranging from on-going social change to changing theoretical orientations—so do the answers, and the completeness of description is inevitably deferred. I believe the positivists of yesterday knew this as well as the later grammatologists. The aims and the nature of the endeavour are, however, clear: namely, the effort to make sense of what the people we seek to understand think and do, and, as Max Weber put it, to grasp how they 'confer meaning and significance' on their lives. Our interpretations, thus, are not merely pictures of empirical reality. They are descriptive, but they are not merely description. In our fieldwork and the subsequent writing, we not only *look* and *listen*, we also *think*. In other words, we inevitably, though not always self-consciously, put ourselves into our ethnographic accounts of others.

As I have reflected over the years upon the nature of anthropological fieldwork and knowledge, I have leaned more and more towards the humanities, and found social and cultural history and literature rich sources of inspiration in my anthropological work. I have noted the need for immense caution implied by Karl Popper's admonition that 'the triumph of social anthropology' may have only been 'the triumph of a pseudo-observational, pseudo-descriptive, and pseudo-generalising methodology and above all marks the triumph of a pretended objectivity and hence an imitation of the methods of natural science' (Banton 1964: 99).

I have also become increasingly conscious of the significance of cultivating a philosophical perspective in the specific sense of comparative ethics. Ethnography merely as knowledge of how other people live their lives can be just baggage, a burden, unless it teaches one to live one's own life better—judged as such in terms of certain ultimate values that enjoy cross-cultural legitimacy. Whether this effort is described as 'the mutual interpretation of cultures', or as the cultivation of 'critical self-awareness' (Madan 1994c: Chapters 7 and 8), the point being made is the same and obvious. It would be trite to try to illustrate such a worldview by citing particular examples: it must inform all that one does and the way one thinks.

CULTURE AND DEVELOPMENT

The years immediately following the completion of my doctoral dissertation at ANU and return to my teaching position at the University of Lucknow in 1959 were marked by some further writing and publication in the area of kinship studies in the midst of two changes of place of work. I spent an academic year as a lecturer at the Department of Anthropology of the School of Oriental and African Studies, London, and then took up (in 1963) a readership of Social Anthropology at Karnatak University in Dharwar. The city is home to a sizeable community of Saraswat Brahmans: they claim descent from Kashmiri Brahmans who, they believe, migrated to the western coast of south India in difficult times long ago. I thought it would be worthwhile to do a comparative study of their family life on the lines of my study of the Pandits of rural Kashmir.

Rather unnecessarily, I got bogged down in learning their language (Konkani), for most of them are proficient in English, particularly the men. I also concentrated on revising my dissertation, written in 1958–59, for publication. *Family and Kinship: A Study of the Pandits of Rural Kashmir* was published in 1965, and remains in print, having been reissued in 1989 in an expanded edition and subsequently reprinted thrice. The reviewers have again been generally kind, although one of them (Stephen Tyler in the *American Athropologist*) called it an 'essay', not a 'scientific treatise'! He changed his assessment in a later published comment as his own perspective on anthropology changed. A recent review of the state of sociology in India regrets the absence of ethnographic studies such as Srinivas's *Religion and Society among the Coorgs of South India* (1952) and *Family and Kinship* (see Béteille 2006: 209).

Even as I was making preparations for a study of the family among the Saraswats of Dharwar, the University asked me to undertake a study of private educational institutions for the National Council of Educational Research and Training (New Delhi). By the time this study was completed in 1965 (see Madan and Halbar 1972), I had decided to move to Delhi. The significance of this study lay in documenting the easy coexistence of primordial (caste, religious) identities, representing a tradition that modernists consider a sign of backwardness, and modern, technical education (including that in engineering and medical sciences) provided by caste and community managed educational institutions. A facile tradition versus modernity model obviously was of little, if any, use. The study covered educational institutions in three districts of the state of Karnataka. Had I not moved to Delhi I would have done a larger, state-level, and more comprehensive study of the subject.

While in Dharwar, which was a small city, although a university town and district headquarters, I become conscious of the interest and importance of studying the organization and culture of private medical practice by individual professionals in the vicinity of hospitals and not too far away from a medical college. It was clear to me that, while in a rural setting (as in Kashmir where I had done fieldwork), work was largely a dimension of the domestic domain; in urban settings the domestic and work domains were considerably differentiated. But I was able to explore the significance of modern occupations and professions only after relocating in Delhi.

MODERN OCCUPATIONS AND PROFESSIONS

In 1965 I was invited by Pierre Bessaignet, a French sociologist and ethnologue, who was the director of the UNESCO Research Centre for the study of urbanization in South and Southeast Asia, to join the Centre in Delhi as it was preparing to be merged with IEG. I would have to head a multidisciplinary research team consisting mainly of sociologists. I had met Bessaignet only once at a seminar in 1961.

I accepted the invitation and joined IEG, a national level research institute recognized by the University of Delhi, in 1966. And I stayed there for the next thirty-one years until I retired in 1997. The decision to move from a university to a research institute, which did not have a regular teaching programme, was taken for partly professional and partly personal reasons. Karnatak University was a provincial university, although good as such, and Dharwar was a small city with limited options for the education of our two children, who were getting to be of school-going age.

Ever since I had begun teaching at the University of Lucknow in 1953, I had put in ten years of service as a teacher, with a break of three years (1956–59) while a doctoral student at ANU, and greatly enjoyed it. Giving up teaching was, therefore, a deeply felt wrench. As it turned out, however, I did not completely lose contact with it. Between 1971 and 1996, I held visiting professorships at five different American institutions, the Universities of Illinois (Champaign-Urbana), Washington (Seattle), Texas (Austin), Smith College, and Harvard, where I taught courses from social theory to religion and comparative ethics. I also taught a course on kinship theory to M.A. students of Sociology at Delhi University for half a dozen years (1972–77) as a guest teacher. Besides, I supervised a number of Ph.D. students at IEG itself. My decades-long engagement with academic life has thus been marked by passages between teaching and research.

At IEG, my first impulse was to go back to Kashmir and study the impact of the radical land reforms of 1950 on the family life of rural Pandits and on Pandit–Muslim relations. The significance of such a study had dawned on me in the course of fieldwork in the mid-1950s (see Madan 1966b), and the time to undertake it seemed opportune. Plans to undertake fresh fieldwork and the study of land records were made in 1967, but had to be abandoned because of intercommunity tension in the Valley caused by the elopement of an adult Pandit girl with a Muslim young man: the Pandits alleged it was a case of forcible conversion and abduction. It was then that I decided to explore the cultural dimensions of socioeconomic development with special reference to modern occupations and development.

The study of private educational institutions in Karnataka had already exposed me to the data collection techniques of the study of 'official' records, interviews and questionnaires, and the analysis of quantitative data. These were also the mainstay of part of my research on modern occupations and professions, 1968 onwards through the 1970s, which proceeded at several levels. Studying the pattern of private (non-institutional) medical practice among doctors in the city of Ghaziabad (near Delhi) involved observation of behaviour in the clinic preceded and/or followed by intensive interviews (Madan 1972c). At the All India Institute of Medical Sciences (New Delhi), the questionnaire was used followed by structured interviews (Madan et al. 1980). Macro studies of modern occupation, and professions in the context of development, involving interstate comparison within India (Madan and Verma 1973) and intercountry comparison within Asia (Madan and Verma 1971) based on official data, entailed the use of statistical analysis (with the assistance of a statistician).

Needless to say, for someone who had begun his research career as a resident fieldworker (I prefer this identification to the conventional but often inaccurate participant observer) in a village, the later studies of educational institutions and modern occupations and professions in urban settings, were a totally different experience, largely impersonal (study of records or analysis of questionnaires), and lacking depth and intimacy where interviews were conducted. Thus, while I was able to demonstrate statistically significant correlations between the magnitude and structure of the professions and levels of economic development, I was never sure that, a few exceptions apart, I really got to *know* the doctors I studied, or attained any deep understanding of the manner in which they related to their professional roles as healthcare providers, researchers, and teachers, and to their broader social environment.

The eight years spent on these researches left me both intellectually and emotionally unsatisfied, notwithstanding professional recognition and, in the case of my study of private medical practice, some public recognition also, of these innovative research efforts. What sustained me during these years was, first of all, an interest in the broader issues of culture and development. Were non-Western societies lacking in cultural resources to modernize? Did all cultures have to conform to a single type of development and modernity? Or, should one be exploring the reality, and not merely the idea, of the diversity of cultures of development (see, for example, Madan 1969, 1976b, 1983a). Nowadays, of course the notion of multiple modernities has wide acceptance, but it was not so in the 1960s and 1970s.

Second, I maintained contact with the village in Kashmir where I had done fieldwork in the mid-1950s through correspondence with some informants, whom I came to recognize as collaborators, and occasional, short visits. This resulted in a number of publications (notably 1972a, 1975a, 1975b, 1981b, 1985, 1987a), reformulating or extending earlier, published work. In a couple of these papers (see 1987a), as already noted earlier, I drew upon works of fiction to explore the realm of moral choices in domestic life, thus attending to an earlier interest in kinship values and maintaining an even earlier and continuing engagement with literature.

Third, I also selectively studied the work of some highly influential Indian and Western scholars, and wrote about some of the different intellectual strands that comprise the sociology of India (1977a, 1983a; see also 1994c and Chapters Six, Seven, Eight, and Nine in this book). Fourth, and perhaps most importantly, 1967 onward, I remained engaged as the principal editor of the journal *Contributions to Indian Sociology* (NS); this responsibility stayed with me for twenty-five years, until 1991 (see Chapter Ten).

My early studies of medical practice found favour with some colleagues at the Department of Social Sciences in UNESCO, notably its director, the Polish sociologist Janusz Ziolkowski; the UN body actually sponsored parallel case studies of institutional medical care in several Asian countries, including India (here, I did a study of the All India Institute of Medical Sciences in New Delhi). I was asked to coordinate the project. Only three of these studies, however, resulted in a publication (Madan et al. 1980).

By the time this work was being brought to a conclusion, I was sure in my own mind that I had to do something new. Not that the area of sociology of work, with particular references to the professions, was not important, but my failure to deeply engage with it was not to be denied. The inadequacy surely was mine, not of the subject. It was time for passage to another subject, but the way I might turn was not immediately clear to me. Around this time, an invitation from Peter Lengyel, editor of the *International Social Science Journal* to write an article on Hinduism (Madan 1977b) suggested a possibility, namely, the comparative study of religious traditions from the sociological-historical point of view.

Previously, I had written about religion only once, an ethnographic account of the festival of Herath among the Kashmiri Pandits (Madan 1961). I had tried to bring out the ritual and secular aspects of the annual event, with the focus more on the latter than the former. I had, however, taught a course on the anthropology of religion at Karnatak University in 1964–65, and much enjoyed dong so. Although the course was structured around Evans-Pritchard's *Nuer Religion* (1956), it led me to read again and closely the classic works of Durkheim (1915) and Weber (1958, 1963), which have been the foundation stones of all my later studies of religious traditions and the ideologies of secularism. I must also acknowledge the influence of the writings of Berger (1967, 1999), Bellah (1970), and Geertz (1966, 1968).

SECULARISM AND INDIA'S RELIGIOUS TRADITIONS

As it turned out, a decision on the next choice in my research career did not have to be taken immediately. Quite unexpectedly, early in 1978, I was invited by the distinguished political scientist Rajni Kothari, who was the Chairman of the Indian Council of Social Science Research (ICSSR) to become the Member-Secretary (Chief Executive) of the Council. After initial hesitation, I accepted the invitation. For the next more than three years, my full-time administrative job afforded me no time for any new research initiatives, although it did not completely exclude academic work.

In my second year with ICSSR, I was expected to participate in an Indo-Soviet seminar on secularization, which was to be held in Tashkant. The Council was a co-sponsor of the seminar, and the anthropologists S.C. Dube and V.N. Basilov were its coordinators. Other commitments made me stay back in India, but I prepared a paper for the seminar (1983b), in which I argued for a historical approach to its subject. My interest in secularization had been aroused by a seminal paper by David Martin (1965). A couple of years later, I had also read M.N. Srinivas's (1966a) discussion of it in his book on social change in modern India. This, then, was my first engagement with a subject that has occupied me ever since; the historical perspective too has stayed with me. I have been, however, interested more in the ideologies of secularism (and fundamentalism) than in the processes of secularization.

After my return to IEG in 1981 (I left ICSSR without completing my five year term), I wrapped up some writing work on culture and development (Madan 1983a), and began my study of the relevant literature on the sociology of religion, secularism, and the history of religious traditions from the specific perspective of secularism. The results of this research, based on published materials and discursive in character, began to appear in the mid-1980s (Madan 1986, 1987b) and have since comprised a book, *Modern Myths, Locked Minds: Secularism and Fundamentalism in India* (1997), and a number of essays most which are included in *Images of the World: Essays on Religion, Secularism and Culture* (2006a), and the present book. The guiding principles of these studies have been a sceptical attitude towards premature generalization and the imperative of historical and cultural contextualization.

At the very beginning of my studies of the subject, the discussion of the evolving connotations of what could be called secularism in Sikh religious and political history (Madan 1986; see also Chapter Four in this book) emphasized both the multivocality of the concept and the untenability of a bipolar, sacred versus secular model of secularization. Enlarging the scope of the discussion, I argued in an address to the American Association of Asian Studies (1987b), that, in the then prevailing circumstances, the Western, secular world view was unlikely to have an easy passage to India in the absence of ideological support from India's three major religious traditions, comparable to Christianity's early distinction between the sacred and secular domains. This, I argued, necessitated a reexamination of the concept of the secular state in the Indian context, and of the appropriate means of securing the same.

Misreading and misrepresenting my analysis as a denial of the ongoing processes of secularization and a rejection of the very idea of a secular state, a number of critics detected a Hindu, right wing political stance in it, notwithstanding my explicit denial that such was my aim (see Madan 2006a: Chapters 3 and 5). Not that nobody got me right, or agreed with my position. I have already cited earlier in the chapter Dumont's appreciation of it. Similarly, political theorist Rajeev Bhargava wrote in a careful review that my address had 'caught secularism in a moment of crisis', and had 'offered a suggestive, plausible explanation for it, and set many scholars down a path on how best to respond to the challenge' (1997: 13).

On my part, I carried forward my studies of the religious traditions of India (Hinduism, Islam, and Sikhism), and also of nineteenth- and twentieth-century reformist rhetorics, for intimations of secularist and fundamentalist tendencies in them. In the light of these considerations, I looked at the Indian constitution and contemporary debates on Indian secularism, to conclude that it was a religio-secular ideal (see Chapter One), and not as an ideology of privatization or marginalization of religion, or of the denial of its social significance, both constructive, as pluralism, and destructive, as fundamentalism. The next step obviously is to develop a defensible pluralist position in culture as well as politics. This is a widely shared concern and not confined to the contemporary Indian situation. It is a methodologically daunting challenge.

CONCLUDING REMARKS

I had wanted to read History when I entered college more than sixty years ago. Had I been able to do so, I would have perhaps become a historian and might have made some original contributions. As I have briefly described, my intellectual journey followed a different path, marked by long engagements as well as winding passages from one theme to another. After first-hand research in the areas of the sociology of the family and the professions, I moved into macro-level comparisons of data on the professions and finally into the study of secularism and religious traditions. Obviously, I am not a historian: that is not the issue. It is not wholly inappropriate, however, to ask in what sense my work on secularism and the study of religious traditions may be called cultural anthropological and sociological. Needless to emphasize, I consider the two disciplines complementary rather than mutually exclusive.

Now, if cultural anthropology is narrowly defined as a body of knowledge about non-Western or non-literate societies and their cultures (African, Asian, and such others), and primarily through fieldwork, then my recent or previous work is not anthropological. But if it is defined as an intellectual effort to understand the other's point of view if it is others one is studying, *and not be shocked by difference*; or if it is to acquire critical self awareness through the exercise of doubt acquired by the comparison of ourselves and selected others *and be surprised*, then I have been and remain an anthropologist. Following Dumont (actually Marcel Mauss and Durkheim), anthropological knowledge may be said to be born of the tension between the view from within and the view from without. As for fieldwork, the point really is that we seek to know through personal experience, and this imposes a clear restriction of scale. The transition from the small scale to the large, from intensive to extensive coverage, usually distinguishes the sociological perspective from the anthropological; and I have done both kinds of work.

I have over the years learnt to distrust sharp disciplinary distinctions as I was taught to do at the very beginning of my academic career by Radhakamal Mukerjee and D.P. Mukerji. In any case, disciplinary spaces have not only fluid, permeable boundaries; they are also always changing through the expectation that they will be open to new questions as these inevitably emerge in course of time. If they are not so open, they soon turn barren. Moreover, one is defined by the disciplinary or interdisciplinary space in which one tries to find one's way about; at the same time, one hopes to have contributed in some measure to the collective endeavour of space expansion and illumination.

Let me, then, conclude by suggesting that an exercise in reflexivity, such as the present narrative, while personally rewarding, might also be of some interest to others cultivating the same field, for no scholar stands on his own in an empty space, as it were. We are always located: in my case in the rich fields successively of family and kinship, the professions, and religious ideas, including Indian secularism.

References

Abdullah, Shaikh Mohammad. 1993. *Flames of the Chinar: An Autobiography*. New Delhi: Viking.
Advani, L.K. 2008. *My Country, My Life*. New Delhi: Rupa & Co.
Ahmad, Imtiaz (ed.). 1973. *Caste and Social Stratification among Muslims in India*. New Delhi: Manohar.
———. 1976. *Family, Kinship and Marriage among the Muslims in India*. New Delhi: Manohar.
———. 1981. *Ritual and Religion among Muslims in India*. New Delhi: Manohar.
Ahmad, Mumtz. 1991. 'Islamic Fundamentalism in South Asia', in Martin Marty and R. Scott Appleby (eds), *Fundamentalisms Observed*. Chicago: University of Chicago Press.
Ahmed, Akbar S. 1986. *Pakistan Society*. Karachi: Oxford University Press.
Ahmed, Rafiuddin. 1981. *The Bengal Muslims 1871–1906: A Quest for Identity*. New Delhi: Oxford University Press.
Amin, Pirzada Mohammad. 2001. *Hazratbal Shrine in Historical Perspective*. New Delhi: Grassroots India Publishers.
Ansari, Ghaus. 1960. *Muslim Caste in Uttar Pradesh*. Lucknow: Ethnographic and Folk Culture Society.
———. 2004. *Umar-i Rafta* (in Urdu), Vol. 2. Delhi: Educational Publishing House.
Anwar, M. Syafi'i. 2007. 'The Clash of Religio-political Thought: The Contest between Radical-conservatism and Progressive-liberal Islam in Post-Soeharto Indonesia', in T.N. Srinivasan (ed.), *The Future of Secularism*. New Delhi: Oxford University Press.
Appell, George N. and T.N. Madan. 1988. 'Derek Freeman: Notes toward an Intellectual Biography', in George N. Appell and T.N. Madan (eds),

Choice and Morality in Anthropological Perspective. Albany: State University of New York Press.
Aron, Raymond. 1967. *Main Currents in Sociological Thought*. New York: Basic Books.
Asad, Talal. 1986. *The Idea of an Anthropology of Islam*. Washington, DC: Centre for Contemporary Arab Studies, Georgetown University.
Avasthi, Abha. 1997. *Social and Cultural Diversities: D.P. Mukerji in Memoriam*. Jaipur: Rawat.
Bailey, F.G. 1958. *Caste and the Economic Frontier: A Village in Highland Orissa*. Bombay: Oxford University Press.
———. 1959. 'For a Sociology of India', *Contributions to Indian Sociology*, III: 80–101.
Baldock, John. 2006. *The Essence of Rumi*. London: Arcturus,
Banton, Michael. 1964. 'Anthropologial Perspectives in Sociology', *British Journal of Sociology*, 15: 95–112.
Barwick, Diome E., Jeremy Beckett, and Marie Reay. 1985. 'W.E. Stanner: An Australian Anthropologist', in D. Barwick, J. Beckett, and M. Reay (eds), *Metaphors of Interpretation: Essays in Honour of W.E.H. Stanner*. Canberra: Australian National University Press.
Basu, Shamita. 2002. *Religious Revivalism and Nationalist Discourse*. New Delhi: Oxford University Press.
Bateson, Gregory and Mary Catherine Bateson. 1987. *Angels Fear: An Investigation into the Nature and Meaning of the Sacred*. London: Rider.
Baviskar, Amita, Nandini Sundar, and Veena Naregal. 2007. 'Editorial', *Contributions to Indian Sociology* (NS), 41(1): 1–4.
Bayly, Susan. 1999. *Caste, Society and Politics in India from the Eighteenth Century to the Modern Age*. Cambridge: Cambridge University Press.
Beliappa, Jayanthi. 1979. 'A Study of the Religious Concepts of the Coorgs', Ph.D. dissertation, Typescript, University of Delhi.
Bellah, Robert. 1970. *Beyond Belief: Essays in Religion in a Post-traditional World*. New York. Harper & Row.
Berger, Monroe. 1977. *Real and Imagined Worlds: The Novel and Social Science*. Cambridge, M.A: Harvard University Press.
Berger, Peter. 1967. *The Social Reality of Religion*. Harmondsworth: Penguin Books.
——— (ed.). 1999. *The Desecularization of the World*. Washington, DC: Ethics and Public Policy Centre.
Béteille, André. 2003. 'Sociology and Social Anthropology', in Veena Das (ed.), *Oxford Companion to Sociology and Social Anthropology*, Vol. 1. New Delhi: Oxford University Press.
———. 2006. 'Sociology and Current Affairs', *Sociological Bulletin*, 55(2): 201–14.

Bhargava, Rajeev. 1997. 'Unlocking Traditional Minds', *The Book Review*, 21(8): 11–13.
———. 2007. 'The Distinctiveness of Indian Secularism', in T.N. Srinivasan (ed.), *The Future of Secularism*. New Delhi: Oxford University Press.
———. 2010. 'The "Secular Ideal" before Secularism: A Preliminary Sketch', in Linell E. Cady and Elizabeth Shakman Hurd (eds), *Comparative Secularism in a Global Age*. New York: Palgrave Macmillan.
Bhattacharya, Swapan Kumar. 1990. *Indian Sociology: The Role of Benoy Kumar Sarkar*. Burdwan: The University of Burdwan.
Bose, Nirmal Kumar. 1941. 'The Hindu Method of Tribal Absorption', *Science and Culture*, 7(1): 188–94. Reproduced in N.K. Bose. 1967. *Culture and Society in India*. Bombay: Asia Publishing House.
———. 1948. *Selections from Gandhi*. Ahmedabad: Navjivan.
Bouglé, Célistin. 1908. *Essais sur le régime des castes*. Paris: Alcan.
Cady, Linell and Elizabeth Hurd (eds). 2010. *Secularism and Politics in a Global Age*. New York: Palgrave-Macmillan.
Carrithers, Michael, Steven Collins, and Steven Lukes (eds). 1985. *The Category of the Person*. Cambridge: Cambridge University Press.
Celtel, André. 2005. *Categories of Self: Louis Dumont's Theory of the Individual*. New York: Berghahn Books.
Chakrabarti, Kunal. 2001. *Religious Process: The Puranas and the Making of a Regional Tradition*. New Delhi: Oxford University Press.
Chandhoke, Neera. 1999. *Beyond Secularism: The Rights of Religious Minorities*. New Delhi: Oxford University Press.
Chatterjee, Margaret. 2005. *Gandhi and the Challenge of Religious Diversity: Religious Plurality Revisited*. New Delhi: Promilla & Co.
Chatterjee, Partha. [1994] 1998. 'Secularism and Toleration', in R. Bhargava (ed.), *Secularism and Its Critics*. New Delhi: Oxford University Press.
Chatterji, Roma. 2007. 'The Nationalist Sociology of Benoy Kumar Sarkar', in Patricia Uberoi, Nandini Sundar, and Satish Deshpande (eds), *Anthropology in the East: Founders of Indian Sociology and Anthropology*. Ranikhet: Permanent Black.
Chaudhuri, Nirad C. 1974. *Scholar Extraordinary: The Life of Professor the Right Honourable Friedrich Max Müller, P.C.* Delhi: Oxford University Press.
Clifford, James. 1986. 'Introduction: Partial Truths', in James Clifford and George E. Marcus (eds), *Writing Culture: The Poetics and Politics of Ethnography*. Berkeley: University of California Press.
Collingwood, R.G. 1970. *An Autobiography*. London: Oxford University Press.
Commons, John. 1934. *Institutional Economics*. New York: Macmillan.
Coulanges, Fustel de. [1864] n.d. *The Ancient City: A Study on the Religion, Laws and Institutions of Greece and Rome*. New York: Doubleday Anchor.

Cunningham, J.D. [1916] 1955. *A History of the Sikhs*. New Delhi: S. Chand & Co.

Dandekar, R.N. 1971. 'Hinduism', in C.J. Bleeker and G. Widengren (eds), *Historia Religionum: Handbook for the History of Religions*, Vol. II. *Religions of the Present*. Leiden: E.J. Brill.

Das, Veena (ed.). 1986. *The Word and the World: Fantasy, Symbol and Record*. New Delhi: SAGE Publications.

Das, Veena, Ramchandra Guha, Dipankar Gupta, and Patricia Uberoi. 1992. 'Editorial', *Contributions to Indian Sociology* (NS), 26(1): 1–2.

Dasgupta, Ajit. 1993. *A History of Indian Economic Thought*. London: Routledge.

———. 1996. *Gandhi's Economic Thought*. London: Routledge.

Dasgupta, Sangeeta. 2007. 'Recasting the Oraons and the "Tribe": Sarat Chandra Roy's Anthropology', in P. Uberoi, N. Sundar, and S. Deshpande (eds), *Anthropology in the East*. Ranikhet: Permanent Black.

Dasgupta, Subrata. 2010. *Awakening: The Story of the Bengal Renaissance*. New Delhi: Random House.

Datta, Bhabatosh. 1978. *Indian Economic Thought: Twentieth Century Perspectives 1900–1950*. New Delhi: Tata McGraw-Hill.

Desai, Mahadev. 1946. *The Gospel of Selfless Action or the Gita According to Gandhi*. Ahmedabad: Navjivan.

Deshpande, Satish. 2003. *Contemporary India: A Sociological View*. New Delhi: Viking.

Dirks, Nicholas B. 2002. *Castes of Mind: Colonialism and the Making of Modern India*. New Delhi: Permanent Black.

Dube, Leela. 1969. *Matriliny and Islam*. New Delhi: National.

Dubois, Abbé, J.A. [1906] 1959. *Hindu Manners, Customes and Ceremonies*. Trs. and ed., Henry K. Beanchamp, 3rd edition. Oxford: Clarendon Press.

Dumont, Louis. 1950. 'Kinship Alliance among the Pramalai Kallar', *The Eastern Anthropologist*, IV(1): 3–26.

———. 1951. *La Tarasque: Essai de description d'un fait local d'un point de vue ethnographique*. Paris: Gallimard, collection 'L'espèce humaine.

———. 1953a. 'Dravidian Kinship Terminology', *Man*, LIII(143).

———. 1953b. 'The Dravidian Kinship Terminology as an Expression of Marriage', *Man*, LIII(34–39).

———. 1957a. *Hierarchy and Marriage Alliance in South Indian Kinship*. London: Royal Anthropological Institute, Occasional Paper No. 12.

———. 1957b. *Une Sous-caste de l'Inde du sud: Organisation sociale et religion des Pramalai Kallar*. Collection 'Le monte d'outre-mer, passé et présent', Ist series I. Paris, The Hague: Mouton.

———. 1959. 'Pure and Impure: M.N. Srinivas', *Contributions to Indian Sociology*, III: 9–34.

Dumont, Louis. 1960. 'World Renunciation in Indian Religions', *Contributions to Indian Sociology*, IV: 38–62.

———. 1962. 'The Conception of Kingship in Ancient India', *Contributions to India Sociology*, VI: 48–77.

———. 1964. *La civilization indienne et nous: Esquisse de sociologie comparée*. Paris: A. Colin. Cahiers des Annales No. 23 (2nd ed., 1975, Coll. 'Uprisme'). (Italian translation by A. Pessali. 1965. Venice: Fondazioné Giorci Cini.)

———. 1966a. *Homo Hierarchicus: Essai sur le système des castes*. Paris: Gallimard, collection bibliothèque des sciences humaines. (English translation by M. Sainsbury. 1970. London: Weidenfeld and Nicolson and Chicago: University of Chicago Press. Same in paperback, with an introduction by M. Douglas. 1972. London: Paladin. For the complete English edition see Dumont 1980a.)

———. 1966b. 'A Fundamental Problem in the Sociology of Caste', *Contributions to Indian Sociology*, IX: 17–37.

———. 1967a. *Homo Hierarchicus: Essai sur le systèmme de castes*. Paris: Gallimard.

———. 1967b. 'Caste: A Phenomenon of Social Structure or an Aspect of Indian Culture?' in A.V.S. de Reuck and Julie Knight (eds), *Ciba Foundation Symposium on Caste and Race: Comparative Approaches*. London: Churchill.

———. 1967c. 'The Individual as an Impediment to Sociological Comparison in Indian History', in Baljit Singh and V.B. Singh (eds), *Social and Economic Change: Essays in Honour of Professor D.P. Mukerji*. Bombay: Allied Publishers.

———. 1970a. *Homo Hierarchicus: The Caste System and Its Implications*. London: Widenfeld and Nicholson.

———. 1970b. *Religion, Politics and History in India*. Paris: Mouton.

———. 1971. 'On Putative Hierarchy and Some Allergies to It', *Contributions to Indian Sociology* (NS), 5(1): 58–78.

———. 1976. 'The British in India', in Charles Moraze (ed.), *History of Mankind: Cultural and Scientific Development*, Vol. V, Part IV, *The 19th Century* London: Allen and Unwin.

———. 1977. *From Mandeville to Marx: The Genesis and Triumph of Economic Ideology*. Chicago: University of Chicago Press. (French version: *Homo aequalis I: Genèse et épanouissement de l'déologie économique*. 1977. Paris: Gallimard, Bibliothèque des Sciences Humaines.)

———. 1980a. *Homo Hierachicus: The Caste System and Its Implications* (revised and complete English edition). Chicago: Chicago University Press.

———. 1980b. 'La dette vis-à-vis des ancêtres et la catégorie de sapinda', *Purusärtha*, 4: 15–38. (English version: 1983. 'The Debt to Ancestors and the Category of Sapindas', in Charles Malamoud [ed.], *Debts and Debtors*. New Delhi: Vikas Publishing House.)

Dumont, Louis. 1981. 'Louis Dumont and the Indian Mirror', Interview by Christian Delacampagne (translated from the French of *Le Monde*, 25 January 1981, p. xv), *Royal Anthropological Institute*, News 43, April, pp. 4–7.

———. 1983a. *Affinity as a Value: Marriage Alliance in South India, with Comparative Essays on Australia*. Chicago: The University of Chicago Press.

———. 1983b. 'A Modified View of Our Origins: The Christian Beginnings of Modern Individualism', *Contributions to Indian Sociology* (NS), 17(1): 1–26.

———. 1986a. *A South Indian Subcaste. Social Organization and Religion of the Pramalai Kallar*. Trs., M. Moffatt and A. Morton. Delhi: Oxford University Press. (Trs. of Dumont 1957b.)

———. 1986b. *Essays on Individualism: Modern Ideology in Anthropological Perspective*. Chicago: The University of Chicago Press. (Shorter version in French: 1983. *Essais sur l'individualisme*. Paris: Sevil.)

———. 1991. *Homo aequalis II. L'idélogie allemande. France-Allemagne et retour*. Paris: Gallimard.

———. 1994. *German Ideology: From France to Germany and Back*. Chicago: The University of Chicago Press.

Dumont, Louis and D.F. Pocock. 1957. 'For a Sociology of India', *Contributions to Indian Sociology*, I: 7–22.

———. 1960. 'For a Sociology of India. A Rejoinder to Dr. Bailey', *Contributions to Indian Sociology*, IV: 82–89.

Durkheim, Émile. 1915. *The Elementary Forms of the Religious Life*. Trs., Joseph Ward Swain. New York: Macmillan.

———. 1938. *The Rules of Sociological Method*. Trs., S.A. Solovay and J.H. Mueller. Glencoe, IU: The Free Press.

———. 1953. *Sociology and Philosophy*. Trs., D.F. Pocock. London: Cohen and West.

———. [1915] 1995. *The Elementary Forms of Religious Life*. Trs., Karen E. Fields. New York: The Free Press.

Durkheim, Émile and Marcel Mauss. 1963. *Primitive Classification*. Trs. and ed., Rodney Needham. Chicago: Chicago University Press.

Eaton, Richard M. 1994. *The Rise of Islam and the Bengal Frontier, 1204–1760*. New Delhi: Oxford University Press.

———. 2000. *Essays on Islam and Indian History*. New Delhi: Oxford University Press.

———. (ed.). 2003. *India's Islamic Traditions*. New Delhi: Oxford University Press.

Eck, Diana. 1982. *Banaras: City of Light*. New York: Alfred Knopf.
Eliot, Charles. 1954. *Hinduism and Buddhism*, Vol. II. London: Routledge & Kegan Paul.
Epstein, Scarlett. 1976. 'The Remembered Village: A Modern Classic', *Contributions to Indian Sociology*, 12(1): 67–74.
Evans-Pritchard, E.E. 1951a. *Social Anthropology*. London: Cohen and West.
———. 1951b. *Kinship and Marriage among the Nuer*. Oxford: Clarendon Press.
———. 1956. *Nuer Religion*. Oxford: Clarendon Press.
———. 1965. *Theories of Primitive Religion*. Oxford: Clarendon Press.
Fenech, Louis E. 2000. *Martyrdom in the Sikh Tradition: Playing the Game of Love*. New Delhi: Oxford University Press.
Field, Dorothy. 1914. *The Religion of the Sikhs*. London: John Murray.
Firth, Raymond. 1951. *Elements of Social Organization*. London: Watts & Co.
Forbes, Geraldine. 1975. *Positivism in Bengal*. Calcutta: Minerva.
Fortes, Meyer. 1949. *The Web of Kinship among the Tallensi*. London: Oxford University Press.
French, Patrick. 2008. *The World Is What It Is: The Authorized Biography of V.S. Naipaul*. London: Picador.
Fuller, C.J. 1992. *Camphor Flame: Popular Hinduism and Society in India*. Princeton, NJ: Princeton University Press.
Gadamer, Hans-Georg. 1975. *Truth and Method*. New York: Continuum, The Seabury Press.
Galey, Jean-Claude. 1982. 'A Conversation with Louis Dumont, Paris, 12 December 1979', in T.N. Madan (ed.), *Way of Life: King, Householder, Renouncer: Essays in Honour of Louis Dumont*. New Delhi: Vikas Publishing House and Paris: Editions Maison des Sciences de l'Homme.
——— (ed.). 1984. *Différences, Valeurs, Hiérarchie. Textes offerts à Louis Dumont*. Paris: Editions de l'Études en Sciences Sociales.
Gandhi, M.K. [1927] 1940. *The Story of My Experiments with Truth*. Ahmedabad: Navjivan.
———. 1946. 'Anasaktiyoga', in Mahadev Desai (ed.), *The Gospel of Selfless Action or the Gita According to Gandhi*. Ahmedabad: Navjivan.
———. 1954. *Prarthanā Pravachan*, Vol. 1. New Delhi: Sasta Sahitya Mandir.
———. 1966a. *The Collected Works of Mahatma Gandhi*, Vol. 19. New Delhi: Publications Division, Ministry of Information and Broadcasting, Government of India.
———. 1966b. *The Collected Works of Mahatma Gandhi*, Vol. 21. New Delhi: Publications Division, Ministry of Information and Broadcasting, Government of India.

Gandhi, M.K. 1969. *The Collected Works of Mahatma Gandhi*, Vol. 32. New Delhi: Publications Division, Ministry of Information and Broadcasting, Government of India.
———. 1971. *The Collected Works of Mahatma Gandhi*, Vol. 44. New Delhi: Publications Division, Ministry of Information and Broadcasting, Government of India.
———. 1979. *The Collected Works of Mahatma Gandhi*, Vol. 75. New Delhi: Publications Division, Ministry of Information and Broadcasting, Government of India.
———. 1983. *The Collected Works of Mahatma Gandhi*, Vol. 87. New Delhi: Publications Division, Ministry of Information and Broadcasting, Government of India.
———. 1997. *Hind Swaraj and Other Writings*, ed. Anthony J. Parel. Cambridge: Cambridge University Press.
Ganguli, B.N. 1973. *Gandhi's Social Philosophy*. New Delhi: Vikas Publishing House.
Geertz, Clifford. 1965. 'Modernization in Muslim Society: The Indonesian Case', in R.N. Ballah (ed.), *Religion and Progress in Modern Asia*. New York: The Free Press.
———. 1966. 'Religion as a Cultural System', in M. Banton (ed.), *Anthropological Approaches to the Study of Religion*. London: Tavistock Publications.
———. 1968. *Islam Observed: Religious Development in Morocco and Indonesia*. Chicago: University of Chicago Press.
———. 1995. *After the Fact*. Cambridge, MA: Harvard University Press.
Gellner, Ernest. 1969. 'A Pendulum Swing Theory of Islam', in R. Robertson (ed.), *Sociology of Religion*. Harmondsworth: Penguin.
———. 1981. *Muslim Society*. Cambridge: Cambridge University Press.
Ghurye, Govind Sadashiv. 1948. *Occidental Civilization*. Bombay: International Book House.
———. 1955. *Family and Kin in Indo-European Culture*. Bombay: Popular Prakashan.
———. 1957. 'Vidyas: A Homage to Comte and a Contribution to the Sociology of Knowledge', *Sociological Bulletin*, vi(2): 1–88.
———. [1943] 1963. *The Aborigines—So-Called—and Their Future*. 3rd ed. entitled *The Scheduled Tribes*. Bombay: Popular Prakashan.
———. [1957] 1963. *The Mahadev Kolis*, 2nd ed. Bombay: Popular Prakashan.
———. [1953] 1964. *Indian Sadhus*, 2nd ed. Bombay: Popular Prakashan.
———. 1968. *Social Tensions in India*. Bombay: Popular Prakashan.
———. [1932] 1969. *Caste and Race in India*, 5th ed. Bombay: Popular Prakashan.

Ghurye, Govind Sadashiv. 1973. *I and Other Explorations*. Bombay: Popular Prakashan.
Goethe, Johann Wolfgang von. 1966. *Goethe: Conversations and Encounters*, ed. and trs. David Lake and Robert Pick. London: Oswald Wolff.
Gold, Anne Grodzins. 1987. *Fruitful Journeys: The Ways of Rajasthani Pilgrims*. Berkeley: University of California Press.
Gowling, Peter G. 1974. 'How Muslim are the Muslim Filipinos?' in P.G. Gowling and R.D. McAmis (eds), *The Muslim Filipinos*. Manila: Solidaridad.
Green, Martin. 1978. *The Challenge of the Mahatmas*. New York: Basic Books.
Grewal, J.S. [1969] 1979. *Guru Nanak in History*. Chandigarh: Punjab University.
Grewal, J.S. and S.S. Bal [1967] 1987. *Guru Gobind Singh: A Biographical Study*. Chandigarh: Punjab University.
Guha, Ramachandra (ed.). 1994. 'Introduction', in *Social Ecology*. New Delhi: Oxford University Press.
Guha, Ranajit. 1983. *Elementary Aspects of Peasant Insurgency in Colonial India*. New Delhi: Oxford University Press.
Halbfass, Wilhelm. 1988. *India and Europe: An Essay in Understanding*. Albany: State University of New York Press.
Hans, Surjit. 1985. 'Historically Challenging Modes of Thought in Sikhism in the Overall Social Context', *New Quest*, 52: 211–21.
Hart, Samuel. 1956. 'Bridging Sociology and Ethics', in Baljit Singh (ed.), *The Frontiers of Social Science*. London: Macmillan.
Herskovits, Melville J. 1952. *Economic Anthropology*. New York: Norton.
Hocart, A.M. 1938. *Les Castes*. Paris: Geuthner.
Hubert, Henri and Marcel Mauss. 1964. *Sacrifice: Its Nature and Function*. Trs., W.D. Halls. London: Cohen and West.
Hume, David. [1757] 1957. *Natural History of Religion*, ed. H.E. Root. Stanford: Stanford University Press.
Huntington, Samuel P. 1997. *The Clash of Civilizations: Remaking of World Order*. New York: Touchstone.
Iyer, Raghavan (ed.). 1986. *The Moral and Political Writings of Mahatma Gandhi. Vol. I: Civilization, Politics, and Religion*. Oxford: Clerendon Press and New Delhi: Oxford University Press.
Jackson, Peter. 1999. *The Delhi Sultanate*. Cambridge: Cambridge University Press.
Jafferlot, Christophe. 1996. *The Hindu Nationalist Movement and Indian Politics*. New Delhi: Viking.
James, Henry. 1937. *The Art of the Novel*. New York: Scribner.
Jarvie, Ian. 1964. *The Revolution in Anthropology*. London: Routledge & Kegan Paul.

Jordens, J.T.F. 1978. *Dayanand Sarasvati: His Life and Teachings*. New Delhi: Oxford University Press.
———. 1998. *Gandhi's Religion*. London: Macmillan.
Joshi, Manoj. 1999. *The Lost Rebellion: Kashmir in the Nineties*. New Delhi: Penguin.
Joshi, P.C. 1986. 'Founders of Lucknow School and their Legacy: Radhakamal Mukerjee and D.P. Mukerji: Some Reflections', *Economic and Political Weekly*, 21(33): 1455–69.
Juergensmeyer, Mark. 1991. *Radhasaomi Reality: The Logic of a Modern Faith*. Princeton, NJ: Princeton University Press.
Karlekar, Hiranmay. 2006. *Bangladesh: The Next Afghanistan*. New Delhi: SAGE Publications.
Karve, Iravati. 1953. *Kinship Organization in India*. Poona: Deccan College.
Kaul, Jayalal. 1973. *Lal Ded*. New Delhi: Sahitya Akademi.
Ketkar, S.V. [1909] 1979. *History of Caste in India*. Jaipur: Rawat.
Khan, Abdul Majid. 1967. 'The Impact of Islam on Sikhism', in *Sikhism and Indian Society*. Simla: Indian Institute of Advanced Study.
Khan, Mohammad Ishaq. 1994. *Kashmir's Transition to Islam: The Role of Muslim Rishis*. New Delhi: Manohar.
———. 1997. *Experiencing Islam*. New Delhi: Sterling.
———. 2004. 'The Rishi Tradition and the Construction of Kashmiriyat', in Imtiaz Ahmad and Helmut Reifeld (eds), *Lived Islam in South Asia: Adaptation, Accommodation and Conflict*. New Delhi: Social Science Press.
Khare, R.S. [2006] 2009. *Caste, Hierarchy, and Individualism: Indian Critiques of Louis Dumont's Contributions*, 2nd edition. New Delhi: Oxford University Press.
King, Richard. 1999. *Orientalism and Religion*. New Delhi: Oxford University Press.
Kopf, David. 1969. *British Orientalism and the Bengal Renaissance*. Berkeley: University of California Press.
———. 1979. *The Brahmo Samaj and the Shaping of the Modern Indian Mind*. Princeton, NJ: Princeton University Press.
Krishnamurty, J. (ed.). 2009. *Towards Development Economics*. New Delhi: Oxford University Press.
Kulke, Hermann. 1986. 'Max Weber's Contribution to the Study of "Hinduization" in India and "Indianization" in Southeast Asia', in D. Kantowsky (ed.), *Recent Researches on Max Weber's Studies of Hinduism*. Munchen: Weltforum Verlag.
Lepenies, Wolf. 1988. *Between Literature and Sciences: The Rise of Sociology*. Cambridge: Cambridge University Press.
Lévi-Strauss, Claude. 1949. *Les structures élémentaries de la parenté*. Paris: Presse Universitaire France.

Lévi-Strauss, Claude. 1967. *The Scope of Anthropology*. Translated from the French by Sherry Ortner Paul and Robert A. Paul. London: Jonathan Cape.
———. [1949] 1969. *The Elementary Structures of Kinship*. Trs., J.H. Bell, J.R. von Sturmer, and R. Needham. Boston: Beacon Press.
———. 1983. *Le regard eloigne*. Paris: Plon.
———. 1985. *The View from Afar*. Trs., J. Neugroschel and P. Hoss. New York. Basic Books, Inc.
Levy, Robert I. with the collaboration of Kedār Rāj Rājopādhyāya. 1990. *Mesocosm: Hinduism and the Organization of a Traditional Newar City in Nepal*. Berkeley: University of California Press.
Lorenzen, David N. 1999. 'Who Invented Hinduism?' *Comparative Studies in Society and History*, 41(4): 630–59.
Macauliffe, M.A. 1909. *The Sikh Religion: Its Gurus, Sacred Writings and Authors*, 6 vols. Oxford: Clarendon Press.
Madan, T.N. 1961. 'Herath: A Religious Ritual and Its Secular Aspects', in L.P. Vidyarthi (ed.), *Aspects of Religion in Indian Society*. Meerut: Kedarnath Ramnath.
———. 1965. *Family and Kinship: A Study of the Pandits of Rural Kashmir*. Bombay: Asia Publishing House. (2nd enlarged edition: 1989. New Delhi: Oxford University Press.)
———. 1966a. 'For a Sociology of India', *Contributions to Indian Sociology*, IX: 9–16.
———. 1966b. 'Politico-economic Change and Organizational Adjustment in a Kashmiri Village', *The Journal of Karnatak University (Social Sciences)*, 2: 20–34.
———. 1967. 'For a Sociology of India: Some Clarifications', *Contributions to Indian Sociology* (NS), 1: 90–93.
———. 1969. 'Caste and Development', *Economic and Political Weekly*, 4(5): 285–90.
———. 1971. 'On the Nature of Caste in India', *Contributions to Indian Sociology* (NS), 5: 1–13.
———. 1972a. 'Religions Ideology in a Plural Society: The Muslims and Hindus of Kashmir', *Contribution to Indian Sociology*, 6: 106–41. (Reproduced in Madan 2001b.)
———. 1972b. 'Two Faces of Bengali Ethnicity: Muslim Bengali or Bengali Muslim', *The Developing Economies*, 10(1): 74–85. (Revised version in Madan 1994c.)
———. 1972c. 'Doctors in a North Indian City: Recruitment, Role Perception and Role Performance', in Satish Saberwal (ed.), *Beyond the Village*. Simla: Indian Institute of Advanced Study.
———. 1975a. 'On Living Intimately with Strangers', in André Béteille and T.N. Madan (eds), *Encounter and Experience: Personal Accounts of Fieldwork*. New Delhi: Vikas Publishing House.

Madan, T.N. 1975b. 'Structural Implications of Marriage in North India: Wife-givers and Wife-takers among the Pandits of Kashmir', *Contributions to Indian Sociology* (NS), 9(2): 217–43.

———. 1976a. *Muslim Communities of South Asia*. New Delhi: Vikas Publishing House.

———. 1976b. 'The Hindu Family and Development', *Journal of Social and Economic Studies*, 4(2): 211–31.

———. 1977a. 'The Dialectic of Tradition and Modernity in the Sociology of D.P. Mukerji. D.P. Mukerji Memorial Lecture at the University of Lucknow', *Sociological Bulletin*, 26(2): 155–76. (Reprinted in *Social Science Information*, 17(6): 777–99 and Madan. 1994c [pp. 3–23]).

———. 1977b. 'The Quest for Hinduism', *International Social Science Journal*, 29(2): 261–78.

———. 1978. 'M.N. Srinivas's Earlier Work and *The Remembered Village*', *Contributions to Indian Sociology*, 12(1): 1–14.

———. 1981a. 'For a Sociology of India', *Contributions to Indian Sociology* (NS), 15(1–2): 403–18.

———. 1981b. 'The Ideology of the Householder among the Pandits of Kashmir', *Contributions to Indian Sociology* (NS), 15(1–2): 223–49.

——— (ed.). 1982a. *Way of Life: King, Householder, Renouncer: Essays in Honour of Louis Dumont*. New Delhi: Vikas Publishing House and Paris: Maison des Sciences de l'Homme.

———. 1982b. 'Anthropology as the Mutual Interpretation of Cultures', in Hussain Fahim (ed.), *Indigenous Anthropology in Non-Western Cultures*. Durham, N.C.: Academic Publishers.

———. 1983a. *Culture and Development*. Delhi: Oxford University Press.

———. 1983b. 'The Historical Significance of Secularism in India', in S.C. Dube and V.N. Basilov (eds), *Secularization in Multi-religious Societies*. New Delhi: Concept Publishing Company.

———. 1985. 'Concerning the Categories Śubha and Śuddha, in Hindu Culture: An Exploratory Essay', in John B. Carman and Frédérique A. Marglin (eds), *Purity and Auspiciousness in Indian Society*. Leiden: E.J. Brill.

———. 1986. 'Secularization and the Sikh Religious Tradition', *Social Compass*, 33(2–3): 257–73.

———. 1987a. *Non-renunciation: Themes and Interpretations of Hindu Culture*. New Delhi: Oxford University Press.

———. 1987b. 'Secularism in Its Place', *The Journal of Asian Studies*, 46(4): 747–60.

———. 1990. 'Images of India in American Anthropology', in Sulochana R. Glazer and Nathan Glazer (eds), *Conflicting Images: India and the United States*. Riverdale, MD: Riverdale.

Madan, T.N. 1991. 'Editorial', *Contributions to Indian Sociology* (NS), 25(1): 189–90.

―――. [1972] 1994a. 'Two Faces of Bengali Ethnicity: Bengali Muslim or Muslim Bengali', in *Pathways: Approaches to the Study of Indian Society*. New Delhi: Oxford University Press.

―――. 1994b. 'D.P. Mukerji 1894–1961: A Centenary Tribute', *Sociological Bulletin*, 43(2): 133–42.

―――. 1994c. *Pathways: Approaches to the Study of Society in India*. New Delhi: Oxford University Press.

―――. 1995. *Muslim Communities of South Asia*, 2nd enlarged ed. New Delhi: Manohar.

―――. 1997. *Modern Myths, Locked Minds: Secularism and Fundamentalism in India*. New Delhi: Oxford University Press.

―――. 2001a. 'The Social Construction of Religious Identities in Rural Kashmir', in T.N. Madan (ed.), *Muslim Communities of South Asia*. New Delhi: Manohar.

――― (ed.). [1976, 1995] 2001b. *Muslim Communities of South Asia: Culture, Society and Politics*, 3rd enlarged ed. New Delhi: Manohar.

―――. 2006a. *Images of the World: Essays on Religion, Secularism, and Culture*. New Delhi: Oxford University Press.

―――. 2006b. 'Holism and Individualism: Louis Dumont on India and the West', in T.N. Madan (ed.), *Images of the World: Essays on Religion, Secularism, and Culture*. New Delhi: Oxford University Press.

―――. 2007a. 'One from Many: Explorations in the Anthropology of Islam. D.N. Majumdar Memorial Lecture at the University of Lucknow', *The Eastern Anthropologist*, 60(1): 1–25.

―――. 2007b. 'Search for Synthesis: The Sociology of D.P. Mukerji', in Patricia Uberoi, Nandini Sundar, and Satish Deshpande (eds), *Anthropology in the East: Founders of Indian Sociology and Anthropology*. Ranikhet: Permanent Black.

―――. 2009. 'Foreword', in Srobona Munshi (ed.), *Redefining Humanism: Selected Essays of D.P. Mukerji*. New Delhi: Tulika Books.

―――. 2010. 'Between the Braying Pestles and the Examination Blues: Childhood Years', in Malavika Karlekar and Rudrangshu Mukherjee (eds), *Remembered Childhood*. New Delhi: Oxford University Press.

――― (ed.). Forthcoming. *Sociology at Lucknow University: The First Half Century*. New Delhi: Oxford University Press.

Madan, T.N. and B.G. Halbar. 1972. 'Caste and Community in the Private and Public Education of Mysore State', in Susan H. Rudolph and Lloyd I. Rudolph (eds), *Politics and Higher Education in India*. Cambridge MA: Harvard University Press.

Madan, T.N. and P.C. Verma. 1971. 'Development and the Professions in Asia: Working Papers', in Ratna Naidu and P.C. Joshi (eds), *Studies in Asian Social Development*. New Delhi: Tata-McGraw Hill.

———. 1973. 'Magnitude and Structure of the Professions in India', *Indian Journal of Labour Economics*, 15(3–4): 207–41.

Madan, T.N. in collaboration with Paul Wiebe, Rahim Said, and Malsin Dias. 1980. *Doctors and Society: There Asian Caste Studies*. New Delhi: Vikas Publishing House (on behalf of UNESCO).

Majul, Cesar A. 1973. *Muslims in the Philippines*. Quezon City: University of the Philippines Press.

Majumdar, D.N. 1958. *Caste and Communication in an Indian Village*. Bombay: Asia Publishing House.

Majumdar, D.N. and T.N. Madan. 1956. *An Introduction to Social Anthropology*. Bombay: Asia Publishing House.

Malinowski, Bronislaw. [1922] 1953. *Argonauts of the Western Pacific*. London: Routledge and Kegan Paul.

———. 1967. *A Diary in the Strict Sense of the Term*. New York: Harcourt, Brace & World, Inc.

Malraux, André. 1968. *Antimemoirs*. London: Hamish Hamilton.

Mandelbaum, David. G. 1970. *Society in India*, 2 vols. Berkeley: California University Press.

Marglin, Frédérique Apffel. 1985. *Wives of the God King: The Rituals of the Devadasis of Puri*. New Delhi: Oxford University Press.

Marglin, Stephen. 2008. *The Dismal Science: How Thinking like an Economist Undermines Community*. Cambridge, MA: Harvard University Press.

Marriott, McKim. 1955a. 'Little Communities in an Indigenous Civilization', in M. Marriott (ed.), *Village India: Studies in the Little Community*. Chicago: University of Chicago Press.

——— (ed.). 1955b. *Village India: Studies in the Little Community*. Chicago: University of Chicago Press.

———. 1969. 'Review of *Homo Hierarchicus: Essai sur le systèmme de castes* by Louis Dumont', *American Anthropologist*, 71(6): 1166–75.

——— (ed.). 1990. *India through Hindu Categories*. New Delhi: SAGE Publications.

Martin, David. 1965. 'Towards Eliminating the Concept of Secularization', in Julius Gould (ed.), *Penguin Survey of the Social Sciences*. Harmondsworth: Penguin Book.

———. 1978. *A General Theory of Secularization*. Oxford: Basil Blackwell.

Martindele, Don. 1961. *The Nature and Types of Sociological Thoery*. London: Routledge & Kegan Paul.

Marx, Karl and Friedrich Engels. 1959. *The First Indian War of Independence*. Moscow: Progress Publishers.
Mathur, J.S. (ed.). 2008. *Gandhi in the Mirror of Foreign Scholars*. New Delhi: Gandhi National Museum.
Mathur, K.S. 1965. *Caste and Ritual in Malwa*. Bombay: Asia Publishing House.
Matilal, Bimal Krishna. 1989. 'Moral Dilemmas: Insights from Indian Epics', in Bimal Krishna Matilal (ed.), *Moral Dilemmas in the Mahābhārata*. Delhi: Motilal Banarsidass.
Mauss, Marcel. 1970. *Gift*. Trs., Ian Cunnison. London: Cohen and West.
———. [1930] 2004. 'Civilizational Forms', in Saïd A. Arjomand and Edward Tiryakian (eds), *Rethinking Civilizational Analysis*. Thousand Oaks, CA: SAGE Publications.
Mayaram, Shail. 1997. *Resisting Regimes: Myth, Memory and the Shaping of a Muslim Identity*. New Delhi: Oxford University Press.
Mayer, A.C. 1978. '*The Remembered Village*: From Memory Alone?' *Contributions to Indian Sociology*, 12(1): 39–47.
McLeod, W.H. 1968. *Guru Nanak and the Sikh Religion*. Delhi: Oxford University Press.
———. 1976. *The Evolution of the Sikh Community*. Oxford: Clarendon Press.
Michaels, Axel. 2005. *Hinduism: Past and Present*. Trs., Barbara Harshav. New Delhi: Orient Longman.
Miri, Mrinal. 2003. *Identity and the Moral Life*. New Delhi: Oxford University Press.
Misra, Satish C. 1964. *Muslim Communities in Gujarat*. Bombay: Asia Publishing House.
Moffatt, Michael. 1979. *An Untouchable Community in South India: Structure and Consensus*. Princeton, N.J.: Princeton University Press.
Mookerjee, Radhakumud. [1928] 1972. *Asoka*. Delhi: Motilal Banarsidas.
Moosvi, Shirin. 2007. 'The Road to *Sulh-I kul*: Akbar's Alienation from Theological Islam', in Irfan Habib (ed.), *Religion in Indian History*. New Delhi: Tulika.
Mukerjee, Radhakamal. 1916. *The Foundations of Indian Economics*. London: Longman, Green & Co., Ltd.
———. 1922. *Principles of Comparative Economics, Vol. I*. London: P.S. King & Son., Ltd. (Reprinted in 2009 by Kessinger Publishing, USA.)
———. 1925. *Borderlands of Economics*. London: Allen & Unwin Ltd.
———. 1926. *Regional Sociology*. New York: The Century Company.
———. 1938a. *The Regional Balance of Man: An Ecological Theory of Population*. Madras: University of Madras.
———. 1938b. *The Theory and Art of Mysticism*. Bombay: Asia Publishing House.

Mukerjee, Radhakamal. 1940.*The Institutional Theory of Economics.* London: Macmillan.
———. 1945a.*Social Ecology.* London: Macmillan
———. 1945b. *The Indian Working Class.* Bombay: Hind Kitabs.
———. 1949.*The Social Structure of Values.* London: Macmillan.
———. 1951. *The Dynamics of Morals.* London: Macmillan.
———. 1956.*'Faiths and Influences', in Baljit Singh (ed.), *The Frontiers of Social Science: In Honour of Radhakamal Mukerjee.* London: Macmillan.
———. 1997. *India: The Dawn of a New Era: An Autobiography.* New Delhi: Radha Publications.
Mukerji, Dhurjati Prasad. 1924. *Personality and the Social Sciences.* Calcutta: The Book Company.
———. 1932. *Basic Concepts in Sociology.* London: Kegan Paul, Trench, Trubner & Co.
———. 1945. *On Indian History: A Study in Method.* Bombay: Hind Kitabs.
———. 1946. *Views and Counterviews.* Lucknow: Universal Publishers.
———. [1942] 1948. *Modern Indian Culture: A Sociological Study*, 2nd edition. Bombay: Hind Kitabs. Reprinted as *Indian Culture: A Sociological Study*, 2002, New Delhi: Rupa & Co.
———. 1954. 'Social Research', in K.M. Kapadia (ed.), *Professor Ghurye Felicitation Volume.* Bombay: popular Prakashan.
———. 1958. *Diversities: Essays in Economics, Sociology and Other Social Problems.* New Delhi: People's Publishing House.
———. 1962. 'Majumdar: Scholar and Friend', in T.N. Madan and Gopala Sarana (eds), *Indian Anthropology: Essays in Memory of D.N. Majumdar.* Bombay: Asia Publishing House.
———. [1943] 1972. *Tagore: A Study.* Calcutta: Manisha Granthalaya.
———. 2002. *Indian Music: An Introduction.* New Delhi: Rupa & Co. Originally published under the title of *An Introduction to Indian Music*, 1945, Bombay: Hind Kitabs.
Mukherjee, Ramkrishna. 1965. 'Role of Tradition in Social Change', in Ramkrishna Mukherjee (ed.), *The Sociologist and Social Change in India Today.* New Delhi: Prentice-Hall.
———. 1977. 'Trends in Indian Sociology', *Current Sociology*, 25(3): 1–193.
Mukherjee, Rudrangshu (ed.). 2007. *Great Speeches of Modern India.* New Delhi: Random House.
Mukherjee, S.N. 1968. *Sir William Jones.* Cambridge: Cambridge University Press.
Munshi, Indra. 2007. 'Patrick Geddes: Sociologist, Environmentalist, and Town Planner', in Patricia Uberoi, Nandini Sundar, and Satish Deshpande (eds), *Anthropology in the East: Founders of Indian Sociology and Social Anthropology.* Ranikhet: Permanent Black.

Munshi, Srobona (ed.). 2009a. *Redefining Humanism: Selected Papers of D.P. Mukerji*. New Delhi: Tulika Books.

———. 2009b. 'Introduction', in Srobona Munshi (ed.), *Redefining Humanism: Selected Essays of D.P. Mukerji*. New Delhi: Tulika Books.

Munshi, Surendra. 2003. 'Revisting Max Weber on India', in H. Hartmut Lehmann and J.M. Ouedraogo (eds), *Max Webers Religionssoziologie in interkultureller Perspective*. Goettingen: Vanenhoeck & Ruprecht.

Nadel, S.F. 1952. *The Foundations of Social Anthropology*. London: Cohen and West.

Nagendra, S.P. 1997. 'D.P. Mukerji as a Sociologist (Centenary Shradhanjali)', in Abha Avasthi (ed.), *Social and Cultural Diversities: D.P. Mukerji in Memoriam*. Jaipur: Rawat Publications.

Nakane, Chie. 1978. '*The Remembered Village*: Memory "Maximized"', *Contributions to Indian Sociology*, 12(1): 33–37.

Nanda, B.R. 1981. *Mahatma Gandhi. A Biography*. New Delhi: Oxford University Press.

———. 1990. *In Gandhi's Footsteps: The Life and Times of Jamnalal Bajaj*. New Delhi: Oxford University Press.

Nandy, Ashis. 1995. *The Savage Freud and Other Essays on Possible and Retrievable Selves*. New Delhi: Oxford University Press.

———. 2001a. *Time Warps: The Insistent Politics of Silent and Evasive Pasts*. New Delhi: Permanent Black.

———. 2001b. *An Ambiguous Journey to the City: The Village and Other Odd Ruins of the Self in Indian Imagination*. New Delhi: Oxford University Press.

Narain, Brij. [1919] 2009. 'Indian versus Western Industrialism', in J. Krishnamurty (ed.), *Towards Development Economics*. New Delhi: Oxford University Press. Originally published in Brij Narain, 1919, *Essays in Indian Economic Problems*. Lahore: The Punjabee Electric Press, pp. 26–40.

Narang, G.C. 1960. *Transformation of Sikhism*, 5th edition. New Delhi: New Book Society of India.

Nasr, Seyyed Hossein. 1993. 'Islam', in Arvind Sharma (ed.), *Our Religions*. San Francisco: Harper.

Nayar, Baldev Raj. 1966. *Minority Politics in the Punjab*. Princeton, NJ: Princeton University Press.

Nehru, Jawaharlal. 1961. *The Discovery of India*. Bombay: Asia Publishing House.

———. 1980. *An Anthology*, ed. Sarvepalli Gopal. New Delhi: Oxford University Press.

Nietzsche, Friedrich. 1974. *The Gay Science: With a Prelude in Rhyme and an Appendix of Songs*. Translated with commentary by Walter Kaufmann. New York: Vintage Books.

Nisbet, Robert A. 1966. *The Sociological Tradition.* New York: Basic Books.
Oakeshott, Michael. 1962. *Rationalism in Politics and Other Essays.* London: Methuen.
Oberoi, Harjot S. 1994. *The Construction of Religious Boundaries: Culture, Identity and Diversity in the Sikh Tradition.* Toronto: University of Toronto Press.
Obeyesekere, Gananath. 1984. *The Cult of the Goddess Pattini.* Chicago: University of Chicago Press.
Olivelle, Patrick. 1998. 'Caste and Purity: A Study in the Language of Dharma Literature', *Contributions to Indian Sociology* (NS), 32(2): 189–216.
———. 2004. *The Law Code of Manu.* New York: Oxford University Press.
Parel, Anthony J. 1997. 'Introduction', in Gandhi, *Hind Swaraj and Other Writings*, ed. Anthony J. Parel. Cambridge: Cambridge University Press.
Parkin, Robert. 2003. *Louis Dumont and Hierarchical Opposition.* New York: Berghahn Books.
Parry, Jonathan. 1991. 'The Hindu Lexicographer? A Note on Auspiciousness and Purity', *Contributions to Indian Sociology* (NS), 25(1): 267–86.
———. 1994. *Death in Banaras.* Cambridge: Cambridge University Press.
Pocock, D.F. 1973. *Mind, Body and Wealth. A Study of Belief and Practice in an Indian Village.* Oxford: Blackwell.
Popper, Karl. 1963. *Conjectures and Refutations.* London: Routledge and Kegan Paul.
Pramanick, S.K. 1994. *Sociology of G.S. Ghurye.* Jaipur: Rawat Publications.
Puri, Baij Nath. 1988. *The Khatris: A Socio-historical Study.* New Delhi: Manohar Publishers and Distributors.
Quinn, James A. 1956. 'Mukerjee, A Pioneer in Social Ecology', in Baljit Singh (ed.), *The Frontiers of Social Science.* London: Macmillan.
Radcliffe-Brown, A.R. [1922] 1964. *The Andaman Islanders.* Glencoe, IL: The Free Press.
———. 1952a. *Structure and Function in Primitive Society.* London: Cohen and West.
———. 1952b. 'Foreword', in M.N. Srinivas (ed.), *Religion and Society among the Coorgs of South India.* Oxford: Clarendon Press.
Raghavan, V. 1980. *The Ramayana Tradition in Asia.* New Delhi: Sahitya Akademi.
Ray, Niharranjan. 1970. *The Sikh Gurus and the Sikh Society.* Patiala: Punjabi University.
Ray, Rajat Kanta. 1984. *Social Conflict and Political Unrest in Bengal, 1875–1927.* New Delhi: Oxford University Press.
Rahman, Fazlur. 1979. *Islam*, 2nd ed. Chicago: University of Chicago Press.
Ricklefs, M.C. 1993. *A History of Modern Indonesia, since c. 1300.* Stanford, CA: Stanford University Press.

Robbins, Lionel. 1932. *An Essay on the Nature and Significance of Economic Science*. London: Macmillan.
Robinson, Francis. 2000. *Islam and Muslim History in South Asia*. New Delhi: Oxford University Press.
Rodinson, Maxime. 1973. *Mohammad*. Harmondsworth: Penguin Books.
Roy, Asim. 1983. *The Islamic Syncretistic Tradition in Bengal*. Princeton, N.J.: Princeton University Press.
———. 2005. 'Thinking over "Popular" Islam in South Asia: Search for a Paradigm', in Mushirul Hasan and Asim Roy (eds), *Living Together Separately: Cultural India in History and Politics*. New Delhi: Oxford University Press.
Roy, Sarat Chandra. 1938. 'An Indian Outlook on Anthropology', *Man* (NS), 172: 146–50.
Rudner, David. 1990. 'Inquest on Dravidian Kinship: Louis Dumont and the Essence of Marriage Alliance', *Contributions to Indian Sociology* (NS), 24(2): 153–73.
Rudolph, Lloyd I. 2006. 'Postmodern Gandhi', in Lloyd I. Rudolph and Susanne Rudolph (eds), *Postmodern Gandhi and Other Essays*. New Delhi: Oxford University Press.
Runciman, W.G. 1097. *Sociology in Its Place and Other Essays*. Cambridge: Cambridge University Press.
Saberwal, Satish. 1978. *Process and Institution in Urban India*. New Delhi: Vikas Publishing House.
———. 2008. *Spirals of Contention: Why India was Partitioned in 1947*. New Delhi: Routledge.
Sachau, Edward C. (trs.). [1914, 1988] 2002. *Alberuni's India*. New Delhi: Rupa & Co.
Samundari, Bishan Singh. 1973. 'Foreword', in Attar Singh, *Secularism and the Sikh Religious Faith*. Amritsar: Guru Nanak Dev University.
Saran, A.K. 1958. 'India', in Joseph S. Roucek (ed.), *Contemporary Sociology*. London: Peter Owen and New York: Philosophical Library.
———. 1962a. 'D.P. Mukerji: An Obituary', *The Eastern Anthropologist*, 15(2): 167–69.
———. 1962b. 'Review of *Contributions to Indian Sociology, IV*', *The Eastern Anthropologist*, 15(1): 53–68.
———. 1963. 'The Marxian Theory of Social Change', *Inquiry*, 6: 70–128.
———. 1965. 'The Faith of a Modern Intellectual', in T.K.N. Unnithan, Yogendra Singh, and Indra Deva (eds), *Towards a Sociology of Culture in India*. New Delhi: Prentice-Hall.
———. 1971. 'Some Reflects on Sociology in Crisis', in Tom Bottomore (ed.), *Crisis and Contention in Sociology*. London: SAGE Publications.

Saran, A.K. 2003. *Meaning and Truth: Lectures on the Theory of Language.* Sarnath: Central Institute of Tibetan Studies.
Sarkar, Benoy Kumar. [1937] 1985. *The Positive Background of Hindu Sociology. Book I: Introduction to Hindu Positivism.* Delhi: Motilal Banarsidass.
Schomer, Karine and W.H. McLeod (eds). 1987. *The Saints: Studies in a Devotional Tradition of India.* Delhi: Motilal Banarsidass.
Seal, B.N. 1924. *Rammohun Roy: The Universal Man.* Calcutta: Saadharan Brahmo Samaj.
Seligman, Adam. 2000. *Modernity's Wager: Authority, the Self, and Transcendence.* Princeton, NJ: Princeton University Press.
Sen, Amartya. 2000. 'Consequential Evaluation and Practical Reason', *The Journal of Philosophy*, XCII(9): 477–502.
———. 2005. *The Argumentative Indian.* London: Allen Lane.
Sen, Ronojoy. 2010. *Articles of Faith: Religion, Secularism and the Indian Supreme Court.* New Delhi: Oxford University Press.
Sen, Surendranath. 1957. *Eighteen Fifty-Seven.* New Delhi: Publications Division: Government of India.
Shah, A.M. 1996. 'M.N. Srinivas: The Man and his Work', in A.M. Shah et al. (eds), *Social Structure and Social Change: An Evaluation of the Work of M.N. Srinivas.* New Delhi: SAGE Publications.
———. 2002. *Exploring India's Rural Past: A Gujarat Village in the Early Ninteenth Century.* New Delhi: Oxford University Press.
Shaikh, Farzana. 2009. *Making Sense of Pakistan.* London: Hurst & Co.
Sharma, Sri Ram. 1962. *The Religious Policy of the Mughal Emperors.* Bombay: Asia Publishing House.
Shils, Edward. 1975. 'Tradition', in Edward Shils (ed.), *Centre and Periphery: Essays in Macro-sociology.* Chicago: University of Chicago Press.
———. 1981. *Tradition.* Chicago: University of Chicago Press.
Singh, Attar. 1973. *Secularism and the Sikh Faith.* Amritsar: Guru Nanak Dev University.
Singh, Baljit (ed.). 1956. *The Frontiers of Social Science: In Honour of Radhakamal Mukerjee.* London: Macmillan & Co.
Singh, Baljit and V.B. Singh (eds). 1967. *Social and Economic Change.* Bombay: Allied Publishers.
Singh, Fauja. 1969. 'Development of Sikhism under the Gurus', in Fauja Singh, Trilochan Singh, Gurbachan Singh Talib, J.P. Singh Uberoi, and Sohan Singh, *Sikhism.* Patiala: Punjabi University.
Singh, Gopal (trs. and annotator). 1978. *Sri Guru Granth Sahab*, 4 vols. Chandigarh: World Sikh University Delhi.
Singh, Harbans. 1964. *The Heritage of the Sikhs.* Bombay: Asia Publishing House.

Singh, Harbans. 1966. *Guru Gobind Singh*. Chandigarh: The Guru Gobind Foundation.
———. 1983. *The Heritage of the Sikhs*. New Delhi: Manohar.
Singh, Jodh. 1967. 'Structure and Character of the Sikh Society', in *Sikhism and Indian Society*. Simla: Institute of Advanced Study.
Singh, Kapur. 1959. *Parāsharprasna or the Baisakhi of Guru Gobind Singh*. Jullundur: Hind Publishers.
Singh, Khushwant. 1953. *The Sikhs*. London: Allen & Unwin.
———. 1963. *A History of the Sikhs*, Vol. I. Princeton, NJ: Princeton University Press.
———. 1966. *A History of the Sikhs*, Vol. II. Princeton, NJ: Princeton University Press.
Singh, Randhir. 1993. *Five Lectures in the Marxist Mode*. New Delhi: Ajanta Publications.
Singh, Trilochan, Bhai Jodh Singh, Kapur Singh, Bawa Karkishen Singh, and Khushwant Singh (eds). 1960. *The Sacred Writings of the Sikhs*. London: Allen & Unwin.
Sinha, Surajit. 1962. 'State Formation and Rajput Myth in Tribal Central India', *Man in India*, 42(1): 35–80.
———. 1986. *Nirmal Kumar Bose: Scholar Wanderer*. New Delhi: National Book Trust.
Smith, Donald Eugene. 1963. *India as a Secular State*. Princeton, NJ: Princeton University Press and Bombay: Oxford University Press.
Smith, Wilfrend Contwell. 1978. *The Meaning and End of Religion*. New York: Harper and Row.
Smith, William Robertson. [1894] 2002. *Religion of the Semites*. Introduction, Robert A. Segal. London: Transaction.
Srinivas, M.N. 1942. *Marriage and Family in Mysore*. Bombay: New Book Company.
———. 1952. *Religion and Society among the Coorgs of South India*. Oxford: Clarendon Press.
———. 1958. Hinduism. *Encyclopaedia Britannica*, 11: 574–77.
——— (ed). [1955] 1960. *India's Villages*. Bombay: Asia Publishing House.
———. 1966a. *Social Change in Modern India*. Berkeley: University of California Press.
——— 1966b. 'The Study of One's Own Society', in M.N. Srinivas (ed.), *Social Change in Modern India*. Berkeley: University of California Press.
———. 1967a. 'Cohesive Role of Sanskritization', in P. Mason (ed.), *Unity and Diversity: India and Ceylon*. London: Oxford University Press.
———. 1967b. *Social Change in Modern India*. New Delhi: Allied Publishers.

Srinivas, M.N. 1973a. 'Itineraries of an Indian Social Anthropologist', *International Social Science Journal*, 25(1–2): 129–48.

———. 1973b. 'Some Comments on Milton Singer's "Industrial Leadership, the Hindu Ethic and the Spirit of Socialism"', in Milton Singer (ed.), *Entrepreneurship and Modernization of Occupational Cultures in South Asia*. Durham, NC: Duke University.

———. 1976. *The Remembered Village*. New Delhi: Oxford University Press.

———. 1988. 'The Image Maker', *The Illustrated Weekly of India*, Bombay.

———. 1993. 'Towards a New Philosophy', *The Times of India*, New Delhi, edit page, 9 July.

———. 1995. 'Sociology in Delhi', in Dharma Kumar and Dilip Mookherjee, (eds), *D. School: Reflections on the Delhi School of Economics*. New Delhi: Oxford University Press.

———. 1996. 'Bangalore as I See It', in *Indian Society through Personal Writings*. New Delhi: Oxford University Press.

———. 1997. 'The Legend on the Wall' and 'The Road to Mercara', in R.K. Narayanan (ed.), *Indian Thought: A Miscellany*. New Delhi: Penguin Books.

———. 2002a. *Collected Essays*. New Delhi: Oxford University Press.

———. 2002b. 'Social Anthropology and Literary Sensibility', in *Collected Papers*. New Delhi: Oxford University Press.

Srinivas, M.N. and A.M. Shah. 1968. 'Hinduism', *The International Encyclopaedia of Social Sciences*, 6: 358–66.

Srinivas, M.N. and M.N. Panini. 1973. 'The Development of Sociology and Social Anthropology in India', *Sociological Bulletin*, 22(2): 179–215. Reproduced in M.N. Srinivas, 2002, Collected Papers, pp. 480–511. New Delhi: Oxford University Press.

Stiglitz, Joseph E. 2010. *Freefall: Freemarkets and the Sinking of the Global Economy*. London: Allen Lave.

Talib, Gurcharan Singh. 1969. 'The Basis and Development of Ethical Thought', in Fauja Singh, Trilochan Singh, Gurbachan Singh Talib, J.P. Singh Uberoi, and Sohan Singh, *Sikhism*. Patiala: Punjabi University.

Taylor, Charles. 2007. *A Secular Age*. Cambridge, MA: Harvard University Press.

Thapan, Meenakshi and Roland Lardinois. 2006. 'Introduction', in Roland Lardinois and Meenakshi Thapan (eds). 2006. *Reading Pierre Bourdieu in a Dual Context*. New Delhi: Routledge.

Thapar, Romila. 1961. *Ashoka and the Decline of the Mauryas*. London: Oxford University Press.

———. 1997. 'Syndicated Hinduism', in G.D. Sontheimer and H. Kulke (eds), *Hinduism Reconsidered*. New Delhi: Manohar.

Thapar, Romila. 2007. 'Is Secularism Alien to Indian Civilization?' in T.N. Srinivasan (ed.), *The Future of Secularism*. New Delhi: Oxford University Press.

Thornton, Robert J. 1985. 'Mach, Frazer, Conrad, Malinowski and the Role of Imagination in Ethnography', *Anthropology Today*, 1(5): 7–14.

Toynbee, Arnold J. 1947. *A Study of History*. Abridgement of Vols I to VI by D.C. Somervell. London: Oxford University Press.

———. 1954. *A Study of History*, Vol. VII. London: Oxford University Press.

———. 1960. 'Foreword', in Trilochan Singh, Bhai Jodh Singh, Kapur Singh, Bawa Harkishen Singh, and Khushwant Singh (eds), *The Sacred Writings of the Sikhs*. London: Allen & Unwin.

———. 1979. *An Historian's Approach to Religion*, 2nd ed. London: Oxford University Press.

Tylor, Edward. [1871] 1913. *Primitive Culture*, 2 vols. London: John Murray.

Uberoi, J.P.S. 1978. *Science and Culture*. Delhi: Oxford University Press.

———. 1984. *The Other Mind of Europe*. Delhi: Oxford University Press.

———. 1991. 'The Five Symbols of Sikhism', in T.N. Madan (ed.), *Religion in India*. New Delhi: Oxford University Press.

Uberoi, Patricia, Nandini Sundar, and Satish Deshpande (eds). 2007. *Anthropology in the East: Founders of Sociology and Social Anthropology in India*. Ranikhet: Permanent Black.

Upadhya, Carol. 2007. 'The Idea of Indian Society: G.S. Ghurye and the Making of Indian Sociology', in Patricia Uberoi, Nandini Sundar, and Satish Deshpande (eds), *Anthropology in the East: Founders of Indian Sociology and Anthropology*. Ranikhet: Permanent Black.

Vardarajan, S. (ed.). 2002. *Gujarat: The Making of a Tragedy*. New Delhi: Penguin.

Wani, Muhammad Ashraf. 2004. *Islam in Kashmir*. Srinagar: Oriental.

Weber, Max. 1930. *The Protestant Ethic and the Spirit of Capitalism*. Trs., Talcott Parsons. London: Allen & Unwin.

———. 1948a. *From Max Weber: Essays in Sociology*. Trs., H.H. Gerth and C.W. Mills. London: Routledge and Kegan Paul.

———. 1948b. 'Science as Vocation', in H.H. Gerth and C.W. Mills (eds), *From Max Weber: Essays in Sociology*, pp. 129–56. London: Routledge & Kegan Paul.

———. 1948c. 'Politics as Vocation', in H.H. Gerth and C.W. Mills (eds), *From Max Weber: Essays in Sociology*, pp. 77–128. London: Routledge & Kegan Paul.

———. 1949a. *The Methodology of the Social Sciences*. Glencoe, IL: The Free Press.

Weber, Max. 1949b. '"Objectivity" in Social Science', in Edward Shils and Henry A. Finch (trs. and eds), *The Methodology of the Social Sciences*, Glencoe, IL: The Free Press.

———. 1958. *The Religion of India: The Sociology of Hinduism and Buddhism*. Trs., Hans Gerth and Don Martindale. Glencoe, IL: The Free Press.

———. 1963. *Sociology of Religion*. Trs., Eprahim Fischoff. Boston: Beacon Press.

Williams, John A. 1971. *Themes of Islamic Civilization*. Berkeley: University of California Press.

Wittgenstein, Ludwig. 1980. *Culture and Value*. Trs., Peter Winch. Chicago: University of Chicago Press.

Wollheim, Richard. 1984. *The Thread of Life*. Cambridge, MA: Harvard University Press.

Wolff, Kurt H. (ed.) 1960. *Émile Durkheim 1857–1917*. Columbus: The Ohio State University.

Wolpert, Stanley. 1988. *Jinnah of Pakistan*. New Delhi: Oxford University Press.

Yalman, Nur. 2007. 'Islam and Secularism: Plato and Khomeini', in T.N. Srinivasan (ed.), *The Future of Secularism*. New Delhi: Oxford University Press.

Zaehner, R.C. 1962. *Hinduism*. London: Oxford University Press.

Zutshi, Chitralekha. 2003. *Languages of Belonging: Islam, Regional Identity, and the Making of Kashmir*. New Delhi: Permanent Black.

Index

Abdullah, Shaikh Mohammad, 8
Abhinavagupta, 59
Abraham, 47, 48
adat law, 55
Ādi Granth, 87, 98
Advani, L.K., 15
Advani, Ram, 149
ahankāra, 81
ahimsa, 19, 103
Ahl-i-Hadīs, in Kashmir, 64
Ahmad, Imtiaz, 9, 66, 67, 71, 72n
Ahmaddiya Muslims, 58
Ahmed, Akbar, 68
Ahmed, Rafiuddin, 58
Ajlāf, 56
Akal Takht, 89
Akali Dal, 98
Akbar, emperor, 11n, 85, 86
  religious tolerance under, 10
  and secular legal structure, 11
al-Biruni, 27, 49
al-Ghazālī, 48
al-Madīnah, 47
Aligarh Muslim University, 151
All-India Sociological Conference, First, 138
Allah, 73

See also Prophet Muhammad
Amar Das, Guru, 85, 87
American Association of Asian Studies, 263
Amin, Pirzada Mohammad, 63n
An Introduction to Social Anthropology (D.N. Majumdar and T.N. Madan), 248
anāsakti (non-possession), 106
Ananthamurthy, U.R., 177n, 184
Andaman Islanders, ethnography of, 33
anekantavād, 17
Angad, Guru, 82–83, 86
Ansari, Ghaus, 65, 66
anthropology, 65, 66, 140, 178, 195, 198, 223, 224, 242, 246, 254, 255
  cultural, 139
  economic, 127, 172
Anthropology in the East: Founders of Indian Sociology and Anthropology (eds, Patricia Uberoi, Nandini Sundar, and Satish Deshpande), xii
Anwar, M. Syafi'i, 53, 54
Arjan Mal, Guru, 86–88

Index 291

Aron, Raymond, 114n, 117
artha, 5
Arthashāstra, 144
Arya Samaj, 20, 97
Asad, Talal, 63
Ashoka, emperor, 10, 11n
  and spread of Buddhism, 11
Ashrāf, 56
Ataturk, Kemal, 21
aurād, recitation of, 64
Aurangzeb, emperor, 68, 91, 93
awareness, 133, 147, 257, 264
  interrogative, 24
Azad, Maulana, 9, 18

Babar, emperor, 77
Bailey, F.G., 30, 199, 205, 206, 226, 227, 228, 231, 233, 252
Bajaj, Jamnalal, 111
Bal, S.S., 83n, 94
Baldock, John, 49
Bangladesh, birth of, 49, 212
  Muslims in, 56
Bangladeshi identity, 58
Basic Concepts in Sociology (D.P. Mukerji), 154, 155
Basilov, V.N., 262
Bateson, Gregory, 3
Baviskar, Amita, 217n, 238
Bayly, Susan, 140
behaviour(al), 31, 32, 33, 39, 46, 59, 70, 127, 131, 260
  change, 201, 223, 254
  patterns, 196
Beliappa, Jayanthi, 34
Benedict, Ruth, 193
Bengal, cultural and religious histories of medieval, 30
Bengal, East, Islamization of, 55–59
  See also Bangladesh
Bengal Renaissance, 120

Bengali intelligentsia, of 1890s, 147
Bengali nationalism, 58
Bengalis, cultural distinctiveness of, 56
Berger, Monroe, 180
Berger, Peter, 262
Bessaignet, Pierre, 258
Béteille, André, 224
Bhagavadgītā, 20n, 41, 92n, 104, 105
Bhāgavat Purāna, 58
bhakti movement, 78
Bharatiya Janata Party (BJP), 14–15, 20, 21
Bhargava, Rajeev, 3, 8, 12, 263
Bhattacharya, Swapan Kumar, xii, 144
Bhutto-Zia conflict, in Pakistan, 68
Biardeau, Madeleine, 228
Bihar, tribal people of, 180
Bogardes, Emory, 173
Bond, Ruskin, 104
Borderlands of Economics (Radhakamal Mukerjee), 129
Bose, Nirmal Kumar, 16, 39, 245
Bose, Satyen, 147, 148
Bouglé, Célistin, 220, 227
Bourdieu, Pierre, xiv
Brahman, 36, 39
Brahmanical culture, 191, 192, 203
Brahmanical intellectualism, 153
Brahmanical tradition, 60, 78
Brahmanical way of life, 41
British rule, 160–61, 163
Buddha, the, 10
Buddhism, 160
  impact of, in Kashmir, 59
  spread of, 11n
Buddhist tradition, concept of, 60
Bukharin, 159
Bureau of Economics and Statistics, 150

Cady, Linell, 21
capitalism, 39, 101
  Gandhi and Weber on, 108–12
  Hinduism and, 40
  Western, 107, 115, 164
capitalist society, 109, 164
Carlyle, Thomas, 129n
Carpenter, Edward, 104, 110
Carrithers, Michael, 102
caste/casteism, 191, 220
  -based social structure, 29
  Brahmanical ritualistic ideology, 140
  and cultural unity, 200
  social interpretation of, 200
  structure of, 140
  system, 29–30, 36, 200, 222, 229, 245
Caste and Race in India (G.S. Ghurye), 140
Celtel, André, 196
census of 2001, 4
Center for Advanced Study in the Behavioral Science, Stanford, 183
Chārvāka, 153
Chakrabarti, Arindam, 176n
Chakrabarti, Kunal, 30
Charar-i-Sharif, military action in, 64
Chatterjee, Bankim Chandra, 120, 167n
Chatterjee, Margaret, 17
Chatterjee, Partha, 15
Chatterji, Roma, 144
  Chattopadhyay, Bankim Chandra, 148
Chaudhuri, Nirad C., 24, 150
Chaudhury, Pramatha, 148
Chauri Chaura incident, 113
Christian asceticism, 81
Christianity, 24, 147
  Muslims conversion to, 53

Civil Disobedience Movement, of Gandhi, 113
civilization(s), 105, 132, 165, 221, 227
  comparison of, 195
  Gandhi and Weber on Western, 108–12
  Study of Indian, and society, 218
class(es), 161–62
  middle, 137, 147, 159, 161
  struggle, 165
  working, 172
Clifford, James, 194n, 255
'collective representation', 33, 220, 222, 223, 252
Collingwood, R.G., 158
Commons, John, 127
communal riots, of 146–48, 16
communalism, 5, 212, 228
Communism, 53
Communist Manifesto, The (Karl Marx and Friedrich Engels), 36
community, 18, 46, 199, 228, 245, 258
  communitarian/communitarianism, 123
  consciousness, 203
'comparative method', xv, 121, 123, 127, 231
Comte, Auguste, 120, 121, 124n, 141n, 143
conflict, 132, 136, 157, 160, 162, 168, 169
  class, 162
  inter-religious, 5
Congress, 14
  Ministry in United Provinces, 150
conscience/conviction, 6, 20, 73, 101, 168
Constitution of India, 7, 12

Contributions to Indian Sociology,
  xvii, 199, 205–07, 209, 211, 217,
  218, 212, 219, 220, 221, 224,
  225–29, 231, 232, 235, 238, 239,
  261
Coomaraswamy, Ananda, 120, 224n
Coorgis, of South India, 29, 34, 222,
  231, 245
  religion and society among, 182
'cosmic', 132, 135
Cosmology, 34, 36
Coulanges, Fustel de, 33, 225
cultural anthropology, xiv, 25, 264
cultural criticism, 58, 95
cultural forms, 26, 29, 59, 92, 167
culture/cultural, composite, 5
  development of, 257–58
  Hindu, 143
  interpretation of, 254–57
  modern Indian, 136, 137
  role of, in ecological relations, 130
  tradition, xi, xiii, xiv
  values, 126
Cunningham, J.D., 89, 90

Dandekar, R.N., 25
Dani, A.H., 65
dār ul-islām (House of Islam), 74
Das, Veena, 234, 236
Dasgupta, Ajit, 106, 111
Dasgupta, Sangeeta, 180
Dasgupta, Subrata, 120
Dayal, Ravi, xvi–xvii
Dayanand Sarasvati, 20
Delacampagne, Christian, 216n
democracy, 6, 53, 169
deprivation, economic and political, 13
Derrett, J.D.M., 228
Desai, A.R., 142
Desai, Mahadev, 105, 106, 112

Deshpande, Satish, xii, 224, 237
*devādasi*s, 43
development, 170, 246
  culture and, 257–58
  economic, 20, 169, 259, 260
  social, 169
dhamma/dharma, 5, 10, 16, 25, 31,
  33, 37, 38, 112
  wheel, 8
Dhar, P.N., 233
Dharmashāstra, 144
dharmayudda (holy war), notion of,
  in Sikhism, 93
dhikr, recitation of, 64
dialectical approach/perspective,
  159, 171, 181, 251
diffusionism, 70, 140, 142
Directive Principles of State Policy,
  13
Dirks, Nicholas B., 24, 140, 228n
Discovery of India, The (Jawaharlal
  Nehru), 11n
Diversities: Essays in Economics, Sociology and Other Social Problems (D.P. Mukerji), 136
Dravidian culture, study of, 197, 214
Dube, Leela, 66n
Dube, S.C., 233, 262
Dubois, the Abbé, 24
Dumézil, Georges, 197, 220
Dumont, Louis, xiv, xv, xvi, 4, 23,
  24, 25, 38, 41, 42, 71, 72, 73,
  98, 102, 129n, 140, 165, 195ff,
  228n, 236, 237, 253, 251, 252,
  254, 264
  academic career of, 196–97
  Contributions to Indian Sociology of, 225–31
  critics of, 213–14
  study of Indian society, 196, 225–31

Dumont, Suzanne Tardieu, 207, 209, 214
Dumont, Victor Emile, 216
Durkheim, Émile, xii, xv, 33, 34, 36, 72, 102, 143, 220, 225, 231
durūd, recitation of, 64
Dutt, Michael Madhusudan, 167n
Dutt, Romesh Chandra, 120
Dynamics of Morals, The (Radhakamal Mukerjee), 131

East India Company, 12
Eaton, Richard, 56, 63n, 72n
Eck, Diana, 43
ecology, human, 130
  social, xv, 129–31, 134, 139, 140, 172
economic theory, xv
economics, xv, 128, 129n, 155
  approach to, 124
  comparative, 129
  'imperative', 128
  Indian, 122, 125
  institutional, 123, 126–29
  and politics, 202
  'regional', 119
  sociology, 123–24
education, 137, 162
egalitarian social order, 55
egalitarianism, 129n
Elementary Forms of Religious Life, The (Émile Durkheim), 220
Eliade, Mircea, 224n
Eliot, George, 180
Elwin, Verrier, 243
empiricism, 175
Engels, Friedrich, 153
Enlightenment, The, 75, 203, 204
environmental degradation, 133–34, 145
epics, later religion of the, 27
epistemology, 19n, 103

Essays on Individualism: Modern Ideology in Anthropological Perspective (Louis Dumont), 203
ethics, xiii, 125, 256
  of responsibility, 113
ethnic and national boundaries, 212
ethnic nationalism, among Muslims, 49
Ethnographic and Folk Culture Society, the, 173n
ethnography, 27, 33, 38, 66n, 67, 69, 140, 194n, 227, 237, 256–57
  of M.N. Srinivas, 182–84
  poetics of, 178–82
European civilization, 35
Evans-Pritchard, E.E., 36n, 179, 180, 198, 224, 250, 252

faith, religious, xiii, 4, 7, 10, 12, 14, 18, 26, 49, 68, 77, 84, 87, 91, 97, 99
family, 192
  caste and, 203
  and marriage, 182, 238, 252
  values, 126
Family and Kinship: A Study of the Pandits of Rural Kashmir (T.N. Madan), 206, 257
Farāizī movement, 58
Fenech, Louis E., 87
fiction (literature), 153, 177n, 180, 252
Field, Dorothy, 88
fieldwork, 42, 140, 183, 184, 195, 197, 198, 260, 265
  on Coorgis in Karnataka, 175, 176, 245
  on Pramali Kallar in Tamil Nadu, 212, 213, 219, 228
  perspectives on, 180, 181
Firth, Raymond, 127
folk Islam, 60

folk religion, 11, 52
Forbes, Geraldine, 121
Foundations of Indian Economics, The (Radhakamal Mukerjee), 122, 124, 125
freedom movement, 6
Freeman, Derek, 250
French tradition, 220
From Mandeville to Marx: The Genesis and Triumph of Economic Ideology (Louis Dumont), 202
Fürer-Haimendorf, Christoph von, 228
Fuller, C.J., 26
functionalism, 34, 244
fundamental rights, 6, 19
fundamentalism, 51, 70, 99

Gadamer, Hans-Georg, vii
Gajendragadkar, P.B., 17n
Galey, Jean-Claude, 210, 213, 216n, 220, 222, 223, 226
Gandhi, Mahatma, 6, 16, 122, 139, 169, 175, 245, 246
  concept of work as duty, 104–06
  pluralism of, xiii, 18–19
  on politics and ethics, 112
  on religion, 16–17
  secularism of, 16–20
  on untouchables, 113
  on values, 170
  and Weber, 101
  on Western civilization, 108–12
Ganguli, B.N., 111
Garuda Purāna, 42, 43
Gérard Bouchard-Charles Taylor Commission, 8
Geddes, Patrick, 121, 122, 123, 130, 139
Geertz, Clifford, 50, 51, 52, 54, 67, 181, 182
Gellner, Ernest, 45, 51, 67, 68, 72

German Ideology: From France to Germany and Back (Louis Dumont), 203
Ghaznavi, Mahmud, 27
Ghose, Aurobindo, 120
Ghurye, G.S., 122, 134, 139–42, 144
Giddings, Franklin, 120, 162
globalization, 145
Gobind Singh, Guru, 77, 90, 91, 94, 91n, 94n, 95, 96n, 99
Goethe, Johann Wolfgang von, 119
Gold, Anne Grodzins, 42
Gottlieb, Manuel, 173
Gould, Harold, 234
Gowling, Peter G., 55
Green, Martin, 115n
Green Revolution, in Punjab, 98
Grewal, J.S., 79n, 83n, 87, 90, 94
Grihasti (householder), 82n
Guha, Ramachandra, 134n, 237
Guha, Ranajit, 57
Gujarat state, BJP government in, 25
  carnage in, 15
Gupta, Dipankar, 237
Gurdwara Act of 1925, 98
Guru Granth Sahib (Holy Book), of Sikhs, 94
Gurumata, 96

Hadīs, 51, 73
Halbfass, Wilhelm, 24
Hamadani, Mir Sayid Ali, 60
Hanafite school of law, 48
Hanbalite school of law, 48
Hans, Surjit, 78, 87, 96n
Hargobind, Guru, 88, 89, 90, 91, 93
Harkat-ul-Ansār, Kashmir, 64
Harmandir Sahib, 87
Harper, Edward, 233
Hart, Samuel, 131

Hayek, F.A., 141n
Hegel, Georg Wilhelm Friedrich, xii, 152, 156
Heller, Clemens, 208
Herskovits, Melville, 127
heterogeneity, 4
hierarchy/hierarchical, 30, 38, 157, 200
  theory of, 201
  view of, 71–72
Hierarchy and Marriage Alliance in South India (Louis Dumont), 197
Hind Swaraj, 104–05, 108, 110
'Hindu' and 'Hinduism', 26
  low caste among, 36
  -Muslim encounters, 28
  religious identity of, 28
'Hindu *dharma*', 28
Hindu dominance, 6
Hindu ethics, absolute relativism in, 41
Hindu personal law, 13
Hindu religious traditions, 25
Hindu revivalism, 14
Hindu Right, 20, 21
Hindu social system, 40
Hindu society, 160, 182, 192
Hinduism, xiii, 15, 23ff, 147, 222
  beliefs in, 34–42
  capitalism and, 40
  and civilizational unity, 141
  conversion to, 53
  'popular', 26
  as ritualistic, 29, 38, 97
  sociology of, xv, 25–28, 41, 42
  'spread' of, 28–30, 39
Hinduization, 39, 40
historiography, 159, 165
Hobbes, Thomas, xii
Hobhouse, L.T., 120, 140
Hocart, A.M., 220, 227

holism, 120, 170, 195, 196, 201, 203
  and hierarchy, 202
Homo Hierarchicus (Louis Dumont), xv, 200–02, 207, 208, 213, 214, 219, 223, 225, 229, 231, 235, 237
  criticism of, 223
Hubert, Henri, 221, 231
human dignity, 157
human rights, 74
humanism, 103, 120, 131, 153, 192
Hume, David, 33, 67, 68
Huntington, Samuel P., 132
Hurd, Elizabeth, 21
Hussain, Dr Zakir, 151

ideas, role of, 40–41
  and values, 203
identity, individual, 4, 145
  religious, 4, 7
ideology, 196, 203
'Īds, 63
imagination, 174, 178, 179, 245
  historical, 180, 181
  literary, 179
  moral, 118, 119, 175, 195
Indian Council of Social Science Research (ICSSR), 208, 262
Indian culture(al), modern, 159–63
  nationalism, 14
Indian history, making of, 163–65
Indian secularism, 3, 264
  Gandhi and, 16–20
  history of, 4–11
  sources of contemporary, 12–16
Indian Sociological Conference, 154
Indian Sociological Society, 142
Indian Sociology: The Role of Benoy Kumar Sarkar (Swapan Kumar Bhattacharya), xiv

Indian Working Class, The (Radhakamal Mukerjee), 137
individual, notion of, 128
individualism/individual, 129n, 154, 203–04
   in Europe, 203
   of the West, 202
Indology, 38, 222, 223
Indonesia, Constitution of, 53
   Dutch rule in, 53
   Islam in, 50–55
   Muslim population in, 53
Institute of Economic Growth (IEG), xvii, 206, 209, 217, 233, 258, 259, 262
Institutional Theory of Economics, The (Radhakamal Mukerjee), 127, 131
institutionalism, 129
International Sociological Association, 141
'intuitive powers', 179
Iqbal, Mohammad, 6, 50n
Islam, xiii, 45ff, 160, 165
   Arab, 66n
   in Bengal, 55–59
   customary law of, 55
   daily prayers in, 63
   early history of, 48
   'lived', 72, 73, 74
   scriptural, 72, 73
   spread of, 47
   way of life in, 46
Islam Observed (Clifford Geertz), 50
Islami Oikya Jote, 58
Islamic civilization, 70
Islamic orthodoxy, 46, 50
Islamic tradition, 67
Islamization, 52, 65, 66, 67, 69, 73
itihāsa, 141n
Iyenger, V. Doreswamy, 215
Iyer, Raghavan, 16, 17, 110

Jāma' Masjid, Srinagar, 62
Jafferlot, Christophe, 14
Jagannatha temple, Puri, study of, 43
Jahangir, emperor, 87, 89
jajmani system, 188
Jamā'at-i Islāmī, 9, 53, 58, 64
Jamā'atul Mujāhidīn, 58
Jackson, Peter, 10n
James, Henry, 174
Janam sākhi, 76
Jarvie, Ian, 178
Jat community, in Punjab, 86, 88
Java, approach to Islam in, 52
Javanese Islam, 67
   and Moroccan Islam, 53
Jews, 47
Jinnah, M.A., 6
jnānyoga, 41
Jones, William, 24
Jordens, J.T.F., 17, 19, 20
Joshi, Manoj, 64
Joshi, P.C., 139, 173
Juergensmeyer, Mark, 43, 44
Justice and Democratic Party (AKP) government, of Turkey, 21

kāma, 81
Kāshī Khanda, 43
Kāshī Mahimā Prakāsh, 43
Kāveri Māhatmya, 33
Kāveri myth, 34
Ka'bah, 47, 48
   and rituals, 48
Kabirpanthi, 43
Kalhana, 60
Kallar, Pramalai, Dumont's monograph on, 197, 212, 213, 218–19, 221
Kamath, H.V., 7
Kannada caste, 'non-Brahmins' among, 31

Kanthapura (Raja Rao), 184
Karlekar, Hiranmay, 59
karma, 31, 33, 37, 38, 191
   doctrine of compensation, 36
karmakānda, 32
karmayoga, 41
karmic bondage/chain, 38, 41
Karnataka, village study of, 175, 184
Karnataka University, 259, 262
Karve, Iravati, 142, 251, 226
Kashmir, 5
   fieldwork in, 260
   Islam in, 59–65, 69–70
Kashmiri Hindus, killing of, 71n
Kashmiri Muslims, 72, 73
   relations with Hindus, 71n
Kashmiri Pandits, study of, 71n, 205, 212, 247, 248, 250
Kaul, Jayalal, 60
Kerala High Court, 16
Kerala, Left Front government in, 15
Kerala State Industrial Development Corporation, 15
Ketkar, S.V., 140
Khālsā (Guru Panth), 94, 95, 96, 97
Khaldun, Ibn, 68
Khan, Mohammad Ishaq, 61, 62, 63, 64, 65, 70, 71, 73
Khare, R.S., 196
Khatri caste, in Punjab, 78, 83, 84, 88
Khawārij ('revolters'), 48
Khusrau, prince, 87
Kierkegaard, Søren Aabye, 182
King, Richard, 24, 28
kinship, 182, 232, 261
   organizations, 226
   system in South Asia, 249
kirpan (sword), in Sikhism, 93–94
Kopf, David, 28, 120, 148

Kothari, Rajni, 262
Krishnamurty, J., 134n
krodha, 81
Kroeber, Alfred, 255
Kshatriya, 36, 41
Kulke, Hermann, 39

Lalla, of Kashmir, 27, 60, 61
Lashkar-e-Tayyiba, 64n
Lévi-Strauss, Claude, 181, 196, 197, 219, 222
Leach, Edmund, 213, 249, 250
Left parties, 14
legislature, 6
Lenin, Vladimir Ilyich, 159
Lepenies, Wolf, 174, 180
Levy, Robert, 44n
liberal humanism, 153
Liberal Islamic Network, Indonesia, 53
Liebniz, Gottfried, 37n
Lingat, Robert, 228
lobha, 81
Locke, John, 202, 203
Lorenzen, David N., 27, 28
Luther, Martin, 20

Mārkandya Purāna, 92
Macauliffe, M.A., 77n, 79, 80, 88
Machiavelli, Niccolò di Bernardo dei, xii
Madan, T.N., 4, 5, 9, 13, 16, 17, 18, 58, 66, 87, 94, 95, 97, 149, 173, 184, 195, 196, 205, 212, 213, 223, 224, 233
Maguindanao, Islam in, 54
Mahābhārata, 35, 41, 57, 114n, 115
Mahadev Kolis, ethnography of, 140
Mahalanobis, P.C., 121
Majul, Cesar A., 55

Majumdar, D.N., xvi, 135n, 136, 152, 173n, 204, 242, 243, 244, 248
Makkah, 47
  pilgrimage to, 62
Malamoud, Charles, 5
Malaysia, Islam in, 54
Malikite school of law, 48
Malinowski, Bronislaw, 178, 179, 181, 249
Malraux, André, 8
Mammon, 107
Mandelbaum, David, 223
Mandeville, 202
mangal-kāvya, 57
Mannheim, Karl, 133
mantra, 32
Manusmriti, 114, 139
Marglin, Frédérique Apffel, 43
Marglin, Stephen, 129n, 133
Marriott, McKim, 30, 226, 231, 236, 255
Martin, David, 91, 99, 262
Marx, Karl, xii, 35, 109n, 120, 152, 153, 154, 156, 159, 163, 167n, 202, 224, 228
Marxism, xv, 152, 153, 165, 170
Marxists, on history of India, 164–65
Marxiology, 136, 152
materialism, 143
  dialectical, 135
Mathur, J.S., 20n
Mathur, K.S., 41
Matilal, Bimal Krishna, 114n
Mauss, Marcel, xv, 72, 183, 196, 197, 220, 221, 231
Mayaram, Shail, 62, 174
Mayer, Adrian, 206, 233
McLeod, W.H., 11, 76, 79, 80, 88, 92
Mead, G.H., 224n

meditation, 61,180
Mehta, Narsi, 111n
Meos, 62
methodological pluralism, 2, 117ff
methodology, 43, 126, 138, 248
  of economic sociology, 123–24
  of Louis Dumont, 198, 224n
  of M.N. Srinivas, 32
  of sociology, 206, 226
Michaels, Axel, 27
Mihārban Janamsākhi, 77
Mill, John Stuart, 120, 124n
Millennium Development Goals, 145
Mindanao, Islam in, 54
minorities, educational institutions of, 13
Miri, Mrinal, 101, 102, 103, 104, 110, 115
Misra, Satish, 66n
Mitra, Ashok, 151
'modern' state, 103
Modern Indian Culture: A Sociological Study (D.P. Mukerji), 136, 137, 159
Modern Myths, Locked Minds (T.N. Madan), xx, 210, 263
modernization, 157, 165–70
  impact on religion, 99
  theories of, 170–72
Moffatt, Michael, 208
moha, 81
moksha, 33, 38
Moosvi, Shirin, 11n
morals/morality, 202, 244
Morocco, Islam in, 50–55, 67
  'classical' style of Islam in, 51
mosque, as public domain in Islam, 62
Müller, Max, 24
mudra, 32
Muhammad, Mir, 60

Mukerjee, Asutosh, 120
Mukerjee, Radhakamal, xiii, xiv, xv, xvi, 119, 148, 151, 153, 172, 240, 242, 244, 248, 265
  contemporaries of, 134–39
  on institutional economics, 126–29
  at Lucknow University, 122–26
Mukherjee, Ramkrishna, xii, 134, 136
Mukherjee, Rudrangshu, 6, 8
Mukherjee, S.N., 24
Mukerji, Ashutosh, 147
Mukerji, D.P., xiv, xvi, 135, 138, 139, 142, 144, 146–73, 177, 243, 244, 245, 265
  and Indian history, 163–65
  on modernization, 165–72
  as a scholar–author, 152–54
  as a teacher, 148–52
  works of, 154–59
Munford, Lewis, 121
Munshi, Srobona, 121, 122, 148, 154
Munshi, Surendra, 40
music, 63, 137, 148
Muslim culture, 59
Muslim League, founded in Dhaka, 58
Muslim society, diversity in, 69
Muslim separatists, 6
Muslim terrorism, 14
'Muslim-ness', 56
mutiny, by soldiers, 12
mysticism, 61

nāthism, 57
Nabī-vaṃśa (Saiyid Sultan), 57
Nadel, S.F., 232, 245, 247, 248
Nagendra, S.P., 173
Nahdlatul Ulamā, 53
Naipaul, V.S., 174, 194

Nakane, Chie, 184
namāz, 47, 59, 73
Nanak Dev, Guru, founder of Sikhism, 75–77, 82, 90
  on concept of God, 80
  followers of, 84
  teachings of, 79, 81
Nanda, B.R., 111n
Nandy, Ashis, 11n, 174, 175, 177n, 184, 194
Narain, Brij, 125
Narain, S.K., 150
Narang, G.C., 89
Narayan, R.K., 184, 185
Naregal, Veena, 238
Narendra Dev, Acharya, 151
Nasr, Seyyed Hossein, 47, 74
Nath Yogi, order, 43
national identity, 13
national movement, 14, 165
nationalism, 14, 26, 52, 120, 169, 228
Nayar, Baldev Raj, 98
Nehru, Jawaharlal, 3, 6, 7, 8, 11n, 97, 150
  secularism of, 97
Nehruvian state, 19
'New Series', 206, 207, 231, 236, 237
Nicholas, Ralph, 234
Nietzsche, Friedrich, 23
Nirmal Kumar Bose: Scholar Wanderer (Surajit Sinha), xiv
nirvana, 179
Nisbet, Robert, xi
nishkāma karma, 106
niti literature, 35
Nitishāstra text, 144
Nuer Religion (E.E. Evans-Pritchard), 262
Nur-ud-din, Shaikh, 28, 61, 63n
  tomb of, 64

Oakeshott, Michael, 167
Obeyesekere, Gananath, 44n, 235
occupation, and profession, 258–62
orthodoxy, notion of, 70

pāpa, 31
Pakistan, creation of, 58
  as Islamic state, 6
Pal, Bipin Chandra, 120
Pancasila, five foundational principles, 53
Panini, M.N., 134n, 173n
Parel, Anthony J., 110
Pareto, Vilfredo, 143
Park, Robert, 130, 131
Parkin, Robert, 196
Parry, Jonathan, 26, 43, 236
Parsons, Talcott, 173
Partition, of India, 159, 165
  impact on Sikh community, 98
  mass killings at, 18
Pathways: Approaches to the Study of Society in India (T.N. Madan), xi, xv, 208
Pattini, goddess, cult of, 44n
patrilineal society, 222
Pax Britannica, 28
personality, development of, 156
  'notion of', 15, 154
Personality and the Social Sciences (D.P. Mukerji), 136, 154
Phillipines, Christians and Muslims in, 54
  Islam in, 50–53, 54–55
Pierce, C.S., 224n
Pignéd, Bernard, 227, 228
Pinter, Harold, 240
planning, economic, 131, 169, 242
  regional, 12, 131
  as state policy, 166
pluralism, 18–19, 96
  cultural, 162

  methodological, 217ff
  participatory, 19
  religious, xiii, 9, 99
Pocock, David, 26, 38, 42, 198, 199, 200, 222, 223, 228, 233
politics, and culture, 161
  Gandhi and Weber on, 112
Popper, Karl, 168n, 256
'popular Hinduism', 26
Positive Background of Hindu Sociology, The (Benoy Kumar Sarkar), 143
positivism, 143, 244, 245, 248
power, Hindu concept of, 92
Pramanick, S.K., xii, 141, 142
prasāda, 41
'principled distance', policy of, 12, 13
'progress', notion of, 155–57
Principles of Comparative Economics (Radhakamal Mukerjee), 126, 127
Prophet Muhammad, 47, 48, 49, 51, 61, 63n, 64, 73
Protestant ethic, 'rationalism' of, 143
Protestantism, 75
Punjab, under Ranjit Singh, 95–96
punya, 31
Purānas, 141n, 236
  later religion of the, 27
Purātan Janamsākhi, 79n
Puritans, 107
purity and pollution, Brahmanical notion of, 82
purushārtha, 154, 209

qānūn (secular law), 48
Quinn, James A., 130
Qur'ān, 9, 45, 48, 50, 51, 52, 61, 70, 73, 104

law, 55
  recitation of, 63
Qur'ānic tradition, 46

Rājataranginī, 60
Rāmāyana, 35, 52n, 57
Rāmkrishna, 144
race, 16, 46, 124n, 192
Radcliffe-Brown, A.R., 32, 33, 34, 182, 193, 194, 205
Radhakrishnan, S., 9
  on Hinduism, 17n
Radhasoami movement, 43
Raghavan, V., 52n
Rahman, Fazlur, 48
Rama-rajya, notion of, 169
Ram Das, Guru, 86
Ramar Sethu (Rama's Bridge), 20, 21
Ranjit Singh, secular state of, in Punjab, 95–97
Rashtriya Swayamsevak Sangh (RSS), 14
Rao, M.S.A., 209
Rao, Raja, 177n, 184
rationality, 169
Rau, M. Chalapathi, 151
Ray, Niharranjan, 78, 79n, 80, 81, 83, 90
Ray, Satyajit, 175
Redfield, Robert, 249
reflexivity, 240ff
  objectivity, 254
  subjectivity, 254
Reformation, 204
region/regionalism, 129, 131
relativism, 41, 132
religion/religious/religiosity, xii, 5, 97, 137, 162
  beliefs and practices, 22
  conversion, 53, 54, 61
  definition of, 33
  ethics, 101
  Gandhi's concept of, 16–17
  identity, 4, 7
  Marxist view of, 153
  pluralism, xiii, 9
  and society, 36
  symbols, 8
  syncretism, 18
  traditions, role of, xii, 162, 262–64
Religion of India: The Sociology of Hinduism and Buddhism, The (Max Weber), 36, 40, 41, 42
Religion and Society among the Co-orgs of South India (M.N. Srinivas), 42, 257
Remembered Village, The (M.N. Srinivas), xiv, 31, 174, 176, 183, 184, 192, 194, 235, 245
Renou, Louis, 197
renunciation, Brahmanical ideal of, 81, 199, 203, 212, 228
Revolution, 68, 163, 204
Rig Veda, 9, 74n
Rishī tradition, 61–62
ritual/ritualism, 42, 59
  'debt', Brahmanical notion of, 199–200
  and pollution, notion of, 182, 191, 221, 224
  purity, 31, 38, 200
  and social solidarity, 31–34
  tradition in Hinduism, 37, 43
Rivers, W.H.R., 140
Robbins, Lionel, 128
Robinson, Francis, 67
Rock of Jerusalem, 47
Rodinson, Maxime, 48
Roman Catholicism, 54
Roy, Asim, 56, 57, 62, 68, 69, 71
Roy, Rammohan, 28, 147, 166
Roy, Sarat Chandra, 180, 181, 243

Royal Anthropological Institute, London, 219
Rudolph, Lloyd I., 19n
Rudner, David, 214
Russell, Bertrand, 141n

sādhāran dharma, 41, 114
Saberwal, Satish, 28, 234
Sachau, Edward C., 27, 49
salvation, 41, 80, 81, 94, 106
sambhava, notion of, 10
sampradāya, 26
sampradāya paramparā, 138
samsara, 36
samskara, 184
Samundari, Bishan Singh, 99
sannyāsī, 17, 78
Sanskritization, 28–30, 40
sapinda category, 199
Saran, A.K., 132, 143, 145, 151, 152, 170, 173, 231, 244, 245, 248, 253
Sarkar, Benoy Kumar, 134, 142, 144
Sarnath pillar, 8
Satyāgrahī, 17, 111
Schomer, Karine, 11
Seal, Brajendra Nath, 121, 132
Science and technology, utilization of, 169
'secular', state, 8
secularism, 3, 77, 81, 90, 97
   definition of, 7
   Indian, xiii, 3
   as political ideology, 5
   and religious tradition, 262–64
   in Sikh history, 262
secularization, patterns of, 5, 99
   notion of, 75–76
'self-cultivation', ideal of, 203
Seligman, Adam, 19n
Sen, Amartya, 11

Sen, Ronojoy, 19
Sen, Surendranath, 12
sevā, 110, 112
Shafiite school of law, 48
Shah, A.M., 24, 26, 32, 38, 40
Shah, K.J., 5
Shah, K.T., 7
Shahjahan, emperor, 89
Shaikhm Farzana, 65
Shaivism, 59
Shakti, cult of, 92
Sharī'ah, 54, 61n, 62, 65
   laws, 53
   way of life, 51, 54
Sharma, Sri Ram, 10
'Shastar Nām Mālā', 93
Shastras, 35
   later religion of the, 27
Shī'ah, 48
Shikoh, Dara, 68
Shils, Edward, xii, 168n
Shiromani Gurdwara Prabandhak Committee (SGPC), 98
Shivaji, and 'Hindu dharma', 28
Shukranīti, 143
Sikh community, relationship with Mughal empire, 90, 95, 96
Sikh identity, 97
Sikh movement, 84
Sikh order, 43
Sikhism, xiii, 75–100
   doctrine of two swords in, 88–95
   and Gurus, 92
   religious tradition, 87, 88, 91, 96, 97, 99
   Sant tradition in, 81
   shabad in, 78, 80
Sind, Islam in, 55
Singer, Milton, 233
Singh, Attar, 99, 100
Singh, Baljit, 173
Singh, Fauja, 84

Singh, Gopal, 86, 90
Singh, Harbans, 77, 85, 89, 92, 93, 98
Singh, Jodh, 81
Singh, Kapur, 79n, 94n, 96
Singh, Khushwant, 76, 79, 80, 82, 83, 89, 91n, 94n, 95–99
Singh, Maharaja Ranjit, 75, 98n
Singh, Randhir, 10
Singh Sabhas, 98n
Singh, Sukha, 75
Singh, Tejeshwar, xvi, xvii
Singh, Trilochan, 80n
Singh, V.B., 152, 173
Sinha, Surajit, xii, 30
Smith, Adam, 120, 128, 202
Smith, Donald Eugene, 12, 82n
Smith, Wilfred Cantwell, 26
Smith, William Robertson, 32
Smritis, 35
   later religion of the, 27
social action, 37, 74, 112, 142n, 169, 196
social anthropology, xv, 32, 37, 74, 112, 169, 196, 224, 245
social behaviour, 128, 131, 159, 196
social interaction, 133
social justice, 13
social mobility, 130, 131
social science, nature of, 154–59
social status, 130, 131
social stratification, 200–01
'social structure', 194
   caste-based, of South Asia, 29
Social Structure of Values, The (Radhakamal Mukerjee), 131, 248
social system, 200–01
'social traditions', 138, 164–65
society, 37
   religion and, 36
Sociological Conference, 152

Sociological Tradition, The (Robert Nisbet), xi
sociology, 25, 38, 138, 140, 225, 245
   history, political science, xiii, 159–60
Sociology of G.S. Ghurye (S.K. Pramanick), xii
Soeharto, President, of Indonesia, 53
Somervell, D.C., 243
Sorabji, Soli, 21
Sorokin, Pitrim, 173
South Asia, Islam in, 55–65
Spanish Islam, 50
Spencer, Herbert, 124n, 148
Sri Lanka, 20
Srinivas, M.N., xiv, xv, xvi, 25, 26, 35, 36, 37, 38, 39, 40, 134n, 142, 173n, 174ff, 222–24, 226, 231, 233, 240, 245, 262
   ethnography of, 182–84, 191–92
   imagined homes and worlds of, 177
   on rituals and social solidarity, 31–34
   short stories by, 185–87, 193
   on 'spread' of Hinduism and 'Sanskritization', 28–30
   'The Image Maker', 187–91, 193
   'The Legend on the Wall', 185–87, 193
Stiglitz, Joseph, 129n, 133
Stopes, Marie, 148
structuralism, 34, 172
Sūfīsm, Sūfīs, 48, 49, 51, 55, 56, 60, 61, 62, 64n, 70, 73, 78, 87
Sultan, Saiyid, 57, 61
Sulu archipelago, Islam in, 54
Sundar, Nandini, xii, 238
Sundaram, Ravi, 174

Sunnī Muslims, 48, 54
supernatural, notion of, 25
superstition, 68
Supreme Court of India, 7, 20, 21
Swadeshi movement, 147
syādavād, 17
syncretism, religious, 18, 67, 70, 71
synthesis, cultural, 141, 157, 162, 165

Tablīghī Jamā'at, impact of, 62
Tagore, Rabindranath, 58, 120, 137n, 139, 147, 148, 166, 167
Taliban, 59, 74
tantra texts, 35
Tarikh-ul Hind (Raihan al-Biruni), 27
Tariqā-i Muhammadiya movement, 58
Tax, Sol, 183
Taylor, Charles, 3, 33
technological innovations, 145
teetotalism, 30
Tegh Bahadur, Guru, 91
Thailand, Muslim insurgency in, 54n
Thapar, Romila, 10, 11, 26
theodicy, notion of, 37n
Thooti, N.A., 122
Thorner, Daniel, 228
Tönnies, Ferdinand, 143
Tocqueville, Alexis de, 9, 227
Todas, 221
Tolstoy, Leo, 104, 105, 111, 110, 115n
tombs, of saints, in Islam, 63
Toynbee, Arnold J., 76n, 82n, 91, 243
'tradition', xi, 162, 172, 168
    and modernity, 166, 177
    taboos of, 168n
Tradition (Edward Shils), xii

transmigration, of souls, 36
'Trends in Indian Sociology', xii
tribal communities, status of, 141
tribalism, Islam and, 68
Trotsky, Leon, 159
trusteeship, concept of, 111
    Gandhi on, 111, 112
Turkey, 21
'two-nation theory', 65

Uberoi, J.P.S., 94n, 143
Uberoi, Patricia, xii, 212, 237
Ulamā', 48, 49, 61, 62
Umayyad Caliphate, 55
Umayyads, 50
Ummah, 46, 48, 50, 59, 65, 69, 73
unity, notion of, 132
'untouchables', 186, 187, 191, 193
University of Lucknow, 122, 125, 259, 242
University Sociological Society, 123
untouchability, practice of, 12
Upadhya, Carol, 141
Upanishads, 35, 37, 157, 228
urbanization/urban process, 192, 258
urbanism, 68
'urs, annual, 63
Usman, 45
Uttar Pradesh, fieldwork in, 199, 228
Uttar Pradesh Labour Enquiry Committee, 150

vākh, 60
Vaishnava order, Hindu, 43
values, 110, 149, 203
    and institutions, 167
    cultural, 126
    ethical, 128
    fundamental, 157–58

social origin of, 131–34
social structure of, 128, 244, 248
traditional, 167
ultimate, 101, 103, 111, 158, 257
'Var Sri Bhagautiji ki' (Guru Gobind Singh), 92
Vardarajan, S., 15
varna, boundaries, 41
varna dharma, 41
Vatuk, Sylvia, 212
Vedanta, 157, 170
Vedantic Hinduism, 9, 18
Vedas, 26, 35
  early religion of, 26–27
Vedic knowledge, 144
vegetarianism, 30
Vidyasagar, Ishwar Chandra, 120
Views and Counterviews (D.P. Mukerji), 153
virtue, practice of, 41, 68, 81, 82
Vivekānanda, 9, 18, 144
Vyakti, 154

Wani, Muhammad Ashraf, 61, 62, 64, 70
Way of Life: King, Householder, Renouncer: Essays in Honour of Louis Dumont (ed., T.N. Madan), 209, 212, 213
Weber, Alfred, 141n
Weber, Max, xii, xiv, 3, 25, 26, 38, 41, 77, 81, 85, 86, 143, 216, 224n, 256

Gandhi and, 101
on belief in Hinduism, 34–42
on politics and ethics, 112
on Protestant ethic, 106–08
on Western civilization and capitalism, 108–12
Western civilization, 75, 92, 103, 104, 202, 227
Western liberalism, 170
Western science, 75, 103
Western sociological tradition, xi, xii
Whitehead, A.N., 141n
Wittgenstein, Ludwig, vii, 224n
Wolff, Kurt H., 225, 226
Wollheim, Richard, 102
Wordsworth, William, 240
work ethic, 101, 105
Wolpert, Stanley, 6

Yalman, Nur, 49
Yeats, W.B., 165
yogīs, 78
yuga dharma, 112

Zaehner, R.C., 115
Zimmerman, Carl, 173
Ziolkowski, Janusz, 261
Zutshi, Chitralekha, 64

About the Author

One of India's most distinguished sociologists, T.N. Madan is Honorary Professor of Sociology at the Institute of Economic Growth, Delhi University, and Distinguished Senior Fellow at the Centre for the Study of Developing Societies in India. He is a Fellow of the Royal Anthropological Institute (London) and Docteur Honoris Causa of the University of Paris X. He received the Lifetime Achievement Award from the Indian Sociological Society in 2008.